The Growth and Structure of International Trade Since The Second World War

The Growth and Structure of International Trade Since The Second World War

Lynden Moore
Lecturer in Economics
University of Manchester

WHEATSHEAF BOOKS · SUSSEX

BARNES & NOBLE BOOKS · NEW JERSEY

First published in Great Britain in 1985 by
WHEATSHEAF BOOKS LTD
A MEMBER OF THE HARVESTER PRESS GROUP
Publisher: John Spiers
Director of Publications: Edward Elgar
16 Ship Street, Brighton, Sussex
and in the USA by
BARNES & NOBLE BOOKS
81 Adams Drive, Totowa, New Jersey 07512

British Library Cataloguing in Publication Data

Moore, Lynden
    The growth and structure of international
    trade since the Second World War.
    1. Commerce—— History——20th century
    I. Title
    382'.09'04   HF499

    ISBN 0-7108-0730-9

Library of Congress Cataloging in Publication Data

Moore, Lynden.
    The growth and structure of international trade since
the Second World War.

    1. Commerce.   I. Title.
HF1411.B744 1985   382'.09   84-11105
ISBN 0-389-20498-6

Typeset in 10/11 point Times by
Mathematical Composition Setters Ltd, Salisbury, Wilts, UK
Printed in Great Britain by
Whitstable Litho Ltd., Whitstable, Kent

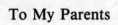

To My Parents

Contents

Contents

List of Tables

List of Figures

Preface

It is the author's belief that a democracy only works effectively if the background to its major policy decisions is understood by a significant number of people. The governments of industrial countries are now faced by persistent demands for greater protection for their agriculture and declining manufacturing industries at the same time as developing countries are endeavouring to gain greater access to their markets. The developing countries are faced with urgent social pressures to reduce poverty but many are in precarious balance of payments positions. Protection by industrial countries affects the trade and financial links between the groups of countries. Economic theory also states that it will reduce the economic welfare of most, if not all, countries. This argument is considered together with the actual changes in trade and commercial policy that have occurred.

Experience of the general pattern of trade has been garnered during the twenty or so years I have been doing research intermittently on the subject. I was able to work intensively on the book during the Hilary Term 1980, which I spent at Nuffield College, Oxford and then the whole of the academic year 1981–2 which I spent at the Institute of Agricultural Economics, Oxford. I am very grateful to both institutions for their hospitality and also to Somerville College which elected me a member of the SCR for the latter period. I am also grateful to the University of Manchester for granting me sabbatical leave for these periods.

I am indebted to George Jones, Michael Artis, Peter Stubbs, Colin Jones, Ashok Desai, Stanley Metcalfe and my father Ronald Moore for reading and commenting on chapters of the book, and I would like to thank Pete Martin for his research assistance with the tables on agriculture; and Jeanne Ashton and her Secretarial Reserve for typing the book.

I am also grateful to Manchester University Press for allowing me to use some extracts from my previous book, under the name of Lynden Briscoe *The Textile and Clothing Industries of the United Kingdom* (Manchester, MUP, 1971).

Lynden Moore

List of Abbreviations

ACP	African–Carribean–Pacific developing countries which have signed the Lomé convention with the EEC
Benelux	Customs Union of Belgium, Netherlands and Luxemburg, established 1948
BTU	British Thermal Units
CAP	Common Agricultural Policy of the EEC
CCC	Commodity Credit Corporation of the US
CEC	Commonwealth Economic Committee, London
CET	Common External Tariff of the EEC
CFP	Compagnie Française des Pétroles
c.i.f.	Cost of Insurance and Freight
CP	Centrally Planned
CPE	Centrally Planned Economies
CPI	Consumer Price Index
CPRS	Central Policy Review Staff
CSO	Central Statistical Office, London
ECE	Economic Commission for Europe
ECSC	European Coal and Steel Community, established 1951
ECU	European Currency Units, established 1979 initially of same value as u.a. but based on a basket of currencies which included the pound sterling
EEC	European Economic Community, from 1957–72 of 6 (France, Germany, Italy, Belgium, Netherlands, Luxemburg), then from 1973–80 of 9 (original 6 plus UK, Denmark, Ireland), 1981– of 10 (the 9 plus Greece)
EFTA	European Free Trade Association, founded 1960
EIU	Economist Intelligence Unit
ENI	Ente Nazionale Idrocarburi
ETA	Eastern Trading Area comprising Russia and Eastern Europe, China, Mongolia, N. Korea and Vietnam
FAO	Food and Agricultural Organisation of the UN

FEOGA	Fonds Européen d'Orientation et de Garantie Agricole—in English The Agricultural Guidance and Guarantee Fund
GATT	General Agreement on Tariffs and Trade
GDP	Gross Domestic Product
GM	General Motors
GNP	Gross National Product
GSP	Generalised System of Preferences
IBRD	International Bank for Reconstruction and Development, now generally known as the World Bank
IEA	International Energy Agency, OECD
IMF	International Monetary Fund
LNG	Liquified Natural Gas
LTA	Long Term Arrangement Regarding International Trade in Cotton Textiles
MAFF	Ministry of Agriculture, Forestry and Fisheries, Japan
MCA	Monetary Compensatory Amounts
ME	Market Economies
MFA	Multi-Fibre Arrangement—that is the Arrangement Regarding International Trade in Textiles
mfn	Most Favoured Nation
MITI	Ministry of International Trade and Industry, Japan
m.t.	Million Metric Tons
m.t.o.e.	Million Metric Tons Oil Equivalent
NIC	Newly Industrialising Country
NIESR	National Institute of Economic and Social Research, London
NIER	National Institute Economic Review produced by the NIESR
OECD	Organisation for Economic Co-operation and Development (includes all the developed market economies) established 1961
OEEC	Organisation for European Economic Co-operation, established 1948 to co-ordinate Marshall Aid; replaced by the OECD in 1961
OPEC	Organisation of Petroleum Exporting Countries (Algeria, Ecuador, Gabon, Indonesia, Iraq, Iran, Kuwait, Libya, Nigeria, Qatar, Saudi Arabia, United Arab Emirates and Venezuela)
PEEE	Primary Energy Equivalent of Electricity
PEP	Political and Economic Planning Institute
R and D	Research and Development

SIC	Standard Industrial Classification
SITC	Standard International Trade Classification published in 1950, revised in 1961 (Rev. 1) and then again in 1975 (Rev. 2)
SMMT	Society of Motor Manufacturers and Traders, London, UK
Tera	Unit multiplied by 10^{12}
u.a.	Unit of account -monetary unit used by the EEC equivalent to the pre 1971 dollar
UAE	United Arab Emirates
UN	United Nations
UNCTAD	United Nations Conference on Trade and Development
UN ECE	UN Economic Commission for Europe
UN ECLA	UN Economic Commission for Latin America
USDA	United States Department of Agriculture
VAT	Value Added Tax

HISTORICAL, FINANCIAL AND COMMERCIAL BACKGROUND TO TRADE

I Introduction

Trade is the most visible of relationships between countries. As such, people's reaction to its growth may vary. Some welcome it as representing a relaxation of political tension between countries. Some regard it with apprehension as a harbinger of new technologies, new tastes and maybe new attitudes. But some will always fear it as a threat to their jobs or livelihood.

In contrast, an international trade economist regards the removal of barriers to trade and its expansion as a means of increasing the level of world output. This is because he would regard the maintenance of full employment as an objective that could be separately achieved, that is as a result of macroeconomic policy. Trade, on the other hand, is the exchange of goods and as such will affect the distribution of production and employment within a country rather than the total level of employment. If each country specialises in the production of commodities for which it has the lowest relative cost of production, then the total output of all countries together will be greater, and each country will have a greater real income. This is a simple account and a somewhat more detailed one with a few qualifications is given in Chapter 7.

Nevertheless, this is the basic argument for the removal of barriers to trade and is the credo on which all the international financial and commercial institutions are based.

A macroeconomist would agree that trade leads to an optimum allocation of factors of production, but might well question the assumption of full employment, particularly as governments appear to have increasing difficulty in simultaneously achieving the macroeconomic targets of full employment, price stability and economic growth. To a macroeconomist, trade represents a link between countries through which changes in aggregate demand and thus employment are transmitted from one country to another. The more open an economy, that is the greater its ratio of trade to Gross National Product (GNP), the more vulnerable it is to shifts in demand in other countries. Generally, the small industrialised countries are very open, with ratios of imports and exports to GNP of between 20 and 50%, the medium-sized ones less so with ratios of 10%, and the US is the least open.

On the other hand, the greater the country's proportion of international trade, the greater the impact of its own fluctuations on the rest of the world.

In terms of these ratios, the US has occupied the most asymmetric position. For instance, in 1960, imports and exports accounted for only 2.9% and 4.0% respectively of her GNP, whereas they accounted for 11% and 16% of world trade (OECD, 1972, pp. 139 and 140). This meant that her government could pursue policies to attain internal objectives as though she were a closed economy, although these might have a considerable impact on the rest of the world. For instance, if she reduced imports by 1% of GNP this would represent a reduction in effective demand on the world market of nearly 4%. But this situation has gradually changed so that US imports now account for 14% of world trade and 9% of her GNP (1982).

The UK occupied an intermediate position with imports and exports representing 17.5 and 14.1% of GNP in 1960 and 9.3 and 8.0% of world trade. The former ratios increased and the latter declined so that the UK has become more vulnerable to transmission and less of a transmitter.

These short-run stabilisation problems are, in fact, not the subject of this book. But they are important because they affect the policies adopted by governments. Inability to maintain full employment has often induced a government to espouse protectionist policies which have affected both the growth and composition of trade.

It is this growth, and the changes in the composition of trade, that form the subject of this book. To begin with, a brief account will be given of the historical development of trade which provided the initial links between countries. The disruption and devastaion of two world wars and the Great Depression in between them also provided the backdrop against which Allies viewed the task of reconstruction as they approached the end of the Second World War. The financial and commercial institutions they established are described in Chapters 3 and 4.

The international institutional structure together with US assistance appear to have contributed not only to the rehabilitation of the war-devastated economies, but also to have provided the basis for a rapid exansion in output and trade for the whole world. This is best documented for the developed countries. The output of countries belonging to the Organisation for Economic Co-operation and Development (OECD) increased by 4.7% p.a. in real terms between 1955 and 1968. However, there were considerable differences between the developed countries with Japan achieving an amazing growth rate of 10.2% p.a. and the next highest Spain, with a growth rate of 7.0% p.a. In contrast the increase in the annual output of the United Kingdom was only 2.8% p.a., that of the EEC (6) 5.3% p.a. and that of the US was lower than the OECD average at 4.0% p.a.

Many developing countries also achieved rapid increases in output (see The World Bank, 1978) particularly the more advanced ones. As can be seen from the Appendix Table A1, Taiwan achieved an increase in real output of 8.3% p.a. Mexico 6.1% p.a., the Philippines 5.6% p.a. and Brazil 5.2% p.a. between 1950–2 and 1964–6. But the rates of increases in the poorest, particularly those in Africa, tended to be much lower.

In order to consider the effect of this increase in output on the standard of living you need also to consider the increase in population. This has been increasing at 2.5% in the middle-income developing countries whereas population growth in the developed countries has been declining from 1.2% p.a. from 1955 to 1968 to 0.8% since 1973. The resulting increase in real output per head of population is shown in the Appendix Table A1. The increase in the demand for goods and services is the net result of increases in *per capita* incomes and increases in population. This expansion in output and income is both partly the result of, but has also contributed to, the expansion of trade.

Expand it did, very rapidly, faster even than national incomes. The value of trade in 1973 was eight times the level in 1953. Part of this increase was just due to a rise in prices. If this is allowed for, the volume of trade in 1973 was almost five times the volume in 1953. One of the main aims of this book is to investigate this expansion and to find out the degree to which areas and countries participated in it and to see which commodities have contributed most to it.

In order to obtain an overall view, it is necessary to begin by grouping both commodities and countries, otherwise the reader will be drowned in a sea of figures (see Chapter 8). Generally, the categories used will be those of the General Agreement on Tariffs and Trade (GATT). It divides countries into Industrial, Developing both oil exporters and non-oil exporters, the Eastern Trading Area (USSR, Eastern Europe and China) and the resource-rich countries of Australia, New Zealand and South Africa.

This classification illuminates one of the sources of friction in the post-war world, namely the relative benefits obtained from trade by the developing and industrialised countries. The developing countries feel that the industrialised countries reap far more of the benefits of international trade than they do. As they were more dependent on exports of primary products, they initially identified the problem as that of an inevitable tendency for the terms of trade between primary products and manufactures to move against the former.

It was this type of dissatisfaction that eventually erupted in the formation of the Organisation of Petroleum Exporting Countries (OPEC) which decided to increase the price of oil four-fold between 1973 and 1974 and has been increasing it erratically since then.

This provided the greatest shock to the international economy since the Second World War. Because oil formed such a large proportion of other countries' imports, for instance 10% of OECD imports, it represented a significant reduction in their real incomes, 2% of the incomes of industrialised countries. But also it posed great problems of macroeconomic adjustment. This shock came on top of the difficulties industrialised countries were already encountering in trying to keep down inflation and maintain employment, and it added to the problems of developing countries.

The OPEC price rise in 1973—4 brought to an end the period of steady growth in industrialised countries that had been evident since 1953. The growth of output in the US and Japan had already begun to slow down in 1968—73. After 1973 the growth rates of all industrial countries fell (See Table A1). Their exports continued to increase, partly because they were required to pay for the increased expenditure on oil. But all countries have found great difficulty in reaching their macroeconomic targets.

This might have happened anyway because a rising rate of inflation was evident from 1967 in most industrialised countries. So also was the increasing difficulty in maintaining the level of employment. All such difficulties in achieving macroeconomic objectives got transmuted into increasingly protectionist commercial policies.

The position of the non-oil exporting developing countries has been variable. All have been badly affected by the rise in the price of oil but most have been able to continue their economic expansion with the aid of additional loans, as discussed in Chapter 3. Some have even achieved the status of Newly Industrialising Countries. But a number of the major borrowers, including the oil producers Mexico, Venezuela and Nigeria, ran into severe difficulties in servicing their international debts in the 1980s and were forced to reduce planned government expenditure and their rate of growth.

These macroeconomic problems have been superimposed on the problems of adjustment to new technology and apparent changes in competitive position of the industrialised countries. The developing countries, always in a precarious position, have achieved different degrees of success in achieving their growth objectives; these objectives themselves have tended to change over time.

The total interaction between various groups of countries, as reflected in their trade, is considered not only in Chapter 8 but by various categories of commodity in Chapters 11–14. Chapters 7 to 9 consider the patterns of trade that emerge in relation to the rationale for trade in terms of factor endowment, technological change and international investment.

2   Historical Background

In order to assess the present structure of international trade and the institutions set up to police it, and to appreciate the controversies that take place about them, a brief description will be given of the historical background.

It is a story of the hegemony in international trade and investment achieved first by Britain and then the US. The overall control by a single power was shaken by the two world wars and the Great Depression in between. Such hegemony also provoked defensive reactions by other countries competing for influence, and a bitter response by many underdeveloped countries who felt that the world trading system was acting against their interests.

One of the problems in assessing the situation is that international trade and development theory tend to develop with the situation but only get accepted by policy makers much later. Thus frequently policy makers are trying to correct what they perceive as a problem when the context in which they are acting has entirely changed. This, as will be seen, can be applied to controversies over the terms of trade, industrialisation, and commodity agreements. However, let us begin by considering the changes which initiated the evolution of the present interdependent world system.

Britain was the first country to industrialise, in the last third of the eighteenth century. The industrial revolution was a revolution in technology and organisation in which inventions went hand in hand with a much greater use and concentration of capital largely in the form of machines. It first appeared in the production of cotton textiles in which production techniques and manning were not ossified by the guild system as they were in the traditional woollen industry, and also in mining and the production of iron and steel and the manufacture of the machinery, particularly transport machinery.

Adam Smith, reflecting on these methods of production, described the economies of the division of labour that could be obtained by each worker performing only one task instead of making the whole item. He regarded them as part of the overall economies of scale, that is reduction in costs that could be obtained when a firm increased its overall output, and commented that they were limited by the size of the market. Thus restrictions on international trade such as those due to tariffs and quotas by limiting the market, kept costs higher than they would otherwise have been.

Ricardo, writing later, is generally credited with the theory of comparative advantage which states that a country benefits by specialising in the production of the commodity in which it has the comparative advantage and exporting it in exchange for a commodity in which it has a comparative disadvantage. By this means it can increase the total quantity of goods available to it. This advantage will accrue to it even though it may have an absolute cost advantage in the production of all commodities.

Both are arguments for free trade, and this was persuasively advocated by a number of reformers and eventually adopted by the British government. The first substantial measure taken was the abolition of the Corn Laws in 1846 which effectively removed agricultural protection. This was succeeded by the reduction and removal of many other tariffs. In many cases this was the product of a most favoured nation (mfn) agreement with another country by which Britain agreed on a reciprocal basis to extend to that country the most favourable terms it was offering to any other country. By the 1860s Britain had achieved free trade.

The removal of tariffs and quotas was probably assisted by the rapid expansion of trade, faster than that of income, that had already begun in the eighteenth century. But equally important was the dependence of the new manufacturing industries on exports for their growth.

Britain could not export manufactures unless other countries could obtain the wherewithal to import them. The movement towards free trade, in particular the removal of agricultural protection, enabled countries to increase their exports of agricultural products to her. She also required increasing quantities of raw materials for her manufactures. Thus right until 1950 she was primarily an exporter of manufactures in exchange for primary products. Both in 1840 and 1950, with not much fluctuation in between, 40% of British imports were Food, Drink and Tobacco. Britain's imports of raw materials accounted for 57% of imports in 1840, reached a trough of 24% in 1930 (probably due to a fall in price) and rose to 38% in 1950. But her imports of other goods incuding manufactures increased from 3.7% in 1840 to a peak of 29% in 1930 and then declined to 22% in 1950. (Deane and Cole, 1967, Table 10, p. 33).

Almost all her exports were manufactures. Coal was the only exception; from 0.5% in 1830 it peaked to 8.7% in 1910 and then declined.

Thus over 90% of her exports were manufactures but the contribution of the different sectors changed considerably over the period. In 1830, 72% of exports were of textiles and clothing, 10% were iron and steel manufactures and 0.5% machinery—chemicals were unrecorded. By 1950, 19% were of textiles and clothing, 10% iron and steel manufactures, 14% machinery, 4% electrical apparatus, 19% vehicles and 5% were chemicals. (Deane and Cole, 1967 p. 31).

This change over the period reflects the inventions and developments that took place—the vehicles, electrical apparatus, chemicals and much of the machinery exported in the 1950s did not exist in the 1830s. But it also reflected the catching up process of other countries, particularly with respect to their acquisition of the technology for manufacturing textiles and subsequently their improvement of it.

Britain's position is however regarded as the paradigm of industrialised power. She was dependent on exports of manufactures to import primary products, and she was better off and the countries from whom she imported worse off the lower the price of primary products relative to those of manufactures. Thus goes the argument buttressed by the extensive trade statistics available. This whole argument implies a high degree of mutual interdependence between Britain and the rest of the world.

Her dependence cannot be gainsaid. Domestic exports peaked at 23% of national income in the early 1870s and imports at 36% of national income in the 1880s. She was a very open economy and thus the difficulty she had in exporting in the 1880s was associated with a significant recession. In the period before the First World War exports had fallen to 15–21% of national income (Deane and Cole, 1967, p. 29). By 1950 they were 21% and by 1953 20% of national income (CSO *National Income and Expenditure 1961*). On the other hand imports ranged between 29 and 30% of national income (Deane and Cole, 1967 p. 29) but by 1950 and 1953 these were 22% of national income (CSO, 1961).

The significance of the British market to the rest of the world declined with time. She accounted for 30% of imports or primary products in 1876–80, but this proportion had fallen to 19% in 1913 which was similar to the proportion she accounted for in 1953. (Yates, 1959, p. 51).

The reason why Britain's imports of commodities were greater than her exports and indeed appear to have been since records began, is because of her net positive earnings on invisibles such as transport and insurance. The net flow of profits, interest and dividends has also been positive although its size has depended on her stock of foreign assets which is the result of her previous level of investment. Estimates of her flow of foreign investment vary from a peak of $6\frac{1}{2}\%$ of national income in the late 1880s and the first decade before the First World War (Yates, 1959, p. 36) to Brinley Thomas's estimate of 9% of national income in 1913 (Brinley Thomas in Dunning, 1972). According to the latter source, it was greater than gross domestic fixed capital formation between 1907 and 1913.

Most of this was portfolio investment, and the plantation type of investment was relatively unimportant. Most of the investment went to the recently developed countries of the US, Canada, Australia and New Zealand. Because Britain had a high propensity to import the kinds of products exported from these countries most of which were primary products (Thomas, 1972, p. 39; Yates, 1959, pp. 55 and 235) the loans did not prove difficult to service.

Britain's dominance in trade and investment, together with the resulting interdependence between her economy and the economies of the major exporters of primary products, led to a mutual interest in the stability of the financial system. This was largely under the control of the Bank of England, which maintained a gold standard system by which sterling was convertible into gold, and tended to adapt to deficits by altering the interest rate. Furthermore because sterling was the currency in which most trade was invoiced and took place, and also because Britain was a major foreign investor, other countries were normally willing to hold sterling as a reserve currency.

Thus under the British hegemony there was a symbiotic relationship between her expanding manufacturing sector and the exports of primary producers. Whether this is regarded as exploitive depends on the possibility of other patterns of expansion.

But exploitive or not, it certainly provoked the envy of other European and North American countries. Their governments began imposing duties on imports of manufactures in order to encourage import substitution. Indeed US tariffs had been rising since 1789 (Rossides, 1977, p. 5) with marked increase after the Civil War of 1861–5 (Saul, 1960, Chs. 6 and 7). After the Meiji restoration of 1868, Japan also began a systematic policy of industrialisation within a tightly protected domestic market by buying technology or training technologists abroad. She did not permit any foreign investment.

This appeared to lead to a reduction in the rate of growth of

British exports of manufactures, particularly of textiles, and they were sent further afield to China, West Africa, and India while those to Europe and North America declined in importance. Japan also increased her exports of textiles.

Britain also appeared to lose her technical lead. This was not only because other countries had acquired her technology in the production of textiles, iron and steel etc. It was also because there was a series of innovations in electricity, chemistry, and the automobile industry, of which the US, Germany and Sweden took much greater advantage than Britain (Thomas, 1972, p. 55), except in man-made fibres where a British firm was astute enough to acquire all the patents (Briscoe, 1971, p. 22).

This resulted in an increasing share of manufacturing exports from North America so that by 1913 it accounted for 10.6% of world exports whereas Britain's share had declined to only 25.3% (Yates, 1959, pp. 50 and 174). However, Britain was the only large country carrying out a policy of free trade. Indeed the general adherence to free trade was so strong that the campaign of Joseph Chamberlain at the beginning of this century to institute Imperial preference failed because any system of preference would first involve imposing duties.

The First World War shook this whole system of world trade. It disrupted economic activity and also resulted in an acute shortage of shipping. It signalled the beginning of the end of the British hegemony which was finalised by the Great Depression that began in 1929, and then the Second World War.

One facet of this was the change in British commercial policy. The shortage of shipping led McKenna, the Chancellor of the Exchequer in 1915, to impose import duties on luxuries or semi-luxuries. These duties were repealed in 1924 and then subseqently reimposed. The First World War also demonstrated the degree to which Britain was dependent on Germany for products such as optical glass and dyes. In order to encourage the establishment of such industries in Britain, very high duties were imposed on precision instruments, synthetic organic chemicals and optical glass under the Safeguarding of Industries Act of 1921.

Britain returned to the gold standard in 1925 but at the pre-war exchange rate with the dollar. As her rate of inflation had been much higher than that of the US the effect was to discourage exports and increase unemployment. The impact of the First World War was also felt in countries which had found it difficult to export to Britain. Those such as India and Egypt with large domestic markets and raw materials such as cotton, expanded their own textile industries. So determined was the Indian government to pursue this policy that after 1921 Britain allowed India to impose a duty on imports of cotton textiles from her.

The result was that at the end of the First World War, Britain faced much greater competition in the case of simpler manufactures such as cotton and jute goods in the home market of many underdeveloped countries, and in the world market increasingly from Japan and later from India. This was against a background of an absolute decline in the volume of international trade in textiles; if 1913 is taken as 100, by 1929 it had fallen to 98 and by 1953 to 70 (Yates, 1959, p. 168).

In the case of the more sophisticated manufactures it was already clear that the US had gained the technological lead. She was the major industrial power to remain unscathed or rather to have profited from the First World War by the maintenance of the high level of demand that it had induced.

The changeover can be seen from Tyszynski's analysis of world trade. He calculated that between 1895 and 1950 the real value of trade had increased at an average cumulative rate of 2.0% p.a. He grouped the various categories of manufactures according to their rate of expansion in international trade. The shares of the categories most subject to technological change were increasing fastest namely, motor vehicles (0.232), industrial equipment (0.140), electrical goods (0.094), iron and steel (0.050), agricultural equipment (0.036) and chemicals (0.017), the trend change in share p.a. is given in brackets. This may be compared with railways, ships etc. (−0.22), drink and tobacco (−0.026), apparel (−0.096) and textiles (−0.333). In the categories of industrial equipment, and electrical goods, UK exports were greater than those of the US in 1913 and smaller in 1929. In motor vehicles and agricultural equipment, US exports were 11% and 100% respectively larger than those of the UK in 1913, and 417% and 755% larger in 1929. Only in chemicals did the UK remain a larger exporter than the US and her lead was very much reduced (Tyszynski 1951, pp. 278, 279 and 283).

Although this may just appear as the supplanting of one country by another, the effect of the US on the international arena was very different. Britain's exports were almost entirely of manufactures, and most of her imports had been of primary products including a high proportion of food and agricultural raw materials. But the US had begun as an exporter of food and agricultural products and although she had increased her exports of manufactures she never specialised to the same extent. The US was inherently more self-sufficient. She also had a much larger economy. Thus trade accounted for a smaller proportion of National Income. Although changes in her level of activity might affect the rest of the world the reverse was not as true. In the long run this also had financial implications. For whereas before the war Britain had been the major creditor nation and the US had been a net debtor country, after the First World War the US began lending more so that she too became a net creditor country. In the 1920s the US accounted for about two thirds of the world flow of foreign investment and much of this was to Germany. In so far as German exports were competitive rather than complementary to those of the US, she found it difficult to service and amortise the loans.

This was the background to the Wall Street crash of 1929 which started off the Great Depression. Investment, production and employment fell in the US and this depression was spread through the rest of the world by balance of payments transactions. Loans were called in and imports fell. This reduced employment in other countries and put them in balance of payments difficulties. The volume of world trade in manufactures fell by 35% between 1929 and 1932 and prices fell by a similar magnitude. The volume of world trade in primary products fell by only 15%, but the price fall was much greater at 50% (GATT, 1958). In order to reduce unemployment and reduce its balance of payments deficit, each country followed what Joan Robinson termed Beggar-my-neighbour policies, that is it devalued or by some other means restricted imports and increased exports. This aggravated the depression for other countries and they were forced to follow suit.

At an international level, the main defensive policies could be classified as financial and commercial, and for both purposes countries gathered themselves into groups.

Britain left the gold standard in 1931 and since then sterling has never been directly convertible into gold. Many countries still held sterling as a reserve currency and many of them later became members of the sterling area.

The US devalued in 1933 but the dollar still remained convertible into gold. Other countries restricted the use of foreign exchange in various ways and Germany formed a currency union with the Balkan states.

The commercial policies adapted by governments could be roughly divided into those covering all commodities and those specific to agriculture. The Ottawa agreement of 1932 establishing the system of Commonwealth preference was of the first variety. Britain at last agreed to abandon free trade and adopt a tariff structure in which the tariffs were generally higher the greater the degree of processing. Duties on raw materials were generally zero. The system of Commonwealth preference was also established, with Britain waiving duties on most Commonwealth goods in return for similar privileges in the markets of other Commonwealth countries. When the duties were not entirely waived a lower rate of duty was imposed.

In addition the British government established an independent tariff commission which recommended changes in tariffs to the Board of Trade. Most of its ι ommendations for higher tariffs appear to have depended on the degree of unemployment in the British industry—they were generally accepted by the government. This was the system of protection for her manufacturing industries that Britain had established by the Second World War. As a means of alleviating the worst effects of the Depression and reducing the level of unemployment it was to a considerable extent successful—unemployment fell from 22% in 1932 to 11% in 1937. This was partly because she had fostered the domestic market for her industries by restricting imports. It may have been partly due to Commonwealth preference which reduced the competition from Japan particularly in textiles in Commonwealth markets; although this may merely have increased the competition by Japan in other countries.

In the US the steady rise in tariffs that had been taking place culminated in the Smoot-Hawley Tariff Act of 1930 which laid the foundation for the present structure of tariffs and raised their rates still further. However, under the Trade Agreements Act of 1934, the President was given the authority to negotiate tariff reductions and agreements. The US also had a Tariff Commission established in 1916 which was a fact-finding agency required to investigate the US need for tariff protection and the effects of the classification schedules and the tariffs and fiscal duties themselves (Rossides, 1977, Part I).

The other industrialised countries also endeavoured to increase their protection in the home or export markets. France, like Britain, had a preferential system with her colonies. Even so, Japan, a relative newcomer, managed to increase her share of world trade in manufactures; in particular her share of trade in textiles increased from 4% in 1913, to 10% in 1929, to 19% in 1937 (Tyszynski, 1951, pp. 286, 278, 279 and 280).

However, endeavours to restrict trade were not limited to manufactures. The reduction and variation in the prices of primary products provoked considerable efforts to control them.

The trade in minerals is dominated by very large multinationals, and their response to the Great Depression was in the formation of cartels to reduce production and maintain prices. But for both tin and copper, these were reinforced by more official schemes which received government support. (Yates, 1943).

But the most systematic intervention was in agriculture.

The major continental European countries—France, Germany and Italy—had followed a protective policy towards agriculture ever since the cereals from the New World, a cheaper source of supply, became available in the last quarter of the last century. In general, the governments supporting these policies appeared to be as much concerned with maintaining the population on the land as with its income. Peasants were regarded as paradigms of thrift, hard work and stability, and they were also regarded—particularly by France—as a reservoir of manpower suitable for the army. After the Second World War they also tended to be regarded as a bulwark against communism. The strategic nature of a domestic agricultural industry which can sustain the population even when imported supplies are cut off has also acquired intermittent importance.

However the dramatic fall in prices with the Great Depression focused attention on incomes, although the relation between prices and incomes does not always appear to have been considered. The need for protection was increased by the small size of holdings which was the result of a Napoleonic form of inheritance. Furthermore it had been intensified by Hitler's and to a lesser extent, Mussolini's drive for self-sufficiency.

Many barriers were placed on trade not only in the form of tariffs but also of quotas. By the end of the 1930s Britain, also the major importer of foodstuffs, had a series of quota agreements. A variety of price-maintenance schemes were introduced; in 1933 for instance, Britain introduced the Wheat Act, a form of deficiency payment scheme. (Tracey, 1964).

But the intervention that had the most far-reaching consequence for international commercial policy was that carried out by the major exporters. It is easiest to consider the policies of the two major categories: the wealthy exporters of agricultural products—Canada, Australia and the US—and the underdeveloped countries.

Of these schemes introduced by the wealthy exporters, that of the US described in Chapter 5 was by far the most extensive and long-lived. The Agricultural Adjustment Act of 1933 introduced the parity price concept, that is the notion of some equivalence between the price of agricultural products and manufactures. The base selected was that of 1910–14. A certain percentage of the parity price was aimed at for the commodities covered by the scheme, namely grain, cotton, groundnuts and flax seed. The Commodity Credit Corporation (CCC) was instituted as a buying agency for this purpose. Clearly, as the US was a major exporter, these provisions had to be buttressed by the subsidy of exports, otherwise the CCC would have continued to accumulate stocks, and also tariffs on imports, otherwise the subsidised exports might have just been reimported (Johnson, 1973).

The institution of a protective policy in the US by which she became insulated from world prices introduced a major distortion in the international market. The scheme was imitated, maybe not intentionally, by the Common Agricultural Policy of the EEC which was established much later.

The other main exporters of agricultural products were the underdeveloped countries. The products affected were food and raw materials.

The most severely affected foodstuffs were coffee and sugar, and of agricultural raw materials, cotton and rubber. The fall in their prices also led to various attempts at commodity control schemes often supported by the government.

The desire on the part of exporting underdeveloped countries for commodity control schemes continued after the Second World War as will be described later in Chapter 4, but a description of the international commodity agreements will not be included in this book.

There are several features of the situation in primary products that might be noted. Firstly, for some products the greater increase in supply than demand was already apparent by 1929. Rowe, for instance, cites coffee, sugar, petroleum, lead and also to a lesser degree, wheat, rubber and tin (Rowe, 1965, p. 79). With a high elasticity of supply with respect to price, this would merely have involved problems of adjustment. But the increase in productive capacity of some products was due to investment that had been carried out much earlier—this included not only minerals but also coffee and rubber. The chaos in the sugar market was due to the fragmentation that had occurred earlier in the market as a whole with beet producers protecting their market (Britain introduced protection in 1924) against the increase in productive capacity of the cane producers.

Finally, another factor that has contributed to changes in the market for agricultural products has been the development of synthetics. This has been hastened by the two world wars, which cut off or threatened to cut off the Axis or Allied powers from the sources of supply of natural raw materials. Thus, the first, rather poor, synthetic rubber was made by Germany during the First World War to counteract the British blockade. Research on it continued and in 1934 Germany began producing two good synthetic rubbers—styrene and nitrile—and production was expanded in anticipation of being cut off from natural rubber supplies yet again. Du Pont of the US had earlier produced neoprene, but production of synthetic rubber in the US and Canada was only undertaken on a large scale at the outbreak of the Second World War. The wars also encouraged the development and increase in production of synthetic fibres as substitutes for the natural ones, and for the war effort. For instance, nylon was commercially introduced in 1938 but the rapid expansion in its production in the Second World War was induced by its use in parachutes.

GATT in *Trends in International Trade* (GATT, 1958, p. 44) endeavoured to take account of the effect of these two elements— protection and the development of synthetics—on trade in agricultural products, by comparing the volume of trade in 1950–5 with that in 1913. Only those products not grown in industrialised countries showed as fast an increase in trade as manufactures, with those also not substitutable by synthetics an even faster increase.

However, another factor applying also to minerals appears to have been the decline in the proportion of natural raw materials and fuels in gross manufacturing output. That is, there has been a decline in the relative demand for natural inputs as compared with manufacturing output.

The overall situation of instability and decline in the world market for primary products on which underdeveloped countries are particularly dependent, has led to their continual sense of grievance. In airing this they have identified as of primary import-ance, changes in the relative prices of primary products and manufactures and price instability.

The study of these received its initial boost in the work of Folke Hilgerdt, who, marooned in the League of Nations in Geneva during the Second World War, decided to study the relationship between industrialisation, trade and the terms of trade. Since then there have been many other contributions by W. A. Lewis, C. P. Kindleberger, Lamartine Yates, P. T. Ellsworth, GATT, John Spraos, etc. They all appeared to agree that there had been a con-siderable fluctuation in the relative price of primary products to manufactures during the inter-war period, mainly due to the Great Depression, but there was considerable controversy as to the evidence of any long-run trend.

The studies of the pre-Second World War are generally based on the British and later the US trade returns. They are calculations of unit, that is average price indexes; for example, the unit value of wheat traded is the value of sales divided by the quantity traded. The increase in the price of any group of commodities that is obtained depends on the weight applied to the unit prices of the individual commodities comprising that group. The weights applied are of expenditure in a particular year. When the weighting is by expenditure in the earlier or fixed year, 0, the index is called a Laspeyres' price index, P_L, and when the weighting is in the later or current period, 1, the index is called a Paasche price index, P_P. Thus, the formula for a Laspeyres' price index comprising n commodities is:

$$P_L = \frac{\sum_{i=1}^{i=n} \left(p_{i0} \cdot q_{i0} \cdot \frac{p_{i1}}{p_{i0}} \right)}{\sum_{i=1}^{i=n} p_{i0} \cdot q_{i0}} = \frac{\sum_{i=1}^{i=n} p_{i1} \cdot q_{i0}}{\sum_{i=1}^{i=n} p_{i0} \cdot q_{i0}}$$

and that for a Paasche price index is:

$$P_P = \frac{\sum_{i=1}^{i=n} p_{i1} \cdot q_{i1}}{\sum_{i=1}^{i=n} \left(p_{i1} \cdot q_{i1} \cdot \frac{p_{i0}}{p_{i1}} \right)} = \frac{\sum_{i=1}^{i=n} p_{i1} \cdot q_{i1}}{\sum_{i=1}^{i=n} p_{i0} \cdot q_{i1}}$$

These unit prices indexes, which were in the pre-First World War period calculated entirely from UK trade statistics, are then regarded as representative of world trade. By 'deflating' or dividing the value of world trade by a price index, an estimate of changes in the volume of trade can be obtained. For instance, the value of trade in year 1 divided by the value in year 0 is:

$$\frac{V_1}{V_0} = \frac{\sum_{i=1}^{i=n} p_{i1} \cdot q_{i1}}{\sum_{i=1}^{i=n} p_{i0} \cdot q_{i0}}$$

If this is divided by the Laspeyres' price index, a Paasche volume index Q_P is obtained of the volume of trade in year 1 divided by the volume in year 0 weighted by the prices in year 1. If a Paasche price index is used, a Laspeyres' quantity index is obtained with the volumes weighted by prices of the earlier period.

International trade economists have found the procedure convenient because they can use the price information available for a few countries, generally the industrial ones, to obtain estimates of world changes in quantities.

Lamartine Yates made a major effort to investigate the developments in international trade that had occurred over the period from 1913 to 1953, which spanned the two world wars and the Great Depression. His task was complicated by the lack of standardisation and changes in classification of the trade statistics. His estimates of some of the main changes in quantity are shown in Table 2.1. The increase in the total volume in trade between 1913 and 1929 shows up clearly, together with its subsequent decline. Because Lamartine Yates is concerned with long-run trends, he does not chart the decline through the years of the Depression but the volume of trade appears to have reached its trough in the early 1930s. However, trade in all the major groups of commodities was lower in 1937 than it was in 1929, although higher than it was in 1913. Furthermore, trade had not increased as fast as manufacturing production between 1913 and 1929 except for minerals—the increase in the latter was due to the very great expansion in crude petroleum, a trade in which hardly existed in 1913.

Over the later period, between 1938 and 1953, the production of manufactures in market economies almost doubled. World trade also increased overall and for the individual categories, except for agricultural raw materials, the volume of which continued to

TABLE 2.1   Quantity Indexes of Trade 1913 to 1953

		World			
	Price Weights	1913	1929	1937	1953
Primary products	1913	100	138	129	
	1953	100		137	
Manufactures	1913	100	129	107	
	1953	100		108	
	World Excluding USSR & E.Europe				
Primary products	1913	100		131	158
	1953	100		139	143
Of which food		100	135	131	156
Agricultural raw materials		100	131	115	103
Minerals		100	155	151	216
Manufactures	1913	100	(124)	109	174
	1953	100		110	176
World export value[3]		100	125	110	160
World manufacturing production[3]		100	155	158[1,2]	310[2]

Notes: 1. 1938
    2. Base 1929 excluding USSR and Eastern Europe.
    3. Derived from League of Nations and UN figures.
Source: P. Lamartine Yates, *Forty Years of Foreign Trade* (Allen & Unwin, London, 1959), Tables 13, 17 and Table 5.

decline. This reflects the substitution by synthetics which has already been mentioned.

However, as mentioned, the dissatisfaction of developing countries has focused less on the quantities traded than on relative prices, that is terms of trade. The terms of trade is generally taken as the ratio of price indexes; if the price index of manufactures rises in relation to that of primary products, the terms of trade is considered as moving against primary products.

TABLE 2.2   Export Unit Values 1913 = 100

	1896–1900	1913	1929	1937	1953	1960[4]	1968[4]
Food total		100	113	85	226[1]	119	214
Cereals		100	107	88	215[1]	170	186
Livestock products		100	137	114	268[1]		
Beverages		100	123	79	352[1]	268	283
Oilseeds and fats		100	92	68	171[1]	157	159
Fruit and vegetables		100	105	69	150[1]		
Sugar		100	84	62	157[1]		
Agricultural raw materials		100	126	110	273[1]	265	238
Fibres		100	133	106	290[1]	235	222
Wood		100	110	106	281[1]		
Wood pulp		100	179	155	434[1]		
Rubber		100	85	87	110[1]		
Hides and skins		100	118	121	359[1]		
Tobacco leaf } Tobacco manufactured }		100	158	154	308[1]		
Oil cake and fodder } Other materials }		100	130	120	324		
Ores and concentrates		100	127	129	235	237	251
Coal and coke		100	105	123	295		
Petroleum		100	157	118	250		
Fertilizers } Other minerals }		100	111	113	200		
Primary products[2]		100	119	102	236		
Manufactures[2]		100	140	124	275		
Primary products[3]		100		96	262	246	251
Manufactures[3]		100		123	272	296	321

Notes: 1. Arithmetical Average of 1912 and 1953 weights and excluding Iron Curtain countries.
2. Weighted at 1913 prices.
3. Weighted at 1953 prices except for 1968 which is at 1963 prices.
4. Estimated from UN figures. Base weights for removing Oil and Fats from UN Agricultural Non-Food index to Food those of 1963.
Source: Lamartine Yates, *Forty Year of Foreign Trade*, pp. 41 and 43.

The export unit values of some of the major categories from 1913 to 1953 are shown in Table 2.2. As can be seen, there is a considerable variation in the unit price rises for primary commodities with the greatest increase to 1953 being shown for wood pulp, and the least for rubber—both are the products of trees but the latter, unlike the former, is substitutable by synthetics. Weighting his indexes with the quantities for 1913, Lamartine Yates calculated that the price indexes of primary products and manufactures had risen to 236 and 275 respectively by 1953 which suggests that the terms of trade moved adversely to primary products by 17%. On the other hand, if they are weighted by quantities in 1953, the price indexes for primary products and manufactures appears as 262 and 272 and the adverse movement of the terms of trade appears to be only 4%.

GATT, taking the same period (but with a base of 1920–38), calculated that the terms of trade of agricultural products in relation to manufactures had increased by 6% (GATT, 1958, p. 44).

Some of Lamartine Yates' series can be extended using UN statistics. These suggest that at least between 1953 and 1968, there was a clear movement of the terms of trade against primary products of 23%. The price of manufactures had risen by 18% whereas the price of primary products as a whole had actually fallen.

This type of finding was given the status of an economic law by Raul Prebisch who asserted that there was an inevitable tendency for the terms of trade between primary products and manufacture to move adversely. He argued that there was an increase in productivity for both, but because primary products were produced under conditions of perfect competition, the benefits of this had to be passed on in the form of lower prices of primary products, whereas manufactures were produced by oligopolistic firms facing monopsonist trade unions. The latter appropriated all the increase in productivity in manufactures in the form of an increase in wages which kept the prices of manufactures up. The result was a persistent tendency for the terms of trade to move against primary products (UN ECLA, 1950).

Prebisch appears to have been influenced by his Latin American background in his discussion of primary products. The agricultural products he was considering may be produced under conditions of perfect competition. But this is scarcely the situation for minerals, the extraction of which is mainly carried out by very large firms—that is of oligopoly with undifferentiated products. Nor is it the situation for plantation crops.

Since then the argument has proceeded on a number of fronts. There has been a further investigation of historical statistics which are generally based on British trade returns. But in these British statistics, import prices are quoted to include the cost of insurance and freight (c.i.f.) and are not the prices of the products as they leave the exporting country which are described as free on board (f.o.b.). Ellsworth has argued that because of the reduction in costs of transport, much of the long-term decline in relative price of primary products (c.i.f.) was not a decline to producers themselves (f.o.b.) (Ellsworth, 1961).

The controversy has continued and so has the concern of developing countries. The UN and now UNCTAD have continued to monitor present trends. They have also been anxious to calculate true price indexes. These are based on the prices of specified qualities of a commodity at specified locations weighted again either by the quantities sold in the earlier or later periods. Any appreciable change in the quality of a commodity over time is then shown up by a divergence between the price index and the unit value index. If there is a relative shift in exports to the higher qualities which are more remunerative, the unit value index of exports will rise more than true prices indexes.

In other words, in dividing the values of a commodity by a true price index, the shift in quality will appear as a change in volume. The most recent UN tabulations of price indexes of primary products are given in the Appendix, Table A1. But these cannot generally be obtained for manufactured goods so unit value indexes have to be used for them and also for commodity trade as a whole.

Let us now turn briefly to consider how prices have changed since 1963, or more importantly since 1968. Price indexes of some of the major commodities in international trade are shown in Table 2.3. As can be seen, by dividing the price index for 1980 by that for 1963, there is a wide variation in price increases. But as prices have also fluctuated, a more systematic approach is necessary. In the present situation of worldwide inflation, the straight calculation of trends or standard deviations would be unsatisfactory in so far as it would incorporate a price rise common to all commodities. Therefore each price index has been divided by the unit value of all exports before making any calculations. Taking the thirteen observations from 1968 to 1980, the standard deviation for the series is first calculated. The trend for the change in real price is then calculated together with its standard error, given in brackets. Finally, the standard deviation around the trend is also calculated.

The strongest trend, as might be expected, is the 13.57% p.a. rise in the price of crude petroleum in real terms. This is sufficient by

TABLE 2.3 Export Price Indexes of Primary Commodities[1] 1975 = 100

	1963	1968	1969	1970	1971	1972	1973	1974	1975	1976	1977	1978	1979	1980	Real Price Indexes 1968–80[2]			
															Increase 1980 1963 %	Standard Deviation %	Trend	Standard Deviation around Trend %
Food	42.7	42.7	44.4	47.4	50	57	88	114	100	104	120	122	137	156	365	*10.29*	−0.61(0.77)	10.45
Wheat	39.6	38.4	37.2	35.6	38	42	79	116	100	86	64	76	95	106	268	24.29	−2.87(1.67)	22.53
Maize	46.3	41.2	45.4	50.9	50	49	89	119	100	102	113	145	176	210	454	12.15	+1.37(0.86)	11.39
Rice	43.3	55.0	48.9	43.3	42	47	89	141	100	72	78	98	92	119	275	27.95	−4.60(1.66)	22.39
Beef	37.6	45.2	48.5	55.7	70	83	110	96	100	105	114	145	178	178	473	17.06	−1.03(1.28)	17.32
Butter	66.0	53.5	52.8	58.8	70	79	76	80	100	103	116	141	163	186	282	14.65	−1.83(0.99)	*13.36*
Oilseed, oils and fats	48.3	47.8	48.8	57.0	57	55	97	145	100	98	120	127	145	130	269	18.34	−2.30(1.24)	*16.71*
Oilseed cake and meals	58.0	61.5	59.8	65.0	65	86	188	114	100	129	152	137	152	156	269	*28.12*	−3.46(1.91)	*25.76*
Fish	34.7	40.9	44.4	52.3	61	75	101	119	100	131	147	179	188	201	579	14.94	+1.74(1.03)	13.90
Sugar	29.3	16.4	19.4	19.9	22	36	48	146	100	57	40	39	48	139	474	*47.84*	+0.67(3.70)	49.91
Coffee	47.0	52.7	55.0	71.9	63	71	87	95	100	200	350	228	242	239	509	*30.64*	+3.40(2.14)	28.86
Cocoa	37.4	49.7	65.0	47.1	37	48	91	133	100	161	308	259	243	192	513	*36.01*	+4.47(2.44)	32.93
Tea	92.8	73.3	70.5	77.9	77	77	79	101	100	112	200	159	158	161	173	22.43	−3.74(1.32)	*17.82*
Fruit	61.7	52.4	54.3	50.0	58	62	76	79	100	91	110	125	133	154	250	12.92	−2.58(0.63)	*8.50*

Table 2.3 (continued)

	1963	1968	1969	1970	1971	1972	1973	1974	1975	1976	1977	1978	1979	1980	Increase 1980/1963 %	Real Price Indexes 1968–80[2]		
																Standard Deviation %	Trend	Standard Deviation around Trend %
Agricultural raw materials	*53.3*	*51.2*	*53.9*	*53.9*	*56*	*64*	*102*	*112*	*100*	*117*	*125*	*134*	*164*	*179*	*336*	*10.33*	*−1.07(0.73)*	*9.87*
Cotton	48.7	49.6	47.7	50.1	55	60	103	119	100	132	127	125	133	156	320	14.66	−1.40(1.05)	14.22
Wool	80.7	59.7	58.9	50.8	46	81	186	126	100	109	118	123	142	161	200	30.33	−3.06(2.16)	29.13
Rubber	91.9	67.1	88.3	70.8	57	58	120	127	100	138	146	177	227	253	275	19.47	−0.84(1.49)	20.04
Hides and skins	51.6	55.7	68.6	60.9	65	133	153	116	100	146	162	206	341	207	401	28.47	+0.55(2.20)	29.65
Wood pulp	32.6	33.5	34.8	40.4	42	40	51	82	100	96	89	78	101	122	374	12.38	−1.03(0.91)	12.24
Timber	44.4	50.6	53.7	51.9	59	74	109	112	100	118	129	142	169	169	381	13.13	−1.14(0.96)	12.90
Minerals and non-ferrous Metals and crude petroleum																		
Iron ore	54.4	51.1	50.0	52.7	56	55	71	80	100	97	92	85	102	121	222	19.81	−4.75(0.55)	7.37
Non-ferrous metals	48.1	72.1	84.1	86.5	74	74	106	131	100	109	117	126	167	186	387	23.48	−5.25(0.89)	12.05
Total of above					51	56	85	108	100	106	117	120	139	159				
Crude petroleum	16.1	16.1	16.1	16.1	19	22	30	100	100	106	117	117	170	295	1832	57.28	+13.57(1.71)	23.03
All primary commodities	32.2	32.2	33.1	24.7	37	42	62	105	100	106	117	119	152	217	674	18.19	+4.13(0.66)	8.86
Manufactures 1963 = 100	100	104	108	114	121	131	152	185	212	212	237	266	304	338	338	8.59	−1.86(0.35)	4.84

Notes: 1. Linked to index based on 1963 at 1971. Indexes of dollar unit prices.
2. Export price indexes deflated by unit value index of world exports given in Table 8.1.
Source: GATT, International Trade, 1980/81 Table A4; 1979/80 Table A5; 1973/74 Table 5; 1972 Table 4.

itself to provide a *positive* trend for primary products as a whole of 4.13% p.a.

For agricultural products, most of the trends are insignificant. Over the period, the only clearly significant ones are a negative trend of −4.6% p.a. for rice, and one of −3.74% p.a. for tea and −2.58% for fruit; the negative one for butter of −1.83% and oilseeds, oils and fats of −2.30% is also nearly significant.

In so far as the trends are significant, the standard deviation around the trend should be considered. In so far as they are not, the first standard deviation should be taken into account—indeed the trend makes little difference to it. These standard deviations are in italics.

The standard deviations for agricultural products are generally high and mostly very much greater than that for manufactures. They are highest for the tropical products—sugar and coffee—but they are also high for wool, hides and skins, oilseed cakes and meal, and maize, some of which are provided by temperate countries.

For the separately identified minerals, iron ore, and non-ferrous metals, there is a significant negative trend of around 5% p.a. Their standard deviation around trend is lower than that of most agricultural products but higher than that of manufactures.

Finally, the significant negative trend for manufactures should be noted. This arises because their price has not risen as fast as that of oil.

Thus, this recent evidence cannot be regarded as supporting the Prebisch thesis. On the other hand, the international economy has been in a state of international macroeconomic disequilibrium in which it is difficult to identify any long-run trend. Furthermore, the period considered is relatively short.

Through most of this book, a longer view is taken.

However, when considering price indexes or unit value indexes over the whole post-war period, certain features of the international economy should be borne in mind. Firstly that, as can also be seen from Table 8.1, from 1953 to the late 1960s, the price of manufactures was stable or only rising slowly—at less than 1% a year. Then in 1968, the price increase began to accelerate. It was this acceleration that provided the Organisation of Petroleum Exporting Countries with the initial pretext for raising the price of oil.

Secondly, an index for the free market price of petroleum is somewhat difficult to obtain because large oil companies extracted most of the oil in the Middle East under profit-sharing and taxation agreements with the governments of the countries concerned. In order to reduce their contribution, the oil companies tended to price crude oil as low as possible so that they appeared to make their profits at the refining stage. However, the UN has now calculated an index—see the Appendix, Table A2. This shows the effects of the initial price rises instituted by OPEC in the early 1970s, and then after the Yom Kippur war, the quadrupling of oil price between 1973 and 1974 and the erratic increase since then. The last major OPEC price rise resulted in the price of crude petroleum rising by $2\frac{1}{2}$ times between 1978 and 1980. The price of oil is largely determined by the OPEC decisions on prices because OPEC producers are willing to back up a price rise by reducing production and because consumers have no immediate substitutes. This is discussed further in Chapter 12.

Thirdly, because of the very large increase in the price of oil and also because of the rapid increase in the volume traded between 1950 and 1973, very different price changes for minerals, primary products or trade as a whole are obtained according to whether the indexes are based on weights for a year before or after 1973. In 1953, crude petroleum had a weight of 10% in primary products as a whole, by 1970 this had risen to 20% and by 1975 to 50% (UN, 1979). Most of the indexes used in this book are based on the weights of 1975. But in order to extend them backwards, they generally have to be linked to an index with an earlier base. In Table A2 a linkage is shown by placing − − round the figure for that year.

3 Financial Background

In this chapter we will consider the financial and economic background against which international trade is taking place.

BALANCE OF PAYMENTS ACCOUNTS

But before we do so we will first of all consider the role of trade in a country's overall balance of payments. A country's balance of payments is a record of all economic transactions carried out between its residents and residents of other countries over a given period of time. For this purpose residents include the subsidiaries of foreign firms. The account is in the form of double entry book-keeping and may be presented in the currency of the country being considered, or in a foreign currency.

The transactions include those in goods, that is visible trade which is the subject matter of this book, services, and financial assets. A transaction is regarded as positive if it adds to a country's supply of foreign exchange and negative if it uses it up. Thus, exports are positive items and imports negative items.

The purchase of financial assets i.e. stocks, shares and bills from the residents or government of another country is regarded as a negative item and vice versa. In order to balance the account it is also necessary that the sale of gold and foreign exchange reserves be regarded as a positive item.

The items in the balance of payments must, in the nature of double entry book-keeping, add up to zero. Any discrepancy is due to errors or incomplete statistical coverage. This is shown as an errors and omissions term or 'balancing item'.

In order to assess the state of a country's balance of payments it is necessary to consider the different accounts that comprise it. *The Current Account* is a record of all transactions in goods and services over the given period of time. It is a flow account and is the foreign counterpart of a country's national income accounts. A subsector of this is the *visible account* which just relates to trade in goods, with which we are basically concerned. In order to exclude the service element from visible trade, imports and exports are valued free on board as they leave the exporting country (f.o.b.) as opposed to (c.i.f.) which means for imports, the inclusion of the cost of insurance and freight. This also means that because a traded item is valued the same by the exporting and importing country, it is possible to draw up networks of trade showing the overall flow of goods from origin to destination. In order also to be able to divide this flow into different commodity categories, international organisations have made great efforts to standardise nomenclature.

Most of the figures in this book are based on the Standard International Trade Classification published in 1950 but which was revised in 1961 (Rev. 1) and then again in 1975 (Rev. 2) to take account of the changing structure of trade. The GATT figures are on the basis of Rev. 1 whereas the OECD figures since 1978 have been on the basis of Rev. 2. The aim of standardisation is to ensure not only that all exports of one country are imports of another, but that net exports, that is exports minus imports, of any particular area of any particular commodity, must be equal and opposite to the net exports of the rest of the world. For instance, if Industrial Areas' net exports of Road Motor Vehicles were $22.6 billion in 1979 this must be equal to negative net exports, or net imports by the rest of the world by the same amount.

An additional complication is that of trade in commodities involving no processing in the country concerned. Some countries, such as the UK, Hong Kong, Singapore, South Africa and centrally planned economies, include this type of entrepôt trade in their reporting of exports and imports; others exclude it. GATT, where possible, excludes entrepôt trade. It now accounts for only a small proportion of trade and therefore makes little difference to the overall picture, and of course makes no difference to net exports. However, in the 1950s, it accounted for a high proportion of the trade of some small developing countries such as Hong Kong and its inclusion suggests a lower growth in exports than has in fact occurred for domestically produced goods.

A country does not have to be in balance on its visible account. Most countries are not. The US ran a fairly large positive balance until the late 1960s but according to GATT statistics has had a negative balance since 1971. Britain has traditionally had a negative balance, the exceptions being 1956, 1958 and 1971. But the advent of North Sea oil and the resulting reduction in imports of fuel has changed this to a positive balance since 1980.

The balance on visible account may be offset by balances on other items in the Current Account; Britain always has a positive balance on sales of services, that is transport, tourism and financial services and a large and growing item entitled 'Other'! She also has a positive balance on flows of interest and dividends. These are often called *invisibles* and include purchases by governments as well as private individuals and firms.

The US has a positive balance on services and so, to a smaller degree, do most other Western European countries. But Japan has a negative balance on services and so do most developing countries.

In addition, there are also gifts sometimes called unrequited transfers. They include all immigrant remittances, and all defence and economic development aid. As these transfers are not made in exchange for any goods or services, they could be included in an account of their own.

The total balance of payments for services, interest and dividends and transfers is called the *invisible balance* and together with the visible balance give the balance on Current Account. For the US before 1970, this was generally positive. For Britain it has fluctuated between positive and negative. For most other European countries it was positive until 1973, but for many developing countries it was negative.

The overall balance on Current Account must be equal and opposite to the total balance of Capital Account transactions.

The capital transactions of a country represent the *changes* in its inter-country loans and debts. An addition to its assets appears as a negative item in the balance of payments. Such foreign transactions may be carried out by individuals or firms within the country concerned. Loans may be long term, i.e. exist for a year or more and then they are generally made by the purchase of financial assets. Such would include all shares or equity which gives the holder part ownership of real productive assets and provides him with a dividend. This is known as foreign direct investment. Alternatively, they may be bonds which are loans to companies or governments entitling the holder to a fixed rate of return per year but imply no ownership.

In addition there are short-term loans. These may be made to a government by the purchase of its bills, such as the purchase of British Treasury bills which have a three-month life. There are also trade bills, bills of exchange, which an exporter sells against his dispatch of goods and which are eventually paid by the importer when he receives them. But these have become relatively insignificant. Of increasing importance is trade credit. This may be extended on imports or exports for the purchase of goods. Countries also sometimes borrow directly, either from the international financial institutions, which we will describe later, or from the international money markets.

EQUILIBRIUM IN THE BALANCE OF PAYMENTS

In appraising these various accounts, how can a government determine whether a country is in deficit or surplus or in equilibrium in its balance of payments overall? Should it consider just one particular account such as that of visible trade, or the current account? This question is important in so far as the selected balance will be an indicator for government action. Furthermore, it is desirable for all countries to use the same indicator, so that the deficits of some countries are balanced by the surpluses of others. Otherwise countries may be following inconsistent policies. For instance, the US might look at her deficit on visible trade and try to correct that, even though her balance on current account is positive. Whereas other countries might look at the current account balance, which over all of them must be negative, (because the US has a positive balance) and try to correct that. Whether countries try to carry out the correction by devaluation or by internal deflationary policies they would be acting inconsistently and the net effect would be a reduction in the world level of activity and the policies would also be self-defeating.

A broader view of a country's international position used to be taken by distinguishing between autonomous and accommodating items in the balance of payments. Autonomous transactions were those carried out by people and firms with regard to their intrinsic profitability. These were regarded as including all items in the current account and long-term capital movements; these comprise the basic balance.

Accommodating transactions were responses to a country's balance of payments position, speculation and anti-speculation and any necessary borrowing. These were regarded as including all short-term capital movements, that is purchases of financial assets or loans that lasted less than a year, and changes in a country's reserves.

A country was regarded as in a balance of payments deficit if the total balance of autonomous items was negative, and vice versa. Under a fixed exchange rate regime, such a deficit would mean that a government would have to use up its reserves, or obtain loans to maintain the value of its exchange rate.

However, there has been a tendency to move from the basic balance concept to a balance for official financing as an indicator of the state of a country's balance of payments. This includes all autonomous items and short-term capital movements. The balance that becomes important is the amount of government intervention required to support the exchange rate, either by the sale of reserves or obtaining loans.

A discussion of the balance of payments has preceded that of financial institutions because the latter are largely concerned with countries' adjustment of the former.

For a government, the balance of payments position of a country with a fixed exchange rate may just represent the constraint within which it may pursue its macroeconomic objectives of full employment and growth. Yet for some countries, such as Britain, balance of payments equilibrium has been raised to the status of an objective in its own right.

Few countries appear concerned about a surplus in their balance of payments, although it is just the counterpart of others' deficits. The onus of adjustment is always placed on the deficit country.

The initial approach to adjustment, both in theory and in practice, was to regard the cause of the imbalance and the means of adjustment as lying in the current account. This may be because most countries have some restrictions on their capital accounts.

The question then became the degree to which adjustment to a deficit was automatic say by the reduction in income (Keynes) or the reduction in money balances (Alexander and H. Johnson) of the country in balance of payments deficit. Alternatively, could equilibrium only be achieved by deliberate government intervention by devaluation, or the imposition of quotas or tariffs on imports? These all had the effect of making imports appear relatively more expensive and thus of inducing their substitution by domestically produced products. Devaluation also led to exports appearing relatively more profitable.

So these measures led to an expenditure switch from foreign to home-produced goods, and thus to an increase in the overall level of demand within the country. In the 1950s and 1960s when most industrialised countries had full employment, such expenditure switching had to be accompanied by some form of internal expenditure reduction, otherwise the resulting excess demand led to inflation which tended to cancel out the initial improvement.

However, during the Great Depression of the 1930s such measures were frequently used by governments, not only to correct a country's deficit in its balance of payments, but often also to reduce its unemployment. But the reduction in the deficit on the visible account that was obtained just represented a reduction in the demand for the goods of other countries, and thus transferred the deficit and unemployment to them. These were therefore called beggar-my-neighbour policies. They represented the means by which the US depression was transmitted to the rest of the world leading to a multiple reduction in income and trade.

INTERNATIONAL FINANCIAL INSTITUTIONS

It was in order to avoid a repetition of such a situation that the Allies met even before the war had ended to discuss the international financial arrangements that should govern trade and capital movements in the post-war world. For this purpose the UN Monetary and Financial Conference met at Bretton Woods in 1944. This set up the International Monetary Fund (IMF) and the International Bank for Reconstruction and Development (IBRD or World Bank). Most of the industrialised countries, apart from Switzerland and those in Eastern Europe, became members, and there was a steady increase in the membership of underdeveloped countries over time.

The World Bank was to be concerned with long-term investment. Initially much of its effort was devoted to the 'restoration of economies destroyed or disrupted by war'. But later it concentrated on investment in underdeveloped economies.

The objectives of the IMF were to provide conditions for 'the expansion and balanced growth of international trade' and 'exchange stability' and 'to avoid competitive exchange depreciation'. Thus, members had to agree on par values of their currencies expressed in terms of gold or US dollars converted into gold, and actual spot values were not to fluctuate from these by more than 1%. Only in the case of 'fundamental disequilibrium' (itself not defined), and then after consultation with the Fund, was a country entitled to change its par value.

So that a country could ride out temporary deficits in its balance of payments without resort to deflationary measures or devaluation, members were also provided with borrowing facilities. Each country's facilities were dependent on the size of its quota. The size of the initial quota allocated to a member appears to have been dependent on a number of different economic factors incuding its GNP, total trade and monetary reserves. The US had the largest quota and the UK the second largest. Each member had to contribute 25% of its quota in gold, and the rest in its own currency, thus providing the Fund with a pool of gold and currencies. A member could borrow from the Fund to cover disequilibrium in its balance of payments, but the conditions laid down for borrowing after the first tranche (25%) were fairly stringent. Initially it could only borrow 25% of its quota within a year[1] and 200% all told. Because of this and because of the restrictions most countries maintained on the conversion of their currency into others, the Fund did not effectively add to the world supply of liquidity in the late 1940s and early 1950s. Only when convertibility for current-account transactions was introduced by most Western European countries in 1958 and the IMF quotas were increased by 50% in 1959, could the IMF be really regarded as an effective force.

ADEQUACY OF RESERVES AND EXCHANGE RATE CHANGES

There was very little addition to gold reserves during the period because a high proportion of the supply of freshly minted gold went for industrial use (chemicals and jewellery) and private hoards, and also because after the war gold continued to be kept at the exchange rate of $35 to the ounce, which did not encourage production. Thus although the proportion of new gold going for monetary uses was 54% in 1954–9, by 1960–5 this had fallen to 30%. In 1966 and 1967 there was a net outflow of gold from monetary reserves.

The increase in reserves largely came from the supply of dollars. In the immediate post-war period there was an acute shortage of them. Many capital goods were required for the rebuilding of war-devastated Europe, and only the US could supply them.

But although the rest of the non-communist world was very dependent on the US, the US was very much less dependent on it; only 4% of her GNP was derived from exports. Hence, her initial insensitivity to the vast problems of reconstruction and re-employment of labour required to place the European Countries on a peace-time footing, and the difficulties they faced in international trade. Britain's position was made more acute by the large sterling balances that had been accumulated during the war by other countries as a payment by her for goods and services provided during the war. At the end of the war these amounted to £3500 million which was accepted as a debt for repayment in due course (Conan, 1966, p. 79). But the US terminated lend-lease in 1945, and when Britain sought a loan fom the US to cover her inevitable deficit, one of the conditions attached to it was the convertibility of sterling. Its introduction in 1947 was estimated to have resulted in a £50 million loss of reserves in a month (Pollard, 1969, p. 360) before it was removed on 20 August (Dow, p. 24). This eventually led to a UK devaluation in 1949, from $4 to $2.8 to £1.

But by this time the US was beginning to be more aware of the total position, and this awareness eventually led to the introduction of Marshall Aid in 1948. This was allocated in accordance with the anticipated deficits of individual European contries, and was conditional on them extending aid to each other and reducing trade barriers between themselves. From 1946 to 1958, US aid and government loans to Europe amounted to $25 billion (Maddison, 1965, p. 162). In addition the Organisation for European Economic Co-operation was set up to administer the Marshall Aid and a series of organisations were set up to improve clearing facilities between European countries. The last of these, the European Payments Union, was wound up when convertibility on current account was introduced by most European countries in 1958.

So, although it was the dollar problem that appeared to dominate the trading situation in the immediate post-war period, this was to a considerable extent alleviated by the US granting of aid and loans and also by the US agreeing to, and indeed encouraging the European countries to discriminate against US goods in favour of imports from each other. This must be remembered in examining the growth of total and intra-European trade.

Meanwhile, other strains had been placed on the world economy. First the communist takeover of Czechoslovakia in 1948, and then the Korean War in 1950, resulted in a drive towards rearmament on the part of North America and Western European countries except for Germany. The Korean War also led to a rapid increase in the demand for primary commodities, the price of which rocketed, placing a further strain on the international economy.

The US ran a deficit on her balance of payments, partly due to her transfers abroad, but mainly due to her net outflow of long-term foreign investment. This was only partly accommodated by an inflow of short-term capital. Other countries were happy to accumulate dollars to begin with to add to what they regarded as their insufficient reserves. However, the eternal problem of reserve currency countries then emerged, that is that other countries are quite willing to continue acquiring their currency if they are confident that it will maintain its real value by, for instance, remaining convertible into gold, but that the more they accumulate, the more they are likely to doubt this. On the other hand the major source of additional liquidity was in fact provided by the US. The UK deficits contributed a small amount but sterling declined in relative importance as a reserve currency. The additions to the world supply of gold for monetary purposes were very small. And as already mentioned, the IMF accounted for only a small proportion of liquidity. Furthermore, although the quotas of members had been increased, the net addition to the reserves of countries was small because 25% of any quota had to be made up by the country's contribution of gold to the IMF.

Economists generally agreed that the need for reserves increased with the level of trade but there ensued a long controversy about the optimal level of reserves in relation to trade, and also the best means of increasing the level. The first approaches were theoretical and most of the models had, in practice, to be modified, to allow for the greater degree of co-operation between central banks. This took its most tangible form in the arrangements negotiated in Basle in 1961 for 'swaps', that is, three months loans allowed to a country when its currency came under speculative attack.

However, the controversy about the form of reserves and their increase continued. On the one hand there have always been proposals to raise the price of gold, thus increasing the value of a component of reserves and encouraging its production. The political objections to this were that it would benefit the gold producers South Africa and Russia, unpopular in the West, and it would also benefit countries such as France who had been least co-operative in countering speculation against the dollar by continuing to demand gold in exchange for her holdings of dollars.

There is also the objection to gold being used as a monetary reserve in that it requires real resources to produce it when it is only going to be buried in bank vaults, such as those of Fort Knox. These arguments, of course, apply to any commodity being used as a monetary reserve.

Eventually an agreement was reached to institute Special Drawing Rights. As enshrined in the first amendment to the IMF, these were reserve assets that did not require any prior contribution of gold or reserve currencies by countries receiving them. As a compromise between the US and UK who wanted them to be wholly owned reserve assets, and the French who wanted them to be merely in the form of a loan over a five-year period, a country was required to maintain an average of 30% of its allocation. The stronger-currency countries were also not required to accept more than double their allocation.

An SDR was valued at $\frac{1}{35}$ of an ounce of gold, that is, it was given the value of a dollar. The initial allocation of $9.5 billion distributed over 1970, '71, '72 was allocated to member countries of the IMF in proportion to their quotas.

The SDR scheme appears to have come into effect at exactly the wrong time. Inflation had already taken an upward turn in 1968 in almost all countries of the world. In monetary terms this appears to have been fuelled by the deficit the US ran to finance the Vietnam War, and in so far as the issue of SDRs provided additional liquidity, it can only have exacerbated inflation.

Meanwhile, the controversy about reserves had been extended into another area, namely the debate about the relative merits of fixed and flexible exchange rates. With freely fluctuating exchange rates in the extreme form advocated by Friedman, no central bank reserves would be required; all adjustments to a balance of payments deficit or surplus would immediately be made by an alteration in the country's exchange rate. This approach was completely contrary to the IMF charter and philosophy. Nevertheless it began to be espoused in government circles, as balance of payments difficulties proved more and more difficult to rectify.

For instance, in the 1960s the UK government had tried hard not to devalue. This was an obvious course of action when the Labour Government came into power in 1964 to inherit a balance of payments deficit of £700 million. But the Labour Party did not want to be the party of devaluation, having already carried out the devaluation of 1949; sterling was also still a reserve currency and thus a devaluation would entail the reduction in the value of this component in other countries' reserves. The Bank of England endeavoured to maintain the value of sterling by borrowing from the IMF and other central banks, and intervening both in the spot and eventually the forward market. A deflationary policy was also adopted by the government in 1966. All was to no avail, and in 1967 Britain devalued. But even this did not immediately correct her balance of payments deficit.

However, it is regarded as having contributed to a worsening of the US position. So that in 1971 the US concluded the Smithsonian agreement by which the dollar was devalued in terms of gold, from \$35 to \$38 an ounce, and thus depreciated in terms of other currencies as well. The convertibility of dollars into gold was removed.

The members to the agreement also agreed to widen the margins of fluctuation of a currency around its parity value from 1% to $2\frac{1}{4}$%. This meant that each currency had a maximum range of fluctuation of $4\frac{1}{2}$% round its parity and that different currencies could fluctuate by up to 9% against each other.

This disturbed members of the EEC who had agreed to the principles of monetary integration and for whom fluctuations in exchange rates created severe difficulties for the Common Agricultural Policy. They formed an organisation called the snake, which restricted their margin of fluctuation to 1% and allowed a maximum range of fluctuation between member countries of 2%.

However, the only consistent members of the snake were Germany and the Benelux countries. In March, 1979 this was replaced by the European Monetary System. The pivotal unit was termed the European Currency Unit and was a weighted sum of the values of the main EEC currencies including that of Britain. Britain, however, is not a member. The other EEC countries who are members can allow their exchange rate to fluctuate by 1% around

its ECU parity level but only $2\frac{1}{4}$% either way from that of another EMS currency, except for Italy whose margin is 6%.
Meanwhile the other large countries had continued their movement towards flexibility in exchange rates. Britain transferred to a managed float in June 1972, the US in 1973. However, as the dollar was still used as the main currency of intervention in the support of other currencies, it was difficult to alter its relative value without the agreement of other countries.

Somewhat belatedly, the IMF officially recognised this general conversion to flexible rates in its Second Amendment of 1978. This included various provisos, one of which was that 'each member must avoid manipulating exchange rates or the international monetary system, in order to prevent effective balance of payments adjustment or to gain an unfair competitive advantage over other members'.

The monetary link with gold was also officially cut by no longer allowing a country to specify the par value of its currency in terms of gold. Since 1974 the SDR had been taken as a numeraire. Its value is determined by a weighted basketful of the major currencies.

Fortunately, the actual conversion to fluctuating exchange rates had occurred long before its official recognition. For without it, adjustment to the major shock to the international economy would have been very difficult.

IMPACT OF OPEC PRICE RISE

This was the OPEC action in quadrupling the price of oil from 1973 to 1974. The rationale for this was that it was required to maintain the purchasing power of oil, which had been eroded by the rapid rates of inflation in the industrial countries and the resulting rise in price of manufactures that the oil exporters wished to buy. However, the increase was far greater than could be accounted for by this, and undoubtedly the other basic motives of OPEC were to maximise their revenue from an export commodity in inelastic demand and to reduce the rate of its depletion.

Oil was an important item in international trade accounting for about 10% of the imports of OECD countries in 1973 and thus the rise in its price had both macro and micro implications.

The macro effects occurred because the rise in price of oil resulted in the revenue of the oil producers increasing very rapidly—even though the high price could only be maintained by reducing output. The OPEC countries were unable to spend all their additional revenue and therefore the surplus they built represented a reduction in purchasing power for the world as a whole. Some Keynesian economists argued that governments should counter the deflationary effect of this by increasing, or at least maintaining the domestic level of demand. Britain and the US also half-heartedly tried to maintain the level of aggregate demand and employment until they were forced by adverse movements in their balance of payments to contract it. This was because the response of most of the other industrial countries was to correct their balance of payments by following a contractionary policy.

The other developing countries were also badly affected. Although their purchases of oil were relatively small they were very dependent on them (see Chapter 12) and their terms of trade moved very adversely. For some of the more populous countries such as Egypt, India and Pakistan, the effect was mitigated by the remittances they received from their nationals who had gone to work in the OPEC countries of the Middle East.

An additional problem was that relative exchange rates were also affected by how the OPEC contries held their surpluses. If they kept them in dollars, this kept up the price of dollars. But in so far as they transferred their holding into sterling or D marks, this lowered the price of dollars and raised that of the latter currencies.

International organisations made considerable efforts to persuade the OPEC contries to 'recycle' that is, lend their oil surpluses to other counries, particularly underdeveloped ones. Some of the recycling that has occurred has been through the international financial institutions, but most of it has gone through the private banking system.

The whole situation is a bankers' nightmare. Bankers have got to encourage recycling in order to keep up the total level of world activity. But this means lending on what is regarded as a less and less creditworthy basis. In addition, the overhang of OPEC surpluses provides a possibility of massive instability between exchange rates. Many countries are afraid to induce any radical changes in their exchange rate because they are afraid of undermining the whole system.

Let us now consider the overall effect of the price rise on the international trading situation. The OPEC countries raised their export earnings from fuel from $37 billion in 1973, to $136 billion in 1978, an increase of approximately $100 billion. Over the same period they raised their imports of manufactures from $16 billion to $78 billion, an increase of $62 billion almost all of which ($54 billion) came from industrial countries. They also increased their imports of primary products (other than fuel) by $10 billion, $8 billion of which was food. Most of the food came from industrial countries and Oceania. This left them with an increase in their trading surplus of $25 billion per annum.

However, when the accounts of the main groups of countries are considered (see Chapter 8) it is clear that the industrial countries over reacted to their potential deficit in trade such that their actual trade deficit declined from − $9.2 to − $4.6 billion between 1973 and 1978. Whereas the non-oil developing countries' trading deficit increased by $28.6 billion between 1973 and 1978 which was considerably greater than the increase in their trading deficit in fuel, which was only $10 billion. The Eastern Trading Areas as a whole remained in balance on their trade although their exports and net exports of fuel were increasing.

Thus the counterpart of the larger OPEC surplus was the increase in the deficit of other developing countries, which they appear to have financed by borrowing on the open market. Because of the OPEC surpluses, credit was easier to obtain, but it was also more expensive than the types of soft loan they had previously obtained fom international institutions.

The decline in the deficit of industrial countries is a reflection of the very contractionary policies they pursued. This represented their difficulty in adjusting and persuading their workforces to adjust without inflation to lower real incomes, due to the decline in their terms of trade. Thus, even if their total output remained the same, less was available for domestic consumption and investment. Secondly, there was the difficulty of adjusting to the higher relative price of fuel which shifted the demand of consumers and producers towards more fuel-efficient products.

The higher price of oil did, of course, induce a search for other non-OPEC sources of oil and other fuels. At the higher price it became profitable to exploit the resources of the North Sea, and Britain is now a net exporter of oil. This did not ameliorate the effect of the original price rise, which raised the price of fuel which both consumers and producers have to pay. But in so far as a country is a net exporter, it benefits from any subsequent rise in price.

The OPEC countries then forced up the price of oil, yet once again, from 1979 to 1980. However, in order to do so they had to reduce their output still further. They now account for less than half the oil produced outside communist areas (*Financial Times*, 10 November 1982).

Their surpluses have also begun to disappear. This is partly because they are now providing a smaller amount. But it is mainly because governments are spending more, in the case of Iran and Iraq in fighting each other. Let us briefly consider the effect of this on the overall growth of trade. The great difficulty encountered by industrial countries in achieving their macroeconomic aims of full employment and price stability, has led them to resort to some very contractionary measures which has in turn led to a fall in investment. There has also been an increasing tendency to resort to beggar-my-neighbour policies, to try and maintain employment in the industries most seriously affected (see Chapter 4). As can be seen from Chapter 8, the result has been a deceleration in the growth of trade and now stagnation, and decline and instability in trade in minerals.

NOTES

1. Or more if the Fund held less than 75% of the value of its quota in the member's currency.

4 Commercial Policy

Now let us turn to consider commercial policy. By this I mean government intervention in a market which discriminates between units of a commodity by their origin or destination.

Over the period, commercial policy has often been used for strictly political objectives. In particular, recent US Presidents appear to regard embargoes on exports to the USSR as appropriate and peaceful means of exerting pressure on it. Thus Carter's response to the USSR invasion of Afghanistan in 1979 was a partial embargo on exports of grain. In response to the discontent of US farmers, Reagan abolished this when attaining office in 1980. But the repression of the Polish free trade union Solidarity and the dissident movement it represented, led Reagan to try and prohibit exports for the natural gas pipeline being laid from Siberia to Western Europe, not only by US firms but also by the foreign firms licensed to use US technology. European governments and firms strongly objected, and in November 1982 Reagan abandoned these sanctions. But the US is still anxious to restrict the sales of high technology to the USSR.

The problem is that either the effectiveness of the embargo is reduced by a general switching of trade partners so that the countries without the trade sanctions are exporting to the USSR; in the case of the grains embargo, these were Argentina, Canada and Australia. Or if complete substitution cannot be carried out because the US is such a large supplier, or the only source of technology, then there is a reduction in sales and that damage is inflicted not only on the USSR but also on the US exporters.

In contrast to these political manoeuvres, commercial policy is generally in the form of tariffs, quotas or export subsidies. An analysis of their effects is given in Chapter 5.

But why are they applied when one of the main tenets of international trade theory is that free trade maximises the level of world production and therefore the potential for world welfare?

One obvious reason for imposing a tariff is to collect revenue. This is still of importance in developing countries, many of which impose duties not only on their imports but also on their exports of primary products. Export duties are particularly high on oil (petroleum) as will be discussed in Chapter 12, and also were on agricultural products in West Africa, as discussed in Chapter 5. But this source of revenue declines in importance as countries industrialise.

Another reason is to encourage the establishement of new industries, the 'infant industry' argument for tariffs. Most countries which industrialised after Britain did so behind tariff barriers; the import duties imposed were generally higher the greater the degree of processing of the product.

But the primary use of tariffs and quotas in industrial countries is to maintain employment or increase producer returns in an import competing industry, particularly 'sensitive', that is declining industries such as textiles, and now steel and cars.

For whatever reason tariffs and quotas are imposed, such government intervention entails the relative prices of goods within a country being different from those on the international market. In economists' jargon, it induces a distortion between the rate at which one commodity can be substituted for another domestically, and on the foreign market. This discriminatory effect is the source of inefficiency, with which we will primarily be concerned.

However, the argument about free trade maximising world production loses its universal validity when countries are not able to maintain full employment. In that case, a government may raise protection in order to reduce domestic unemployment and increase domestic output.

This is because of its expenditure-switching features, that it shares with a devaluation. For instance, if a 20% duty was imposed on all imports and a 20% subsidy given to all exports, this would be similar in its effect on the goods market to a devaluation of 20%. The increase in the aggregate demand for domestic goods which would lead to increased employment at home would be at the expense of a reduction in the demand for foreign goods and hence the transmission of unemployment abroad. It would be a beggar-my-neighbour policy.

Thus, the Great Depression of the 1930s gave an upward impetus to all forms of protection in a way that was ultimately self-defeating. Each country, by employing such measures, transmitted its unemployment to others with the net result of a contraction in trade and stagnation of output, as described in Chapter 2.

Furthermore, the endeavours of countries to protect themselves by forming preferential trading blocks as described in Chapter 2, sometimes led to great political dependence of the less developed or smaller members on the industrialised member country. The most tragic example of this is the dependence of the Balkans on Nazi Germany.

It was with this experience in mind that the Allies regarded the regulation of trade as a priority in their plans for a better post-war world.

The US drew up a proposal for an International Trade Organisation. Meanwhile, as a committee worked on a draft charter, the major countries signed as an interim agreement, the General Agreement on Tariffs and Trade (GATT) by which the participants agreed to extend most favoured nation status to each other and agreed to reduce tariffs.

Then in 1947–8, the United Nations Conference on Trade and Employment was held in Havana. It drew up the Havana Charter which put forward a series of objectives, namely:

(1)   To assure a large and steadily growing volume of real income and effective demand, to increase the production, consumption and exchange of goods, and thus to contribute to a balanced and expanding world economy.

(2)   To foster and assist industrial and general economic development, particularly of those countries which are still in the early stages of industrial development, and to encourage the international flow of capital for productive investment.

(3)   To further the enjoyment by all countries, on equal terms, of access to the markets, products and productive facilities which are needed for their economic prosperity and development.

(4)   To promote on a reciprocal and mutually advantageous basis the reduction of tariffs and other barriers to trade and the élimination of discriminatory treatment in international commerce.

It also drew up a code of conduct to govern international trade and investment.

Among other things there was a general demand for the lowering of trade barriers. Specific proposals included those for:

(a) the gradual elimination of quotas on trade (except when used to deal with balance of payments disequilibrium);

(b) the extension of most favoured treatment to all member countries, that is the application of the same tariff on their products. Certain preferential trading areas were excluded from this including the Commonwealth preference scheme;

(c) a removal of price discrimination (defined as the difference between a country's domestic price and foreign price). In cases of discrimination a country was entitled to apply countervailing duties;

(d) a reduction of tariffs.

A plan was put forward for the International Trade Organisation to supervise the enforcement of such measures. In the event the US Congress refused to ratify it. Meanwhile the General Agreement on Tariffs and Trade accepted the main provisions of the Havana Charter.

However, the initial liberalising of trade between European countries in the early 1950s was largely achieved under the provisions of the 'Marshall Plan' administered by the OEEC as mentioned in the previous chapter. Quotas on manufactures were removed and foreign exchange restrictions lifted. In the early post-war period because of the dollar shortage the US allowed discrimination against her goods, but by the late 1950s this had also been removed. By 1958 there was general foreign exchange convertibility for current-account transactions.

The formation of GATT extended the degree of multilateralism in trade because its member countries extended most-favoured-nation (mfn) status to each other and to each new member. However many countries were very reluctant to extend the same to Japan. They complained of her past 'unfair competition' of which they cited instances of 'dumping, exploiting labour, violating copyright laws, and patent rights', and the 'sudden flooding' of markets to destroy competition. (Patterson, 1966, p. 274.) The US and Japan said that with the new laws and institutions this would be unlikely to recur. However, many continued to fear that Japan would be a 'particularly aggressive, international competitor in labour intensive goods' (Patterson, 1966, p. 275). But the US, who was responsible for her post-war rehabilitation, continued to press her case and in 1955 Japan was admitted to GATT, although fourteen of its members including Belgium, France, the Netherlands and the UK entered reservations on their own behalf and that of thirty dependencies (Meyer, 1978, Patterson, 1966, p. 286). Britain, as one of them, continued to negotiate trade and quotas every year, until in 1962 she negotiated a trade treaty setting down the annual quotas for imports from Japan which were generally increased over the period 1963–5. The most limiting was that for cotton yarn which was zero over the whole period. In 1956 Japan also agreed to a 'voluntary' restraint of some of her textile exports to the US. But by the 1970s most countries had removed their special provisions with respect to Japan.

It was difficult to compare the protective structure of different countries until industrialised countries agreed to adopt the Brussels nomenclature for tariff classification. Some comparative schedules for Western European countries and the US were drawn up by

TABLE 4.1   Tariffs on Textiles—ad valorem equivalent mfn.
percentages

| | Basic rate 1 January 1957[1] | | | | 1 January 1960 | | |
	Germany	Benelux	France	Italy	CET of EEC	US	UK
Raw materials							
Wool—sheep or lambs' not carded or combed	0	0	0	0	0	0–47	0–10
Cotton—raw, not carded, combed, bleached or dyed	0	0	0	6	0	0–8	0
Yarn							
Woollen yarn ⎫ not for retail sale	6	4	4–6	12 ⎫	6	25–39	7.5–10.0
Worsted yarn ⎭				⎬			
Cotton yarn not for retail sale	5–15	0–10	15–20	15–22	10	$6\frac{3}{4}$–27	7.5–24
Cloth							
Woven fabrics of wool or fine animal hair (not containing synthetic or artificial fibres)	12	18	15	20	16	28–90	17.5–24
Cotton gauze					15	n.i.	25
Terry towelling of cotton ⎫	10–14	12–18	20–25	20	18	20	17.5–24
Other cotton woven fabrics ⎭					17	17.5–34.5	17.5
Carpets and mats							
Carpets and rugs, knotted or coiled of wool (and fine animal hair)	20	24	80	35	40	$11\frac{1}{4}$–30	10–20
Carpets—other	19–21[2]	24[2]	20[2]	25[2]	23	8–50	20–42

Table 4.1 (continued)

	Basic rate 1 January 1957[1]				1 January 1960		
	Germany	Benelux	France	Italy	CET of EEC	US	UK
Other made up textile products							
Blankets	14[2]	15–25[2]	15–25[2]	18–22[2]	19	17–83	20–42
Bed, table, toilet or kitchen linen, curtains, etc.	15	24–30	20–30	20–30	22	10–65	17.5–42[3]
Tarpaulins, sails, awnings, sunblinds, tents					19	15–41	20–42
Clothing other than knitted or crocheted							
Men's and boys' outer garments	15	24	20–22	20–22	20	10–42.5	20–33.3
Women's and girls' outer garments	15	24	22–25	20–22	20	10–42.5	17.5–33.3
Men's and boys' undergarments including shorts	15[4]	24[4]	22[2]	15–30[4]	20	5–42.5	20–33.3
Women's, girls' and infants' undergarments	15[5]	24[5]	25–30[5]	20–30[5]	22	10–42.5	20–33.3

Notes: 1. Basic rates for the calculation of the Common External Tariff (CET) of the EEC except for Italy, ignores the 10% reduction made in 1951. Rates are often higher if the yarn or cloth of the stated fibre is mixed with other fibres.
2. Of wool.
3. If cotton—higher with mixture of man-made fibres or silk.
4. Containing over 50% of man-made fibres, underwear.

Sources: Political and Economic Planning, *Tariffs and Trade in Western Europe* (London, Allen & Unwin, 1959); Political and Economic Planning, *Atlantic Tariffs and Trade* (London, Allen & Unwin, 1962).

PEP. The tariffs on raw or basic materials were generally zero or very low. Apart from that the general feature of industrial countries' tariff schedules is that tariffs tend to be higher the greater the degree of fabrication of a commodity. Take as an example the schedules for textiles and clothing in the UK in 1960 shown in Table 4.1. There were no tariffs on raw cotton or wool, but they were 7.5% on yarn, 17.5% on cloth, and 20% for bed linen and carpets, which are further processed, and generally higher still for clothing which undergoes even more processing.

However, for the UK the continuing influence of arrangements arrived at during the 1930s was still apparent. Commonwealth preference meant that duties on imports of many products from Commonwealth countries were zero and others were at a preferential rate. The products covered by the Safeguarding of Industries Act of 1921, which included precision instruments and synthetic organic chemicals still attracted very high rates of duty.

Other countries also had particular industries which they heavily protected often for historical reasons. But high rates on cars in Norway and Switzerland were more excise than protective duties as there is no domestic industry. However, the general picture that emerged was of zero or low rates of duty in Scandinavian countries and Switzerland and much higher duties in other continental countries.

As examples the schedules for textiles and clothing, and motor vehicles in the major European countries and the US are shown in Tables 4.1 and 4.2. The basic rates in Germany and the Benelux were somewhat lower than those of France and Italy in 1957. These basic rates were used as the basis for establishing the Common External Tariff (CET) of the EEC. They are somewhat higher than the rates actually being charged at the time because they do not include the 10% cut agreed to in 1951.

US duties were very complicated and difficult to compare, particularly for textiles and clothing where they varied greatly according to fibre content. For motor vehicles and components, US tariffs tended if anything to be lower than the UK ones and the CET.

In retrospect, the mid-1950s appears to be the time when multilateralism in trade, a primary objective of the Havana Charter, was most nearly achieved. But it was soon to be abandoned.

In the earlier part of the period the only move away from this multilateralism was the formation of customs unions and free trade areas.

They received general approval in the Havana Charter and Article XXIV of GATT in so far as they increased freedom of trade

TABLE 4.2 *Tariffs on Motor Vehicles and Components*—ad valorem *equivalent mfn.*
percentage

	Basic rate 1 January 1957				1 January 1960		
	Germany	Benelux	France	Italy	CET of EEC	US	UK
Rubber tyres	19	24	22	28	22	8.5–12.5	20–33.3
Internal combustion piston engines							
Automobile with more than 250cc.	12	15	25	25	19	10–15	30
Electrical starting and ignition equipment for internal combustion engines for motor vehicles							
(a) Starting motors	8	12	20	16.5	14	10.5	17.5–30
(b) Sparking plugs	8	12	25	40	18	10.5	17.5–30
Electrical lighting and signalling equipment, windscreen wipers, defrosters and demisters							
(a) Lighting equipment					17	10.5–30	27.5–39
(b) Sound signalling equipment					14	10.5–30	20–30
(c) Other					15	10.5–15	15–30
Motor vehicles with engines							
(a) For transport of persons	17–21	24	30	35–45	25–29[1]	8.5–10.5	22.5–30
(b) For transport of goods	21	24	30	35–40	25–28[1]	10.5	15–30
Special purpose motor vehicles—breakdown lorries, road sweepers, etc.					25	10.5	30
Chassis for vehicles fitted with engines					29	0–11.5	15–30
Bodies for vehicles					24	0–11.5	30
Parts and accessories for motor vehicles	19	6–24	25	20–40	19	10.5	15–30

Note: 1. Higher rate for those with spark ignition or compression ignition engines.
Sources: Political and Economic Planning, *Tariffs and Trade in Western Europe*, (London, Allen & Unwin, 1959); Political and Economic Planning, *Atlantic Tariffs and Trade*, (London, Allen & Unwin, 1962).

between member countries. But such agreements were to cover a substantial part of the trade of member countries, and their duties and other regulations concerning trade with third, that is non-member, countries were not to be higher or more restrictive than before. They were also to include a schedule for the completion of the union or free trade area within a reasonable period of time.

In the Havana Charter some mention was made of compensation for those countries who would be adversely affected. But the clause mentioning compensation was eventually removed from GATT and was not a feature of any subsequent arrangements.

EUROPEAN ECONOMIC COMMUNITY

However, the effect of unions on third countries did become an issue with the formation of the European Coal and Steel Community (ECSC) in 1951. The signatories—France, Germany, Italy, Belgium, Netherlands and Luxembourg—agreed to remove all barriers on trade between them in coal and steel, but these provisions were not extended to the rest of the world. The Scandinavian countries and Austria in particular were concerned about the effect of it on their exports of steel to the ECSC and later about the evidence of price discrimination being practised by producers in the ECSC between their internal and external markets. (Patterson, 1966, pp. 125–38.)

But this, together with the customs union between Belgium, the Netherlands and Luxembourg (Benelux) the treaty for which was signed in 1939 but which could not be put into effect until 1948, were just precursors to the full customs union of the six countries established by the Treaty of Rome signed in 1957 called the European Economic Community (EEC).

The impetus for this greater economic integration was that it would lead to a greater degree of political co-operation and integration which would prevent another world war ever starting because of conflicts between European countries, in particular France and Germany.

The provisions of the Treaty of Rome were both very broad and very imprecise. But it specified free trade between member countries in manufactures and agricultural products, and the institution of a common external tariff. The Common External Tariff (CET) was meant to be the arithmetic average of the member countries' tariffs, that is the basic rates shown in Tables 4.1 and 4.2. But the rates for certain commodities were negotiated with an upper limit.

The treaty also provided for the removal of discriminatory

practices between member countries which could affect trade. In addition, it provided for the removal of restrictions on the mobility of capital and labour and that is why it is generally referred to as the common market.

The Treaty of Rome also provided for the present institutional structure with the Commission (EEC civil service), Council of Ministers of the member countries (political decision-making body), the European Parliament (representative body).

The influence of this institutional structure on the commercial policy pursued by the EEC should not be underestimated. The Commission initiates policies which are presented to the Council, which generally amends them sometimes beyond recognition. For instance, each year the Commission presents its proposals for agricultural prices but the Council representing the member countries has generally raised them. Because the finance of the Common Agricultural Policy (CAP) is compulsory, as laid down by the treaty, once the price level is set expenditure becomes determined in an open-ended way; it entirely depends on agricultural production. Thus, the protection of agriculture is built into the constitution of the EEC.

With respect to the other industries the Commission is primarily concerned with the standardisation of the conditions of competition of industries in different member countries and the removal of restrictive practices.

But since 1973, as member countries have found increasing difficulty in both maintaining full employment and controlling inflation, the Commission has shown increasing interest in the position of individual industries. Information and consultation concerning these are obtained from a series of committees, which generally consist of representatives of the industries, employers' federations, trade unions and maybe some independent members. The effect of this method of gaining information is to make it very strongly orientated towards the interest of the industry concerned with very little account taken of interests of consumers. The European Parliament provides no effective counterweight as it is also far more responsive to the lobbying of the producer interests. For instance, in *The Report on the Crisis in the Textile Industry* drawn up by The Committee on Economic and Monetary Affairs of the European Parliament with rapporteur M. T. Normanton and adopted in 1977, the interests of consumers are not once mentioned.

In the international sphere the EEC has, since its inception, negotiated as a body within GATT. In 1980 the negotiation of quotas on imports was also transferred from member countries to the Commission.

EUROPEAN FREE TRADE ASSOCIATION

Britain disliked certain elements in the EEC. These included the Common Agricultural Policy (CAP) described in more detail in Chapter 5, her inability to continue with Commonwealth preference in such a union, and its supra-national aspects. Thus, when she found herself excluded from the EEC she proceeded to found the European Free Trade Area with Norway, Sweden, Denmark, Switzerland, Austria and Portugal in 1959, with Finland becoming an associate member in 1961. This was purely a free trade area in manufactures with all barriers on trade in them between member countries being removed. Because there was no common external tariff some rules of origin had to be included to prevent all goods from outside just entering EFTA through the country with the lowest tariffs. EFTA had no political objectives or central organisation other than a secretariat.

But Britain continued negotiations for membership of the EEC. It was made clear to her that accession to the CAP was a condition for entry. In negotiations the EEC also made quite clear that India and Pakistan were going to be granted no privileged status as for instance was afforded to former dependencies of France. Furthermore, although Hong Kong as a British dependency should have been eligible for association under Part IV of the Treaty of Rome, she was specifically excluded, and was only admitted to the generalised system of preferences with the exclusion of her exports of textiles and shoes (Young, 1973, p. 153).

In 1973 Britain was admitted together with Ireland and Denmark. The remaining members of EFTA then combined with the EEC to form a free trade area in manufactures.

OTHER FREE TRADE AREAS

There have also been numerous attempts to establish free trade areas in the developing world. Sometimes the main objective has been, as with the EEC, to achieve greater political integration by means of economic integration; such have been the Arab unions between Egypt and Libya, and Egypt and Syria and in 1965 an Arab Common Market open to all Arab League states. But these have been more temporary than those designed to assist economic development, in particular, by expanding the market for the manufacturing industries set up within the participating countries behind protective barriers. The most notable of these are the Central

American Common Market (CACM) established in 1958, and the Latin American Free Trade Association (LAFTA) created in 1960, which grew to include all the major Latin American countries. In Africa, the best established was the East African Common Market consisting of Kenya, Tanzania, and Uganda, which had been functioning since the early 1920s, but it suffered from the suspicion of the latter two countries that Kenya was deriving most of the benefits from it, and also from the political troubles in Uganda, and it collapsed in 1978. These arrangements have only covered a fraction of the trade of the participating countries which in turn has been only a small proportion of world trade. So from a world point of view these agreements have no significant effect. (Patterson, 1966, pp. 139–271.)

Meanwhile GATT had persisted in its attempts to reduce the level of protection. It organised a whole series of tariff-reducing sessions, the most important of which were the Dillon round in 1962 and the Kennedy round from 1964–7, and the Tokyo round, 1973–9. Each country refers to its tariff reductions as 'concessions' which have to be met by 'concessions' on the part of the other countries which will assist its exports. That is, in these negotiations each country acts in the interest of its existing domestic producers and seldom the efficiency of its economy as a whole. Although, of course, the rationale for the negotiations themselves is an improvement in world efficiency. The result of these rounds was a gradual lowering of tariffs on trade in manufactures.

For instance, the tariffs on motor vehicles were reduced over the post-war period. As can be seen from Table 14.2 the CET was lower than the previous French and Italian duties, and in later rounds of tariff bargaining this was reduced still further so that by 1972 the import duties on cars for the EEC, and UK were 11%. France also removed her quota on imports of cars in 1959.

Japan began the period with very heavy barriers to imports. She had removed her quotas by 1967 but in 1968 still had tariffs of 40% on small cars, 35% on large cars and 30% on trucks and buses. Under the Kennedy round she agreed to reduce these by 50%. Most of the pressure for reduction has come from US producers who also object to the excise duties on large cars being so much greater than on small cars.

But in 1970, Japan reduced her import duty on small cars to 20% in exchange for Italy expanding her imports quota on Japanese cars to 1000 units. (Duncan, 1973.)

By 1978, Japan had abolished all import duties on cars although difficulties in registration appear to represent some form of non-tariff barrier.

However, the protection of agricultural products and of 'sensitive' items, that is the products of declining industries, were generally excluded from these cuts by industrialised countries (UNCTAD, 1975). These exclusions were noted by developing countries many of whom had only recently acquired their independence.

They found themselves faced with a series of international institutions in whose establishment they had not participated. While it was obvious that trade had increased very rapidly, they were doubtful about the degree to which they were benefiting. In particular, they felt that the lack of any reduction of agricultural protection discriminated against them. These doubts were expressed and rationalised by Prebisch who developed his theory of the inevitable adverse movement of the terms of trade of primary products discussed in Chapter 2.

In order to mollify them, the UN Assembly set up the United Nations Conference on Trade and Development (UNCTAD) which met for the first time in 1964. A considerable amount of research was carried out by it to investigate the argument about the terms of trade. Numerous proposals were put forward, the most significant of which were the demands for commodity stabilisation schemes, access for primary products, preferences for manufactures exported from developing countries, and most recently, the transfer of technology to developing countries. The United Nations Industrial Development Organisation (UNIDO) also proposed in 1972 that developing countries should aim to supply 25% of the world trade in manufactures by 2000 AD. In effect, the developing countries were demanding preferential treatment or assistance through improved trading opportunities for their own economic development.

This involved the abandonment of the laboriously negotiated extensions of the mfn status to new member countries in favour of a lower tariff on imports of commodities, particularly manufactures, from developing countries. The industrialised countries eventually agreed to this. The EEC introduced a generalised system of preferences (GSP) scheme in 1971, the US and Canada in 1973, and Japan also in the 1970s. But in all cases these were hedged with numerous restrictions. One of these was the tariff quota, that is the quantity of imports from developing countries that would be eligible for this discount. The other was the limit placed on the use of the preference scheme by any single country—this might be a fraction of the tariff quota, or it could be some given overall value. For the US, in 1976, preferential treatment was denied 'to any article from any beneficiary who provided more than $29.9m. or

50% of total U.S. imports of the article in the previoius year'. (UNCTAD, 1978, p. 17.)

However, because the developing countries did regard the GSP as important, they were reluctant to have the mfn tariff of industrialised countries cut because this would reduce their margin or preference. In objecting to this, the developing countries had abandoned the basic objectives of GATT. The GSP bore a faint resemblance to Commonwealth preference which had only been possible when the UK abandoned her free trade policy. But the Commonwealth system as such never included a quota (the UK only had quotas on agricultural products, coal and steel in the 1930s), only preferential treatment.

The underdeveloped countries in turn had also imposed a whole range of duties, foreign exchange restrictions and quotas on their imports. In the first place, they were generally imposed to protect their nascent industries. But later, particularly when the South East Asian and West African countries had used up the foreign exchange reserves they had accumulated during the Second World War, and then during the Korean War boom, they were used for balance of payments reasons because the countries were reluctant to devalue or devalue sufficiently to achieve equilibrium in their foreign balance. In certain countries, most noticeably India, the duties were differentiated so that very high duties were imposed on luxury goods, such as air-conditioners, and low ones on investment goods.

GATT has officially recognised the claim of underdeveloped countries for special treatment, and their right to raise tariffs on their imports at the same time as they demand special preferences for their exports of manufactures to industrialised countries. The pressure on them to liberalise their trade has largely come from the World Bank, which has conducted a number of studies which indicate the costs of such distortionary policies.

OFF-SHORE PROCESSING

Ironically, perhaps, the greatest assistance the developing countries have received for exporting manufactures has been from large vertically integrated firms in industrial countries which have endeavoured to minimise their costs of production by transferring labour-intensive processes to developing countries. US and German firms have taken advantage of their tariff code which allows duties to be imposed only on the value added abroad and not the total value of imported items if the home country supplied the original inputs. In the US tariff schedule they have to come under items 806.3 and 807.0.

The processes carried out are not only for the traditional labour-intensive industries such as clothing, but also include labour-intensive processes in many of the high technology industries particularly the assembly of electronic equipment. In 1969, Helleiner estimated that imports under Item 807.00 of the US tariff schedule were $367 million with a 43% value added abroad of $159 million. Metal products, that is office and electronic equipment, were the most important, accounting for $125 million of value added abroad (Helleiner, 1973, p. 41).

OECD estimates also show a rapid growth, with German imports under such provisions rising from DM 386 million in 1962 to DM 2.6 billion in 1976. In the 1980s they accounted for 25–30% of German output of clothing. (Noelke and Taylor, p. 305.) In the US such imports rose from $61 million in 1966 to $2.8 billion in 1976 (OECD, 1979A).

The countries involved are generally neighbouring countries, that is Mexico and Puerto Rico for the US, and East Germany and Yugoslavia for Germany, but they also include a number of Asian countries, in particular Hong Kong, Taiwan, South Korea, and Singapore (Helleiner, 1973).

These special tariff provisions, as the EEC has had cause to emphasise, only apply when the inputs are supplied by the importing country.

BUY-BACK ARRANGEMENTS

Another bizarre feature of the commercial scene is 'buy-back' arrangements by which a firm from an industrial country builds a plant generally in an Eastern European country and accepts part of the output of that plant as payment for it. Much of the EEC's car imports from Eastern Europe come under such schemes.

Both of these are methods of gaining access to the markets of western industrial countries and bypassing the growing trade barriers. But they have in no way dampened the demand by developing countries for less discrimination against their products.

THE TOKYO ROUND, 1973–79

In the Tokyo round GATT both drew attention to the interests of developing countries and provided them with technical assistance in the negotiations. But, in general, the tariff reductions achieved for industrial products were greatest for non-electrical machinery, wood products, chemicals and transport equipment mostly of interest to industrial countries, and were least for textiles, leather and rubber sectors which are of more interest to developing countries. (GATT 1979, p. 120.)

However, much of the Tokyo round was given to a consideration of the non-tariff barriers to trade which became increasingly important as tariffs were reduced.

One of these was subsidies. Almost all industrial countries ascribed to the 1960 Declaration Giving Effect to the Provisions of Article XV1:4 of the GATT which prohibited export subsidies on industrialised products. But non-signatories and developing countries were free to use them. With respect to primary products, however, governments agreed that they should 'seek to avoid' export subsidies and should not apply them so as to secure 'more than an equitable share of world export trade' in the product concerned.

However, the negotiators had considerable difficulty in dealing with subsidies granted directly to an industry. Could these not be regarded as the legitimate activity of a government concerned with a country's economic and social problems?

Let us take an example. There are no protective duties imposed on ships and under the Tokyo Agreement all customs duties were removed on the importation and repair of civil aircraft. (GATT, 1979, p. 180).) This reflects the concern of governments with the state of their shipping lines and now their airlines. But the actual production and trade in these products is largely determined by government subsidies. These may be direct production subsidies, or in the case of aircraft, subsidies for research and development.

Little progress was made in this matter apart from an agreement to regard minerals as manufactures rather than primary products and thus not open to export subsidies by industrialised countries.

It was reaffirmed that countervailing duties should only be imposed by the importing country when such subsidised products caused, or threatened to cause, damage to domestic producers, and that they should not be greater than the subsidy. (GATT, 1979 p. 129–31.)

More success was achieved over government procurement. Previously a government had been able to discriminate in favour of domestic producers when acquiring goods for its own use. But in the Tokyo round it was agreed to end this discrimination for purchases over SDR 150,000 (approx. US $195,000) and to open tendering procedures.

Another form of non-tariff barrier is the quota. From the beginning GATT had permitted the use of quotas on a temporary basis for a country in balance of payments difficulties. But together with the OEEC it had made great efforts to negotiate their removal for any other purpose. By the mid-1950s they had been largely successful (it could be said that quotas were an implicit feature of trade agreements with the Sino-Soviet bloc. But these must be regarded as outside the scope of the present discussion in so far as they are not conducted through commercial channels).

ORGANISATION OF TRADE IN TEXTILES AND CLOTHING

However, the disappearance of quotas was short-lived. The earliest overt reappearance of them was in textiles and clothing. A short description will be given of how they have gradually spread to encompass almost all the trade between industrialised and developing countries in these products, and the great difficulty GATT has had in controlling, let alone liberalising, them.

As already explained, most of the major European countries were reluctant to open their markets to Japanese goods. Thus, the US became the main market for Japanese exports of textiles. The US government was concerned about them but did not wish to impose tariffs or quotas on them directly because this would undermine its efforts to achieve a greater liberalisation in world trade. Instead it persuaded the Japanese government to introduce 'voluntary' export restraints between 1957 and 1962. This provided the first major precedent for the increasing use of quantitative limits on trade and a step back to the situation in the 1930s (Woolcock in Turner et al., 1982, p. 31).

Their first overt introduction in Europe was by the UK in 1959 in response to an influx of cotton textiles from underdeveloped countries entering under Commonwealth preference duty-free. These increased so fast that in 1958 Britain became a net importer. The reaction of the government was similarly to try and control the inflow of imports by concluding voluntary imports quotas on the products from India, Hong Kong and Pakistan. This merely had the effect of encouraging the entry of cotton textiles from elsewhere, and gradually Britain extended this to imports from all developing countries. She also had to extend it to the cotton cloth equivalent of clothing—still, however, favoured by the exporting country because it involved a higher value added. These quotas on cotton goods in turn encouraged the imports of goods made of man-made fibres or a mixture.

The same type of situation occurred in all western industrialised countries. Cotton textiles were described as 'sensitive' items, in effect items on which industrialised countries were unlikely to remove protection. Indeed there was such a proliferation of quotas that GATT decided they could only be controlled by agreement. In 1961 a short-term (one-year) agreement on cotton textiles was signed. In October 1962 this was replaced by the Long-Term Arrangement Regarding International Trade in Cotton Textiles (LTA) which was to last for five years and then be renewed for another five years. Cotton textiles were defined to include yarn, piece goods, made-up articles, garments and other textile manufactured products in which cotton represented 50% or more by weight of fibre content.

In the LTA the objectives of expanding international trade and promoting the development of less developed countries and providing opportunities for them to increase their foreign-exchange earnings from the sale on the world market of products they could efficiently produce were recognised, at least in the preamble. But it was also recognised that in some countries a situation had arisen which they felt caused or threatened to cause 'disruption' in the market for cotton textiles. Market disruption was defined as serious damage to domestic producers or actual threat thereof which was not caused by technological change or change in consumers' preferences. The conditions in which it occurred were:
(i) a sharp and substantial increase, or potential increase, of imports or particular products from particular sources;
(ii) that these products were offered at prices which were substantially below those prevailing for similar goods of comparable quality in the market of the importing country.
Because of the second element this has always tended to discriminate against the exports of developing countries in spite of the initial statement to the contrary.

The LTA did, however, represent an attempt to modify the restrictions imposed by the industrial countries in so far as the participating countries agreed not to intensify them and also to increase their quotas by 5% a year (except in exceptional circumstances when increased by 0–5% a year). The following countries also agreed to specific increases in their quotas by 1967: Austria 95%: Denmark 15%; the EEC 88%; Norway 15%; Sweden 15%. The high increases in Austria and the EEC reflect their extremely low level of quotas in 1962.

Canada and the UK each signed protocols refusing to expand access to their domestic markets in this way because of the substantial volume of cotton textiles they imported from less developed countries and Japan in relation to their own production of cotton textiles.

As had been anticipated in the LTA (LTA Article 6) it led to endeavours to substitute other fibres for cotton in order to circumvent it.

There was a rapid expansion in trade in textile of other fibres. Some of the more advanced countries, Hong Kong, South Korea, and Taiwan also traded up into clothing of man-made fibres. Their producers found this particularly advantageous when they could import yarn and fabric at low prices because of liberal trading policies (Keesing and Wolf, 1980, p. 35). Faced with rapidly expanding imports of non-LTA products the US in 1971 negotiated agreements for quota limits on man-made textiles from Japan and clothing from Taiwan, South Korea, and Hong Kong. It then persuaded the other industrial countries to negotiate an agreement through GATT to cover not only cotton but also wool and man-made fibre textiles and clothing. Japan was the exception in so far as although she has been faced with quotas on most of her exports, she herself has not found it necessary to impose them (Keesing and Wolf) on her imports.

This GATT Arrangement Regarding International Trade in Textiles, generally called the multi-fibre agreement (MFA) came into force at the beginning of 1974 for four years. It covered tops, yarns, piece goods, made-up articles, garments and other textile manufactured products of cotton, wool, man-made fibres, or blends in which these fibres represented either the chief value of 50% or more by weight (or 17% or more by weight of wool) of the product.

The objectives of the MFA were similar to those of the LTA but an additional reason for protection was allowed, namely the maintenance of a *viable* level of production in countries with small markets and exceptionally high levels of imports and low levels of domestic production, i.e. some of the Scandinavian countries. It provided for the negotiation of bilateral agreements on base levels and growth rates between participating countries. The quotas on trade were to be increased by at least 6% a year, but in exceptional circumstances if market disruption would recur or it would affect a country's minimum viable production, a lower growth rate would be allowed.

The US having already established some bilateral agreements took full advantage of the first MFA. But the EEC, needing to reach agreement on the distribution of the quotas between member countries as well as with exporting countries, and with inadequate information on recent trade, found it more difficult to do so. As a result the first bilateral agreement with a supplier was not reached until 1975. Meanwhile, imports into the EEC were increasing rapidly by 41% over the two years after the MFA, in contrast with an increase into the US of only 3%. The EEC responded by an even more restrictive approach (Noelke and Taylor, 1981, p. 251).

In the negotiations for the renewal of the MFA in 1977 the EEC insisted on making the quota restrictions even more severe by dividing the commodities according to sensitivity. Eight products: cotton yarn, cotton fabric, fabrics of synthetic fibre, T-shirts, pullovers, trousers, blouses and shirts were described as extremely sensitive and put in Group I. Group II included other sensitive products whose market penetration exceeded 20% for the Community as a whole. Group III consisted of other textile products, Group IV other clothing, and Group V articles for technical use. 1976 was taken as the reference year in which 60% in volume terms of the EEC textile imports were of items in Group I and almost half the remaining imports were of Group II (Noelke and Taylor, 1981, p. 255–6).

The Council of Ministers then fixed global ceilings for imports from low-cost producing countries for each of the eight most sensitive items and the growth rate for these was set at 1–2% p.a. For Group II it was set at 4% p.a. Growth rates for Groups II, IV and V were set in relation to their market penetration levels. Products whose market penetration was between 5% and 20%, or products with more than 20% market penetration, but which came from one or two suppliers only were given growth rates of around 6%. For others whose market penetration was less than 5% the growth rate could exceed 6% p.a. (Noelke and Taylor, 1981, p. 256).

Another problem was the allocation of quotas between the EEC member countries, 'burden sharing' as it was described. It was agreed that the ideal allocation which the Community would aim for was Germany 28.5%, Benelux 10.5%, France 18.5%, Italy 15%, Denmark 3%, Ireland 1%. But by 1981, the UK, Germany and Benelux still had a higher percentage in most of the eight sensitive products, and France had a lower percentage except in T-shirts. (Noelke and Taylor, 1981, p. 257.)

The replacement of a multilateral system of trading by a bilateral system provided an even greater scope for protection. Under the guise of helping the least developed countries the EEC was relatively more 'generous' with its quotas to countries with relatively little productive capacity, such as Sri Lanka, at the expense of the bigger producers. Thus quotas for Hong Kong were generally reduced by between 11 and 13%, for Taiwan there was a 60% reduction between 1977 and 1978 for knitwear and trousers and

75% for T-shirts, knitted shirts and blouses (Consumers Association, 1979, p. 17).

But in many cases, the supplier country's exports were so small that it was not worth negotiating an individual quota. To protect itself against unforeseen surges in imports from one of these countries the EEC introduced the basket mechanism. The basket for any product was the total of imports from outside the EEC. The Community set a certain percentage of this total as the trigger point for imports of a particular product. When the supplier country's exports to the EEC exceeded this the EEC could demand to negotiate a quota. The trigger points were set at 0.2% for Group I products, between 1 and 1.5% for those of Group II, and between 3 and 5% for those of Groups III, IV and V.

The EEC could not legally impose restrictions on those countries with which it had preferential trade agreements. These included most of the Mediterranean countries (including Portugal) and the ACP countries which had signed the Lomé Convention. These agreements guaranteed these countries access to the Community for their manufactured goods. Thus the EEC has endeavoured to persuade them to accept self-limitation on their exports to the EEC.

The 1982 negotiations aroused much bitterness, particularly between the EEC and her four major suppliers, Hong Kong, South Korea, Macao, and Taiwan, which together account for 40% of EEC imports. The EEC eventually modified the *reduction* in quotas it was requiring from, for instance, Hong Kong to 8.3 and 6.3 in the most sensitive category of T-shirts, sweaters, trousers, blouses and skirts, in comparison with its original demand of a reduction of 12% (*Financial Times*, 2 December 1982).

THE EXTENSION OF QUOTAS TO OTHER PRODUCTS

The use of quotas to protect 'sensitive' industries has become more and more pervasive. The appellation 'sensitive' appears now to be applied to any declining industry exposed to competition from less developed countries, and the decline is often thought of in terms of employment rather than output. Little effort is made to ascertain how far it is just due to an increase in productivity. Although Anne Krueger, investigating changes in employment in US industries from 1970 to 1976, found that most of it was accounted for by the combination of changes in demand for the product and changes in labour productivity and very little by changes in imports. This was true whether industries were defined broadly (2-digit SIC) with, for instance, textiles as one industry, or narrowly (4-digit SIC) with the textile industry having broken down into cotton weaving, synthetic weaving, etc. (Anne I. Krueger, 1978). The situation has been exacerbated since 1973 by the increasing difficulty the industrialised countries have had in reaching their macroeconomic targets. Their efforts to reduce inflation have led to persistently high and increasing levels of unemployment. Furthermore, the phenomenon known as de-industrialisation by which is meant a reduction in employment or even output by manufacturing industry, which in terms of employment became apparent in the UK after 1966, began to appear also in other EEC member countries. In an endeavour to check this there has been frequent resort to 'voluntary' agreements backed by the threat of official ones.

Furthermore, this has now become extended to trade between industrial countries themselves. Much of it has been directed at Japan who, effectively excluded from trade in textiles, transferred her efforts to other industries. One of the most important of these has been trade in road motor vehicles, which is discussed in Chapter 14. From the early 1960s Japan's exports of passenger vans and commercial vehicles increased rapidly first of all to the Asian countries around her, then to the US, then to non-producing European countries, and then to the larger European countries. Italy still had an import quota on Japanese cars which had been raised to 2400. British manufacturers negotiated a 11% market share agreement in 1975, France a 3% one in 1978. Later, in 1980, when Japanese exports to the EEC increased by 23% in terms of units when the overall market was in decline, all the other EEC countries also imposed limits, Netherlands and Luxembourg of no increase on the 1980 level and Belgium of a 7% decline on the 1980 level, and Germany of a 10% p.a growth on 1980 sales of 252,000 units. Both the US and Canada negotiated voluntary restraint agreements with Japan in 1978.

These are some of the most overt restraints on trade. There are many others, but information on them is 'classified' and even GATT who only discovered their extent in the course of negotiations on the Tokyo round, does not appear to know the quantities involved. In theory, the transfer of the right of deciding quotas from individual EEC countries to the Commission in 1980 should shed further light on them. But countries appear to have many other devious means of restricting imports by, for instance, their issue of licences, etc.

EEC countries have under constant surveillance imports of many consumer durables and investment goods ranging from colour TVs and tubes to numerically controlled machine tools, and have imposed 'restraints' or quotas on many of them—particularly those from Japan. France is the most protectionist in this respect.

The ECSC acts as a European cartel in steel production, endeavouring to raise prices and reduce the output of European producers. But the EEC has also been forced to conclude an agreement with the US whereby from 1 November 1982 to 1985, EEC exports are limited to 5% of the US market for the eleven main categories of steel products and 5.9% for pipes and tubes (*Financial Times*, 22 October 1982).

Thus, even the stalwarts of a free-trade system in manufactures, the US and Germany, have succumbed to protectionism. Furthermore, there are many demands within both the US and the EEC to dispense with the non-discrimination and multilateral framework of GATT, the idea being that the US and the EEC could each bargain with other countries or groups to get trade barriers on their exports reduced. Japan would be a particular target for this, as her tariffs on many products are extremely high. However, although she could dispose of her overall trade surplus, she would be unable to remove her surplus on trade with other industrialised countries because this is required to pay for her large deficit in fuel.

5 Agricultural Policies Affecting Trade

So far we have considered the institutional arrangement governing trade in manufactures. We mentioned that GATT tried to include agricultural products in its negotiations with very little success. Let us now consider some of the government policies that have been pursued.

AGRICULTURAL POLICIES OF INDUSTRIALISED MARKET ECONOMIES

Let us begin by considering agricultural policies of industrialised countries. Traditionally their governments have intervened to protect their agriculture and they continue to regard it as a crucial industry even though it accounts for a low and declining proportion of their GDP and employment.

The objectives they pursue are various. Halting depopulation is important to some of the smaller European countries with extensive mountainous regions, particularly if they are anxious about their borders. The stability and security of food supplies is often mentioned, and on occasions an increase in farm output is regarded as desirable. In the past, a sizeable agricultural sector has also been regarded of strategic importance in the event of war, but this view has declined in importance with the advent of nuclear weapons and the devastation and fallout that would result from their use. However, the primary objective of agricultural policy in almost every industrialised country, is the maintenance of farm incomes.

The method of protection varies considerably, the basic structure often begin a relic of the past. But the operable variable is invariably regarded as the price of agricultural commodities, and farmers are always regarded as benefiting from a rise in the price of their product and suffering from a fall in its price.

The systematic and extensive protection that emerged in the 1950s was the cumulative effect of the response of governments firstly to the Great Depression described in Chapter 2, then to the transport difficulties of the Second World War, and lastly to the fear of a world-wide food shortage that existed in the immediate post-war period.

The protection was lowest in the countries whose economies were very dependent on agricultural exports, namely the land-abundant countries of Australia, New Zealand and Canada, and also Denmark and the Netherlands.

US AGRICULTURAL POLICY

However, although the US is a major exporting country, Roosevelt's government of the New Deal, faced with the collapse of agricultural prices and incomes in the 1930s, introduced an extensive system of price support with the Agricultural Adjustment Act of 1933. This was designed to raise the prices of agricultural products to their purchasing power in 1910–14, termed their parity price. It operated through the Commodity Credit Corporation (CCC) which was established to provide loans against a farmer's crops at the specified minimum price. At the end of the loan period, the farmer could either pay back the loan in cash, which he would normally do if the market price was above the set minimum price, or he could pay it back in kind. Thus, when market prices were high, the CCC merely acted as an agency for providing credit, but when prices fell below the minimum, it accumulated stocks. There was also some provision for supply control.

This original Act has subsequently been amended and modified by a whole series of additional ones. The concept of parity, although still based on 1910–14, was altered in 1950 to allow for changes in the relative cost of production of commodities.

This minimum loan price was initially set according to some relationship between actual supply, which included the carry-over from the previous year, and the 'normal' or desired supply. But if supply was greater than required, the price could not be lowered below 75% of parity. Later, modifications were introduced so that the loan price could be moved nearer the world price and could be topped up by a payment conditional on producers participating in a programme of supply control. This total payment per bushel is regarded by the US Department of Agriculture as the support price, but it is not a price in the ordinary sense of the term as the amount a producer would get from an additional unit of production. This can be regarded as the actual market price, or if he is participating in a set aside programme, the return he would get which would involve breaking the agreement.

This support system was legally required to cover maize, wheat, rice, cotton, peanuts, tobacco, milk, and butter fat, wool, mohair, barley, oats, grain sorghums, tung nuts and honey. Others which may be supported at the discretion of the Secretary of Agriculture are cotton-seed, flax-seed, soyabeans, dry edible beans, and crude pine gum (OECD, 1967A, p. 565). But the CCC does not intervene at all in the market for meat, eggs and fresh fruit and vegetables.

The price support scheme has always been buttressed by some form of supply control exerted through the control of acreage. During the early post-war period, it was centred on acreage allotments for different crops, which were apportioned to individual farms, and the farmer was only entitled to price support if he complied with this arrangement. In 1956, an acreage reserve (Soil Bank) programme was introduced by which payments were made to farmers who planted less than their acreage allotment of the six basic commodities in greatest surplus, that is maize, cotton, wheat, rice, tobacco and peanuts. The amount of crop land diversion was extended by the Agricultural Act of 1961, particularly for wheat. In 1967 and 1968 this was removed for wheat but then reintroduced. In 1970 this was modified slightly by continuing to make payments on the land the farmer took out of cultivation (set-aside) but allowing him to allocate the remaining area between crops as he wished.

The change in acreage and production that actually occurred between five-year periods centred on 1950 and 1970 can be seen in Table 5.1. the acreages of wheat, maize, cotton, tobacco and groundnuts were certainly reduced by 20% or more and barley by a mere 4%. But it should be noted that the acreage under wheat and maize was reduced by no greater proportion than that for cereals as a whole—certain cereals subject to very little government intervention such as buckwheat and oats showed a much more rapid decline.

Furthermore, for cereals and groundnuts, farmers were able to compensate for a reduction in acreage by an increase in yield so that the production of the major cereals actually increased, wheat by 32%, maize by 68% and barley by 60%. The production of rice, whose acreage had increased by 7%, more than doubled. The production of groundnuts increased by 55% in spite of a reduction in acreage. There was a decline in the production of cotton and tobacco but it was not nearly as great as that of their acreages. This suggests that endeavours to keep price up but to reduce

TABLE 5.1 The Effect of the US Supply Control Schemes.

	Area Harvested[1]			Production[1]		
	1950	1970 1000 acres	% Change	1950	1970 1000 metric tons	% Change
Wheat	68,588	48,083	−30	31,048	46,886	+32
Rice milled	1858	1986	+7	1266	2692	+113
Rye	1696	1303	−23	524	851	+62
Maize shelled for grain	73,778	57,910	−22	74,305	125,534	+68
Barley	10,118	9750	−4	5850	9389	+60
Oats	37,725	16,678	−56	18,950	12,761	−33
Sorghum	7627	14,050	+84	3896	19,374	+397
Total food grain	72,142	51,372	−29	32,838	44,429	+35
Total feed grain	129,248	98,388	−24	103,001	166,060	+61
Total cereals	201,390	149,760	−26	135,839	210,489	+55
Cotton	24,213	11,364	−53	3105	2408	−22
Tobacco	1666	875	−47	959	805	−16
Groundnuts	2258	1461	−35	839	1301	+55[2]

Notes: 1. Five-year averages centred on year shown.
2. Exaggerated because 1950 data gross weight, 1970 data net weight.
Totals are totals of those shown.
Source: USDA Agricultural Statistics 1967 & 1980.

production by government directives to reduce acreage are relatively ineffective. This may just be because it induces farmers to employ more factors of production in the form of labour and capital and more inputs such as fertilisers per acre of land. Furthermore, if technological change in the form of the introduction of higher yielding crops is not exogenous, the maintenance of artificially high prices may also have hastened it and encouraged a greater speed of adoption.

In order to prevent these price-support schemes being undermined, the government also intervenes in the import market. In 1954, the market was protected by a system of quotas for milk products (milk and cream, butter and cheese), wheat and wheat products, rye, groundnuts and cotton. In 1964, quotas were also imposed on imports of beef, veal and mutton.

The sugar market is entirely organised by a system of quotas with which the US endeavours to maintain roughly half its domestic market for home producers.

The US also had a series of tariffs imposed mainly on processed agricultural products. Most of them were specific, but in 1952 their *ad valorem* equivalent ranged up to 41% for cigarettes, and 40% for distilled alcoholic beverages. By 1971, the *ad valorem* equivalents appeared to have fallen (OECD, 1974A, p. 94; OECD, 1956), pp. 300–01).

The fundamental problem arising from this type of policy has been the accretion of stocks. In the immediate post-war period, the US and Canada were the only countries that had any appreciable stocks of temperate agricultural commodites. Those of the US were far the largest and in relation to the international trade were most significant in cereals, that is, wheat and coarse grains, and in milk products (cheese, butter and dried milk) and cotton and tobacco.

A contributing factor was the phasing out of US government donations abroad for relief of approximately $52 billion p.a in the late 1940s which accounted for over two thirds of US agricultural exports. Exports then fell after 1951 and there was a bumper harvest in 1952. By 1954, stocks stood at an all-time record of 23.5 million metric tons of wheat and 30 of coarse grains equal to the total quantity entering world trade for one and two years respectively. In butter and cheese, US stocks in relation to international trade were somewhat lower but she was not a major supplier; in dried milk, for which she was, her stock was equal to more than a year's international trade. Her stock of cotton of 2.125 million metric tons represented almost three times her annual exports and was nearly equal to one year's total trade. Her stock of tobacco appeared to be greater than one year's trade.

Furthermore, much of the rise in stocks from 1953 to 1954 appears to have been financed by the CCC, whose ownership of stocks rose by $3 billion.

Thus, the US government was very concerned to reduce its level of stocks; they were costly to finance and also represented a threat to the stability of the international market. However, both the US government and FAO were concerned about the security of world food supplies, and also the very low level of food consumption and nutrition in some countries.

The US government wished to dispose of its stocks in such a way as not to undermine its price support system at home or the international market. At home, it disposed of some stocks by subsidised programmes for school children and the needy. But most of the stocks had to be disposed of abroad. The US government endeavoured to avoid disruption by selling or giving its products to consumers or governments who could not afford to purchase the commodities on the open market. Under Title I of the Agricultural Trade Development and Assistance Act of 1954 (PL 480) and Section 402 of the Mutual Security Act of 1964, it sold products against local currency. Under Title II of PL 480, the President could also donate agricultural commodities to meet famine or other urgent relief requirements. Under Title III, agricultural commodities could be bartered for strategic materials, and under Title IV they could be provided under long-term loans. Certain exports such as those under the International Wheat Agreement were subsidised directly.

PL 480 was superseded in 1966 by the Food for Peace Act which contained the same general provisions. However, the shift from sales for local currencies to sales for dollars under liberal credit schemes, which had already been occurring, was to be continued and 1971 was set as the date by which the change-over to commercial sales was to be completed (FAO, *State of Food and Agriculture*, 1967, p. 57).

Statistics on the distribution of agricultural exports under Title I of PL 480 show the most prominent recipients in the late 1950s and 1960s as being India, Pakistan, UAR (Egypt), Korea and Brazil, with South Vietnam increasing in importance (USDA, *Agricultural Statistics*, 1959, Table 824 and 1967, Table 832). But by 1978, Egypt was the largest recipient of food aid followed by Indonesia, with Bangladesh, the rest of Pakistan, and Korea still figuring prominently. Portugal also became an important recipient in 1979 (USDA, *Agricultural Statistics*, 1980, Table 779).

The contribution of government-assisted exports under the schemes to total exports can be gauged by looking at Table 5.2.

TABLE 5.2 US Exports of Agricultural Commodities—Total and under Government Programmes
$ million

	1955–7			1960			1970			1979		
	Total	Under gov. prog.	% of total exports	Total	Under gov. prog.	% of total exports	Total	Under gov. prog.	% of total exports	Total	Under gov. prog.	% of total exports
Total	3789.4	1398.0	37	4516.8	1312.9	29	6721.4	1035.8	15	31,975.4	1441.7	5
Total grain of which:	1120.3	710.5	63	15,589	886.9	57	2285.5	632.8	28	12,399.6	1073.1	9
Wheat and flour	681.1	468.8	69	868.8	649.9	75	941.6	390.5	41	4775.3	599.0	13
Rice	112.6	62.0	55	136.2	73.7	54	322.3	150.0	47	884.2	122.5	14
Corn	172.6	88.4	51	277.3	71.0	26	828.5	34.8	4	6058.8	222.9	4
Soyabeans	174.1	11.7	7	299.9	24.5	8	1069.0	0.2	0	5444.4	67.0	1
Soyabean oil	69.5	48.8	70	109.0	72.2	66	138.7	85.3	61	705.7	117.7	17
Cotton	723.9	296.3	41	825.7	155.9	19	346.6	133.0	38	1896.2	14.6	1
Tobacco (unmanufactured)	342.0	36.1	11	341.9	69.1	20	561.9	23.0	4	1292.2	28.5	2
Milk products [a]	226.4	172.9	76	92.3	50.9	55	98.1	82.3	84			
of which: Milk nonfat dry	65.1	60.5	93	51.1	40.7	80	78.3	74.9	96	27.4	22.8	83

[a] Data for 1955–7 include cheese, butter, butter oil and ghee. Data for 1960, 1970 and 1979 are for evaporated and condensed, whole dried and nonfat dried milk only.

Sources: USDA, *Agricultural Statistics*; 1980, Table 777; and 1972, Table 820; US Department of Commerce, *Statistical Abstract of the United States*; 1962, No. 902; 1959, No. 861.

From 1955–7, they accounted for 37% of all agricultual exports, but this proportion gradually declined over time to 5% in 1979; thus it is now insignificant.

The main commodities included in these programmes and the percentage of their trade that came under them is also shown in Table 5.2. More than half the assisted exports are of cereals of which in 1955–7 two thirds was wheat, and this latter proportion rose to 73% in 1960. The actual quantity of wheat exported under these programmes rose from 7821 thousand metric tons from 1955–7 to a peak of 15,428 in 1964. This indicates their primary function as that of surplus disposal in so far as rice would, in many cases, have been the preferred cereal of recipient countries. But the actual quantity of rice coming under these programmes did increase from an average of 576 thousand metric tons from 1955–7 to 1269 from 1970–2. The quantity of coarse grains entering these programmes has fluctuated and if anything declined from the 3 billion tons of 1955–7. However, it is clear that although this assisted trade has become insignificant now, it was an important factor in US grain exports in the 1950s and 1960s.

The other commodities for which government export assistance was important were soyabean oil, cotton, tobacco and milk products. It has faded into insignificance in trade in cotton and tobacco, the acreage and production of which has fluctuated but scarcely increased so that the CCC stocks of them are now relatively low. The assisted exports of butter and cheese also appear to have been a temporary phenomenon. But assisted exports of dried milk and soyabean oil continue, probably because milk and vegetable oils are products most urgently required in famine relief and also under special aid programmes for children. They, nevertheless, represent a very small proportion of the total outlay of these programmes, three quarters of which now goes on cereals.

This distribution of the US agricultural surplus was welcomed by many as a means of improving the living and nutritional standards of some of the poorest people in the world. It was also argued that these surpluses could be used directly or indirectly as wage payments in investment projects. But many agricultural economists both inside and outside the US considered that they discouraged agricultural development in the recipient countries. Furthermore, great resentment was shown by the developing countries themselves when the US endeavoured to use this as a political weapon, in particular withholding it from India and Pakistan while they fought each other in 1971.

As a reaction to this type of criticism and also because of the cost of this operation, the US was already endeavouring to reduce the production of commodities in surplus by the increasingly restrictive acreage provisions that have already been described.

However, the whole picture changed as the Sino-Soviet bloc shifted from being a small net exporter to a net importer of food as will be mentioned in Chapter 8. As will be described in Chapter 11, it became a major importer of cereals. World trade demand in the 1970s increased so dramatically that the US government with its Agricultural Acts of 1970 and 1972 felt able to remove much of the price-support elements and in 1972 removed restrictions on acreage for cereals.

It has been necessary to consider US agricultural policy and the way it has changed over the period since the Second World War because it has been so intimately tied up with her trading position, and because she is the world's largest exporter of agricultural products.

BRITISH AGRICULTURAL POLICY

But now let us turn to consider the position of those countries which, in the early part of the period, were large importers. Let us begin with Britain, at that time the largest importer of agricultural products in the world, with imports of $6.5 billion in 1951.

Britain followed an entirely different type of policy. She admitted most agricultural products duty free. But the Agricultural Act of 1947 stated the aim of raising net farm output 50% above the pre-war level. In order to achieve this she instituted for the major agricultural products a system of guaranteed prices for cereals (wheat, rye, barley, oats and mixed corn), fatstock (cattle, sheep, lambs, pigs), wool, milk, eggs, potatoes and sugar beet. In so far as the market prices for cereals and fatstock did not reach the guaranteed prices, the differences were made up to the farmer by a system of 'deficiency payments'. In the case of milk, wool, eggs and potatoes and sugar beet, all marketing was carried out by a central board and any deficiency payments were made payable through it. There was also a stringent control of the acreage under sugar beet which was determined by the government each year in accordance with the capacity of its sugar factories and its commitments under the Commonwealth Sugar Agreement of 1951 by which the UK agreed to buy specific quantities of sugar at negotiated prices from each Commonwealth exporter. These Commonwealth sugar prices were generally above the world market prices.

The various sectors of the horticultural industry were protected during the period of peak domestic production by relatively high specific duties and sometimes nil quotas. But for most of the year, markets were quite free, with scarcely any import duties. Tariffs were employed only on items of minor importance. For the major products listed above, accounting for two thirds of gross agricultural revenue in the 1950s, the system of guaranteed prices and deficiency payments was used.

The guaranteed prices were negotiated each year for the coming year between farmers' representatives and the government. As the government found it difficult to keep the negotiated price down, its open-ended commitment became embarrassing as agricultural production steadily increased and with it its subsidy bills.

It thus tried to limit its commitment. For instance, in 1964 Britain concluded a whole series of agreements with those countries who traditionally supplied her with cereals to keep their shipments above a certain minimum price. As this minimum price was generally below the world market price, it is unlikely that this had much effect. She also negotiated some 'voluntary' quota agreements for the imports of butter in 1961, bacon in 1964, and cheese. In 1962, she had to replace the butter agreement with an official system of quotas in order to protect her traditional suppliers, particularly New Zealand.

In addition to these guaranteed prices, farmers also received production grants and subsidies on inputs such as fertilisers. Indeed, British government assistance to agriculture, ranging from £250–£350 million a year in the 1960s, was split fairly evenly between the two kinds of support.

Thus, British protection of her agriculture lay almost entirely in subsidies to producers most of which were related to output.[1] Consumers could purchase commodities at world market prices. This, therefore, could be described as a policy for low food prices. This system was very different from that of the other major European countries.

CONTINENTAL EUROPE AND THE EUROPEAN ECONOMIC COMMUNITY

When the major continental countries had recoverd from the Second World War, all their governments were still intervening in the markets for agricultural products.

Germany continued with import agencies which effectively

maintained a minimum import price by the imposition of variable levies on imports and the restriction on supplies for grains, milk products and fats, and meat and livestock. Adenauer's government in 1949 also stated its aim of increasing agricultural output.

In France, the government in the immediate post-war period merely aimed at self-sufficiency, but after 1948 it made a deliberate attempt to increase exports of basic agricultural products. The government instituted an extensive system of intervention, the most important features of which were a system of guaranteed prices which were often indexed, strict control over imports, and assistance for exports often by direct subsidies.

Italy continued with Mussolini's policy of a high price of wheat maintained by a state buying monopoly and control of imports.

The Benelux countries found it more difficult to achieve free trade between themselves in agricultural products than manufactures, mainly because Belgium and Luxembourg were reluctant to allow the Netherlands to dominate their markets. A series of compromises were adopted which included the recognition of the right of member countries to set their own minimum prices for agricultural products and restrictions on intra-Benelux trade in them.

Thus the conflict of agricultural interests between countries was exacerbated by the steady expansion in output resulting from the protection afforded by their governments. This was the background to the negotiations for the EEC (Tracy, 1964).

By signing the Treaty of Rome in 1957, the six countries— France, Germany, Italy, the Netherlands, Belgium and Luxembourg—agreed to open their agricultural markets to each other in the same way as they did for manufactures. But in other respects the provisions for agriculture were more extensive, and there was specific provision for a common agricultural policy (CAP).

Article 39 of the treaty states:

1. The common agricultural policy shall have as its objectives
    a) to increase agricultural productivity by developing technical progress and by ensuring the rational development of agricultural production and the optimum utilisation of the factors of production, particularly labour;
    b) to ensure thereby a fair standard of living for the agricultural population, particularly by the increasing of the individual earnings of persons engaged in agriculture;
    c) to stabilise markets;
    d) to guarantee regular supplies; and
    e) to ensure reasonable prices in supplies to consumers.

Article 40 states:

...a common organisation of agricultural markets shall be effected...
[it] may comprise all measures necessary to achieve the objectives set
out in Article 39, in particular, price controls, subsidies as to the production and marketing of various products, arrangements for stock-piling and
carry-forward, and common machinery for stabilising importation or
exportation.

...A common price policy, if any, shall be based on common criteria and
on uniform methods of calculation.

In practice, the chief difficulties the member countries had in
opening up their markets and achieving common prices were due
to their very different previous levels of protection: the low level in
the Netherlands, the high level in Germany, with that of other
countries somewhere in between. Furthermore, there was also some
divergence in relative prices between different countries. Wheat,
and in Germany rye, as the bread grains, were much more heavily
protected than the feed grains in the larger countries, with the result
that their prices were very much higher. But the situation in the
Netherlands reflected that in the world market, where the prices of
barley and soft wheat were nearly the same.

This also proved a major problem in setting the common prices.
These were supposed to represent the average of those ruling in the
different countries but in fact, when they were finally agreed to in
July 1957, they were nearer the high German ones than the low
Dutch ones. The agreement actually raised prices particularly of
cereals to the largest producer, France.

The common prices all hinge on the target prices for commodities, which are set by the Council of Ministers on recom-
mendations from the Commission just before the harvest year.
These apply throughout the EEC or are fixed for a particular point
in it; for instance, the target price for cereals is set for Duisburg in
Germany, a marketing centre where there is the greatest deficit in
grain. All other prices in the system such as the 'threshold' or
'sluice gate' price, and the 'intervention' price for a commodity are
set in relation to its target price.

The 'threshold' or 'sluice gate' price is, in effect, a minimum
import price acting like a ring fence round the EEC as a whole.
Because the EEC prices are set by the Council of Ministers and only
change gradually, they are inevitably and intentionally much more
stable than the world prices which have fluctuated considerably
since 1967. Thus the degree of protection they represent has also
fluctuated. But as can be seen from Table 5.3, the percentage

TABLE 5.3 Agricultural Protection in the EEC—Minimum Import Price Divided by the World Price.

%

	Soft Wheat	Durum Wheat	Rice	Barley	Maize	Sugar	Pork[1]	Butter	Skimmed Milk	Olive Oil	Oilseeds	Beef and Veal live Animals
1967/68	185	200	117	160	160	438	147	397		166	200	175
68/69	195	214	138	197	178	355	134	504	365	173	203	169
69/70	214	230	186	203	159	298	137	613		160	155	147
1970/71	189	232	210	146	141	203	134	481		155	131	140
71/72	209	254	205	185	176	186	131	171	112	153	147	133
72/73	153	181	115	137	143	127	147	249	145	125	131	112
73/74	79	116	60	96	98	66	131	320	156	96	77	110
74/75	107	120	81	107	106	41	109	316	139	113	80	162
75/76	124	145	137	117	128	109	113	320	266	217	127	158
76/77	204	236	166	147	163	176	125	401	571	192	121	192
77/78	216	218	128	206	203	255	137	388	494	211	153	196
78/79	193	216	157	225	201	276	155	403	458	200	161	199
79/80	163	159	131	161	190	131	152	411	379	193	185	204

Note: 1. The calendar year of the first half of the agricultural year is given, i.e. 1979 for 1979/80.

Sources: Commission of the European Communities, *The Agricultural Situation in the Community*, 1980, p. 196; 1978, p. 202; Eurostat, *Yearbook of Agricultural Statistics*, 1970, p. 134; 1973, p. 183; 1972, p. 199.

protection, that is the percentage increase in the internal over the world prices, has been around 100% for grains. In 1968/69, it began by being somewhat lower for beef and veal and pigmeat, but by 1979/80, this had risen so that it represented an additional 104% for beef and veal and 55% for pigmeat. The CAP price for butter was initally in 1968/9 504% of the world price but in spite of efforts to bring it down, it is still 411% of it, thus representing a tariff level of 311%. The apparent protection afforded to sugar producers began by being very high at a mark-up of 255% but due to instability in the world market, it has fluctuated considerably and in 1979/80 was only an additional 31%

Thus, by comparing the EEC minimum 'entry price' with the offer price of third (non-member) countries, the CAP appears to afford the greatest degree of protection to producers of milk products, then to cereal producers, and lastly to meat producers.

The minimum import prices are brought into effect by the imposition of variable levies on imports. These are set by the administrative body of the CAP, the Agricultural Guidance and Guarantee Fund (FEOGA). They are applied to cereals, milk products, sugar, olive oil, eggs, poultry, pigmeat, and beef and veal. Beef and veal imports are also liable to customs duties. In the case of meat, the target and 'sluice gate' price or minimum import price, takes account of the higher cost of feed grains facing the EEC producer. The only protection for lamb used to be in the form of an import duty and an agreed limit on imports from New Zealand, but this has been modified recently by allowing Britain to reintroduce some deficiency payments.

In 1973/74, the world prices of cereals and sugar rose so much that as can be seen from table 5.3 the threshold prices were lower than them. The CAP system then went into reverse with levies being imposed on exports. But occasions such as this when the EEC price has been kept lower than the world one are rare.

The system was designed to keep internal prices above world prices by levies on imports. But, as will be discussed in the next chapter, it only works to the extent that the product continues to be imported. In fact the relatively high and stable prices have encouraged production so much that whereas in 1956–69, the EEC of the six produced 85% of its requirements of cereals and 104% of sugar, by 1969/70, this had risen to 91% for cereals and 110% for sugar (EEC Statistical Office, 1971, p. 77). Some EEC countries, in particular France, had hoped that Britain would absorb some of their surpluses when she entered in 1973. But Denmark and Ireland, both agricultural exporters, joined with her. In fact, the trend continued such that in 1979/80 the EEC was overall self-sufficient in cereals, with a surplus in soft wheat and a deficit in maize, and she produced 124% of her requirements in sugar and in 1980 115% of her requirements in skimmed milk powder, 105% in cheese, 119% in butter and 102% in eggs (Commission of the European Communities, 1983 pp. 244 and 245).

However, in the absence of imports there is a buttress to the price support system in the form of intervention buying. This is the procedure by which FEOGA can, or is obliged to, purchase a commodity for stock when its price falls to an intervention level; this intervention price is around 70–80% of the target price for feed grains but nearer 90% for beef and hard wheat. This procedure is used for cereals, butter and skimmed milk, beef, wine, and olive oil.

Thus, just as for the US, the maintenance of an internal price level well above world market levels has entailed the accumulation of stocks. In the EEC, the chief constituents of them have been cereals, milk products and beef. For instance, on 31 December 1979, out of a total value of stocks in public storage of 2142.5 m u.a. ($2,937 m), 22% were of cereals (16.4% wheat, 5.1% rye), 45% milk products (33.8% butter, 10.8% skimmed milk), 28% beef, 3% olive oil, and 3% tobacco (Commission of the European Communities, *9th Financial Report on the European Agricultural Guidance and Guarantee Fund*, p. 68).

In the same way as the US, the EEC has endeavoured to dispose of these stocks without undermining its internal price system. The domestic measures it has used are discussed in the next chapter. But in almost all cases, the EEC has had to export a considerable proportion of them. In doing so, the EEC has shown very much less concern about upsetting the world market than the US. It has negotiated some direct sales with the USSR and India but most of the money allocated for export refunds just represents the difference between the internal price of the products and their world prices. The average degree of subsidy it represents is shown in Table 5.4. Food aid has been aggregated with the export refunds. The former just represents a donation at world market prices which attracts an additional amount of export refund and it is, therefore, difficult to separate out the complete cost of a donation. The average rate of subsidy has been very high for milk products. This is mainly a reflection of the very high internal price of butter compared with the world price. The average subsidy on exports of cereals appears to have fluctuated inversely with the world price as you would expect it to do. The percentage export refund on eggs and poultry appears to fluctuate between 16% and 25%. It may be higher for beef and pork but so far it has not been possible to

TABLE 5.4 EEC Exports of Agricultural Products to Third Countries and Associated Export Refunds.

		1972 EEC (6)				1973 EEC (9)				1979 EEC (9)			
	SITC	Exports	Export refunds	Food aid	Average subsidy %	Exports	Export Refunds	Food aid	Average subsidy %	Exports	Export Refunds	Food aid	Average subsidy %
			million u.a.				million u.a.				million u.a.		
Cereal total	04	704.0	555.8		79	1074.2	468.8		44	2030.3	1184.7	80.0	62
Rice	042	37.2	47.9		129	34.7	10.5		30	93.4	41.7		45
Milk & Milk products													
Milk & cream	022	561.5	155.8	50.5	37	878.5[3]	744.5[1]	56.2	91[3]	2252.7[3]	2087.9	161.0	100[3]
Butter	023					483.1		27.5		1206.2			
Cheese	024					208.7	416.4[1]			592.1	75.2		
Skimmed milk						186.7		28.7		454.4	94.7		
Sugar	06	272.4[2]	65.8		24	485.6	51.6		11	911.1	685.1	0.3	75
Meat													
Bovine cattle	001.1	46	7.4		16	52.1	2.7		16	100.2	270.2		
Beef	011.1												
Swine	001.3	205.9	49.3		24	5.0	90.6		24	4.7	78.4		
Pork	011.3												
Poultry live	001.4	42.7	11.8		22	13.4	17.8		16	48.3	70.5		23
Poultry meat	011.4	12.1				97.7				229.5			
Eggs	025					20.9	3.7		18	44.9			

Table 5.4 (continued)

SITC	1972 EEC (6) Exports	Export refunds (million u.a.)	Food aid	Average subsidy %	1973 EEC (9) Exports	Export refunds (million u.a.)	Food aid	Average subsidy %	1979 EEC (9) Exports	Export refunds (million u.a.)	Food aid	Average subsidy %
Fruit and vegetables	332.1	33.1		10	555.1	25.8		5	1083.6	34.5		3
Wine	411.7	0.3			393.8	0.4			839.7	4.6		1
Tobacco	13.8	–			165.7				436.2	3.7		1
Total (ex. for fish)	4542.1	953.8	50.5	22	7134.7	1442.4	56.2	21	14,812.9	4723.7	259.0[4]	34

Notes: 1. 124 m.u.a. expenses for export of ghee from intervention stocks and 292.4 m.u.a. for expenses for export of butter from intervention stocks.
2. Includes sugar beet that is SITC 054.82.
3. Total of milk and cream, butter and cheese.
4. Total expenditure by EEC member countries for EEC Commission.

Sources: Commission of the European Communities, *Financial Report on the European Agricultural Guidance and Guarantee Fund, 2nd Annex VI*, p. 77; Eurostat *Yearbook of Agricultural Statistics 1976–9*, p. 14; 1975, p. 14; 1974, p. 13.

calculate it. But the percentage refund for fruit and vegatables has declined from 10% in 1972 to 3% in 1979. The overall percentage subsidy on agricultural exports appears to have increased from just over a fifth in the early 1970s to a third in 1979.

The CAP was conceived of in a framework of fixed exchange rates. Since 1971 industrialised countries have gradually abandoned them and it has proved more and more difficult to retain common prices. Appreciating countries such as Germany have been very reluctant to reduce prices to their farmers by the extent of the appreciation, and depreciating countries such as France have been reluctant to raise prices to their farmers signalling as it would an encouragement to greater production. Thus, special 'green' rates of exchange have been introduced to translate the negotiated target prices into domestic currencies. These 'green' exchange rates have been kept relatively stable but can only be changed in the direction that the actual exchange rate has moved. In so far as the green rate of exchange for the Deutschmark is lower than the actual exchange rate, agricultural imports from other EEC countries must be taxed and the exports of German agricultural products subsidised. Obversely, for a depreciating country, the green rate will be higher than the true rate of exchange and imports of agricultural products will be subsidised and exports taxed.

Clearly the degree to which a country requires a subsidy or tax partly depends on the units in which the target price was set. It was initially set in European units of accounts (u.a.s) which were equal to the pre-1971 value of the dollar. But from 13 March 1979 it was set in European currency units (ECUs) initially of the same value but which represented a basket of currencies in which the pound was included.

These subsidies and taxes on intra EEC agricultural trade also depend on the relative fluctuations of the currencies. If all the EEC currencies fluctuated together against the dollar, none would be required. In fact, the Commission and certain member countries, mostly notably France, have made persistent efforts to persuade member countries to join a monetary union to stabilise EEC exchange rates. But it is not clear that either the European Monetary Union or the European Monetary System reduced exchange rate fluctuations to any appreciable degree and Britain has always refused to join. The UK exchange rate has fluctuated considerably in relation to the others with the result that initially she was obtaining subsidies on agricultural imports from the EEC but now they are being taxed.

The subsidies and taxes on EEC agricultural trade are called Monetary Compensatory Amounts (MCAs). If the system was neutral, you might expect them to balance out but, in fact, they have represented a form of additional support amounting in 1979 to 7% of the total, two thirds of which was on intra-Community trade. By 1980 this had fallen to 2% and the EEC member countries have agreed to try and phase them out (Commission of the European Communities, 1980 pp. 232–7).

The problems of coordination and agreement have become greater as the EEC has become extended to include, in 1973, Britain, Ireland and Denmark, and in 1981 Greece. All negotiated transitional arrangements. Nevertheless, the addition of one major importer plus three countries heavily dependent on exports of agricultural products added to the strain associated with the system. Because of the differing importance of agriculture in the different countries, the CAP now acts as a vehicle for large net transfers between different countries and across their foreign exchanges. Germany and Britain are the main contributors.

Furthermore, expenditure on agriculture has grown so much that EEC expenditure is now becoming greater than the revenue it obtains from 'its own resources', that is, from customs duties, trade levies, sugar levies and 1% VAT, the first and last of which accounted for more than 80% of the revenue. With no provision for deficit financing and reluctant to reduce more than marginally the level of agricultural prices in the Community, the Commission has put forward plans for imposing levies on producers of surplus products. Surplus is defined in relation to national requirements. There is also a move to exempt small producers. Both measures are detrimental to efficiency—the first because it discourages specialisation according to comparative advantage—Irish low-cost milk producers would pay it whereas Italian high-cost producers would be exempt. The second measure would benefit the higher-cost small producers at the expense of the frequently more efficient large producers.

JAPANESE AGRICULTURAL POLICY

To complete this discussion of agricultural policies in industrialised countries, let us consider Japan. She has traditionally followed a very protective policy with respect to her agriculture (McCrone, 1962). The basis for her present protective system is the Food Control Act of 1942 and the Agricultural Basic Law 1961. This system has features common to both the EEC and US policy. Her apparent objective was to be as self-sufficient as possible, to maintain incomes of farm families at levels similar to those of other

Japanese families, in particular those whose chief earners are employed in manufacturing, but at the same time to acknowledge Japan's position as a major trading nation that benefits from the liberalisation of trade. Thus, implicit in the objectives is the notion of parity, in this case of incomes, while the advantages of trade are recognised (Bureau of Agricultural Economics, (BAE), 1981).

Japanese agriculture is traditionally based on the production of rice, which remains both economically and psychologically the most important crop. Under the Food Control Act the government was a monopoly buyer of rice through the Ministry of Agriculture, Forestry and Fisheries (MAFF) Food Agency. The purchase price of rice was set by a formula relating it to actual costs and imputing labour at the industrial wage level. The government then sold it at a lower price to consumers but this price was still three to five times the world price (BAE, 1981. p. 29). Clearly, in order to maintain prices at this level, the government has also got to be able to control imports. This system was slightly modified in 1969 by no longer requiring the delivery of a certain amount of rice to the government; however, the government still provided financial assistance for it.

The effect of such a high price for rice was to encourage production. But it also contributed to the reduction in *per capita* consumption which occurred after 1962. After 1965, Japan ceased to be a net importer of rice and except for four years in which she had a bad harvest, always produced more than she consumed. In order to reduce the inevitable accumulation of stocks, the government disposed of some of them in school lunch programmes and as livestock feed. Two million tons were exported between 1969 and 1972 at concessional terms to developing countries like Korea, Indonesia and Pakistan. But she also introduced a rice diversion programme in which farmers were paid to transfer rice land to the production of other commodities in which Japan was not self-sufficient.

The need for this is partly due to the change in demand that has come about because of the rapid increase in *per capita* income and change in tastes, the effect of which has outweighed the straight expansionary effect of a 1% p.a. increase in population. The reduction in the consumption of rice was initially associated with an increase in human consumption of wheat, but more recently with a very rapid increase in the consumption of livestock products. Total consumption of meat per head increased from 3.51 kilos p.a. in 1960 to 20.77 kilos in 1978. *Per capita* consumption of milk products in wholemilk equivalents has risen from 12.1 kilos p.a. in 1955 to 59.3 in 1978 (drinking milk from 5.5 to 32.1, butter from

0.08 to 0.5 and cheese from 0.01 to 0.7) (BAE, 1981, p. 101). These actual levels of consumption are much lower than in other industrialised countries. Nevertheless, their rapid rate of increase has been associated with a rapid increase in imports.

In exerting its control over imports, the government generally appears to have been concerned to stabilise internal prices and achieve a high level of self-sufficiency.[2] At the wholesale level, dairy product prices are about three times and beef prices between three and four times international prices (BAE, 1981, p. 29). They are to some extent joint products in so far as 60% of beef comes from the dairy herd. But the production of beef has been increasing more slowly than that of consumption, whereas Japan tends to produce a surplus of some dairy products.

It has controlled imports of beef by a system of quotas, and in order to fulfil its objectives it raised them from 3.0 thousand tons in 1958 gradually to 24.56 thousand tons in 1968 to 160 in 1973, nil in 1974, and then 134.8 in 1980. The government sets a target price for milk products, that is butter, skimmed milk powder and condensed milk and allows imports in when prices are likely to exceed these levels. Under this system, imports have tended to rise, except since 1974 for butter imports which have fluctuated. Deficiency payments are also made on milk. The effect of these arrangements is that the officially calculated self-suffieciency ratios were in 1978 at 89% at about the same level in 1960, but for beef they have fallen from 96% in 1960 to 73% in 1978.

Japan does appear to have been more successful in increasing her output of pork and poultry meat, both of which increased by 94% between 1969–71 and 1979 (FAO, *Production Year Book*, 1979). The self-sufficiency ratios for these products have, therefore, remained higher; in pork they only declined from 96% in 1960 to 86% in 1975 and then rose again to 90% in 1978 (BAE, 1981, p. 16).

There has also been an increase in consumption of grains other than rice. Consumption for food has fluctuated but generally appears lower than it did in 1955. Most of this is of wheat but earlier on, in 1955, 45% was of barley (BAE, 1981, p. 48). Most domestically produced wheat and barley is delivered to the MAFF Food Agency, which pays considerably more than the import price. Imports of wheat and barley are controlled through a global quota system. Any tariffs on these have been suspended but the government nevertheless usually makes money on the difference between the import price and the domestic price at which the Food Agency sells them.

Consumption for feed has increased extremely rapidly, and in

1978 at 16 million tons was eleven times its level in 1955; 54% of this was of maize, and 32% was of sorghum. Indeed, this has been the requisite for the increase in Japanese production of livestock products. There are scarecely any barriers on imports of feed grain. Indeed, Japan appears to have deliberately fostered imports of maize from India and Thailand. As a result almost all supplies come from abroad.

The system of protection for sugar is very complicated and is aimed at stabilising the internal price and encouraging domestic production. Prices to producers appear on average 80% above the import c.i.f. price. In 1978 Japan produced 22% of her requirements.

With respect to other agricultural commodities, there was a major effort to liberalise trade between 1968 and 1972 by removing the quantitative limits on imports. Some of the main products liberalised included ham, bacon and pigmeat, margarine, coffee, apples, grapefruit, and a variety of processed products such as cornflakes, spaghetti, macaroni and sausages. A preferential tariff system for developing countries was also introduced in 1971 by reductions of 20–100% in import duties. In October 1972, in order to try and reduce its external trade surplus, the Japanese government also decided on (a) further liberalisation of import restrictions, (b) 20% tariff reduction for processed agricultural products, (c) expansion of import quotas by at least 30% over the previous year and their increase to 7% of total domestic consumption for products having a quota below that level (OECD, 1974B).

The official Japanese calculation of their overall self-sufficiency ratios shows it declining from 93% in 1955 to 74% in 1977. The Australian Bureau of Agricultural Economics has criticised this as taking account of the final products and not taking sufficient account of the inputs required to produce them. They made a calculation in terms of 'original calories', that is including the input of feedingstuffs required for the livestock products and this shows the ratio as falling far faster, from 84% in 1955 to 44% in 1977. This is because of the very rapid increase in the importation of feedingstuffs for the domestic livestock industry.

However, the criticism appears misdirected as the real problem is one of aggregation. In order to aggregate their self-sufficiency ratios, the Japanese use their wholesale prices. These are very much higher than the world price for rice but are roughly at the same level for the feed grains maize and sorghum. Hence, the weight attached to the production and self-sufficiency of rice is far too great. World prices do, after all, represent the opportunity cost to the Japanese economy of acquiring commodities—as will be argued in the next chapter.

Now let us turn to consider how these protective policies pursued in industrialised countries show up in the prices to producers and consumers. The next chapter provides a theoretical analysis of the effect of protection, the resulting price rises for producers and consumers and the determinants of changes in quantity supplied and purchased. But in anticipation of that, let us just see whether we can see any systematic effect of protection in the markets of the industrial countries.

OECD has estimated comparable consumer price indices for all items, and for food, beverages and tobacco, which we will term 'food', since 1960. Eurostat also provides a breakdown of the consumer price indices for the different categories of food, bread and confectionery, meat, milk, butter and cheese, and comparable information is provided by the USDA for the US. The same sources also provide producer price indices for all agricultural products, and these are broken down into crops and livestock since 1968 for the EEC countries and back into history for the US. The annual price increases to producers and consumers since 1968 are shown in Table 5.5.

In the US, as described earlier, protection has been declining since the mid-1960s. Between 1967 and 1971, food prices to both producers and consumers were not increasing as fast as the Consumer Price Index (CPI), but between 1972 and 1975 they increased more rapidly with the rapid increase in world market prices. Since then, the prices to consumers have been increasing roughly in line with the Consumer Price Index, whereas prices to producers have been increasing more slowly. Over the whole period, taking the base as 1967, the price index to producers stood at 241.4, to consumers at 234.5, whereas the RPI stood at 217.4. But the difference was largely due to a change in the world market situation.

Among the EEC countries experience varied. Because member countries began with different levels of protection and also because the way the common prices were converted into domestic currencies which depend on the actual exchange rate and the green exchange rate and the way these changed over time, the relative price changes have been different. In Germany, the Netherlands and Belgium, the price of food has systematically risen at a slower rate than the Consumer Price Index since 1960. In Italy, it began by rising at a slower rate, but since 1973 the price of food has been increasing at a slightly faster rate than other items, as it has been doing all along in France.

TABLE 5.5 *Agricultural Price Rises to Producers and Consumers in the US and EEC.*
% per annum

	Producer Price Rises				Consumer Price Rises				
					USDA and Eurostat Estimates			OECD Estimates	
	1968–79	1968–73	1973–9		1968–79	1969–73	1973–9	1969–73	1973–9
United States				*US—CPI*					
Total	8.1(7.4)	11.9(7.3)	5.1(7.5)	Food	6.9	4.9	8.5	4.9	8.5
Crops	7.6	11.8	4.1	Bread and cereals	7.7	6.7	8.8	6.7	8.8
Livestock	8.6	12.0	5.8	Meat	7.1	4.9	9.3		
				Dairy products	8.3	9.5	7.1		
					6.6	4.5	8.5		
EEC									
Germany				*German—CPI*					
Total	3.0	3.6	2.5	Food and beverages	4.6	5.4	4.6	5.3	4.7
Crops	4.0	3.2	4.8	Total	4.0	4.8	3.6	4.8	3.8
Livestock	2.6	3.7	1.9	Bread and cereals		7.0			
				Meat		6.3			
				Milk, butter, cheese		4.2			
France				*France—CPI*					
Total	7.9	8.2	7.7	Food and beverages	8.6	6.1	10.7	6.0	10.7
Crops	8.4	7.7	8.4	Bread and cereals	8.7	7.4	10.3	7.3	11.0
Livestock	7.5	8.5	6.7	Meat		6.2	13.4		
				Milk, butter, cheese		8.7	8.9		
						7.3	10.0		
Italy				*Italy—CPI*					
Total			15.0	Food and beverages	11.4	6.5	16.3	6.6	16.3
Crops			15.5	Bread and cereals	11.3	6.9	16.0	7.0	17.6
Livestock			14.5	Meat	12.6[1]	6.0	17.1		
				Milk, butter, cheese	12.2[1]	8.7	14.7		
					13.9[1]	7.0	18.5		
Netherlands				*Netherlands—CPI*					
Total	3.5	4.8	2.2	Food and beverages	7.2	7.1	7.3	6.7	7.2
Crops	4.2	5.1	3.0	Bread and cereals	5.8	6.1	5.3	5.7	5.4
Livestock	3.1	4.7	1.8	Meat	7.6[1]	6.3	8.1		
				Milk, butter, cheese	5.3[1]	7.9	3.8		
					5.7[1]	5.3	5.6		

Table 5.5 (continued)

Producer item	1968–79	1968–73	1973–9	Consumer item	USDA & Eurostat 1968–79	USDA & Eurostat 1969–73	USDA & Eurostat 1973–9	OECD 1969–73	OECD 1973–9
Belgium — Total			2.9	*Belgium*—CPI	6.8	5.1	8.4	5.2	8.4
Crops			5.3	Food and beverages	6.9	4.9	6.8	5.0	6.9
Livestock			1.6	Bread and cereals	8.4[1]	6.2	10.0		
				Meat	6.0[1]	6.4	5.9		
				Milk, butter, cheese	5.1[1]	3.6	5.5		
United Kingdom — Total	11.7	8.3	13.0	*UK*—CPI	11.9	8.0	15.6	8.0	15.6
Crops	11.0	9.8	13.5	Food and beverages	12.2	9.2	16.0		16.9
Livestock	10.6	9.7	12.9	Bread and cereals					
				Meat		14.6	14.0		
				Milk, butter, cheese		8.6	18.2		
Ireland — Total	13.5	11.9	15.5	*Ireland*—CPI	12.2	9.3	15.0	9.3	15.0
Crops	12.2	9.4	15.0	Food and beverages	12.3		14.5	10.8	15.6
Livestock	14.0	12.4	15.0	Bread and cereals			17.0		
				Meat			15.2		
				Milk, butter, cheese			15.1		
Denmark — Total	8.3	11.4	7.0	*Denmark*—CPI	8.7	7.0	10.8	6.9	10.8
Crops	8.9	10.1	9.1	Food and beverages	8.6		10.2	8.7	10.8
Livestock	8.2	11.8	5.3	Bread and cereals			13.2		
				Meat			9.8		
				Milk, butter, cheese			11.0		
Japan				*Japan*—CPI				7.5	10.0
				Food				8.2	10.2

CPI = Consumer Price Index, US bracketed figures All Foods.

Notes: 1. 1969–79.

Sources: Commission of the European Communities, *The Agricultural Situation in the Community 1980 Report*, pp. 180, 181, 191, 192; USDA, *Agricultural Statistics 1981*, pp. 449, 450; pp. 443 and 557; Eurosta: *Yearbook of Agricultural Statistics 1974*, pp. 262 and 263; OECD, *Consumer Price Indices*, Sources and methods and historical methods (OECD, March 1980).

In Denmark and Ireland, consumer prices for food were increasing more slowly than the CPI up to 1968 and then began to increase faster even before they entered the EEC. But producer prices appear to have increased more slowly than the CPI, at least after 1973.

Britain, whose initial protective system was so different, showed the greatest changes in adjusting to the CAP. Her producer prices increased more slowly than the CPI, but since 1970 her food prices to consumers have increased faster than that of other items. In Britain, food has been one of the leading sectors in inflation.

Thus, although the main objective of the CAP was to open member country markets to each other and achieve a uniform price, it has had markedly different effects on the economies of member countries.

This very different experience with respect to the relative price of food serves to explain the very different levels of public consciousness and concern in the EEC countries about the expense and distortions of the CAP.

The situation may be compared with that of Japan, whose level of protection is even higher than that of the EEC. From 1960 to 1968 her food prices were increasing at about half the rate of the Consumer Price Index (CPI). A better comparison can be made by taking food out of the CPI because it forms such a large component—even by 1975, 39% of consumers' expenditure was on food. By so doing, food prices are shown to have risen at one third the rate of other items between 1960 and 1968. Since then, they have been increasing at a somewhat faster rate.

The situation in the EEC may also be compared with that in the traditional exporters, namely the US, Canada, Australia and New Zealand. In general, the price rise of food and other products appeared as broadly in line between 1960 and 1968. But then for the US and Canada there was a fairly sharp rise in the relative price of food in the early 1970s. This reflects to a large extent the increase in price of cereals on the world market.

This raises the question of the degree to which we would expect a similar rise in price to consumers and producers in view of the amount of services required to convey agricultural products to the consumer. The increase in producers' prices since 1968 in the US and EEC is shown in Table 5.5. By comparing these with the CPIs in Table 5.5, some idea of the change in real prices to agricultural products can be obtained.

Again, experience in member countries of the EEC differs. In Germany and the Netherlands, real producer prices appear to have declined. In France they appeared to be increasing from 1968 to

1973 and then declined, a decline which is shared by Italy, Britain, Denmark and Belgium. However, in all of the main EEC countries, the price of cereals appears to be increasing faster than that of livestock.

As far as can be judged from the scattered information available, this is also true on the consumption side, namely that cereal products (bread and confectionary) are increasing faster in price than livestock products (meat and milk, butter and cheese). This suggests that the level of protection for cereals is being better maintained than for livestock products.

In contrast, in the US the price of livestock has been increasing faster than that of cereals since 1973 but this does not appear reflected in the price to consumers.

These prices changes may all be contrasted with the situation in the world market in which according to GATT the price of food increased by 56%, the price of beef by 62%, of butter by 114%, wheat 20% rice 3% and maize 98% between 1973 and 1979.

AGRICULTURAL POLICIES AFFECTING TRADE IN DEVELOPING MARKET ECONOMIES

Now let us turn to consider the situation in developing countries. Their governments are generally following policies diametrically opposed to those of industrialised countries. They are concerned with keeping the price of agricultural products, in particular food, down to their rapidly growing urban population, purportedly to protect low-income consumers and to encourage the rapid growth of manufacturing. As Brown states (Schulz, 1978), the assumptions underlying the approach are:

(1) that aggregate agricultural production is not very responsive to price changes;
(2) that the chief beneficiaries of higher prices would be the larger size farmers;
(3) that higher food and other agriculture-related prices such as clothing would most adversely affect low-income consumers; and
(4) that manufacturing growth depends upon large transfers of income (profits) and foreign exchange from agriculture to manufacturing.

Thus, the policies have been designed to keep agricultural prices relatively low compared with world prices.

Many different systems are employed for this purpose. Those established longest are for export crops. Indigenous and colonial governments have found that some of the easiest taxes to collect have been those on trade. The developing countries' exports were initially primary products and this system of export taxes has been continued up to the present day such that they are imposed on most exports of tea, coffee and raw materials such as rubber, cotton and jute.

Sometimes government intervention is more extensive. In West Africa, that is Ghana and Nigeria, marketing boards were established to purchase all agricultural products, chiefly cocoa, palm kernels and groundnuts, for export during the Second World War. These marketing boards were retained afterwards initially for the purpose of stabilising prices to producers; but they soon became vehicles for taxing them and the producers themselves were only paid 20–80% of the international price of the product. Furthermore, this system has been adopted in other countries, notably Kenya.

But in addition to this, the governments of developing countries have frequently intervened in the markets for staple foodstuffs. Sometimes they set up government agencies to purchase foodstuffs at relatively low prices for their 'fair price' shops which kept the price down to indigenous farmers. But they do not generally control the price of livestock products.

In addition to this, the import of grain and other foodstuffs subsidised by the industrialised countries has also tended to lower the price to indigenous farmers. Sometimes the government has also subsidised imports, as in Egypt of wheat, and in Sri Lanka of rice and sugar. All these measures depress the price of staple foodstuffs which may benefit consumers of them but they also discourage production, as will be discussed in the next chapter. Also should be mentioned the overvaluation of the currency and the workings of multiple exchange rates which have the effect of taxing exports and subsidising imports.

EASTERN EUROPE AND THE USSR

Finally, let us consider the situation in Eastern Europe and the USSR. Here governments appear to have been increasing their support of agriculture. This has largely taken the form of the increasing deficits of the state trading companies which purchase agricultural products from peasants and collectives to sell in the cities. The burden of the increasing consumer subsidies is implicitly recognised by the governments of Eastern Europe which have almost all introduced economic reforms during the last few years involving large increases in the prices of agricultural products, particularly livestock products.

Notes

1. But the schemes for sugar and milk were self-financing and disposals from the breeding herds of poultry, pigs, cattle and sheep were not covered. No payments were made on broilers, fruit and vegetables, and only small ones on potatoes.
2. Ratio of self-sufficiency by products

$$= \frac{\text{Total domestic production}}{\text{Total domestic consumption}} \times 100\%$$

(domestic consumption = domestic production + net imports − increase of stocks). It can be measured in terms of quantities or at wholesale prices of a given year (OECD, 1974B, Table 5, p. 19).

6 A Theoretical Analysis of Commercial Policy and Empirical Results

A brief outline of commercial policy since the second World War was given in the last chapter. The policy objectives ranged from the avowed intention on the part of most underdeveloped countries to foster their own manufacturing industry, to the defensive policies industrialised countries have carried out with respect to their agricultural and manufacturing industries. In addition a number of preferential trading agreements were considered.

In order to consider the actual effect commercial policy has on international trade some theoretical framework must be employed; without this, it is impossible to identify the significant elements in the policy let alone assess the result. Indeed in the post-war period the theory has been developed side by side with the commercial policies.

In order to span the gap that often exists between empirical results and pure theory, I will begin with a brief account of some assumptions and definitions that are common to them all.

With respect to demand, the assumption is that with tastes and incomes constant the quantity consumers purchase of a commodity over any given period of time will be inversely related to its price. If the relationship at any point is described in terms of a price elasticity of demand e_d:

$$e_d = \frac{\% \text{ change in quantity demanded}}{\% \text{ change in price}}$$

Because of the inverse relationship it is mathematically negative. But economists generally consider it as though it has been multiplied by -1. This convention will be retained here. It affects all the succeeding statements.

Thus e_d is assumed to lie between 0 and ∞. If it is 0 the quantity consumers purchase remains the same whatever the price and therefore their expenditure varies by the same percentage as the price. If it is $+1$ the quantity consumers purchase will increase (decrease) by the same proportion as price falls (increases) so the total expenditure on the commodity remains the same. From the point of view of international trade it is not only the aggregate demand of all consumers in the world market that is important but also the way it appears to an individual country. If the country is 'small' in relation to the world market it will appear as though it is facing an infinitely elastic demand curve for its exports—that is it can sell any amount of them at a given price even though the overall elasticity of demand for the product may be less than ∞.

Likewise it is assumed that if technology and the supply of factors of production remain constant the quantity produced per unit of time will be directly related to price. This relationship at any point is described by the price elasticity of supply

$$e_s = \frac{\% \text{ change in quantity supplied}}{\% \text{ change in price}}$$

This is assumed to lie between 0 and ∞. Again it is not only the total supply elasticity to the world as a whole which is assumed to lie between 0 and ∞ that is important but also the way it appears to an individual country. If the country is 'small' the supply of imports to it will appear infinitely elastic at the world price—that is it cannot affect the world price by altering its purchases.

Further it should be remembered that countries are not likely to specialise completely. Indeed commercial policy would be of little importance if they did. Most countries that import, say, wheat, will also produce some domestically. In that case the overall domestic demand for wheat will be called the demand for an importable. The elasticity of demand for *imports* e_m depends on the elasticity of home demand and supply of importables e_m and e_h. That is

$$e_m = \frac{e_{dm}D + e_h H}{D - H}$$

where D is the original quantity consumed domestically and H the quantity originally supplied by home producers. That is, the elasticity of demand for imports is higher than for importables because it is the net result of changes in both the quantity demanded and supplied to the home market.

If for instance

$$e_{dm} = 0.5$$

$$e_h = 2.0$$

and the initial consumption D is 100 units of which 50 are supplied by home producers. Then

$$e_m = \frac{0.5 \times 100 + 2.0 \times 50}{100 - 50} = 3.0$$

Likewise with the export market if there is some domestic consumption of the exportables, the elasticity of supply of *exports* e_x will depend on the elasticity of supply of exportables e_s and the domestic elasticity of demand for exportables e_d. As the commodity is exported the original amount of the commodity produced domestically, S, must be greater than the quantity consumed domestically, D. Thus

$$e_x = \frac{e_s S + e_d D}{S - D}$$

and e_x will be greater than e_s.

Having defined some of the terminology we can now approach the theory.

PARTIAL EQUILIBRIUM ANALYSIS

This chapter will be confined to a partial equilibrium analysis. Consideration is limited to the market for the product itself and it is assumed that changes in its production and consumption do not have appreciable effects on the rest of the economy. The changes in quantities produced and purchased with changes in money prices can be expressed directly with supply and demand curves as shown in Figure 6.1 The market demand curve D_H for a commodity represents the quantities consumers would be willing to purchase over a given period of time at different prices assuming their tastes and incomes remain constant. Consumers are assumed to go on acquiring units of the commodity until the value of the last (marginal) unit to them is just equal to its price. The lower the price the more units they will buy. This means that the value to them of the intra-marginal units is greater than their price. This difference is termed consumers' surplus and is equal to the area under the demand curve minus total consumers' expenditure on the product.

A supply schedule represents the quantity that would be supplied over the same period of time at any given price assuming technology and the supply of the factors of production remain constant. Producers are willing to increase production of the commodity until the cost of providing the last unit is just equal to its price. The difference between the total revenue they gain and the cost of production is termed producers' surplus. It is equal to the difference between the area under the supply curve and the total revenue gained. The supply schedule of domestic producers S_H is assumed to slope upwards because additional units can only be produced at a higher cost. But the foreign supply schedule S_W is assumed to be indefinitely elastic, that is a horizontal straight line, because it is assumed that the home market is very small in relation to total world supplies.

The equilibrium is the same as under a general equilibrium in so far as consumers equate the value of their marginal unit to its price and producers expand their output until the cost of their marginal unit is equal to its price. Price here can be taken as a proxy for the marginal value of goods in the economy. Although, as already stated, in partial equilibrium analysis the market for the commodity is analysed in isolation as though changes in production and consumption in it did not affect the rest of the economy.

As the observations to determine demand and supply curves must in practice be made over a period of time, prices should be regarded as in real terms, that is after an allowance has been made for the effect of inflation.

Clearly, as the curves only show a relationship between price and quantity, any changes in the factors assumed constant for any particular curve will change its position. For instance, as *per capita* incomes increase, you would expect consumers' purchases of, say, textiles to increase even though the real price of textiles remains constant. This would appear as a rightward shift in the demand curve for textiles, and would be referred to as an increase in demand for textiles. Indeed, in this book an 'increase' or 'decrease' in demand or supply refers to a shift in the whole schedule, that is a change in its parameters. Any movement along such a schedule is described as such.

Figure 6.1 illustrates the market for an importable assuming consumers do not differentiate between the home-produced and imported product. With free trade, imports enter the domestic market at the international price OP_1, which then becomes the domestic price. Consumers will purchase OQ_1, where the value of the last unit to them is just equal to OP_1. Domestic producers will produce OQ_2 where their marginal cost is equal to OP_1. The quantity Q_1Q_2 will be imported and $Q_2 FCQ_1$ will be spent on it. This free-trade situation is used as the criterion for assessing the effect of different forms of protection.

There are many protective devices. One of the most common is an *ad valorem* duty, that is a duty imposed as a percentage of the value of an import. The other forms of protection will be expressed

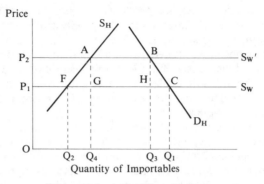

Figure 6.1: A Tariff on Imports

where possible in terms of their *ad valorem* equivalent—that is as a tariff which would have a similar effect on domestic prices and the quantity of imports.

TARIFF

If such an *ad valorem* tariff is imposed it will raise the price of imports to domestic consumers by the full amount of the tariff if it is non-prohibitive and the foreign supply schedule is infinitely elastic. The foreign supply schedule will appear to shift to S_W' at price OP_2 (see Figure 6.1). Consumers will transfer their purchases from foreign to home producers until the price of the product from both sources is the same. That will lead to a reduction of Q_2Q_4 in imports. Imports will also be reduced by Q_3Q_1 because consumers now purchase fewer units of the commodity because its price is higher. Consumers now appear to be spending Q_4ABQ_3 on imports. But ABHG represents tariff revenue. So from the point of view of the trade account, they are only spending Q_4GHQ_3 on imports compared with their original expenditure of Q_2FCQ_1. This reduction in expenditure is equal to the reduction in the quantity of imports $Q_2Q_4 + Q_3Q_1$ times the original price OP_1.

The effect of the tariff can be considered in terms of its distributional effects; producers gain from the higher prices and consumers lose and the government gains tariff revenue. But it can also be considered in terms of its overall effect on the economy.

Many people regard a reduction in expenditure on imports as intrinsically good. But this is misleading, as it implies that the country is not in macroeconomic equilibrium. In terms of this analysis, the loss in welfare is the reduction in consumer surplus P_1P_2BC against which may be set the government's gain in revenue from the import duty of ABHG, and a gain in producers' surplus of P_2AFP_1. There is, therefore, a net loss of AFG + BCH which can be crudely estimated as equal to half the reduction in imports times the absolute value of the tariff, or half the reduction in expenditure on imports times the proportional tariff. It is due to the distortion between prices on the world and home market which leads to a misallocation of resources in production and of consumers' expenditure.

Clearly the size of the welfare loss depends on the height of the tariff because that determines the difference between the domestic and international price. But with a straightforward *ad valorem* duty, the price on the domestic market will fluctuate in accordance with changes in the international supply—if there is a glut, the price on the international market will fall and so will that on the domestic market.

QUOTA ON IMPORTS

This is one of the reasons that producers often prefer quotas as a form of protection. This is a quantitative restriction on imports. To be effective it must reduce imports below their free-trade level. In that case, a quota would have exactly the same effect on the price in the domestic market as a tariff which reduced the quantity of imports by the same amount.

This can be seen in Figure 6.2. The free trade situation is identical to that in Figure 6.1. The effect of a quota is best analysed by aggregating the home and world supply schedules as S_A. At prices below OP_1 all supplies will be provided by home producers and thus they account for the first part of the aggregate supply schedule. At price OP_1, foreign suppliers are prepared to provide an infinite amount, and thus under free trade the aggregate supply schedule would be infinitely elastic. But with a quota, that is a quantitative limit of FJ = AB, when this has been supplied the consumers can only obtain additional units from home producers, and thus the aggregate supply schedule coincides once more with the home supply schedule as JBS_A displaced from the origin by the amount of the quota.

By assumption, the reduction in imports of $Q_2Q_4 + Q_3Q_1 = Q_5Q_1$ is the same as in Figure 6.1 and thus the price rise P_1P_2 is the same and so is the loss in consumers' surplus and gain in producers' surplus. However, in the case of a quota of AB, the difference

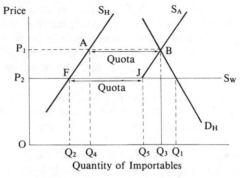

Figure 6.2: A Quota on Imports

between the expenditure on imports of Q_4ABQ_3 and the cost of obtaining them $AB \times OP_1$ does not necessarily go to the government in the form of revenue. Indeed, it will only do so if the government auctions the quota rights, or also imposes a tariff of the same amount. Generally, the benefits of economic rent associated with the quota will accrue to the organisation to whom the quota rights are allocated. This may be the importing firm, the foreign government, or a foreign firm. In spite of the importance of these quota rights, it is often not clear from quota agreements how these are allocated in the first place. However, generally in 'voluntary' agreements negotiated by industrialised countries to protect their 'sensitive' industries, the exporting firm or government gains them. This appears particularly true of those negotiated by the UK and US. In cases where quota rights are allocated to exporting firms, a market may develop in the quota rights themselves as has occurred in Hong Kong for textile quotas. The allocation of quota rights to the exporting country represents some compensation for the quotas imposed on its exports but the total revenue of the exporting country will only remain the same if the elasticity of demand for imports from that country by the importing country is equal to 1. This is unlikely to occur in the long run in which other exporting countries can arise to take its place.

Many underdeveloped countries have in the past also used quotas to limit their imports of consumer and intermediate goods. The effect is the same—it raises the price on the domestic market and enables those to whom the quotas are allocated to reap the benefits.

The disadvantage of quotas as seen from consumers' eyes and advantages as seen from producers' eyes is that they feel it provides a more certain form of protection. The amount imported does not depend on the variation in world supplies or prices but only on the size of the quota. On the other hand, the domestic price then becomes responsive to shifts in the domestic demand and supply schedule.

THE MONOPOLY EFFECT OF A QUOTA

It is also possible for there to be only one domestic producer of the commodity. In that case a quota will change the market from a competitive one to a monopoly and there will be additional welfare costs due to the resulting divergence between prices and marginal costs.

In order to analyse this, we have to replace S_H with the marginal cost (MC) curve of the monopolist as in Figure 6.3. From the monopolist's point of view instead of facing an infinitely elastic demand schedule at OP_1 as under free trade, or OP_2 with a tariff, he now faces the domestic demand schedule D_H minus the amount $AB = FK$ supplied by the quota shown as D_H' in Figure 6.3. The competitive equilibrium where $MC = Price$ is not his profit-maximising equilibrium. He is concerned with his marginal revenue from selling one additional unit of the commodity. This is equal to the price, less the reduction in price he has to sustain on all previous units which depends on the elasticity of the market demand schedule. With a downward-sloping demand schedule, his

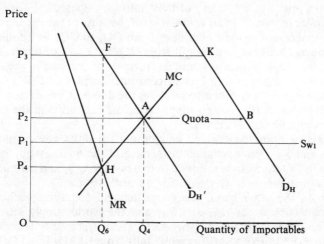

Figure 6.3: When a Quota leads to a Monopoly

marginal revenue must always be less than the price and his profit-maximising position is where MC = MR. Output is lower than in the competitive situation at OQ_6 instead of OQ_4 which leads to a rise in the domestic price of P_2P_3. There is an additional welfare loss of P_2P_3KB of consumers' surplus and a change in producers' surplus of P_4P_3FH minus P_4P_2AH. This is equal to the net efficiency loss of the triangle HFA. There is also an increase in value of imports on the domestic market of $P_2P_3 \times$ quota AB. Note that the change in the producer's surplus is only equal to his additional profit if the MC curve is a long-run one and includes capital as well as direct costs.

This analysis can also be applied to a small number of large firms in so far as in this type of situation they always have an incentive to form a cartel and behave like a monopoly.

VARIABLE IMPORT LEVY

From the home producers' point of view, the most secure form of protection in terms of price stability is a variable import levy designed to bring the price of imports up to a minimum import, or threshold price. This has been adopted in particular for the protection of agriculture both in the US and now by the EEC.

Let us assume that the minimum import price is OP* and that the initial home demand and supply schedules are D_{H1} and S_{H1} and the world supply schedule is S_{W1} as in Figure 6.4. In order to bring the price of imports up from the world price OP_1 to the minimum import price of OP*, a levy of P_1P^* must be imposed. The analysis is similar to that of an *ad valorem* tariff; because of the rise in price, consumers reduce their purchases from OQ_1 to OQ_3 and domestic producers increase their output from OQ_2 to OQ_4. Consumers bear the whole cost of protection in the form of an increase in the price they have to pay with a loss of consumer surplus of P_1P^*LC.

However, this system also insulates the domestic price from both fluctuations in the foreign supply schedule and shifts in the home demand and supply curves.

Say the domestic demand and supply schedules now change to D_{H2} and S_{H2}. Price remains the same and the quantity purchased falls to OQ_5 and home production increases to OQ_6 and the quantity imported falls to Q_5Q_6 (as for an ordinary tariff).

If on the other hand, the home demand and supply schedule remain constant at D_{H1} and S_{H1} and the world supply schedule shifts upwards to S_{W2} at price OP_2, the variable levy is reduced from P_1P^* to P_2P^*, tariff revenue falls from KLMN to KLQP but everything else including imports remains constant.

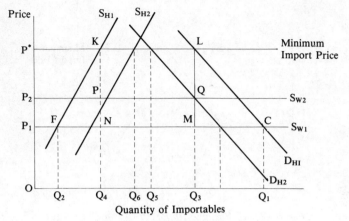

Figure 6.4: A Variable Import Levy

In this type of situation, consumers cannot benefit from an increase in supply by either domestic producers or foreign producers but on the other hand they do not face higher prices when there is a reduction in supply. The effect of fluctuations in home demand and supply is entirely reflected in trade. The effect of fluctuations in world supply is entirely reflected in changes in the height of the tariff. Both will affect tariff revenue. Stability of price on the domestic market has been acquired at the cost of adding to instability in the rest of the world both by transmitting the full effect of any changes in home demand and supply through changes in trade, and by preventing any response by domestic consumers and producers to changes in world market conditions.

However, as this system entirely depends on imports entering the domestic market at a fixed price, it only works if the protection is less than prohibitive.

If, for instance, demand and supply shift to D_{H3} and S_{H3} (see Figure 6.5) home producers can supply at price OP* more than enough to satisfy domestic consumers. How then can price OP* be maintained on the domestic market? Only, as many governments have discovered, by purchasing the surplus LK and removing it from the domestic market.

In the EEC, this process is institutionalised in the CAP. As mentioned in Chapter 5, FEOGA is the intervention agency which purchases this surplus although at a price somewhat below the minimum import price. Originally it was hoped that FEOGA would be able to later sell off this stockpile when supplies of the commodity fell. But the support prices were so high that this never occurred.

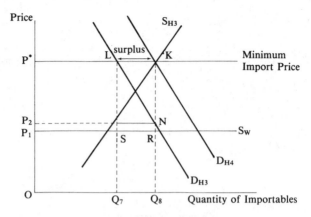

Figure 6.5: A Variable Import Levy with Surpluses

As it was neither financially nor physically feasible to continue accumulating stock, FEOGA was faced with the option of complete destruction or 'valorisation' of the stockpile which has always been regarded with abhorrence by the world community, or with selling it on an alternative market.

If it is to be sold within the EEC, the alternative market must be that of another product. This involves 'denaturing' the commodity to ensure that it is not sold back into its original market; thus wheat is sprayed with green dye and sugar is mixed with carbon so that they can be sold as feedingstuffs but cannot re-enter the market for human food. Sometimes more expensive processes are applied; for instance, part of the wine lake is being distilled to produce industrial alcohol. Thus additional costs are incurred and the return obtained is often very much lower than the intervention price. This policy may also disrupt the secondary market.

The alternative is to sell the product on the international market. In that case the cost to the intervention agency per unit is the difference between the intervention price and world price OP_1, that is P_1P^*. It is also necessary to continue imposing the variable duties on imports and indeed subject them to the strictest surveillance otherwise the subsidised exports just re-enter the system.

The EEC has incurred considerable internal criticism for undertaking such subsidised exports, on the grounds that the EEC taxpayers are financing the subsidy of products for foreign consumers. However, if the price at which they are sold is just the world price and the EEC's exports are sufficiently small not to affect it, this is inaccurate: the subsidy just represents the cost of disposing of an expensively acquired stockpile. The complaints arise because the protection of domestic producers is entirely at the expense of domestic consumers, so that consumers cannot purchase the product at its world price.

Complaints by other exporting countries about the effect of these EEC-subsidised exports on their markets are also somewhat misdirected. Their markets are just affected by the EEC's policy of protection whether this protection leads to import substitution or to additional exports by the EEC.

The US pursued a similar type of agricultural policy with the Commodity Credit Corporation (CCC) acting as the intervention agency. It accumulated large stocks which it often used as aid for developing countries. Nevertheless, it was accused of undermining the agricultural markets in the developing countries to which they were sent. At one point it also subsidised exports of cotton whereupon the domestic textile producers bitterly complained that the US government was giving foreign textile producers an unfair competitive advantage. Eventually, the US government subsidised home consumption of cotton as well.

The subsidisation of domestic consumption does, of course reduce the distorting effects of this type of protection on consumption. Let us assume that the original demand curve was D_{H2} in Figure 6.4 and the effect of the subsidy is to make it appear to producers that it is D_{H1}, i.e. the subsidy per unit is the vertical distance between the two demand schedules QL. Because the product now appears cheaper, the consumers will purchase Q_5Q_3 more of it than they did when the price appeared to them as OP* and imports will increase by the same amount. But because the subsidy per unit is only QL which is less than the LM required to compensate them fully for protection, they are still purchasing less than they would do under free trade. The government expenditure on the subsidy is P_2QLP^* whereas the tariff revenue obtained assuming S_{H1} is the domestic supply schedules is KLMN.

In the situation depicted in Figure 6.5, the institution of consumer subsidies may be sufficient to avoid the accretion of surpluses, if, for instance, it raised the apparent demand curve from D_{H3} to D_{H4}. However, although it removes most of the distortion on the consumer side, the government expenditure on the subsidy P^*KNP_2 is much greater than the previous cost of disposing of the surplus LKRS.

In practice, the subsidisation of consumption has generally been marginal. In the case of the EEC, subsidies have been placed on milk for school children, occasionally on beef and butter for old age pensioners, and butter for non-profit making institutions. In the US, they have largely taken the form of food stamps which have been distributed as a form of poor relief.

This digression has served to demonstrate the ramifications of a highly protected system and how all efforts to modify its effects either contribute to difficulties for other producers or entail considerable government expenditure.

SUBSIDY TO PRODUCERS

Let us now turn briefly to an analysis of the type of protective system employed by Britain for her agriculture before she joined the EEC, that is a subsidy to producers (see Figure 6.6). In this case, imports can enter freely at the world market price OP_1. There is thus no loss of consumer surplus. The subsidy to domestic producers shifts the apparent supply schedule to S_H' which is vertically below the actual supply schedule S_H by the amount of the subsidy. Home producers now increase their output by Q_2Q_4 because they are actually receiving a price of OP_2. The cost to the government is the subsidy per unit P_1P_2 times the number of units being produced, that is OQ_4.

Subsidies can, therefore, be regarded as a preferable form of intervention in so far as they do not introduce other distortions in allocation into the system. But they have to be financed. It is the cost of financing them that has deterred governments. Furthermore, the raising of revenue may also be distortionary if it is in the form of either taxes on commodities or marginal taxes on earnings.

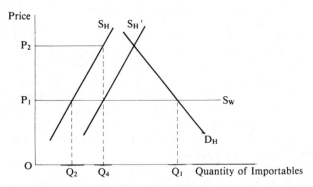

Figure 6.6: A Subsidy on Production of Importables

INTERVENTION IN THE EXPORT MARKET

Now let us turn to the export market (see Figure 6.7). Supply is now greater than demand and this is demonstrated by drawing the supply schedule S_H to the right of the demand schedule D_H. If the country is small it can be regarded as facing an infinitely elastic demand schedule D_W for its exports. With free trade, it would produce OQ_2 of which OQ_1 would be sold on the domestic market and Q_1Q_2 exported.

The effect of a tax on exports is to make it appear as though the world demand schedule for exports had fallen to $D_W{'}$. Producers will thus transfer part of their output from the export market to their domestic market until the price they receive in both markets is the same, that is OP_3. This will lead to an increase in domestic consumption of Q_1Q_3. The producers will also reduce their output by Q_4Q_2 in response to the reduction in price they receive. The total effect will be a loss in producers' surplus of P_1VYP_3, a gain in consumer surplus of P_1P_3ZU, and tariff revenue of $RSYZ$, thus leading to a net welfare loss of URZ and SVY which is roughly equal to half the reduction in quantity of exports $(Q_1Q_3 + Q_4Q_2)$ times the absolute tariff which is P_1P_3.

It might be thought that the countries are so anxious about their balance of payments that they would never employ such devices. But many countries do so apparently under the belief that the supply of exports to the world market is inelastic—this would imply that the total supply of exportables is inelastic and so is demand in the home market. Alternatively they may be assuming that the

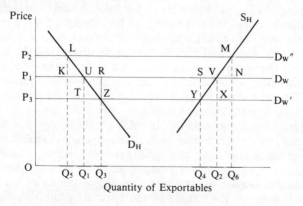

Figure 6.7: A Tax or Subsidy on Exports

country is not facing an infinitely elastic demand schedule but one with an elasticity below 1 and by restricting the quantity of exports to the world market the country can raise its total foreign-exchange earnings.

SUBSIDY ON EXPORTS

Exports can also be subsidised. This is more likely to be carried out by an industrialised country. The effect of doing so is to make it appear that the world demand schedule has increased. Let D_W'' be the apparent demand schedule. The above process will go into reverse with Q_5Q_1 of the product being transferred from home consumers to exports and producers increasing their output by Q_2Q_6. The total welfare effect will be a gain in producers' surplus of P_2MVP_1 and loss in consumer surplus of P_1P_2LU, and a subsidy on the exports of Q_5Q_6 of LKNM. The net welfare loss will be KLU and VMN.

By now the reader may well be feeling that although the analysis sounds fine in theory its application may well be more difficult. This is true. One of the chief problems is that the effects of protection depend on the elasticities of demand and supply and for many products these are not known. However, there has been a considerable effort on the part of agricultural economists in general and the USDA in particular to calculate them for agricultural products (see Rojko, 1978). Using these ranges of estimates, Bale and Lutz (1981) estimate for 1976 the effect in terms of changes in production, consumption, exports and employment of governmental interference in the price system. They take as their standard the international price of the product at the border of the country. They take some of the main products within each country—wheat, maize, barley, sugar and beef in France, Germany and the United Kingdom, the same plus rice minus maize in Japan—for all of which the internal price is considerably above the international price. They also consider countries that discriminate against their agriculture, namely Argentina, Egypt, Pakistan, taking the four main agricultural commodities in each of them, e.g. for Egypt wheat, rice, maize and cotton, plus Thailand which discriminates in favour of maize and sugar and against rice and rubber. Yugoslavia as an example of a centrally planned economy is also taken; she discriminates against wheat and maize and in favour of beef.

Calculations are then made of the effect of protection for the selected commodities in the countries concerned, using the high and low estimates of the elasticities of supply and demand. Thus the calculations provide a range of effects on production and consumption and therefore exports. For instance, the rate of protection for wheat in France is estimated at 26% and this, together with the high estimates of elasticities of supply of 1.28 and of demand of 0.30, is calculated to increase exports by 4.748 million tons. Whereas assuming the low elasticities of supply of 0.42 and demand of 0.10 leads to an increase in exports of only 1.560 million tons.

The highest rates of agricultural protection are in Japan. The most significant one facing both consumers and producers is for rice. The range of elasticities is given as between 0.08–0.24 for supply and 0.06–0.18 for demand. The effect of protection is then calculated as leading to additional exports of between 7.606 and 20.020 million tons of rice. As Japan did, in fact, import 22 thousand metric tons of rice in 1976 the calculation shows the degree of import substitution rather than the actual amount of exports.

In contrast, the developing countries discriminated against their agriculture and this led to higher levels of imports then they would have had otherwise. The greatest degree of discrimination was shown by Egypt whose domestic price of wheat was 48%, of rice was 35%, of maize was 52%, and of cotton was 34% of the world price, thus representing negative rates of protection. She exported 211 thousand tons of rice and 165 of cotton. She imported 2918 thousand tons of wheat and 459 of maize. This discrimination led to imports being much higher than they would have been otherwise by 1153–3534 thousand tons of wheat, 1533–4639 of rice, 557–1704 of maize, and 83–250 of cotton. Thus, were the discrimination to be removed, she would have exported more rice and cotton, would have become an exporter of maize, and might have been an exporter of wheat.

The welfare effects of these protective policies were that in developed countries there was a considerable redistribution of income away from consumers towards producers. The largest absolute transfer appears to be under the low elasticity assumptions in Japan with a loss of $6869 million to consumers in Japan and a gain of $5132 to producers. In developing countries, the transfer was the other way around and the study showed the largest absolute transfer to consumers was in Egypt at $1436 million under high elasticity assumptions, and the largest loss to producers was $2232 million under high elasticity assumptions in Argentina. The net loss taking government revenue also into account was highest in absolute terms in Japan and then Egypt. In relation to GNP it was highest in Egypt at 10.58% and then in Pakistan at 3.04% under high elasticity assumptions.

This exercise is limited to a few agricultural products and is only partial in nature. It only considers the immediate effect of protection on trade and not the result of complete adjustment, which would be extremely difficult to calculate. However, it does give some idea of the order of magnitude involved.

Another area in which this type of calculation has become important is in calculating the effect of the CAP on EEC member countries, particularly Britain. In this case, an important feature is not only the effect on trade but also on the distribution of income. But let us now turn to consider the analysis of preferential trading.

PREFERENTIAL TRADING

In addition to the variety of protective devices already mentioned, another element became of increasing importance through the period, namely preferential trading. This was first exhibited in the formations of customs unions and free trade areas and then later on in the generalised system of preferences (GSP).

In signing a free trade area agreement, countries agree to remove all impediments in the way of tariffs or quotas on trade between themselves but retain their previous tariff on imports from outside countries. In order to avoid these imports all coming through the member countries with the lowest external tariff, such an agreement limits free trade status to member countries' products. These are specified by its rules of origin. In EFTA, a product was accorded free trade status if 50% of its value was accounted for by production within EFTA or if certain processes had been carried out within EFTA.

In a customs union, all impediments on trade between member countries are removed and a common external tariff (CET) is imposed on goods from outside.

Viner led the way in developing the theory of customs unions. He pointed out that although trade is freer between member countries, there is now discrimination between member and non-member countries. He distinguished two aspects of the situation, one in which production is transferred from a high-cost to a lower-cost source of production, say from the home country to the partner country because tariffs have been removed from the latter country's products; this he terms *trade creation*. The other occurs when production is transferred from a low-cost source to a higher-cost source of production, say from a third country to a partner country because tariffs are no longer imposed on products from the latter—this he termed *trade diversion*. Trade creation he regarded as always beneficial, and trade diversion as detrimental (Viner, 1950).

This is to look at benefits and costs entirely from the production point of view—he assumed that the commodities were always consumed in the same proportion. It was left to Lipsey to point out that there was also a consumption angle. Indeed, the consumer benefits occured in both cases and might even outweigh the losses in the case of trade diversion (Lipsey, 1957).

To show the general situation, I will use a diagram employed by Kindleberger (see Figure 6.8). This is in terms of partial equilibrium analysis. (Kindleberger and Lindert, 1978).

The world schedule to the market is S_W or S_W' with a tariff, the partner's supply schedule is S_P and the domestic supply schedule is S_H. Before the formation of the customs union, all imports come from the rest of the world as they appear cheapest. The price on the domestic market is equal to the world price OP_1 plus the tariff P_1P_2 and is thus OP_2. Consumers purchase a quantity OM_3 and the output of domestic producers is OM_4. M_4M_3 is imported from the rest of the world requiring a foreign exchange expenditure of ADM_3M_4 and providing a tariff of BCDA.

If a customs union is formed, the tariff is removed on the partner's goods but not on those from the rest of the world and thus goods from the partner country appear cheaper at OP_3. If OP_3 is less than OP_2 prices on the domestic market fall. All imports are then acquired from the partner country and are greater at M_6M_5. There is a gain in consumers' surplus of P_2CEP_3 and a loss in producers' surplus of P_2BFP_3 due to the lower price, and also a loss

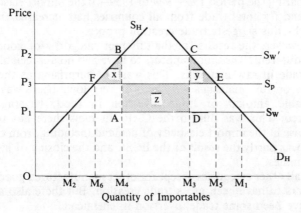

Figure 6.8: Trade Creation and Trade Diversion

in tariff revenue of ABCD which is equal to a net gain of $x + y - z$. z can be regarded as the trade diversion effect on transferring purchases from a low-cost producer W to a higher-cost producer P.

This is fine in theory but how can the effects of the formation of EFTA or the EEC actually be calculated when neither demand nor supply schedules can be assumed to be static? Herewith lies the problem in calculating the economic effect of any institutional change, namely that in order to do so you have to make an assumption about what would have happened in the absence of that change. Several approaches to that problem are reflected in the exercises carried out for the effect of the formation of EEC and EFTA.

Balassa, in his investigation of the effects of the formation of EEC, assumes that the income elasticity of demand for imports would have remained the same in its absence.[1] By income elasticity, he means the annual rate of change of imports to that of GNP measured at constant prices. Thus the effect of integration is assumed to be the residual. He then calculates this income elasticity of imports for a period 1953–9 before any tariff cuts were instituted and compares it with the periods afterwards, 1959–65 and 1959–70 for total imports of the EEC, and intra-area imports and extra-area imports.

From this type of analysis a rise in the income elasticity of demand for intra-area imports would indicate gross trade creation (due either to substitution for domestic or third-country sources of supply). A rise in the import elasticity from all sources would indicate true trade creation. A fall in the import elasticity from third countries would indicate trade diversion. He calculated that comparing the period 1953–9 with 1959–70 the import elasticity of demand for total trade from all countries had increased from 1.8 to 2.1—this suggests trade creation proper.

However, the results for the different categories of goods were very different. The union appears to have had no appreciable effect on trade in raw materials. This was not surprising as the initial tariffs on raw materials were zero or very low. There was a considerable amount of trade diversion in food, beverages and tobacco. This was due to the CAP. In fuels there has been an increase in the import elasticity of demand including from outside. This was partly the result of the ECSC and the closing of high-cost coal mines.

In all other categories except for other manufactured goods there appears to have been gross trade creation. But there also appears to have been some trade diversion in chemicals.

In general the net trade creation that has occurred has been in manufactures. So has this led to industries shrinking in some countries and expanding in other countries? This cannot be answered by an analysis with such large categories.

The NIER did endeavour to analyse the pattern of trade in manufactures more fully by smaller SITC categories by comparing the trade of EEC countries in 1958 with it in 1969. Over that period exports of countries had become more similar rather than more different. (Major and Hays, November 1970, pp. 34–5). This had led proponents of the EEC to argue that the benefits of the EEC have come from rationalisation of production within industries rather than benefits in the form of trade creation leading to greater specialisation by industries. But there is no independent evidence of this.

EFTA

A similar type of analysis has been carried out for the effects of EFTA. The pre-integration period 1954–9 is compared with the post-integration period 1959 to 1965.

In this case imports were related to apparent consumption. The average annual change in the share of imports from 1954 to 1959 were extrapolated from 1959 to 1965 and compared with the actual share of imports in apparent consumption. This was done for imports from all areas and imports from other EFTA countries and imports fron non EFTA countries.

In so far as imports fron non EFTA countries were lower than estimated by extrapolation from 1954–9 this is regarded as trade diversion, and in so far as imports from EFTA countries were higher than the extrapolated estimate this is regarded as trade creation. The results were that by 1965 the value of trade creation amounted to $373 million and trade diversion amounted to $457 million (EFTA, 1969).

If individual commodities are considered, the greatest amount of trade creation appears to have taken place in textiles and clothing. The countries who chiefly benefited were the UK and Portugal. A considerable amount of trade creation also took part in pulp and paper products, partly due to lower-cost Scandinavian producers expanding production at the expense of higher cost, i.e. British producers.

The largest amount of trade diversion appears to have taken place in machinery, but there was also a considerable amount in textiles and clothing, metals and metal manufactures.

In all these exercises the implicit assumption is that an appropriate means of assessing any economical integration is to compare what would happen if there had been no reduction in tariffs with the effect of reducing barriers to trade with the partner country.

But as we are considering the situation from the point of view of the world as a whole, it appears more appropriate to compare the effect of reducing or removing impediments on trade with member countries, with that of a non-discriminatory reduction in trade barriers, an approach that was first used by Cooper and Massell (1965). Their argument was that although the removal or reduction of a tariff on imports from a country may have trade-creating as well as trade-diverting effects, the former without the latter could be obtained by a non-discriminatory removal of tariffs.

GENERALISED SYSTEM OF PREFERENCES

The arguments against this with respect to the Generalised System of Preferences (GSP) is that a preference in favour of under-developed countries, although it may be trade diverting in the location of production to developing countries, nevertheless by improving the welfare of the poorer countries at the expense of the wealthier improves the welfare of the world as a whole. However it is not clear why a worse allocation of resources would automatically lead to a better distribution of income without some very stringent assumptions about rigidities in production and demand patterns.

Furthermore, in practice the GSP has been hedged round with even further restrictions. One of the most prevalent is a tariff quota. This involves the preference on exports from a developing to industrial country being available up to a certain limit and above that limit the full tariff being paid. So although the developing country may get the benefits of the quota rights if they are allocated to her of such preferential exports, immediately the quota is reached her additional exports bear the normal tariff. Indeed for exports to some industrial countries the cost of exceeding the quota is extremely high in so far as the exporter loses the whole of her preferential rights if she does so. This applies on trade with the US to countries supplying 50% or more of the total value or $25 million of US imports of the articles.

Secondly, if there is a tariff quota and this is effective for a particular country, that is its marginal exports incur the full mfn duty, then the price on the market will not fall and although the initial exports will be allowed in at a lower duty than before the benefits of this may never be gained by the exporter—particularly when control is being exerted at the importing end.

Thirdly, if the proportion of the tariff quota that can be utilised by one country is limited then this will assist other developing countries at its expense. There are also the complaints of UNCTAD that because of the restrictions and because other developing countries were unable to utilise the remainder of the quota this restricted exports from developing countries as a whole. But exports will not be any lower than they would have been with no GSP.

In general, because the tariff quotas were smaller than the imports from developing countries the latter faced the mfn tariff at the margin. Thus the GSP does not encourage exports from them. Furthermore the benefit of the reduction in the tariff on the intra-marginal units could not go to the exporting country unless it controlled the licences.

Furthermore, the US under its Trade Reform Act of 1973 excluded entirely import-sensitive items such as textile products, footwear, watches and certain steel products. In any case the restrictions on industrialised countries' imports of textiles and clothing have become increasingly severe under successive MFA agreements, as has been related in Chapter 4.

THEORY OF EFFECTIVE PROTECTION

The analysis of protection was also extended by the theory of effective protection. This theory allows for trade not only in final but also intermediate products—an aspect that has been ignored or assumed non-existent so far.

Certain elements of the analysis remain the same as before. That is, the effect of a small country imposing a non-prohibitive tariff will be to raise the price of the product on the domestic market by the same amount. Thus consumption, that is the quantity purchased of the final product, will fall due to this price rise.

The theory of effective protection is concerned with the degree of protection afforded to a particular industry or process of production supplying a final good. Using Corden's notation, let us assume that the industry's activity j produced a final product also termed j. (Corden, 1971 pp. 35–7). This industry is placed between two international markets, that of the final good j, and that for its input i.

Let us also assume that a fixed physical amount of i is required to produce any unit of j. At free-trade prices a_{ij} is the share of i in the total cost of producing commodity j. Thus, if p_j is the price of the commodity j and p_v is the value added by activity j

$$p_v = p_j(1 - a_{ij}) \tag{1}$$

The value added by j is raised by any nominal tariff t_j placed on its final product j. On the other hand it is reduced by a nominal tariff t_i imposed on its input i by an amount depending on a_{ij}. Thus if $p_v{}'$ is the value added under protection

$$p_v{}' = p_j[(1 + t_j) - a_{ij}(1 + t_i)] \tag{2}$$

where the nominal rates are the *ad valorem* equivalents of all tariffs and quotas.

The effective rate of protection g_j for industry j is defined as the percentage increase in its value added due to protection. Thus

$$g_j = \frac{p_v{}' - p_v}{p_v} \tag{3}$$

Substituting equations (1) and (2) in (3), we obtain the general equation for the effective rate of protection

$$g_j = \frac{t_j - a_{ij}t_i}{(1 - a_{ij})} \tag{4}$$

If there is more than one traded input, this generalises to

$$g_j = \frac{t_j - \sum a_{ij}t_i}{(1 - \sum a_{ij})}$$

The effective rate of protection g_j will only be equal to the nominal rate of protection t_j if $t_j = t_i$ or if there is vertical integration such that $a_{ij} = 0$.

Most countries are observed in a situation in which they already have a protective system. In that case although the physical input-output coefficient is assumed to remain the same, in terms of price it may be different. The protection distorted coefficient $a_{ij}{}'$ then is

$$a_{ij}{}' = a_{ij} \frac{(1 + t_i)}{(1 + t_j)} \tag{5}$$

and the formula for the effective rate of protection becomes:

$$g_j = \frac{1 - a_{ij}'}{\dfrac{1}{1 + t_j} - \dfrac{a_{ij}'}{(1 + t_i)}} - 1 \tag{6}$$

The introduction of the theory of effective protection in the 1960s provided an additional basis for the developing countries' complaints that the industrialised countries discriminated heavily against their manufacturing industries. As seen from Chapter 4, the tariffs of industrialised countries were generally zero or very low on raw materials, and then tended to escalate with the degree of processing of the product. This led to the effective rates being higher than the nominal; that is industrialised countries were protecting their own manufacturing industries even more heavily than they appeared to be from their ordinary tariff schedules.

APPLICATION OF THE THEORY OF EFFECTIVE PROTECTION TO COTTON TEXTILES

The theory of effective protection was thought to be particularly applicable to textiles in which there was a considerable amount of trade at each stage of manufacture, and for which the conversion rates of fibre into yarn and yarn to cloth could be regarded as fixed.

In Table 6.1, some calculations are made of the effective rates of protection for cotton yarn and sheeting in the US, UK, Germany and France using data for 1968. (This was prepared by the Textile Council of the UK. It used data supplied by the Werner Textile Associates which almost certainly understated the average labour costs for Germany and France.) In Table 6.1, the first five columns are of costs excluding what is termed 'profit'. Columns 6 to 8 are of tariffs (somewhat lower in 1968 than they were in 1960; see Table 4.1). The US tariff schedule is so complicated that it is difficult to know what the *ad valorem* equivalent is but the average duty collected has been taken as the rate for grey cloth.

Using the mfn tariffs, the apparent effective rates of protection are calculated for the UK, Germany and France using equation (6). The effective rates do appear much higher than the nominal rates and they also appear higher for weaving than spinning.

But by the late 1960s, the industrialised countries were protecting their textile industries not only with tariffs but by a whole series of quota restrictions negotiated under the LTA and imposed otherwise (see Chapter 4). We therefore need an *ad valorem* equivalent of these.

TABLE 6.1 Costs, Tariffs and Effective Rates of Protection in Cotton Textiles in some of the Larger Industrialised Countries in 1968.

	Costs of Production pence					mfn Rates of Protection			Apparent Effective Rates of Protection[5]				Effective Rate of Protection using Hong Kong Costs for Yarn and Cloth[4,6]		
	US	UK	Germany	France	Hong Kong	US %	UK %	CET %	UK %	Germany %	France %	US %	UK %	Germany %	France %
Spinning d/lb															
Cotton-clean	33.4	31.7	31.9	31.2	30.1	(0)	0	0							
Spinning	13.7	15.1	12.5	11.1	6.6										
of which labour	6.1	8.3	5.7[1]	4.7[1]	3.2										
depreciation	1.1	2.4	3.4	3.4	1.3										
other	6.5	4.4	3.4	3.0	2.1										
Total yarn	47.1	46.8	44.4	42.3	36.7		7.5	8[3]	27.6	35.6	39.4	92.8	88.3	55.6	26.7
Weaving d/yd															
Yarn	33.0	32.8	31.2	29.6	25.7										
of which labour	9.2	9.1	5.7	5.0	2.6										
depreciation	0.6	1.2	1.9	1.8	0.8										
other	7.4	5.5	7.0	5.4	5.6										
Total grey cloth	50.2	48.6	45.8	41.8	34.7	(16.4)	17.5	16.3[3]	45.6	39.1	42.9	73.8	59.9	48.6	22.9

Table 6.1 (continued)

Coefficients under protection a_{ij}		
	Cotton to yarn	Yarn to cloth
UK	.677	.675
Germany	.713	.681
France	.738	.708

Compared with Hong Kong + 10% travel costs *apparent nominal rates* %

	Yarn	Cloth
US	16.7	31.5
UK	15.9	27.3
Germany	10.0	20.0
France	4.8	9.5

Hong Kong coefficients a_{ij}
Clean cotton into yarn = .820
Yarn into cloth   = .741

Notes:
1. Figures appear true of only the most efficient firms—other sources suggest 6.2 for France and 7.9 for Germany.
   Sheeting 92", 60 × 60, 20s/20s.
2. Average duty collected—US rates are very complicated.
3. Highest of range 6%–8% for yarn and 13.3 to 16.3% for woven cotton fabrics.
4. Allowing for transport costs of 10% from Hong Kong to other countries.
5. $g_j = \dfrac{1}{\dfrac{1}{(1 + t_j)} - \dfrac{a_{ij}'}{(1 + t_i)}} - 1$
6. $g_j = \dfrac{t_j - a_{ij}t_i}{(1 - a_{ij})}$ where a_{ij} is the Hong Kong coefficient.

Source: The Textile Council *Cotton and Allied Textiles*. (Manchester, The Textile Council, 1969), Ch, 5, Addendum, p. 45 and Appendix XIII, p. 161.

For this purpose, Hong Kong was taken as the point of complete free trade. Her coefficients of clean cotton into yarn of 0.820 and yarn into cloth of 0.741 were taken as the free-trade coefficients. Transport costs were regarded as about 10% from Hong Kong to the industrialised countries; thus yarn costing 36.7d per pound could be supplied at 40.37d per pound, and cloth costing 34.7d per yard could be supplied at 38.17d per yard. The difference between these and the costs of production in the industrialised country is regarded as representing the tariff equivalent of the quotas imposed on imports from developing countries. These nominal rates were considerably higher than the mfn rates except for France. The effective rates of protection calculated from them were higher still as can be seen from the last four columns. But interestingly, the effective rates of protection were higher for spinning than weaving for all countries. The obverse of this is that Hong Kong's comparative advantage was greatest in spinning where her value added was 6.6d per pound, approximately half that in industrialised countries except for France (whose labour costs are almost certainly understated) whereas in weaving, the value added at 9.0d per yard was generally more than half that in industrialised countries. Hong Kong here represents the marginal low-cost producer—she was both an exporter and importer of cotton yarn and cloth.

The high tariff on yarn, of course, discriminates against the weaving industry but restrictions on imports of cloth are sufficient to provide it with a high effective rate of protection, albeit not as high as for spinning. It might also be noted that the quantitative restrictions mean that the rates of protection in France and Germany are different even though they are both surrounded by the same Common External Tariff (CET).

PROBLEMS IN CALCULATIONS OF EFFECTIVE RATES

Non-trade inputs

Certain difficulties in applying the theory should now be considered in so far as the way they are dealt with will affect the estimates of the effective rates.

Firstly, physical inputs into the final product may not always be traded. Herein lies a problem. Should non-traded inputs be treated as on a par with the value added by industry and thus benefiting in the same way from protection, termed the Corden method? Or should a non-trade input be regarded like imports as in infinitely elastic supply, termed the Balassa method?

Let p_v be the value added by the industry concerned and p_h be the value added by non-traded inputs and Δp_j be the increase in price of the final product due to the imposition of a tariff of t_j on it. Then the Corden method would show an effective rate of protection of

$$\frac{\Delta p_j}{(p_v + p_h)}$$

whereas the Balassa method would show an effective rate of protection of

$$\frac{\Delta p_j}{p_v}$$

The Corden method leads to lower estimates of effective protection for industry j than does the Balassa method.

Most calculations provide a set of results for each method.

Indirect taxes and subsidies
The other problem is the degree to which indirect taxes should be taken into account. After all, a tax on the consumption of an input i raises the price of i to industry j in the same way as a tariff on the imports of i. But a subsidy on the production of i will have no effect on j, in so far as i's price to the industry j will be determined by the price at which imports of i can enter the domestic market.

In contrast, a consumption tax on j will not alter the effective protective rate for j so long as imports of j can enter at the same price. Whereas a production subsidy for j will raise the value added in the production of j and thus the effective rate of protection for j.

Often the reason for very different estimates of effective protection in a country lies in the degree to which indirect taxes have been taken into account.

Allowance for over-valuation of the exchange rate
Finally, there is the degree to which the system of protection is being used as a substitute for devaluation of the exchange rate.

As must be obvious from the notation, the theory of effective protection, although developed as a partial equilibrium theory, is also used on input-output tables to assess protective rates for all industries. However, it is perfectly possible to find that all industries receive positive effective protection. Therefore, in order to find its effect on the allocation of resources, it is first necessary to find out the devaluation that would be required if all protection were to be removed but the same balance of trade achieved. This percentage should then be subtracted from the effective protective rates to give the net effective rates of protection. In so far as this is positive for an industry, the overall system of protection is increasing the returns to factors employed in it, and thus encouraging an allocation of resources to it. On the other hand, the reverse applies to industries receiving negative net rates of protection, even though the simple effective rate of protection appeared positive.

However, the actual increase in output will depend on the elasticity of supply of factors of production to the industry. The greater this is, the greater the increase in output.

But effective protection may also be expected to affect the relative returns to factors of production. If they can only be employed in fixed proportions, the increase in return to any particular factor will be inversely related to its elasticity of supply. If it is in infinitely elastic supply to the industry, it will not benefit at all from protection. On the other hand, a factor of production in very inelastic supply, such as cultivable land is to agriculture, would benfit from the protection of the industry. If there is some degree of substitution between the factors of production or between a factor and a traded input, these above conclusions need to be modified.

EFFECTIVE PROTECTION IN THE US

There have been a number of calculations of the effective rates of protection for the US and UK. Using the 1958 input-output table, Baldwin calculated the effective rates of protection for industry groups in the US for 1958, 1964 and forecast them for 1972 by which time the Kennedy round cuts were to be completed (Baldwin, 1970). He obtained positive rates for agriculture which appeared to decline from 1958 to 1972, negative rates for other primary industries such as forestry and fishery protection, iron and ferroalloy mining, stone and clay mining but positive rates for crude petroleum and natural gas. Most manufacturing industries received positive rates of protection except for paper and allied products, farm machinery and equipment, and in 1964 and 1972 miscellaneous textile goods and floor coverings. The latter appears inconsistent with our previous discussion of textile tariffs but is probably due to the high degree of effective protection on yarn which he calculates to be 95% in 1964, which is not far off our calculation of 93% in 1968—see Table 6.1

EFFECTIVE PROTECTION IN THE UK

Baldwin also calculated the effective rates of protection for industry groups in the UK on the basis of the 1954 input-output table for 1954 and forecast it for 1972. He included indirect taxes and for 1972 the effect of the export rebate and employment subsidy then in force. He obtained positive rates of 28% for agriculture, forestry and fishing and negative rates for mining and oil refining. He obtained a mixture of rates for manufacturing with negative rates for aircraft, shipbuilding, printing and publishing, woollen and worsted, and hosiery and lace, due to the tariffs and excise duties on their inputs.

A later study of the manufacturing sectors in the UK by Barker and Han (Barker and Han, 1971) using the input-output tables for 1963 showed negative rates for a number of industries producing intermediate products such as oil refining, coke ovens, light metals, other non-ferrous metals, cement, and paper and board, but also pharmaceutical and toilet preparations, soap, oils and fats, industrial engines, aircraft, and printing and publishing. Most of the rates were positive and higher than those of Brown. The highest were those for motor vehicles of 56.9%, other vehicles 44.6%, insulated wires and cables 34.3%, cans and metal boxes 33.2%, hosiery and lace 21.4%, pottery and glass 20.5%, and production of man-made fibres 18.5%.

EFFECTIVE PROTECTION IN DEVELOPING COUNTRIES

Under the auspices of the World Bank, Balassa calculated the structure of protection in some developing countries—Brazil, Chile, Mexico, West Malaysia, Pakistan and the Philippines. Allowing for over-valuation of the exchange rates, he calculated that the nominal and effective rates of protection to agriculture, forestry and fishing, and also mining and energy, were generally negative. The rates of protection to manufacturing tended to increase with the degree of processing and the effective rates of protection were always higher than the nominal rates. Sometimes they were extremely high—for instance, 915% for consumer durables in the Philippines (Balassa, 1971).

Occasionally, the effective rates or protection for manufacturing were both high and negative as, for instance, the − 1,433% for consumer durables in Pakistan. This was due to the denominator being negative $1 - a_{ij} < 1$ and meant that the imported contents were worth more than the finished item. The actual degree of protection in Pakistan was so high that it had induced the establishment of industries with negative value added—such that the economy was sustaining a net loss for every unit produced.

As already discussed, the effective rate of protection assumes constant physical input-output ratios, although it can be calculated using free-trade prices or prices under protection. However, if the physical coefficients are not fixed and there is any possibility of substitution between inputs, the estimates using coefficients under free trade and protection may well differ. Thus, Balassa makes estimates for both, and the effective rates of protection using domestic input-output ratios generally appear lower than those using the free-trade ones.

However, with all the refinements, the same general conclusion emerges as from other studies, namely that the developing countries discriminate against their agriculture and often other primary products, and in favour of their manufacturing, particularly of consumer durables. In contrast, the industrialised countries discriminate in favour of their agriculture. The US and UK in the 1950s and 1960s appeared to discriminate against their other primary industries, apart from oil and gas, and the estimates of the effective rates of protection of manufacturing industries are dependent on the protection of industries providing their inputs and the allowance that is made for indirect taxes.

It would be difficult to make a calculation of effective rates of protection in the last ten years in so far as it would involve an initial calculation of the *ad valorem* equivalents of the many quotas and voluntary export restraints that have crept in.

NOTES

1. B. Balassa, 'Trade Creation and Trade Diversion in the European Common Market', *Manchester School*, June 1974.

The Overall Picture and Explanation of Flows

7 The General Equilibrium Approach to Trade

So far in considering trade and commercial policy we have always taken a partial equilibrium approach; we have assumed that the market for a commodity could be considered using supply and demand curves without considering the repercussions of any changes in it on the rest of the economy. This is sufficient if we are just concerned with the direct effect of any government intervention or are only concerned with small changes. But this approach is inadequate if we are investigating the overall position of a country, or group of countries in international trade. We are then concerned with trade as a reflection of the direction and degree of specialisation within the economy. Government intervention in the form of tariffs and quotas not only affects the market for the commodity on which they are imposed but it also affects the country's overall position in trade.

This is the province of pure trade theory, which is a general equilibrium analysis. By this is meant equilibrium not only in the market for goods, as described in Chapter 6, with prices being such as to equate quantity demanded with quantity supplied, but also equilibrium in international trade such that the value of each country's exports equals the value of its imports.

The starting point of it is the theory of comparative advantage. In this case we will make it more specific by defining it in relation to the *marginal* costs of production; a country has a comparative advantage in the production of a commodity X if its relative marginal cost of production is lower than in other countries. Furthermore, comparative advantage is taken as a determinant of the direction of trade as well as an argument for trade.

Let us consider the concepts involved using the very simple comparative static textbook mode. We will consider the major results without going through all the theory, which is given in the major textbooks. In this model there are posited only two commodities both of which are traded, say agricultural products and manufactures, and two countries. I will take the first country, A, and assume that the other is the rest of the world. Country A is relatively small in relation to the rest of the world and therefore cannot affect the international price. There are no transport costs. Perfect competition is assumed so that prices are equal to marginal costs of production.

The situation in country A is then considered before and after trade. In each case we must consider the production and consumption of the two goods. The situation is illustrated in Figure 7.1. The curve HH' indicates the outer boundary of production possibilities of A. It is assumed that the supply of factors of production in a country is fixed and that there is no mobility of factors such as labour or capital between countries. Country A will be producing along the production possibility curve if there is full employment, complete mobility of factors of production between agriculture and manufacturing, and perfect competition. The last ensures that each factor of production is paid the value of its marginal product and this is equated between the two industries. Thus no additional output can be obtained by any reallocation of the factors.

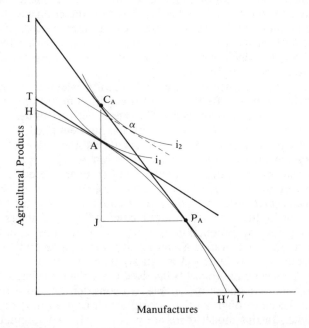

Figure 7.1: Country A with a Comparative Advantage in Manufactures—Production and Consumption before and after Trade.

Let us assume that these conditions are fulfilled. Then more manufactures can only be produced at the cost of less agricultural output, with the marginal cost of producing an additional unit of manufactures, that is the domestic rate of transformation (DRT) of agricultural products into manufactures at any point on the production possibility curve being shown by its slope. Thus this DRT is assumed to increase the greater the production of manufactures—the production possibility is concave to the origin.

Demand is introduced by means of community indifference curves shown as i_1, i_2 in Figure 7.1. Each represents the different collections of the two commodities between which the community would be indifferent—thus it is taken as a contour level of satisfaction or welfare for the community as a whole. To remain on the same community indifference curve, the country must be compensated for a reduction in consumption of one commodity by an increase in the consumption of another. The marginal trade off between the two, known as the domestic rate of substitution (DRS), is shown by the slope of the community indifference curve at that point. Any community indifference curve is an aggregate of the indifference curves of individuals. However, the particular indifference curve for individuals that are associated with any particular community indifference curve clearly depends on the distribution of income. Problems associated with this will be ignored and when a country reaches a higher indifference curve, it will be regarded as achieving a higher level of welfare.

The quantity produced before trade is assumed to be at the point A at which the production possibility curve just touches a community indifference curve. At that point, consumers maximise their satisfaction in so far as they are on the highest community indifference curve possible, and the amount of agricultural products they are prepared to substitute at the margin for an extra unit of manufactures (their DRS), shown by the slope of the community indifference curve, is equated to the price of manufactures in terms of agricultural products shown by the heavy price line AT. In a closed economy this price, in turn, is equated under perfect competition with the marginal costs of production of an extra unit of manufactures in terms of agricultural products foregone (the DRT).

When the relative marginal cost of production, DRT, is compared with the international price of manufactures in terms of agricultural products as shown by the line II', that is the foreign rate of transformation (FRT), it can be seen that country A has a comparative advantage in the production of manufactures; it can produce an additional unit of manufactures by giving up fewer units of agricultural products than is required for exchange on the world market.

Thus, when the country is opened up to trade, it will produce more manufactures at the cost of a reduction in its agricultural output until the marginal cost of production is equal to the world prices as at P_A—Figure 7.1. In this case of increasing costs, trade has led to specialisation in manufacturing, but at the point of equilibrium it still has an agricultural industry, albeit one smaller than before.

This greater return from producing manufactures leads to a higher income for consumers which they in turn spend on the goods. They move on to a higher community indifference curve. But as manufactures are now relatively more expensive, they will consume relatively less of these and more of agricultural products than they would have done if prices had remained the same—consumption will be at C_A not α.[1]

The benefits to country A will accrue both from the reallocation of production and from the reallocation of consumption. If for any reason production is fixed, consumers, by reallocating their purchases in response to international prices, can reach a higher community indifference curve than without trade. But with perfect internal mobility of factors and thus a readjustment of production as well as consumption, an even higher community indifference curve can be reached.

So trade enables a country to enjoy a higher level of consumption and thus welfare than would have been possible if it had been restricted to domestic production. The benefit a country derives from trade is measured by comparing its consumption with trade shown by C_A with the maximum level of satisfaction it can achieve without trade shown by A. This difference can be measured in terms of manufactures or of agricultural products, and either at the pre-trade or post-trade relative price.

The trade a country undertakes is the difference between its production and consumption. With consumption at C_A and production at P_A imports of agricultural products must be C_AJ and exports of manufactures must be JP_A. This right-angled triangle is sometimes called the trade triangle. The degree to which the country will increase its exports of manufactures in response to an increase in their relative price will depend on the one hand on the degree to which the production of manufactures can be substituted for that of agricultural production, and on the other hand on the change in consumption which will depend on the rate at which consumers will substitute the cheaper agricultural products for the more expensive manufactures in conjunction with the income effect by which they will wish to increase their consumption of both goods as their real income rises.

OFFER CURVES

The relationship between the quantity the country is willing to trade and the price of its exportables can also be shown by an offer curve which is really just the plotting of the trade triangles (see Figure 7.2). Each point on the offer curve represents a point at which the country would be in internal and external equilibrium given the country's terms of trade, that is the price of exports in terms of imports. This is shown by a straight line from the origin O to any point on the offer curve such as OF.

The better a country's terms of trade, the higher it is on its offer curve.

If there were only two countries in the world, international equilibrium would be determined where their offer curves crossed. But so far we have assumed that one country is the rest of the world. How can we obtain the latter's offer curve?

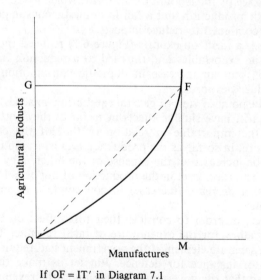

If OF = IT′ in Diagram 7.1
Then exports JP$_A$ in Diagram 7.1 = OM
and imports C$_A$J in Diagram 7.1 = OG

Figure 7.2: Country A's Offer Curve – She is Offering Manufactures in Exchange for Agricultural Products

The offer curve of any group of countries is derived by summing their offer curves radially, that is, summing the quantities of the two commodities that each country would export or import at any given terms of trade so as to obtain a point on the group's offer curve at that terms of trade.

If the group is the rest of the world, then its offer curve may appear very elastic, indeed infinitely elastic, that is a straight line from the origin, so that the single country cannot affect its terms of trade. This also means that although the individual country benefits from trade, the benefits to the rest of the world are not significant.

BARRIERS TO TRADE

Now let us consider the effect of governmental intervention in international trade. Remember that we are continuing to assume full employment.

In Chapter 6, Figure 6.1, we saw that the effect of a duty on imports was to raise the price of the importable above the international price by the amount of the tariff, which led to an increase in domestic production and a fall in domestic consumption, both of which combined to reduce imports.

Likewise, a tariff on exports (Figure 6.7) reduced the domestic price of the exportables and thus led to a reduction in domestic production and an increase in domestic consumption, both of which reduced exports.

From the point of view of general equilibrium analysis, these two types of tariff have similar effects in so far as they both raise the price of the importable in relation to that of the exportable. Furthermore, in so far as the production and consumption of one can only be increased at the expense of the other, they both lead to an increase (decrease) in the production of importables (exportables) and a decrease (increase) in consumption of importables (exportables).

However, in order to consider their total effect on trade, you must also allow for the expenditure of tariff revenue. This could enter as a separate element if the government had requirements of its own, for instance for defence. But let us make the simpler assumption that the government redistributes the revenue back to the consumers. Then this will provide them with some compensation for the real income loss of the change in prices. The effect of the tariff on trade will, therefore, depend on the price response of consumers and producers to it, both of which will tend to reduce imports and increase exports. In other words, the offer curve will move inwards and the country will move away from its position of optimum economic efficiency.

However, if the country (or a group of countries) faced an offer curve on the part of the rest of the world that was less than infinitely elastic, it would not be in a position where it was maximising its own real income with free trade. Because of its monopoly position, there would be a divergence between the price and the marginal revenue it obtained from its exports. That is, DRS = DRT ≠ FRT. This could be removed by the imposition of a tariff. The optimum tariff would be that which equalised the marginal return for a unit of exports to its internal price—both measured in terms of the other commodity. But it would be improving its own position at the expense of that of the rest of the world.

EXPLANATION FOR DIFFERENCES IN COMPARATIVE ADVANTAGE

Now let us turn to consider some of the explanations for differences in comparative advantage. Clearly, they could reside in the differences in tastes and demand patterns in different countries. But most modern theories regard the source of the difference as being on the supply side.

In order to neutralise the effect of consumption, it will be assumed that consumers in different countries have the same tastes and their income elasticity of demand for the products is 1. Therefore, as income rises, there is no change in the distribution of consumption between the two commodities unless price changes.

RICARDIAN THEORY

Ricardo considered labour to be the only factor of production and provided various *ad hoc* explanations as to why the relative costs of production varied between different countries, such as differences in climate, differences in the fertility of the soil, etc. But there is no reason for these to vary with the quantity produced. Therefore, the Ricardian production possibility curve is taken to be a straight line with no variation in marginal costs. Thus, if a country exposed to international trade finds that it has a comparative advantage in manufactures, it will specialise completely in them producing none of the other commodity under free trade.

HECKSCHER-OHLIN THEORY

In contrast, Heckscher and Ohlin regarded the difference in countries' relative endowments with factors of production, land, labour and capital as the sources of comparative advantage. In the simple exposition, let us assume only two factors of production—land and labour—which are homogeneous, that is of uniform quality, throughout the world. Let us assume that agriculture is land-intensive and manufactures labour-intensive, such that at any set of factor prices, agriculture uses relatively more land in relation to labour.

In a movement from any point along the production possibility curve, more manufactures can be produced only by reducing the output of agricultural products. But this releases more land and less labour than was previously employed in the production of manufactures. In adjusting to these less advantageous factor proportions, the marginal cost of producing manufactures in terms of agricultural products foregone goes up the greater the quantity of manufactures produced. That is, the production possibility curve is concave to the origin as for instance HH' in Figure 7.1.

If we make the assumption that producers have the same technological knowledge and are equally efficient, then the shape of countries' production possibility curves will depend entirely on their relative endowments with land and labour. If their demand conditions are identical, this will also determine their comparative advantage. In figure 7.1, country A, as has already been seen, has a comparative advantage in manufactures; assuming the Heckscher-Ohlin theory, this is because she is relatively well endowed with labour. In contrast, in Figure 7.3, country B has a comparative advantage in agricultural products because she is relatively well endowed with land and therefore her relative price of producing agricultural products before trade DB is lower than the world price II'. Without trade country B will produce and consume at B. If opened up to trade they will both move to their equilibrium position, where their domestic prices are equal to the world price; country B will specialise in the production of agricultural products to produce at P_B and will export them in return for manufactures, whereas A, as already mentioned, will do the reverse.

If A and B are the only trading countries or groups of countries in the world, A's exports or manufactures will be equal to B's imports, and B's exports of agricultural products will be equal to A's imports. The terms of trade, that is the relative price of manufactures in relation to agricultural products, will be inversely related

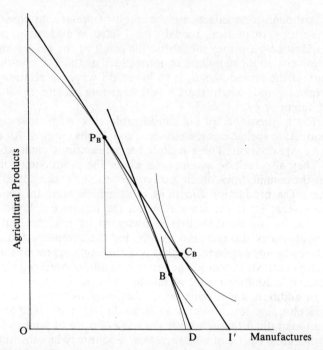

Figure 7.3: Country B with a Comparative Advantage in Agricultural Products – Production and Consumption before and after Trade

to the amount traded. The position of equilibrium will depend on the demand and supply conditions in both countries; it will be where their offer curves intersect. This position in turn would be affected by tariffs.

FACTOR PRICE EQUALISATION

However, let us assume that A and B move from a position of autarchy to a free-trade equilibrium. They each specialise in the commodity using most intensively the factor with which they are relatively well endowed. This increases the demand for it and thus its relative price. Whereas the resulting fall in the demand for the scarce factor leads to a fall in its price. Thus, in A the price of labour rises and the price of land falls, whereas in B the price of land rises and the price of labour falls. Will this tendency towards factor price equalisation lead to an actual equality in real wages and rents throughout the world?

Although these effects are the result of the assumptions under-lying this theoretical model, they have considerable political implications. Do they mean that the result of the US trading with relatively labour-abundant countries such as India and in the early part of the period Japan, is to lower US wages in relation to the return to land? Might the US real wage rate become equal to that of Japan or even India?

These questions led to considerable theoretical investigation. Samuelson spelled out the stringent conditions required for factor-price equalisation. These include the assumptions made above.

They also include assumptions about the production functions for the commodities which are assumed to be the same in all countries. The production functions must exhibit constant returns to scale—that is, if the amount of all the factors employed in the production of manufactures is increased by x%, the output of manufactures also increases by x%. But there must be diminishing returns to any single factor that is if the employment of the other factors remains the same, the increase in output obtained with each successive additional unit of labour will fall.

In addition, there must be no factor-intensity reversal; that is agricultural production must require relatively more land to labour than manufacturing whatever the relative price of land to labour. If the relative price of land increases, labour may be substituted for it in both agriculture and manufacturing but this will never proceed so much faster in agriculture that agriculture becomes relatively labour-intensive. This is known as the strong Samuelson assumption.

An example of this type of production function is the Cobb-Douglas, where if Q is the quantity of output and T is the amount of land and L the amount of labour and K a constant:

$$Q = KT^{\alpha}L^{1-\alpha}$$

If these conditions hold, there is a one to one relationship between commodity prices and factor prices.

According to Samuelson, this will also hold if the number of commodities is increased. The result will also hold for more factors provided there is an equal or greater number of commodities and there is no complete specialisation of a country in a commodity—although there appears to be some controversy as to whether all countries should produce all commodities or not (Samuelson, 1949).

This analysis and these conditions may appear far removed from those in the real world. But this rigid framework of two goods and two factors and these stringent assumptions have provided the basis for the comparative static analysis of economic expansion.

ECONOMIC EXPANSION

Economic expanion is an increase in the productive capacity of a country illustrated by an outward shift in a country's production possibility curve. It may be due either to an increase in the supply of factors of production, or to technological progress which increases the amount that a country can produce with the existing factors. In pure trade theory, the effect of such economic expansion is analysed by first considering the changes in production and consumption that would occur at constant terms of trade.

Due to an increase in the supply of a factor:
Let us first consider the effect of economic expansion that is due to an increase in the supply of labour, due, say, to an increase in population. This will move the production possibility curve outwards but more at the manufacturing than the agricultural end because manufactures are labour-intensive. Indeed, if the above assumptions are made and relative prices are kept constant accord ing to Rybczynski's theorem (Rybczynksi, 1955), the production of manufactures (Man) will increase more than proportionally and the output of agriculture (Ag) will fall absolutely (see Figure 7.4).

What about the change in demand? This will be due to an increase in the workforce earning the same average wage as before (as commodity prices have been kept constatnt so also must factor returns). Strictly speaking, the community indifference curves now represent preferences between commodities rather than levels of welfare, as it is invidious to compare levels of welfare on the same community indifference map with different numbers of people. However, assuming the indifference curve map remains the same, consumption of the two commodities will increase proportionally, that is along a straight line from the origin.

The effect on trade will depend on whether the country is initially an importer or exporter of manufactures. If it is an importer, the more than proportional increase in output of manufactures and absolute decline in agricultural output, together with the proportional increase in consumption, will lead to an inward movement of the country's offer curve from OF_1 to OF_2 (see Figure 7.4a and 7.4c). It will now offer less agricultural produce (because its production is lower and consumption greater) to the rest of the world in exchange for fewer manufactures. The economy will, therefore, become more closed. Of course, if the increase in the supply of labour is sufficiently large, it may reverse the direction of trade.

Now let us consider the position of country A which is initially an exporter of manufactures (Figures 7.4b and 7.4d). In this case, an increase in the supply of labour causes her offer curve to move

7.4a: Labour-intensive manufacturers (Man) the importable — Country B

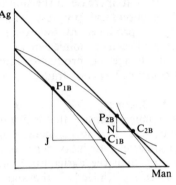

7.4b: Labour-intensive manufacturers (Man) the exportable — Country A

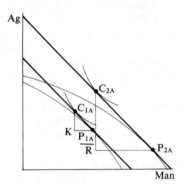

7.4c: Offer curves of Country B

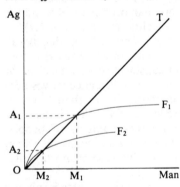

7.4d: Offer curves of Country A

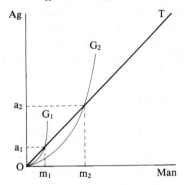

International terms of trade OT.

Before economic expansion

Country B exports $OA_1 = P_{1B}J$ agricultural products in exchange for $OM_1 = C_{1B}J$ manufactures.

After economic expansion

Country B exports $OA_2 = P_{2B}N$ agricultural products in exchange for $OM_2 = C_{2B}N$ manufactures.

Country A exports $O_{m1} = P_{1A}K$ manufactures in exchange for $Oa_1 = C_{1A}K$ agricultural products.

Country A exports $O_{M2} = P_{2A}R$ manufactures in exchange for $Oa_2 = C_{2A}R$ agricultural products.

Figure 7.4: The Effect on Trade of Economic Expansion due to an Increase in the supply of Labour

outwards with A exporting more manufactures (manufacturing output has increased more than proportionally, whereas consumption has only increased proportionally) and importing more agricultural produce (output has fallen whereas consumption has increased) at constant terms of trade. Country A has become more open to trade.

Due to technical progress:
What about economic expansion due to technological progress? Here we are very limited by our assumption of only two commodities. We can only consider technological progress that consists of an exogenous reduction in the real cost of producing one of the commodities (see Findlay and Grubert, 1959).

As might be expected, this leads to a rise in the production of the commodity in which technological progress takes place. At constant terms of trade it will also generally lead to a fall in the production of the other commodity. The only possible exception to this is when the technological change saves the factor used most intensively in the production of the other commodity. If, for instance, technological change in the production of manufactures led to a reduction in the proportion of land to labour required at constant factor prices, this would be termed land saving. In this case, the output of agriculture might not fall.

But in all other cases technological change in one commodity with constant terms of trade will lead to an increase in its production and a fall in the output of the other commodity. The effect of the biased growth and production on trade can be analysed as previously for growth due to an increase in factor supplies.

Clearly this model is simplistic and very restrictive. Nonetheless, this approach of regarding changes in trade as the net result of changes in production and consumption will be used in the analysis of commodity trade. It is also desirable to differentiate the shifts at constant prices from the changes that are a response to changes in price. The latter may be the result of adjustment in the international market or government policy. Unfortunately it is seldom possible to separate them in practice.

But there is still the question of whether the underlying changes in production can be attributed in this way to an increase in the supply of factors and their efficiency leading to the biased type of growth described above. This depends on the validity of the Heckscher-Ohlin theory.

TESTS OF RICARDIAN AND HECKSCHER-OHLIN THEORIES

Let us now briefly consider some of the empirical tests of the two theories. Clearly, in the real world there are far more than two commodities and the more stringent assumptions of perfect competition do not hold. Nevertheless, MacDougall did attempt to test Ricardian theory by comparing US and British trade in manufactures in 1937 (MacDougall, 1951). Because of tariffs on each other's goods, the analysis had to be carried out for their exports to third countries. A country was taken to have a comparative advantage in the production of a commodity if the ratio of its output per worker to that in the other country was greater than the ratio of its money wage rate. In 1937, the US wage level in manufacturing was approximately twice that of Britain, and for those industries in which productivity was more than twice that of the UK, the US did export more than the UK. This served to confirm the Ricardian theory. Furthermore, attempts to allow for capital as another factor of production by considering the horsepower per worker did not prove of any explanatory value: 'there [was] little tendency for Britain to export more than America of products requiring a low ratio of capital to labour, and vice versa'.

Leontief then attempted to apply the Heckscher–Ohlin theory to the US (Leontief, 1954). He assumed two factors of production— labour and capital. Using the input-output tables of the US economy for 1947, he could calculate the amount of capital and labour used directly and indirectly in the output of each industry. He then estimated what would happen if the US reduced both its imports and exports by $1 million each. Exports were cut by the same proportion over all commodities. The same procedure was used for competitive imports, i.e. imports that could be produced in the US. Non-competitive imports, that is, coffee, tea and jute were assumed to remain unchanged. He then calculated the change in requirements for capital and labour that would be required based on the average coefficients contained in the input-output matrix. He came to the paradoxical conclusion that US exports embodied considerably less capital and somewhat more labour than an equivalent amount of imports.

Within the Heckscher-Ohlin theory of comparative advantage, this was a paradox, as all agreed that the US had a relative abundance of capital to labour compared with the rest of the world.

Various attempts were made to maintain the Heckscher-Ohlin

theory and at the same time to explain away this result. One suggestion put forward by Leontief was that the quality of the factors was not the same—indeed, that one man year of American labour was equal to three man years of foreign labour. In that case, the US would have a relative abundance of labour.

It has also been pointed out that the analysis was limited to the consideration of only two factors of production, labour and capital, and that land is also of considerable importance, particularly in the production of agricultural commodities. Indeed, if natural resources are taken into account, the result disappears.

It should also be pointed out that Leontief assumed similar factor intensities of commodities within the US and outside it. An import was described as capital-intensive if any import substitution would have involved a capital-intensive method of manufacture. That is, he implicitly made the strong Samuelson assumption that a commodity produced by a relatively capital-intensive method of manufacture within the US would also be produced by a capital-intensive method of manufacture outside the US.

This induced empirical investigation. But for this, a production function was required which would allow it. Minhas, Samuelson and Solow developed the constant elasticity of substitution (CES) production function which exhibited constant returns to scale, diminishing returns to a single factor, and an elasticity of substitution of one factor for another which was constant for a commodity but which might differ between commodities. Thus, if capital could be substituted for labour more easily in the production of chemicals than textiles as wages rose, then even if chemicals were comparatively labour-intensive at low wage rates, they might be comparatively capital-intensive at high wage rates. Taking countries with widely different wage levels such as the US and Japan or India, Minhas claimed to have discovered factor intensity reversals in certain pairs of industries such as textiles and non-ferrous metals, pulp and paper and chemicals (Minhas, 1962). But the work of other economists suggests that the elasticity of substitution is very near to one, particularly when natural resources are allowed for, which would rule out any factor intensity reversals.

This is a brief account of pure trade theory that will be familiar to many readers of this book. The originators may have been Ricardo and Heckscher and Ohlin but subsequent developments of them, particularly of the latter by Samuelson, have converted them from fairly loose wide-ranging theories to closely specified mathematical models. This has enabled them to be used for analysing economic expansion as above, and also international investment.

How far can this type of economic theory be regarded as empirically valid and how far as useful in explaining trade?

Firstly, it should be pointed out that the Heckscher-Ohlin theory is the only one to relate a country's pattern of trade to its factor endowment and distribution of income. It is, however, clear that the very rigid formulation of it is very limiting. Even though there have been attemps to generalise the Heckscher-Ohlin theory for a large number of factors and commodities, there are still problems in empirical application and testing. What, for instance, is meant by a factor and a commodity? The factors generally considered are capital, physical and human, labour—often divided according to skill, and land, but this can scarcely be regarded as homogeneous. But the classification of commodities then also becomes difficult. Ideally, you want each group of commodities intensive in a particular factor. Agriculture can be separately classified. But it is difficult to separate in this way the various branches of manufacturing.

There is also the perennial problem that is rarely considered, namely that the grouping of commodities by their production characteristics may be very different from grouping them by their consumption characteristics, e.g. rubber will be included under agricultural raw materials, synthetic rubber will be included in other semi-manufactures as part of manufactures, and yet from the point of view of the consumer, they may appear, if not identical, at least as highly substitutable. In fact, in the SITC, the broad groups are according to production characteristics, but the sub-divisions within them are more according to consumption characteristics. The GATT classification used in the next chapter is a compromise and is more consumer-oriented.

If there are assumed to be only two factors of production, a large number of commodities can be considered by arranging them in order of factor intensity. The dividing line between exportables and importables would then depend on the equilibrium position of the country, which, in turn, would depend on the relative demand for the different commodities. There have been quite a number of empirical investigations using this approach, particularly of the US exports and imports of manufactures. Leontief's was one of the first. But others have introduced modifications

ECONOMIES OF SCALE

One of the most important qualifications has been to allow for economies of scale. In empirical work this is generally interpreted as meaning that the size of the home market might influence a country's competitive position—it is assumed that a domestic firm has a preferential position in the home market. Therefore, the larger the home market, the more a firm can exploit economies of scale, and the lower its costs will be. The work done on this tends to show that its importance varies. In an early OEEC study of the US and UK, it appeared that the more capital-intensive the type of production, the more important the size of the home market (Paige and Bombach, 1959).

Additional assistance in this respect is provided on the same demand side by Linder's hypothesis that specialisation is determined by demand as much as supply (Linder, 1961). A country will export commodities for which there is a relatively large home market and with which it can, therefore, exploit economies of scale. Thus, the US exports large cars, the European countries and Japan export small ones. This type of theory is particularly helpful in explaining why a country both exports and imports the same commodity.

INNOVATION AND INTERNATIONAL DIRECT INVESTMENT

Another modification has been to drop the assumption of perfect knowledge, namely that producers are faced with the same production functions. The importance of innovation and the 'technological gap' theory and its ramifications are considered in Chapter 9. Associated with this is a theory of international direct investment. This has so far been precluded by assumption and yet it is an important feature of the world economy. In theoretical investigations, the effect of the mobility of capital on trade depends on the assumptions made about the other factors of production and technological know-how (Corden in Dunning, 1974). Some of the empirical studies of it will be considered in Chapter 10.

THEORIES CONCERNED WITH SPECIFIC FACTORS

There are also other explanations of trade which lie outside the main body of theory. A number of them are concerned with production that depends on the use of specific natural resources. These include the available theory (Kravis, 1956), the vent for surplus theory (Myint, 1958) and the staple theory (Caves, 1965). Myint was concerned with the historical expansion in output of agricultural products and minerals for export in West Africa and South East Asia, and the staple theory was applied to the development of North America and Australia whereby the production of one commodity after another was started as agricultural land was cleared and one mineral after another was discovered. The significant feature of these developments was that there was a rapid increase in output and exports without any apparent diminution in the output of other goods. This suggested the existence of factors which had previously lain idle. But it should be pointed out that the expansion of production was often associated with considerable immigration into North America and Australia, and use of indentured labour in South East Asia and Africa.

However, as world demand increases, the relative scarcity of these natural resources becomes apparent. Indeed, for deposits of fossil fuels and other minerals, consumption itself uses up the resources, and the rate of depletion in relation to the known level of resources has raised the possibility that they may eventually be exhausted (Meadows et al. 1974). Concern about the rate at which their oil reserves were being used up contributed to the OPEC's decision to raise prices.

These theories all have elements of realism missing from the pure trade theory. They identify particular aspects of production which are difficult to subsume under a theory of comparative advantage which implies that all countries could produce any commodity. But they are insufficient by themselves to identify the equilibrium position of a country or group of countries which is the main objective of pure trade theorists.

APPROACH ADOPTED IN THIS BOOK

First it must be emphasised that the author is concerned, just as the theorists are, with the relationship between trade and specialisation. It is not enough just to say that the US or UK exports so many cars, so much steel, so many chemicals. It is also of interest to know the degree to which this reflects specialisation in the production of cars, steel and chemicals—that is a situation in which output is greater than domestic absorption. In order to obtain this, the author has calculated not only exports but also net exports, that is, exports minus imports, for the country concerned. The difference between the two gives an indication of intra-industry trade. This occurs when there are considerable economies of scale, as mentioned above, and also when consumers require a great variety. Thus, a country's specialisation is shown by its net exports.

It is regarded as 'offering' on the world market its net exports in exchange for those products for which it is a net importer. But because a large number of commodity categories are considered, the direct relationship of 'offers' to relative price will not be considered.

The position of individual countries will be considered in the analysis of commodity trade in Chapters 11–14. Their changes in specialisation over time will be considered as the net result of changes in production and consumption. But it has not proved possible to make the clear distinction, as in pure trade theory, of changes in production that are due to exogenous shifts in the supply of factors or technological change, and those that are a response to relative price changes.

However, it is difficult to get an idea of the overall change in trade by looking at individual countries. For this purpose, the countries are grouped, as by GATT, according to economic status, as that is the way they are ranged in debates on trade and commercial policy. Thus, we have groups of Industrial countries, Developing countries, and the Eastern Trading Area.

We are then concerned with the trade relations of these groups of countries and how they have changed over time. The total exports of a group of, say, motor vehicles, is merely the sum of exports of all members of the group. If all the imports of motor vehicles is subtracted, this leaves the net exports of motor vehicles by the group. This removes all trade between members of the group and shows how it specialises in relation to the rest of the world.

The positive net exports of the group are what it 'offers' for the net imports it obtains from the rest of the world. But we cannot make the assumption of pure trade theory that the value of exports is equal to the value of imports. Trade in goods is only one element in the current account; there is also trade in services and interest on international capital flows, for which the Western industrial countries generally have a positive balance. It is also possible for countries or groups of countries to run deficits on their current accounts—this, as has been discussed in Chapter 3, must be financed by a positive balance on their capital account. Nevertheless, although the overall balance of trade may not be zero, the net balances for the different categories of commodities show the direction of specialisation.

One of the aims of this book is to show how this specialisation has changed over time. In the real world this is somewhat difficult to measure because all net export positions are shown in value terms at current prices. However, a rough idea of the increase in real net exports can be obtained by comparing their monetary increase with the increase in the price index over the period. It is also possible to get quantitative changes for some commodities. Furthermore, clear indications of change are obtained when net exports move from being positive to negative or vice versa.

The best range of trade and price statistics is provided for industrial countries. It has, therefore, been possible to draw up histograms showing the changes in the volume of trade balances and therefore specialisation over time

An additional dimension to this can be provided by the ordering of the commodity groups. It might have been possible to arrange the commodity groups in order of capital or labour intensity of production. This has not been done for a number of different reasons. Firstly, as mentioned, there is considerable mobility of capital, which reduces its value as a determinant of production in any specific location. More important is that most of the major groups contain commodities which require very different labour and capital intensities in their production. For instance, the category fuels contains oil and gas which are very capital-intensive, but also coal is relatively labour-intensive.

Instead, the ordering is made according to what the author regards as the more significant determinant of trade, particularly between the major groups of countries, namely the use of specific factors of production, and the importance of technological innovation. This will be discussed further in the next chapter.

NOTE

1. α , the consumption at the new level of income but pre trade prices, is constructed by drawing a dashed line parallel to the original price line so that it touches the new indifference curve.

8 The General Structure of International Trade

Now let us turn to consider the actual changes in international trade. In this chapter we will be concerned with the position of the world as a whole with respect to changes in the overall level of trade and changes in its structure. We will also be concerned with the position of the different groups of countries.

WORLD TRADE

The earliest overall figures obtainable are for 1953 and this also appears a good date from which to start, as by then post-war reconstruction can be regarded as completed, and also the level of prices and activity during the Korean war boom of 1951 had largely subsided.

The general changes that have occurred in trade are shown in Tables 8.1 and 8.2. In the first table, 8.1, commodities are divided into three broad categories of Agricultural Products, Minerals and Manufactures, for selected years between 1953 and 1982. The second table, 8.2, provides a greater commodity breakdown but only in terms of value and the earliest year for which this can be obtained is 1955.

VALUE OF WORLD TRADE

The first section of Table 8.1 shows the changes in the total value of trade. The dominating impression conveyed by these figures is of rapid and consistent expansion; the value of merchandise trade in 1980 was 28 times its value in 1953 and 21 times its value in 1955. But this expansion temporarily ceased with a decline in 1981 and 1982. Since then expansion has been resumed.

The relative importance of the three categories has also changed. Agriculture, which in Table 8.1 is broadly defined to include not

TABLE 8.1 *World Exports $ billion and Indexes of Unit Value, Volumes and World Commodity Output 1963 = 100.*

World Exports	1953	1955	1963	1968	1969	1970	1971	1972	1973	1974	1975	1976	1977	1978	1979	1980	1981	1982
Value $ billion																		
Total	71	93	154	240	274	312	351	416	574	836	873	991	1125	1303	1638	1990	1960	1845
Ag. Products[a]		33	45	54	58	64	69	83	121	148	150	166	188	213	262	299	292	272
Minerals[a]		17	26	41	45	51	57	65	96	215	207	241	266	276	400	567	547	493
Manufactures	32	42	82	140	165	190	217	259	347	459	501	566	648	788	945	1095	1090	1049
Unit Values (1963 = 100)																		
Total	100	99	100	105	107	114	121	130	161	227	244	249	271	297	354	423	418	403
Ag. Products[a]	110	(110)	100	100	104	107	113	125	185	235	225	230	255	262	300	330	314	292
Minerals[a]	99	101	100	111	116	122	136	147	192	445	460	510	550	563	780	1200	1320	1254
Manufactures	95	94	100	104	108	114	121	131	152	185	212	212	232	266	303	337	323	314
Volume (1963 = 100)																		
Total	54	(64)	100	149	166	178	189	208	231	239	232	258	269	284	300	305	304	300
Ag. Products			100	121	125	135	137	149	147	142	149	163	166	183	196	203	209	209
Minerals		(65)	100	144	151	165	164	173	195	190	176	184	188	193	201	185	162	153
Manufactures	51	(54)	100	166	187	204	220	244	280	304	290	328	344	364	382	400	415	410
World Commodity Output 1963 = 100																		
All commodities			100	133	143	146	151	161	180	185	183	196	205	214	222	224	226	223
Agriculture			100	115	118	119	123	122	128	130	134	137	139	145	146	146	152	154
Mining			100	129	134	143	147	153	171	174	171	181	191	190	199	196	190	183
Manufacturing			100	141	153	159	165	179	197	203	200	216	227	238	249	253	254	249

[a]Including fuels and non-ferrous metals.
Bracketed figures are estimates.
Source: GATT International Trade 1977/78, 1974/75, 1978/79, 1979/80, 1980/81, 1981/82. See table A1. 1982/83.

TABLE 8.2 *Value of World Exports by Main Commodity Groups.*

	Billion Dollars									% of total 1955	% of total 1982
	1955	1963	1968	1973	1978	1979	1980	1981	1982		
Primary Products											
Food	20.42	30.07	37.63	86.39	162.60	194.50	223.40	223.30	208.5	21.9	11.3
Raw materials	12.13	14.23	16.12	34.61	52.05	67.90	75.25	68.95	62.5	13.0	3.4
Ores and minerals	3.44	5.03	7.80	14.91	24.50	33.90	42.65	38.25	34.0	3.7	1.8
Fuels	10.26	15.73	23.09	63.48	223.60	329.40	471.50	470.15	426.0	11.0	23.1
Non-ferrous metals	3.62	4.72	9.52	17.28	27.80	37.55	52.55	38.75	34.0	3.9	1.8
Total Primary Products	49.87	69.82	94.12	216.70	490.60	663.20	865.50	839.40	765.0	53.5	41.5
Manufactures											
Iron and steel	4.25	7.40	11.41	28.46	57.15	70.60	76.55	73.80	69.0	4.6	3.7
Chemicals	4.91	9.66	17.67	41.87	100.60	130.80	153.95	148.80	143.0	5.3	7.8
Other semi-manufactures	4.47	7.13	12.03	28.95	65.20	79.90	92.40	83.80	78.0	4.8	4.2
Engineering products	19.59	41.83	75.03	187.97	439.05	509.00	593.00	605.60	586.0	21.0	31.8
Machinery specialised[1]	6.43	14.47	23.06	52.46	117.45	136.10	158.85	158.30	148.0	6.9	8.0
Office and telecommunications	6.82	2.88	5.67	17.21	38.80	48.10	57.90	60.95	64.0	0.9	3.5
Road motor vehicles	3.32	7.16	15.84	41.01	99.45	115.75	127.45	128.55	125.5	3.5	6.8
Other machinery and transport equipment[2]	7.72	14.54	25.13	62.04	147.90	168.90	198.80	206.20	202.0	8.3	11.0
Household appliances	1.30	2.78	5.33	15.25	35.40	40.15	48.15	51.55	46.5	1.4	2.5
Textiles	4.72	7.03	9.88	23.35	40.70	49.55	55.55	55.10	51.5	5.1	2.8
Clothing	0.80	2.21	4.40	12.59	28.35	34.30	40.35	41.30	41.0	0.9	2.2
Other consumer goods	3.00	5.63	9.61	24.26	57.50	70.75	83.30	81.55	80.5	3.2	4.4
Total Manufactures	41.73	80.88	140.03	347.45	788.50	944.90	1095.10	1090.00	1049.0	44.7	56.9
Total Exports	93.30	154.70	237.80	574.30	1303.00	1634.70	1988.90	1959.60	1843.0	100.0	100.0

Note: 1. For 1955, 1963 and 1968 is agricultural and industrial machinery and machine parts n.e.s.
2. For 1955, 1963 and 1968. Power generating machinery, other engineering products and scientific instruments and other transport equipment.

Sources: GATT *International Trade* 1979/80, 1980/81, 1982/83; GATT *Networks of World Trade* (Geneva, 1978) Tables A1, A2 and A3.

only crops and livestock but also fishery and forestry products, declined in relative importance from 35% of the value of trade in 1955, 29% in 1963 to 15% in 1982. From Table 8.2 it can be seen that most of this reduction is due to the relative fall in the value of trade in food from 22% of all trade in 1955 to 11% in 1981. The rest of it is due to the relative decline in importance of raw materials, which include textile fibres, rubber, and forestry products, from 13% of trade in 1955 to 3.4% in 1982.

In contrast, minerals (Table 8.1) accounted for an increasing proportion of trade; 17% in 1955 and 1963, and 27% in 1982. However, this category comprises fuels, ores and minerals, and non-ferrous metals, which have fared very differently. The increase appears entirely due to fuels (Table 8.2) which represented 11% of international trade in 1955, declined slightly to 10% in 1963 and 1968, and then rose from 11% to 20% from 1973 to 1974 due to the OPEC price rise, then fluctuated upwards and in 1982 represented 23.1 of the value of trade. The relative value of trade in ores and minerals declined slowly from 3.7% of trade in 1955 to 3.3% in 1963 and 1.8% in 1982.

The value of trade in manufactures has been increasing faster than the average so that whereas they accounted for 45% of international trade in 1953 and 1955, this had risen to 53% an 1963 and 57% in 1982. This increase was largely accounted for trade in engineering products which as can be seen from Table 8.2, increased as a proportion of world trade from 21% in 1955 to 33% in 1973 and 32% in 1982. Rapid increases in the value of trade were also shown by chemicals, other consumer goods, and clothing. Changes in the value of trade are of course the result not only of changes in the quantities traded but also of changes in price. In the next two sections of Table 8.1 the changes in unit values and volume of trade are given for trade as a whole and for the major categories.

PRICE CHANGES SINCE 1953

The unit value indexes of trade in total and of the different categories, incorporate 1975 weights. The unit value index for all trade (see Table 8.1) suggests that overall prices were steady from 1953 to 1963, then rose slowly by 5% from 1963 to 1968, and then from 1968 onwards the increase in prices accelerated. But after 1980, the overall price level began to fall.

However, there was a considerable change in relative prices with agricultural prices falling from 1953 to 1963, stabilising from 1963 to 1968 and then increasing erratically but overall as fast as those of manufactures. From 1978 to 1981, the relative price of agricultural products and manufactures appeared almost the same as in 1963. But as can be seen from Table 2.3, Chapter 2 and Appendix Table A1, this conceals diversity of experience. Between 1963 and 1980, the price of coffee, cocoa, fish and sugar had increased far more than that of manufactures but that of tea and wool far less.

Likewise, Table 8.1 shows that the price of minerals increased more slowly than that of manufactures from 1953 to 1963 but then accelerated so that it was increasing at a faster rate even before the OPEC price rise of 1972–4. But again this conceals disparate movements. The price of iron ore increased more slowly and non-ferrous metals faster than manufactures both between 1968 and 1980 (see Table 2.3). The price of crude petroleum hardly moved at all between 1950 and 1970 but then began its very rapid increase (see Table A1).

The price of manufactures is taken as the reference because they are the largest element in international trade and because their price shows less deviation around trend (see Table 2.3) and because it appears to be a more consistent reflection of experience of its different categories. For instance, Table 8.1 shows an increase of 196% in the price of manufactures from 1970 to 1980, whereas UN figures show that the price increase of the large category of machine and transport equipment was 138%. Since 1980, the price of both has fallen slightly.

CHANGES IN THE VOLUME OF TRADE

GATT calculated the indexes of the volume of trade by deflating the value of exports by the export unit values or price indexes. They can be compared with the indexes of world output shown in the last section of table 8.1.

The overall volume of world trade increased fairly steadily and at a greater rate than output until 1974. Thus, countries were trading an increasing proportion of the output of their commodities and as such becoming more open, with their economies more dependent on world trade. This is borne out by the figures of trade and Gross National Product (GNP) of individual countries. You can, however, exaggerate its impact, particularly for trade in manufactures. It is perfectly possible for a country's exports to equal 100% of its GNP. All this means is that its exports must have contained a high import content, not that everything the country produced went across its borders.

Over the period as a whole, the volume of trade in manufactures has increased the most; it doubled between 1953 and 1963, then tripled between 1963 and 1974 and then, after a slight drop in 1975, increased more slowly by a further 37% by 1981. Between 1981 and 1982 it declined slightly.

The volume of trade in the other products did not increase as fast. Trade in agricultural products increased by 49% between 1963 and 1972, it then declined slightly to 1974 and then increased again. It is now just over twice as great as it was in 1963.

The volume of trade in minerals has fluctuated much more than that of manufactures. It increased so that in 1973 it was almost twice its level in 1963 but then fluctuated. Since 1979 it has been declining, so that in 1982 it was only 53% above its level in 1963, that is only 78% of its level in 1973. It does, however, include fuels as well as other minerals and these have shown disparate trends.

So far we have just considered trade from the point of view of overall flows of output and exports. Can we say anything about the relative position of countries or groups of countries?

Their interrelationships are best shown by a trade network in which, as explained in Chapter 3, trade flows are classified by their origin and destination. For this purpose all trade must be measured f.o.b. in order that the value of exports should appear the same to the exporter as importer, and thus the value of exports is equal to that of imports. This also means that the net exports of one country are equal to the net imports of the rest of the world. A network can be drawn up for total trade or for trade in any particular commodity, and the information is generally provided for a period of years.

If each country was specified separately the network itself would be vast. In order to make it more comprehensive GATT groups the countries according to economic status as that is the way they are ranged in debates on trade and commercial policy. Thus we have Industrial countries comprising North America, Western Europe, and Japan; The Eastern Trading Area (ETA) comprising Russia and Eastern Europe, and China, Mongolia, North Korea and Vietnam. Most of the others are Developing countries and since 1970 GATT has divided them into the traditional oil exporters (OPEC) and the Others. This classification leaves out the resource-rich countries of Australia, New Zealand and South Africa, but their trade is included in the total.

What does such a network reveal? Firstly the dominant position of the industrial countries; in 1955 world exports were $93.3 billion and of those $56.7 billion, that is 61% were from industrial countries and 63% of these in turn were to other industrial countries. That is, 38% of world trade was carried out between industrial countries. This proportion tended to increase so that in 1968 it stood at 51% but after 1973 it declined, and in 1981 was 41% of total trade.

Exports by all developing countries were \$23.75 billion in 1955, representing a quarter of the world trade, and 70% of these went to industrial countries, GATT has calculated that in 1970 12% of world exports were accounted for by non-OPEC countries, henceforth called non-oil or other developing countries, and 6% by oil exporters. The OPEC price rise led to a rapid rise in the latter from 7% in 1973 to 15% in 1974.

The Eastern bloc has continued to account for approximately 10% of world trade.

However, in this book it is not the network itself that we will be concerned with but the degree of participation in trade of the groups of countries and the relative specialisation of these groups in relation to the rest of the world, and how these have changed over time. But we must first consider their balance of trade.

BALANCE OF TRADE

Initially, these groups of countries were broadly in balance for overall trade (see Chapter 3) with the deficits of the non-oil Developing countries being largely balanced by the surpluses of the oil exporters. From 1973 onwards, the industrial countries and non-oil exporting developing countries were in deficit. These deficits together with those of Australia, New Zealand and South Africa, were, of course, the counterpart of the OPEC surplus. But whereas the industrial countries' overall trade deficit was smaller than their fuel deficit, the developing countries' was considerably larger, whether considered in terms of its level or in terms of its absolute change from 1973 to subsequent years. This represents a much greater adjustment to counter their adverse balance of payments by industrial countries and apparently none by non-oil developing countries, as discussed in Chapter 3. In so far as this adjustment consists in maintaining or increasing exports while reducing imports, this should be borne in mind when looking at trade in other commodities.

The general participation of the groups could be considered in terms of either their exports or their imports. In the following Tables 8.3, 8.4 and 8.5, exports have been selected as the most significant indicator. The exports of each group are just obtained by adding up the exports of all countries in that group, and this has been done for the commodity classes as well as total trade. For the

TABLE 8.3 Industrial Countries—Exports (E) and Net Exports (NE) 1955–82
$ Billion

	1955		1963		1968		1970		1973		1975		1980		1981		1982	
	E	NE	E	NE	E	NE	E	NE	E	NE	E	NE	E	NE	E	NE	E	NE
Primary Products																		
Food	8.68	−5.86	14.56	−6.34	19.22	−7.15	24.43	−8.09	51.05	−10.36	66.17	−8.84	131.75	−4.05	134.55	−4.10	124.40	−0.60
Raw materials	4.70	−4.39	6.34	−4.13	7.83	−4.11	9.35	−4.11	17.44	−8.07	18.90	−5.06	40.90	−10.20	37.05	−7.85	32.80	−7.50
Ores and minerals	1.59	−1.19	2.41	−1.60	4.02	−1.60	5.16	−3.56	7.10	−5.08	9.17	−7.97	20.10	−12.70	16.45	−12.10	13.80	−11.00
Fuels	3.23	−2.98	4.04	−6.81	5.20	−11.81	7.24	−14.54	13.71	−36.08	27.78	−102.12	83.75	−280.65	91.65	−268.65	93.00	−222.10
Non-ferrous metals	2.01	−1.03	2.79	−1.03	5.60	−2.50	7.21	−3.00	10.23	−3.87	11.21	−2.71	32.25	−7.75	25.05	−5.25	21.50	−4.40
Total Primary Products	20.21	−15.43	30.14	−19.93	41.85	−28.05	53.41	−33.30	99.55	−63.45	133.25	−126.70	311.80	−315.30	304.75	−289.75	295.50	−245.50
Manufactures																		
Iron and steel	3.63	1.38	5.74	1.49	9.13	1.96	13.81	2.90	23.78	6.75	38.75	15.65	62.40	21.20	59.60	20.40	54.70	19.50
Chemicals	4.27	1.64	8.29	2.63	15.43	4.65	19.95	5.45	36.46	9.14	54.17	15.89	124.20	34.45	125.55	22.75	120.10	29.30
Other semi-manufactures	3.86	1.00	9.65	0.83	9.86	1.11	12.40	1.31	23.31	1.35	30.77	4.56	74.20	8.80	66.00	11.10	61.00	10.10
Engineering products	16.75	7.89	35.19	11.96	64.22	18.91	88.42	23.29	159.60	37.08	237.00	79.95	498.00	153.00	507.30	169.80	485.90	154.40
Machinery special.[1]	5.12	2.27	11.41	4.00	17.97	6.55	24.39	8.29	41.61	13.95	67.75	29.81	127.60	52.10	126.50	57.45	115.70	52.20
Office and telecomm.	0.77	0.30	2.64	0.67	4.98	1.18	8.20	1.77	14.57	2.77	19.33	4.72	47.60	7.85	47.95	7.90	49.90	8.00
Road motor vehicles	3.19	1.68	6.74	2.24	14.69	3.31	20.32	4.28	37.71	6.74	53.94	15.45	118.40	29.35	119.65	34.40	116.80	29.10
Other machin. & trans.[2]	6.46	3.18	12.15	4.37	21.68	6.76	28.69	7.69	52.76	12.51	80.48	27.47	166.75	57.35	173.04	62.85	167.20	59.70
Household appliances	1.21	0.47	1.68	0.69	4.90	1.12	6.82	1.26	12.95	1.82	15.45	2.50	38.40	6.40	40.20	7.20	36.30	5.40
Textiles	3.78	1.75	5.31	1.20	7.55	0.51	9.54	1.69	17.12	1.82	19.73	3.16	38.40	4.55	36.25	5.8	33.50	4.70
Clothing	0.56	0.14	1.51	0.07	2.82	−0.29	3.98	−0.71	6.92	−3.89	9.00	−3.79	20.15	−11.10	18.45	−12.00	18.10	−12.30
Other consumer goods	2.31	0.97	4.41	0.62	7.58	0.03	10.14	0.03	18.43	0.45	24.34	0.47	62.00	0.50	59.00	2.50	57.70	1.20
Total Manufactures	35.50	15.09	65.96	18.78	116.60	28.50	158.24	33.95	285.60	52.70	414.75	115.90	886.90	211.40	872.60	230.70	831.50	207.50
Total Exports	56.70	0.00	99.05	−0.55	160.70	−0.55	215.80	1.50	391.30	−9.20	558.40	−7.30	1217.30	−99.20	1195.60	−52.70	1135.00	−31.50

Notes: For 1955, 1963 and 1968

1. For 1955, 1963 and 1968 Agricultural and Industrial machinery, machinery parts n.e.s.
2. For 1955, 1963, 1968 and 1970 Power generating machinery, other engineering products and scientific instruments and other transport equipment.

Source: GATT, *International Trade 1978/79 & 1981/82, 1982/83*; GATT, *Networks of World Trade by Areas and Community Classes 1955–1976* (Geneva, 1978) Tables A2 and A3.

TABLE 8.4 Developing Countries—Exports (E) and Net Exports (NE) 1955–82
$ Billion

	1955 E	1955 NE	1963 E	1963 NE	1968 E	1968 NE	1970 E	1970 NE	1973 E	1973 NE	1975 E	1975 NE	1980 E	1980 NE	1981 E	1981 NE	1982 E	1982 NE
OIL EXPORTERS																		
Fuels							14.88	14.72	37.38	37.24	107.55	106.55	282.20	276.35	258.65	252.50	210.00	—
Total Primary Products							17.20	15.60	41.15	37.40	111.25	101.70	292.70	264.90	266.45	234.65	216.50	186.50
Total Manufactures							0.45	-7.15	0.95	-15.00	1.75	-44.15	6.10	-93.30	5.55	-112.45	5.00	-110.50
Total Exports							17.65	7.85	42.10	21.40	113.00	55.10	298.50	167.50	272.50	117.70	222.00	71.00
	ALL DEVELOPING COUNTRIES						*OTHER DEVELOPING COUNTRIES[3]*											
Primary Products																		
Food	8.70	4.82	10.64	4.98	12.33	5.19	13.30	6.13	22.05	9.00	31.24	11.33	59.40	19.90	58.50	17.85		
Raw materials	4.86	3.39	4.72	3.13	4.80	2.83	4.51	2.36	7.69	3.29	7.06	2.52	16.35	5.20	13.85	3.50		
Ores and minerals	1.13	.98	1.62	1.38	2.29	1.92	2.81	2.33	4.12	3.26	6.30	4.95	12.50	8.75	12.00	8.10		
Fuels	5.90	2.96	9.48	6.29	15.07	10.89	3.21	-1.20	5.98	-3.52	17.69	-9.96	56.00	-19.85	64.40	-12.30		
Non-ferrous metals	1.23	1.00	1.43	1.00	2.89	2.15	3.56	2.64	4.40	2.94	4.06	2.00	9.40	4.15	6.55	2.45		
Total primary prod.	21.83	13.15	27.88	16.80	37.39	23.00	27.41	12.49	44.25	14.95	66.35	10.85	153.65	18.00	155.30	19.00	146.50	18.50
Manufactures																		
Iron and steel	0.04	-1.23	0.14	-1.41	0.31	1.83	0.58	-1.86	0.95	-3.39	1.23	-5.47	4.55	-9.10	5.10	-8.70		
Chemicals	0.25	-1.44	0.39	-2.23	0.69	-3.78	0.89	-3.58	1.83	-6.08	3.04	-9.51	9.85	-19.70	10.35	-18.45		
Other semi-manufactures	0.32	-.84	0.57	-.91	0.96	-1.22	1.47	-0.82	3.39	-0.36	3.59	-1.78	10.85	-3.00	11.15	-3.25		
Engineering products	0.17	-6.29	0.46	-10.23	0.97	-15.60	1.88	-14.88	5.91	-21.13	9.39	-35.19	34.30	-72.30	39.25	-73.65		
Machinery specialised[1]	.05	-1.94	.10	-3.39	.18	-5.09	0.33	-5.20	0.81	-7.49	1.34	-12.30	4.15	-26.90	5.15	-28.00		
Office and telecomm.	.01	-0.23	.01	-.53	.18	-0.91	0.27	-1.08	1.28	-1.62	1.95	-2.28	8.15	-2.95	9.15	-2.35		
Road motor vehicles	.01	-1.27	.03	-1.82	.04	-2.78	0.11	-2.60	0.38	-3.72	0.70	-5.92	2.10	-13.50	2.50	-13.50		
Other mach. & transport[2]	.09	-2.43	.22	-3.85	.36	-5.81	0.76	-5.11	1.80	-7.99	3.15	-13.29	11.65	-28.45	13.20	-29.70		
Household appliances	.01	-.43	.10	-.64	.21	-1.01	0.41	-.89	1.64	-.31	2.25	-0.40	8.25	-0.50	9.25	-0.10		
Textiles	.66	-1.29	1.10	-.83	1.58	1.03	1.88	-0.69	4.05	0.13	4.45	-0.02	11.65	1.00	12.70	0.65		
Clothing	0.08	.67	0.30	-.07	0.88	.38	1.38	-.69	3.82	2.93	5.36	4.32	14.70	11.40	16.80	12.85		
Other consumer goods	0.31	-.66	0.51	-.63	0.82	-.60	1.79	0.25	3.18	.97	4.19	1.09	13.90	4.40	15.20	4.40		
Total Manufactures	1.82	-11.90	3.47	-16.30	6.21	-23.70	9.89	-20.64	23.15	-26.90	31.25	-46.85	99.80	-87.50	110.55	-85.55	107.50	-71.00
Total Exports	23.75	.80	31.85	-.40	43.65	-1.60	38.20	-9.30	68.30	-14.60	98.80	-39.50	255.80	-26.20	268.00	-74.40	255.50	-60.50

Notes: 1. and 2. See notes to Table 8.3.
3. 1955, 1963 and 1968. All Developing Countries.
Sources: GATT, International Trade 1978/79 1979/80, 1980/81 and 1981/82, 1982/83; GATT, Networks of World Trade (Geneva, 1978).

TABLE 8.5 Eastern Trading Area—Exports (E) and Net Exports (NE) 1955–82
$ Billion

	1955 E	1955 NE	1963 E	1963 NE	1968 E	1968 NE	1970 E	1970 NE	1973 E	1973 NE	1975 E	1975 NE	1980 E	1980 NE	1981 E	1981 NE	1982 E	1982 NE
Primary Products																		
Food	1.80	0.13	2.90	0.27	3.80	0.11	3.85	-0.43	6.64	-1.81	8.99	-3.67	15.00	-12.45	14.40	-15.00		
Raw materials	1.20	-0.14	1.50	-0.45	2.00	0.36	2.41	0.08	3.88	0.18	4.54	0.35	8.80	-0.90	11.20	-1.10		
Ores and minerals	0.50	0.02	0.70	-0.01	0.95	0.09	1.12	0.03	1.73	0.11	2.71	0.07	4.30	0.00	4.30	-0.15		
Fuels	1.10	0.33	2.10	0.85	2.55	1.14	2.97	1.23	5.66	2.48	14.72	6.89	42.55	24.60	50.40	28.20		
Non-ferrous metals	0.25	-0.03	0.37	0.01	0.64	0.06	0.91	0.07	1.70	0.34	1.85	0.09	3.30	0.05	3.00	0.40		
Total Primary Products	4.85	0.32	7.57	0.09	9.94	1.66	11.26	0.97	19.60	1.30	32.80	3.70	77.00	11.40	83.30	14.50	88.00	20.00
Manufactures																		
Iron and steel	0.55	0.03	1.40	-0.05	1.75	-0.12	2.40	-0.23	3.23	-1.55	4.93	-4.23	7.40	-4.60	7.15	-3.20		
Chemicals	0.32	-0.04	0.88	-0.08	1.31	-0.44	1.56	-0.50	2.74	-0.86	4.42	-1.98	9.20	-3.75	9.85	-2.65		
Other semi-manufactures	0.22	-0.04	0.60	0.15	0.83	0.09	0.99	0.02	1.58	0.04	2.17	-0.28	4.50	-0.05	4.45	0.15		
Engineering products	2.55	-0.06	6.00	0.10	9.50	-0.52	11.95	-0.43	21.22	-1.92	30.15	-7.15	56.65	-6.25	55.30	-3.80		
Machinery special.	1.25	0.03	2.90	-0.06	4.80	-0.64	5.65	-0.53	9.83	-1.88	14.03	-4.44	26.30	-3.90	25.85	-2.35		
Office and telecomm.	0.04	0.00	0.23	0.01	0.50	-0.04	0.80	-0.09	1.32	-0.14	2.00	-0.26	3.45	-0.40	3.35	-0.50		
Road motor vehicles	0.10	-0.07	0.62	0.11	1.03	0.13	1.43	0.12	2.62	0.08	3.55	-0.33	6.55	0.45	6.00	0.50		
Other machin. & trans.	1.10	-0.09	2.10	0.00	2.97	-0.01	3.72	-0.01	6.94	-0.03	9.66	-2.27	18.40	-2.35	18.25	-1.35		
Household appliances	0.06	-0.03	0.15	0.04	0.20	0.04	0.35	0.08	0.51	0.05	0.90	0.14	1.95	0.00	1.85	-0.05		
Textiles	0.27	0.05	0.60	0.11	0.72	0.03	0.83	-0.04	1.76	0.09	2.07	-0.38	4.50	0.20	5.30	0.40		
Clothing	0.15	0.01	0.40	0.03	0.69	-0.04	0.85	0.00	1.77	0.27	2.26	0.25	5.00	1.80	5.15	2.00		
Other consumer goods	3.00	2.77	5.63	4.88	9.61	8.71	1.61	0.38	2.41	0.76	3.24	1.03	6.00	2.05	6.20	1.90		
Total Manufactures	4.40	-0.13	10.83	-0.46	15.96	-0.76	20.19	-0.82	34.70	-3.20	49.25	-12.75	93.30	-10.50	93.40	-5.30	97.00	-2.50
Total Exports[1]	9.45	0.55	18.75	0.80	27.00	1.50	32.90	1.30	57.20	0.60	85.50	-6.30	178.00	6.40	185.00	15.20	193.00	24.00

Notes: 1. Total exports and imports given by GATT are always greater than the sum of the components indicating unallocated trade. See notes to Table 8.3.
Sources: GATT *International Trade 1979/80, 1980/81, 1981/82, 1982/83;* GATT, *Networks of World Trade,* (Geneva, 1978) Tables A1, A2 and A3.

Tables, 1955, 1963, 1968, 1970, 1973, and 1975 have been selected as representative years and they are shown together with the latest available figures, that is for 1980 to 1982. The division of developing countries into oil exporter and non-oil exporters since 1970 is also shown in table 8.4

As discussed in Chapter 7, the specialisation of these groups of countries is even more important in so far as it indicates the effect of international trade on resource allocation. The overall specialisation of the groups is shown by their net exports. These are total exports minus imports. Thus the net exports of a group excludes all intra-group trade. Because most trade occurs between industrial countries their net exports appear small in relation to their total exports. Nevertheless it does show the exchange that is taking place with the rest of the world.

Now let us return to the overall picture as depicted in Table 8.3, 8.4 and 8.5. The impression they convey is one of expansion in exports of all areas and for all categories of goods over each successive period. (The only exception to this is the developing countries' exports of raw materials which actually declined in money terms between 1955 and 1968). But as already mentioned, part of this general increase in value, particularly after 1968, is due to inflationary price increases.

Let us now examine the net export balances of the different groups of countries as showing their direction of specialisation, and their relative changes in exports and net exports as providing some idea of the changes in structure.

OVERALL SPECIALISATION

Firstly it is clear that during the whole of the period that industrial countries as a whole were net exporters of manufactures and net importers of primary products. Obversely, the developing countries were net importers of manufactures and net exporters of primary products. The Eastern Trading Area countries, accounting for a relatively small amount of trade were net exporters of primary products and net importers of manufactures.

PRIMARY PRODUCTS

Now let us turn to consider the changes over time. Let us first consider primary products. In 1955 the most important of these was food. Gatt's definition of food includes not only what can be eaten but also beverages and tobacco, oilseeds, and products and animal oils and fats (SITC Rev. 1, section 0, 1 and 4 and division 22). Both industrial and developing countries each exported $8.7 billion of food and thus each accounted for 43% of world trade. But the industrial countries increased their exports much faster so that in 1981 they accounted for 60% of world trade.

A similar picture emerges for raw materials although the overall increase is much lower. Raw materials are defined to include all rubber whether natural, synthetic or reclaimed, textile fibres, hides and skins, wood, lumber and cork, pulp and paper (SITC Rev. 1, section 2 excluding 22, 27, and 28). Developing countries exported slightly more with $4.8 billion compared with the industrial countries $4.7 billion in 1955; that is 40% and 39% of world trade respectively. But exports by industrial areas increased much faster so that by 1981 they accounted for 55% of world trade.

Exports of ores and minerals were less important to industrial countries with $1.59 billion and developing countries with $1.13 billion in 1955. But both groups of countries increased the value of their exports by between six and seven times.

However, it is clear the developing countries were not the major suppliers of these primary products and their relative position has declined over time. Even in 1955 they accounted for less than half world exports of food, raw materials and ores and minerals, and by 1981 non-oil developing countries accounted for only 26%, 20% and 31% respectively. The $8 billion of non-fuel primary product exports by oil developing countries would only add a small amount to the percentage.

FUELS

Only for fuels were the developing countries the predominant suppliers, accounting for 58% of world trade in 1955. Almost all their exports were of petroleum products, as can be seen from Chapter 12. Their position was then reinforced by the OPEC price rise, so that in 1973 they accounted for 68% and in 1974 78%. But, of course, only the developing countries exporting oil benefited from this—in Table 8.4 they are differentiated from the others after 1970. In the subsequent discussion, they are termed oil developing areas in contrast to non-oil developing areas.

As discussed in Chapter 11, OPEC could only maintain the higher price level by reducing its output. But at the same time, the higher price encouraged the production of oil and other fuels elsewhere. Thus, by 1981, OPEC's share of world exports had fallen to 55% and by 1982 to 49%.

Other developing countries and the ETA, which had in 1973 each supplied 9% of world exports, increased their proportion to 14% and 11% respectively in 1981. The proportion supplied by industrial countries was 22% in 1982 just as it had been in 1973, although it dropped in the period in between.

However, we are concerned with the specialisation of groups of countries. Net exports are more relevant. As can be seen from Table 8.3, the net import of fuels by industrial countries were initially increasing with a tripling in value terms between 1973 and 1975. However, since 1980, net imports in terms of value have been falling. This has been paralleled by a decline in the net quantity of petroleum imported between 1979 and 1982 of -19% p.a. for North America (-18% p.a. for the US), $-7\frac{1}{2}\%$ p.a. for Japan, and -11% p.a. for Western Europe with EEC(10) -13% p.a. (GATT, *International Trade*, 1982/83, p. 76).

The net imports of fuels by other developing countries in terms of value also increased from 1970 until 1980 since when they have been declining.

In contrast, the ETA has continued to expand its net exports of fuels. It benefited indirectly from the OPEC price rises.

NET EXPORTS

Food

To try and clarify the picture of trade in primary products let us consider net exports. Even in value terms developing countries' net exports of food were increasing only slowly to begin with from $4.82 billion in 1955 to $4.98 in 1963 and $5.19 in 1968. In 1981 the net exports of food by non-oil developing countries were $17.85 billion. The net exports of food by oil developing countries cannot be directly calculated because their exports of primary products other than fuels at $7.80 billion in total in 1981 are not broken down by commodity group. But their imports of food were $20.90 billion in 1981. Thus their net imports of food must have been somewhere between $13.10 billion, if all their exports of primary products other than fuel were of food, and $20.90 billion if they had no exports of food. Even if we take the lower figure, net exports of food by all developing countries appear at $4.75 billion in 1981 to be only 95% of their value in 1963. But food prices were 328% of their level in 1963 (see Table 2.3) so that the net exports of food by developing countries must have fallen greatly in real terms.

The counterpart to this is shown by the position of industrial countries. Their net imports of food were increasing very slowly in real terms until 1970 since when they have fallen, so much that in 1981 industrial areas as a whole were almost in balance. This indicates a gradual reversal of specialisation.

The Eastern Trading Areas have changed from being overall a small net exporter in 1955, 1963, and 1968 to a net importer of food in the 1970s.

Raw Materials

Now let us turn to trade in raw materials. The developing countries' net exports of raw materials declined in value between 1955 and 1968. This represents a real decline because although prices were very slightly lower in 1968 than 1963 this is not sufficient to account for it.

The value of net exports of raw materials by non-oil developing countries more than doubled between 1970 and 1980. But as prices in 1980 were 332% of their level in 1970 this represents a real reduction of about a third. Obversely, industrial countries' net imports of raw materials have increased more slowly than the price index and, therefore have declined in real terms.

Manufactures

Now let us turn to trade in manufactures as shown in Tables 8.2, 8.3, and 8.4. As can be seen, exports of manufactures by developing countries increased much faster than those from industrial countries such that whereas they only represented 4% as compared with 85% respectively of international trade in manufactures in 1955, by 1982 this had risen to 11% compared with 79%. The proportion supplied by the Eastern Trading Area (ETA) declined slightly from 11% in 1955 to 9% in 1982.

To get a clearer view we should also look at net exports. For industrial countries these were in 1982 11.05 times their level in 1963 at current prices. But the price index stood at 314 (see Table 8.1) so the real increase was 252%. For developing countries there is a divergence in the fortunes of oil-exporting and other developing countries. If other developing countries are regarded as entirely responsible for net imports of Manufactures in 1963, then their value increased to 436% of that level in 1982. With a deflation by the price index this represents a real increase of only 39%. Because of the initial assumption this is perhaps somewhat misleading. Indeed if we confine ourselves to the last twelve years, the real net imports of manufactures of non-oil developing countries appears in 1982 to be only 25% greater than their level in 1970. The increase for oil developing countries is much greater with their net imports of manufactures in 1982, $5\frac{1}{2}$ times their level in 1970 in real terms. Both have shown a downturn since 1980.

It is also interesting to look at the situation for different categories of goods. In terms of value the exports by all areas of each category of goods appears to have increased. But as can be seen since 1970 those of the non-oil developing countries have been increasing faster than those of industrial areas. Exports of the ETA have also been increasing, not as fast as those of industrial countries for engineering products and chemicals, but slightly faster in textiles and clothing.

Now let us consider the balance of trade in the various categories. Let us begin with the industrial countries. Imports of the simpler manufactures appears to have increased faster than exports so that for clothing, industrial countries as a whole have changed from being net exporters in 1955 to net importers in the 1970s, and for textiles and household appliances net exports in monetary terms have increased very slowly and therefore in real terms must have declined. On the other hand, net exports of engineering products as a whole continued to increase at a fast rate until 1981. In terms of value they were in 1981 $7\frac{1}{3}$ times their level in 1970. The UN price index for machinery and transport equipment was 235% of its level in 1970 and therefore in real terms net exports in 1981 must have been three times their level in 1970. But since 1981 they have declined. Net exports of other manufactures, particularly chemicals, have also been increasing very fast, much faster than the manufacturing price index and therfore have certainly increased in real terms.

The counterpart of this is represented by the trade balances of other countries. In 1955 and 1963 all developing countries were net importers of each individual category of manufactures. In 1970 the non-oil developing countries were small net exporters of other consumer goods: by 1980 these net exporters had rapidly increased and they were also net exporters of textiles and clothing. On the other hand, their net imports of engineering products as a whole have consistently increased in real as well as money terms until 1981 and their net imports of chemicals increased until 1980.

There is less information on exports of manufactures by oil developing countries because in total it is so small and, therefore, the net balances cannot be worked out. But they do import every category of manufactures.

This total picture is illuminated by GATT's calculations of changes in volume of trade and the main classes of goods of the industrial countries and developing countries between 1963 and 1976, as shown in Table 8.6. This shows up very clearly the

TABLE 8.6 *World Trade Export and Import Volume Indexes—Industrial and Developing Areas 1963 to 1976.*

		Value 1970 $ billion		1963	1968	1970 = 100	1971	1972	1973	1974	1975	1976	Increase from 1963 to 1976 %
Industrial Areas													
Manufactures	E	165		49	81	100	107	118	134	147	140	157	220
	I	134		46	80	100	108	121	137	145	131	152	230
Primary products	E	46.2		65	86	100	102	111	126	125	120	131	102
	I	76.5		65	88	100	103	113	125	119	111	123	89
Food	E	24.4		65	86	100	106	116	133	131	133	145	123
	I	32.5		71	90	100	105	116	125	117	119	—	68[2]
Raw materials	E	9.4		75	89	100	101	109	124	123	100	118	57
Ores and minerals	E	5.2		58	92	100	87	91	110	112	110	117	102
	I	22.3[1]		71	90	100	97	106	122	117	100	—	41
Fuels	E	7.2		59	79	100	98	112	113	114	108	111	88
	I	21.8		51	82	100	107	115	127	125	111	123	141
Developing Areas													
Manufactures	E	13.8		46	71	100	105	125	151	164	166	203	341
	I	39.1		59	81	100	105	110	125	155	169	184	212
Primary products	E	41.1		67	88	100	103	112	122	118	111	—	66[2]
	I	15.6		70	92	100	104	111	127	131	137	—	96[2]
Food	E	14.5		81	93	100	101	110	114	102	117	—	44[2]
	I	8.2		72	92	100	108	111	123	133	148	—	106[2]
Raw materials	E	8.5		73	86	100	101	111	123	123	97	—	33
Ores and minerals	I	2.9		63	86	100	108	122	155	154	141	—	124[2]
Fuels	E	18.1		53	86	100	106	114	129	128	112	—	111[2]
	I	4.6		70	95	100	93	103	119	114	111	—	59[2]

Notes: 1. Imports Raw materials and Ores and Minerals.
2. Increase to 1975.
E = Exports.   I = Imports.
Source: GATT *Networks of World Trade by Areas and Commodity Classes 1955–76* (Geneva, 1978), Tables DI and EI.

development of trade in manufactures; for both groups, exports and imports of manufactures were increasing more rapidly than in other products. The greatest increase was in the volume of exports from developing countries, which in 1976 were almost $4\frac{1}{2}$ times as great as in 1963. They were increasing faster than imports which in 1976 were approximately three times their level in 1963. Obversely, over the whole period the volume of exports by industrial countries had increased by a slightly lower amount than their volume of imports, 220% compared with 230%. But this apparent difference was entirely due to the situation before 1973. Since then the volume of exports of manufactures by industrial countries has been increasing faster than their volume of imports, whereas the imports of manufactures by developing countries have been increasing faster than their exports. This reflects the need of industrial areas to pay OPEC countries (included with developing countries) for the higher price of oil with manufactures.

The impact of OPEC can be broadly assessed by looking at the volume of trade in fuels. Up to 1972 the volume of exports of fuels by the developing countries was increasing faster then their volume of imports—thus the area as a whole was becoming more of a net exporter. Exports increased again in 1973 but then fell so that in 1975 their volume of exports was lower than in 1972. On the other hand the industrial countries' volume of fuel imports increased more rapidly than exports until 1973 after which they declined. Their volume of exports has remained round their 1973 level.

In food the divergent trends remain throughout the period. The volume of exports by industrial countries has almost consistently increased faster than their volume of imports. In the last few years shown imports fluctuated but not much above the 1972 level. Whereas the developing countries' volume of imports has increased faster than their volume of exports. Thus in food industrial countries and developing countries do appear to be moving from their traditional position of net importers and net exporters.

Less information is available on other primary products but the imports of industrial countries do appear to have been badly affected by events since 1973.

SPECIALISATION CURVES

These GATT volume indexes have been used as the basis of histograms showing the real trading position, that is the net exports and imports at 1970 prices of industrial countries with respect to the rest of the world for 1963, 1970 and 1975. The category of ores and minerals has been disaggregated from that of raw materials using GATT network figures of values and prices indexes. Furthermore, it has been possible to extend the figures for certain categories to 1982 where price indexes have been available.

The GATT categories have been arranged from left to right in diminishing order of their use of specific factors. By specific factor is meant one that is geographically fixed and used in any quantity only for the commodity in question such as oil fields or mineral deposits. It must also be in short supply. By short supply is meant not only that there is a finite limit to the amount of the factor available but also that any expansion of production involves increasing cost. In the case of oil and other mineral deposits this would not only be the cost of extraction but also the cost of prospecting and establishing extraction facilities.

Fuels are regarded as the most dependent on specific factors, then ores and minerals, then non-ferrous metals which often come as by-products of the extraction of other ores. Raw materials are regarded as more dependent on specific factors than is food since both natural rubber and cotton and jute production are limited by climatic factors. This is also true of certain food products—tea, coffee, cocoa and bananas—but these do not form such a high proportion of trade in food; most often tropical products are substitutable by temperate products.

Moving from the centre to the right the commodity categories are arranged in increasing order of their technological input as defined in Chapter 9. The production of textiles and clothing involves only a well-established technology and this is increasingly becoming true of road motor vehicles. The commodities most dependent on technological progress and a high expenditure on research and development are chemicals and electronic and electrical goods included in other engineering products. (See Chapter 9).

It must be emphasised that the arrangement is not according to labour or capital intensities in production. Most of the categories include capital-intensive and labour-intensive products. Fuels for instance include the very capital-intensive oil production and labour-intensive coal production.

The intermediate range of production includes those with a well-established technology requiring little highly skilled labour and which are not dependent on any geographically fixed specific product. Indeed, textiles and clothing are often regarded as prime examples of footloose industries whose raw materials have a very high value in relation to weight and the production of which can therefore be easily transferred from one country to another.

This is less true of iron and steel, nevertheless the larger develop-

ing countries have all made great efforts to establish their own production. Increasingly this is also true of cars.
Food production does require a specific factor—land. But in so far as all countries have an agricultural industry, and many tropical products are substitutable at the margin by temperate products, as will be described in Chapter 11, food can be added to the group. All these intermediate products are very susceptible to government intervention in trade. As described in Chapter 5, there is a very long record of intervention in agriculture, and there is an almost equally long record of government protection for textile industries. Intervention in the iron and steel industries is more recent and has generally taken the form of more direct intervention to reorganise or subsidise the industry. The amount of intervention in trade in cars has only recently become apparent.

Now let us consider what has actually happened. Figure 8.1 shows the histograms for the industrial countries' trade balances at 1970 prices. Let us call the histograms for any particular year a curve. In Figure 8.1 there are three curves for 1963, 1970 and 1975. For certain categories it has also been possible to draw the position for 1982.

In this kind of diagram the index number problem looms large. That is, the measurement of changes in volume or in price depends on weighting. Most of the information for the individual categories is derived from the GATT volume figures and is therefore weighted by relative prices in 1970. This affects the estimate for the group itself and it also affects the relative size of histograms for the different categories; the histogram for fuel would look relatively much larger if all the measurements were made at the prices of the late 1970s.

However let us consider what changes have occurred in real terms, that is at constant prices. The most obvious is the movement of the edges of the curve. Net imports of fuel were increasing from 1963 to 1970 and then to 1975. On the other hand net exports of the more technologically advanced goods chemicals, and other engineering products were increasing and so also were road motor vehicles. Changes in the trade balances of the other goods appeared relatively small. Net imports of ores and minerals increased slightly and those of non-ferrous metals decreased, but difficulties in calculations render these suspect. Net imports of raw materials and food have declined since 1970 whereas those of iron and steel and wood semi—manufactures have increased. The categories of textiles and clothing have had to be amalgamated because of insufficient breakdown of the import figures, and they show a movement from a small positive balance in 1963 to a very small negative balance in

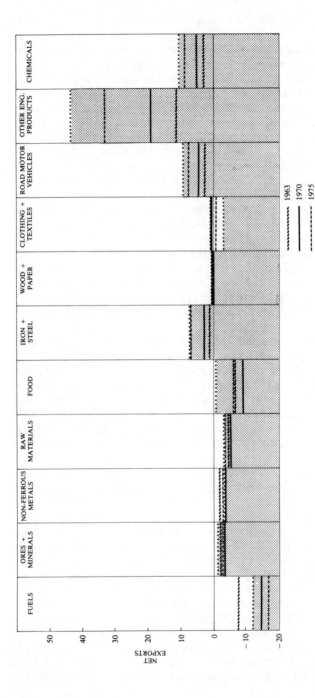

Figure 8.1: Industrial Countries Overall Specialisation in 1963, 1970, 1975 and 1982 — Histograms of Net Exports at 1970 Prices in $ Billion

Figure 8.1 (continued)

Source: Most figures for 1963, 1970 and 1975 derived from GATT, *Networks of World Trade 1955–76* (GATT, Geneva, 1978) Tables EI and FI some of which are shown here in Table 8.6.

These were extended from 1975 to 1982 using the figures for current values as shown in Table 8.3 deflated by the price index based on 1975 published in the *UN Monthly Bulletin of Statistics.*

The net exports of textiles and clothing and chemicals in 1983 were deflated by the unit value index of manufactured goods exports. The current value of net exports of other engineering products for 1982 and 1975 were deflated by the price index for machinery and transport equipment and that for road motor vehicles by the price index for road motor vehicles. Net exports of ores and minerals for 1975 and 1982 were deflated by the UN index for minerals from which fuels had been removed using 1975 weights.

The change in the value of net exports of iron and steel between 1975 and 1982 was assumed to increase in proportion to the increase in the tonnage of steel exported between 1975 and 1981 as shown by, OECD, *The Iron and Steel Industry in 1975* (OECD, Paris 1977) and OECD, *The Iron and Steel Industry in 1981* (OECD, Paris, 1983).

1975. But as can be seen from the other tables this is the net result of a positive balance of textiles and a negative balance for clothing. It has been possible to estimate some of the figures for 1982 using unit prices indexes based on 1975. This shows a decline in the net imports of fuel to below the 1970 level. The reduction in net imports of food continued until in 1982 the industrial countries were almost in balance. The net exports of road motor vehicles and other engineering products continued to expand. The figure for chemicals is calculated using the price index for manufactures.

The same type of histogram has been drawn up for industrial countries comparing 1973, the year prior to the OPEC price rise, with 1982, but in this case deflating the net exports for the two years by a price index with 1975 weights—that is, taking the relative weights after the OPEC price rise (see Figure 8.2). The net imports of fuel then appear relatively much more important.

At current prices, industrial countries' net imports of fuel were, in 1982, six times their level in 1973. However, the increase is almost entirely due to a rise in their price. As will be seen in Table 12.9, their net imports of fuel in terms of million tons of oil equivalent, and their net imports of oil, increased only slightly between 1973 and 1979 and, as already remarked, the net imports of oil into industrial countries have been declining by 12.5% a year since 1979.

Thus a comparison of the trade position of industrial countries in 1982 with that in 1973 at constant 1975 prices shows how they have paid the increased price of their net imports of fuel. From Figure 8.2, it can be seen that industrial countries have reduced their net imports of other primary products—that is, ores and minerals, non-ferrous metals, raw materials and food. They have increased their net exports of the technologically advanced products—that is, chemicals and all machinery, except household appliances and road motor vehicles. To a lesser extent, they appear to have increased their exports of iron and steel, other semi-manufactures and textiles. Their net imports of clothing have increased, but they have moved from net importers to net exporters of other consumer goods which include footwear, furniture, luggage, glassware, pottery, etc.

In Figures 8.3, 8.4 and 8.5 we can also see the position of the US, the EEC (10) and Japan. The difference between the specialisation curves of these three and the way each has responded to the higher price of fuels is an illustration of their differing endowments with natural resources.

The US, the best endowed with natural resources, has slightly reduced her net imports of fuel, moved from a small net importer

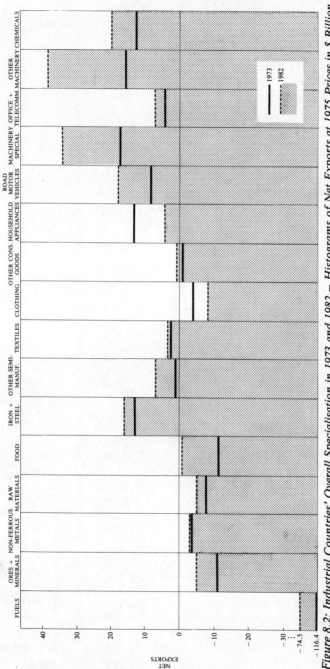

Figure 8.2: Industrial Countries' Overall Specialisation in 1973 and 1982 – Histograms of Net Exports at 1975 Prices in $ Billion Exports f.o.b., imports c.i.f.

Notes: Net exports of iron and steel estimated from the changes in net exports of steel in tons. For EEC (10), Japan and Industrial Countries net exports of steel in 1981 taken as proxy for 1982.

Source: GATT, *International Trade*, 1981/82 and 1982/83. Current values deflated by export price indexes (1975 = 100) derived from the *UN Monthly Bulletin of Statistics*.

OECD *The Iron and Steel Industry in 1975* (OECD, Paris, 1977).
OECD *The Iron and Steel Industry in 1981* (OECD, Paris, 1981).

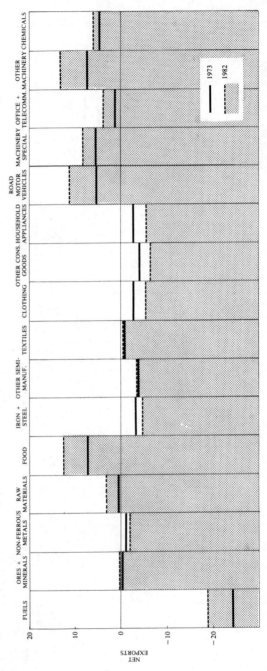

Figure 8.3: US Specialisation Curves for 1973 and 1982 – Histograms of Net Exports at 1975 Prices in $ Billion

For notes and sources see Figure 8.2.

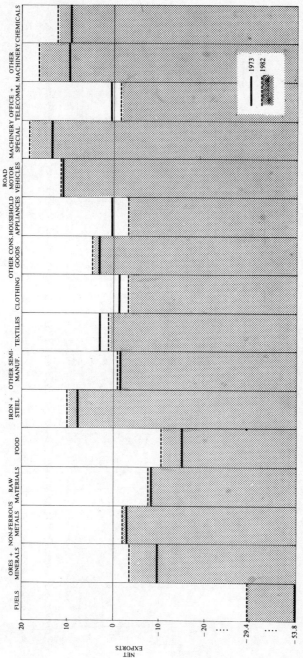

Figure 8.4: EEC(10) Specialisation Curves for 1973 and 1982 — Histograms of Net Exports at 1975 Prices in $ Billion

For notes and sources see Figure 8.2.

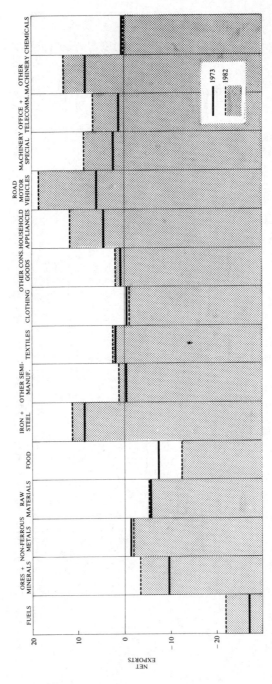

Figure 8.5: Japan's Specialisation Curves for 1973 and 1982 – Histograms of Net Exports at 1975 Prices in $ Billion

For notes and sources see Figure 8.2.

to a net exporter of ores and minerals, and increased her net exports of raw materials and food. As can be seen from Table 11.3, by 1973, the US was already the largest net exporter of agricultural products and subsequent developments have just reinforced her position.

The EEC, which comprises countries with very different resource endowments, has reduced its net imports of all the classes of primary products in real terms—most importantly those of fuels, ores and minerals and food.

Japan, which is least well endowed with natural resources—having scarcely any fuel or mineral deposits and little agricultural land in relation to her population—has reduced her real net imports of fuel and ores and minerals. But her real net imports of non-ferrous metals and raw materials remained roughly the same and her real net imports of food increased.

Turning to the right-hand side of Figures 8.3, 8.4 and 8.5, it can be seen that the US has increased her real net exports of the four technologically advanced sectors of chemicals, other machinery (and transport equipment), office and telecommunications equipment, and machinery for specialised industries. The EEC (10) has achieved an even greater increase in real net exports of chemicals but it has moved from a net exporter to a net importer of office and telecommunications equipment.

Japan has scarcely any net exports of chemicals; her industry was expanding into petrochemicals, a position from which she has had to retreat with the higher price of oil (JETRO, quoted in Sinha, 1982, p. 134). But her net exports of the other categories of specialised engineering equipment have generally increased; in particular, she has become a major net exporter of office and telecommunications equipment. She has also greatly increased her net exports of road motor vehicles and household appliances. Indeed, she appears to have entirely paid for the higher price of fuel she must import by increased exports of engineering and transport equipment.

Now let us consider categories of products in which trade intervention has become increasingly important. Figure 8.3 shows that the US real net imports of most of these products have increased between 1973 and 1982. But her net imports of textiles appear the same, and those of other semi-manufactures have only increased slightly.

Thus, in relation to the rest of the world, the US appears to specialise in food and raw materials and high technology products, although she has not increased her real net exports of high technology machinery by nearly as much as Japan. This may be associated with changes in the rate of technological innovation and expenditure on research and development discussed in Chapter 9, and also the pattern of her direct foreign investment discussed in Chapter 10. With her increased net exports of these products, the US has paid the higher price of fuels and also imported more of the intermediate products.

With respect to intermediate products, the EEC appears to have increased its net exports or reduced its net imports of all products except textiles and household appliances.

Taking the situation of the EEC as a whole, it has adjusted to the higher price of fuel by reducing net imports of fuel and other primary mineral products from the rest of the world. The EEC (10) has expanded its net exports of food, as already discussed in Chapter 5, largely due to the Common Agricultural Policy, and most of the intermediate products. This latter partly reflects the intervention policies which have restricted imports of textiles and clothing from developing countries and road motor vehicles from Japan (see Chapter 4). There are some restrictions on imports of household appliances but as can be seen, the EEC has, nevertheless, moved from the position of a small net exporter to a net importer from the rest of the world. The EEC has successfully expanded its net exports of the three technologically advanced sectors of chemicals, other machinery and transport equipment, and machinery for specialised industries. But it has moved from a net exporter to a net importer of office and telecommunications equipment.

Japan, the least well endowed with natural resources and thus the most heavily dependent on imports of fuels and raw materials, has shown the greatest increase in exports of manufactures. She has increased her exports of all manufactures, except chemicals and clothing. Her net exports of machinery and transport equipment in 1982 were several times their level in 1973 in real terms. These increases have been required to pay for the higher price of fuel and also to pay for her increased imports of food.

The position of these three at current prices in 1982 can be seen in Figure 8.6. This brings out the somewhat complementary nature of the US and Japan. The US is the major net exporter of food, Japan the major net importer. Japan is the major net exporter of iron and steel, household appliances, and road motor vehicles and the US is the major importer. It is not surprising that the US accounts for 27% of Japanese exports of manufactures, and that Japan accounts for 15% of US exports of food.

The US, EEC (10) and Japan are all net exporters of machinery

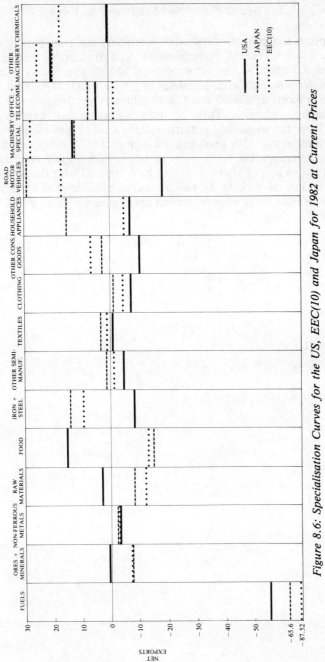

Figure 8.6: Specialisation Curves for the US, EEC(10) and Japan for 1982 at Current Prices

For notes and sources see Figure 8.2.

for specialised industries and other machinery and transport equipment. These are largely investment goods, and as can be seen from Tables 8.3 and 8.4, the net exports of $57.45 and $62.85 billion respectively by industrial countries in 1981 are half accounted for by net imports of $28.00 and $29.70 billion respectively by non-oil developing countries. Then of industrial countries' exports of machinery for specialised industries, 22% went to non-oil developing countries and 15% to oil exporters, and of other machinery and transport equipment, 21% went to non-oil developing countries, and 13% to oil exporters. This can be compared with the average distribution of exports of manufactures by industrial countries where in 1981, 17% went to non-oil developing countries and 11% to oil exporters.

9 Technological Gap Theory and the Product Cycle

The technological gap theory was developed by industrial economists to explain the changes that were taking place in the 1950s and 1960s in the production, trade and investment in manufactures. It was based on the observations of firms, mostly American. As such it represents a partial equilibrium approach—the overall position of a country's balance of payments is never considered. But this has enabled it to be investigated in considerable detail (Posner, 1961; Hufbauer, 1966; Hirsch, 1965; Vernon, 1966).

According to the theory, a firm innovates in order to strengthen its competitive position. Innovation is generally conceived of as the introduction of new products. However, to extend this theory to an explanation of trade it is necessary to argue that a firm's innovation in the production of a commodity enables it to export the commodity even though its manufacture costs more than if undertaken elsewhere. That is, the firm's competitive position lies in its superior knowledge, not lower costs of production. This only provides a basis for exports from the home country if the firm restricts the transmission of the knowledge. Once the knowledge is transferred elsewhere by licence, direct investment, or imitation, the advantage disappears.

TECHNOLOGICAL GAP THEORY

Thus, in the technological gap theory of trade, a theory of innovation, trade, and direct investment are all combined. The argument is that when an innovation is made by a firm in one country, it will initially produce for the home market. As it expands production, it will also eventually export some of the commodity. The time elapsing between the beginning of commercial production in the first country and the purchase of the product by the second country is called the demand lag. The basis of the exports from the first country to the second is the technological advantage of the first. But gradually, as trade expands, the firm in the first country has to consider whether it is not better to supply the second country by producing there, rather than exporting from the first country. The inducement for the original firm to set up a subsidiary or to license an indigenous firm to produce the commodity in the second country will be greater if factor costs are lower there, and also if there are impediments to trade in the form of high transport costs or tariff barriers. Alternatively, production may be started in the second country because of imitation by another firm. For whatever reason production starts in the second country, the length of time that elapses between production in the first and second country is called the imitation lag of the second country. Exports from the first to the second country are regarded as function of the difference between the demand lag and the imitation lag.

The general argument is buttressed by an assumption of economies of scale in production. These are of two kinds—static, that is, due to declining long-run average cost curves, and dynamic economies, that is, where the cost curves fall over time because of the learning process undergone by the firm. Sometimes these dynamic economies of scale are regarded as a function of the time over which the firm has been producing the commodity, and sometimes of the total quantity produced by a firm, but they are generally assumed to be irreversible. Both types of economies of scale will tend to favour production in the first country. Indeed, production will only be transferred to the second country if consumption there is large enough to support a plant which can exploit sufficient economies of scale to make costs there competitive with exports from the first country, allowing, of course, for the costs incurred in transport and tariffs. If, in addition, the technology used is easily transferable as blue prints or in a package which includes skilled personnel, then this will encourage production in the second country by, as it were, speeding up the dynamic economies of scale.

PRODUCT LIFE CYCLE

As already mentioned, this theory of technological change implicitly assumes that the objective is the production of new commodities. Associated with this is the theory of the product life cycle. It is argued that the nature of a manufactured product and its production process changes over time.

As an illustration, let us assume that a new product, say the motor car, is launched on the US market. Initially, cars are produced in small batches and a high proportion of skilled labour is used in their manufacture. Proximity to the market is very important so that the producers can respond rapidly to the needs and wishes of buyers and remedy any defects. Because of the frequent changes in design and production, a high proportion of skilled manpower is required.

However, as knowledge is acquired about the best design and production methods, both become more standardised. Proportionally less skilled manpower is required and mass-production techniques are introduced. Henry Ford, for instance, introduced the assembly line. This lowers the average costs of production and enables prices to be cut and thus extends the market to those with lower incomes. It is at this point, when the product is becoming standardised and prices are falling, that production is most likely to be transferred to other consuming countries.

Thus, in the second stage of the product cycle, production is transferred to the countries which have previously been the largest importers, assuming, that is, that their costs are lower, their markets large enough to support a feasible size of plant, and there are the necessary supplies of skilled labour.

The third stage is reached when the commodity and process of production become completely standardised. Then a market will be supplied from the cheapest location. Where this is, of course, depends not only on the price of factors of production but also on transport costs and impediments to trade in the form of tariffs and quotas.

The transfer of production may be by the direct foreign investment of the innovating firm. The firm will undertake this if it considers it the best method of maximising its return from the innovation. Alternatively, it could license another firm to start up production, or it could just sell its know-how or the use of its patent directly.

The technological gap theory, modified by the theory of the product cycle, is descriptive. Empirical backing is provided by case studies of particular firms and industries. It is essentially an account of the behaviour of individual firms.

But it also provides an explanation for exports of manufactures outside the general equilibrium theory. As such, a considerable amount of effort has gone into testing it.

Firstly, there is the problem of identifying the innovation. The OECD in a comprehensive study carried out in the late 1960s, entitled *Gaps in Technology* first distinguishes three successive phases in the innovative process which they describe as:

(I) *Invention*, which occurs when the *feasibility* of a new product or production process is postulated or established. Invention is often accompanied by the taking out of patents.

(II) *Original Innovation,* which occurs when *for the first time*—a firm sells a new or better product or production process, *with resulting commercial success.* A strong performance by a firm, industry or country in originating innovations is likely to be reflected by a strong competitive position in world markets for product groups with rapid rates of innovation.

(III) *Diffusion of Innovation,* whereby a new or better product or production process is produced or adopted by a wider number of firms. A high rate of increase in the diffusion of a new or better production process is likely to be reflected by a high rate of increase in productivity.
(OECD, 1970), p. 183

The OECD committee then compiled a list of what they regarded as the 110 major innovations in manufacturing occuring between 1945 and 1966. US firms had accounted for 60% and European firms 38%, of which UK firms were responsible for 14% and German ones for 11%(OECD, 1970, p. 185).

THE LOCATION OF INNOVATION

Why should innovations have been so heavily concentrated in a few countries, with the US predominating? According to both Vernon and the OECD, the ultimate cause of the US preponderance in innovation was the response of US firms to their domestic environment. The US market was very competitive. Most of the firms were large and their products differentiated from those of their competitors. In order to outwit its rivals, each firm endeavoured to introduce new products. US average *per capita* income was one of the highest in the world and the total market in terms of GNP the largest. Its high-income consumers appeared avid for new fashions and new products on which they could spend their money. Thus, the launching of new products was not difficult.

These high incomes were a reflection of high wages which, in turn, represented the high opportunity cost of labour. Thus the greatest inducement to innovate was in labour-saving products both for consumers in the form of washing machines and drip-dry shirts, and producers in the form of labour-saving machinery.

European and Japanese firms did not have the same advantage; national markets were smaller and *per capita* incomes lower. But the formation of the EEC could be regarded as being a step towards the creation of a larger market.

These may be regarded as the demand factors determining innovation. The supply factors Vernon regarded as being the easy availability of credit in the US and the availability of skilled manpower. This is because the prerequisite innovation is expenditure on research and development (R and D). Times have long since passed when innovation represented the sporadic bursts of inspiration of solitary scientists. As Freeman stated (Freeman, 1974), innovations are now the products of teams of scientists and engineers deliberately set up for the purpose.

The implicit assumption of the technical gap theory was that innovation took the form of the development of new commodities. This tended to be confirmed by evidence that new products, or the improvement of existing ones, were the main objectives of R and D expenditure by US firms in the mid-1960s (OECD, 1970, p. 188).

However, because of the extreme difficulty in identifying innovation, R and D expenditure is often taken as a proxy for them. But to take the inputs as a proxy for the outputs, you must implicitly be assuming a high correlation between them. The OECD *Gaps in Technology* confidently asserts that there is a direct relationship between innovations and expenditure on R and D (see, p. 254, para. 520). This also tends to be confirmed by information on patents and royalties.

Furthermore, R and D expenditure could be regarded as investment in the acquisition of knowledge, an investment less tangible than in fixed capital equipment, or even in human skills, but nevertheless an expenditure of effort and resources now to increase productivity in the future.

Thus, both as a proxy for innovation and as a particular kind of investment, R and D expenditure has been treated as a possible additional determinant of international trade. This is one of the reasons why so much effort has been expended on the collection of comparative data.

Let us now consider some of these statistics on R and D (see Table 9.1). These are largely derived from OECD sources. As countries accounting for almost all the innovations by the preceding definition are members of it, this does not appear too misleading. However, estimates do not appear entirely consistent between the different sources and, therefore, their absolute values should be treated with circumspection.

The figures for total R and D expenditure as given for 1963–4, (column 1) include all research expenditure whether undertaken for economic or social purposes or defence. A more relevant figure for this study is that carried out in the 'industrial sector'. The

TABLE 9.1 Resources Devoted to Research and Development.

	Expenditure $ million[1]			Total R&D Manpower FTE 1000s			Research Scientists and Engineers FTE 1000s			Government financing of Industrial R&D	
	Total 1963–4 (3)	Industrial 1963–4 (4)	Industrial 1975 (2)	Total 1963–4 (6)	Industrial 1963–4 (5)	Industrial 1975 (2)	Total 1963–4 (3)	Industrial 1963–4 (5)	Industrial 1975 (2)	1963–4 (5) %	1975 (2) %
Major R&D Effort											
US	21,075	13,510	24,164	963.5		767.8	696.5	346.3	362.8	56.9	35.6
Japan	1060	593	5658	289.3	178.5	308.7	197.2	60.0	145.2	6.4	1.7
Germany	1436	920	5881	187.0	133.3	186.2	105.0	17.7	61.6	7.8	17.9
UK	2160	1369	2964	282.9		180.2	159.5	41.8	61.7	33.9	30.9
France	1650	730	3643	150.7	80.6	120.8	95.6	18.0	29.4	29.8	25.4
Medium R&D Effort											
Italy	291	185	996	45.9		40.3	30.3	8.0	13.7	0.9	6.5
Netherlands	330	195	938	42.5	27.3	28.2	31.3	3.3	4.6	1.1	3.6
Sweden	257	176	848	24.2	17.6	23.5	16.5	11.7	8.1	26.7	15.9
Canada	425		681	29.4	14.2	21.5	23.9	5.8	9.0	14.9	11.2
Belgium	137	95	531	18.7	12.5	18.3	15.6	2.3	2.7	4.1	8.4
Switzerland			917			17.5					1.5
Australia (1973)			(440)			16.1			4.9		

Table 9.1 (continued)

	Expenditure $ million[1]			Total R&D Manpower FTE 1000s			Research Scientists and Engineers FTE 1000s			Government financing of Industrial R&D	
	Total 1963–4 (3)	Industrial 1963–4 (4)	Industrial 1975 (2)	Total 1963–4 (6)	Industrial 1963–4 (5)	Industrial 1975 (2)	Total 1963–4 (3)	Industrial 1963–4 (5)	Industrial 1975 (2)	1963–4 (5) %	1975 (2) %
Small R&D Effort											
Spain		8	158	8.4	1.5	11.1		0.3	2.6		1.1
Austria	23	15	(157)	6.5	4.4	8.3	3.2	1.0	1.9	0.1	3.5
Denmark			166			6.1			1.5		6.7
Finland			131			6.1			1.7		6.0
Norway	42	22	183	5.6	3.1	5.8	3.8	1.0	2.1	23.6	23.0
New Zealand			(26)			1.6					21.0
Ireland		4	20	2.5	0.4	1.1		0.2	0.4	8.7	4.7
TOTAL			48,520			1771.4			724.5		

Note: 1. At current exchange rates FTE = Full Time Equivalent.

Sources: 2. OECD *Trends in Industrial R&D in Selected OECD Member Countries 1967–1975* (OECD, Paris, 1979).
3. OECD *Gaps in Technology Analytical Report* (OECD, Pairs, 1970).
4. OECD *The Overall Level and Structure of R&D Efforts in OECD Member Countries* (OECD, Paris, 1967), pp. 99 and 108.
5. OECD *Statistical Tables and Notes. A Study of Resources Devoted to R&D in OECD Member Countries in 1963/64* (OECD, Paris, 1968) Tables E6, E7(a) and (c), and E2.
6. OECD *Patterns of Resources Devoted to Research and Experimental Development in the OECD Area 1963–71*, Table 1, Annex A, Table 11.

'industrial sector' comprises all private and public enterprises and industrial research institutes. It covers agriculture, mining, manufacturing and service industries. 'Industrial R and D' comprises all R and D performed in the sector, whatever the source of funds. As can be seen, by comparing column 2 with column 1, industrial R and D accounts for nearly two thirds of the total. A more recent figure for 1975 is shown in column 3. All three columns give expenditure at current prices converted from the home currency to dollars at the current exchange rate. Herewith lie some problems. Firstly, in so far as the relative salaries of research scientists and engineers may differ in the different countries—for instance, they are lower in Britian and considerably lower in Japan than in the US. Therefore, an equivalent amount of research is cheaper outside the US than inside it and thus the figures overstate the US research effort. Secondly, there is the problem of comparison over time in particular because the price of R and D personnel appears to have risen more than the price index. There is also the change in the relative exchange rates.

In order to avoid these problems, the total manpower involved is given in full-time equivalents (FTE) in columns 4, 5 and 6. Within this total, the Research Scientists and Engineers—that is those with degrees or the equivalent—are distinguished (see column 7, 8 and 9), but we can only obtain those in industry for 1975.

However, these figures do reveal certain aspects of the situation. The US carries out far more R and D however it is measured. In 1963–4, the UK appeared to be the next largest R and D spender in industry, followed in succession by Germany, France and Japan. However, by 1975 the ordering of countries below the US had changed quite markedly. Germany was the next greatest spender followed by Japan, France, and then the UK.

This impression should be qualified by the employment figures. Japan is second to the US in the employment of all personnel and also qualified scientists and engineers. The reason for the discrepancy is that qualified manpower costs less in Japan than in Europe and North America.

According to the OECD, the overall position is that between 1959 and 1967, industrial R and D at constant prices increased by about two thirds in the OECD as a whole but at a slightly lower rate in the US and UK of about 60%. Between 1967 and 1975 the resources devoted to R and D for the area as a whole remained static. However, there was a redistribution within it with the real resources devoted to R and D in the US and UK declining and those of Germany and Japan increasing, with little change in France (OECD, 1979, p, 5).

But not all R and D expenditure represents the responses of firms to competition. A significant element in the overall picture is the role of the government. A high proportion of the total industrial R and D in some of the countries was financed by the government—56% in the US, 34% in the UK, 30% in France and 27% in Sweden in 1963–4 (see column 10 and 11 in Table 8.1), thus including the two highest-spending countries. Much of this was spent on nuclear, space and defence R and D. This is clearly quite outside the technological gap theory of innovation as being a response to market conditions. The question is whether this has 'spin offs' of innovations useful in other sectors. Or does it, as is sometimes argued, just compete with other R and D for scarce skilled manpower?

But neither R and D expenditure nor manpower is evenly distributed between different industries nor would you expect it to be. It is far more important for 'science based' industries than others. In its earliest report the OECD defined 'science based' or 'research intensive' industries as those 'based not on a once-and-for-all dose of technology, but for which a continuous stream of new products and processes is necessary in order to keep in the market'.

Measuring this by the ratio of R and D expenditure to sales or value added, in the ratio of employment on R and D to total employment, The OECD classified the industries as follows:

Science based	Mixed	Average	Non-Science based
Aircraft	Machinery	Non-ferrous metals	Textiles
Electronics	(non-electrical)	Ferrous metals	Paper
Drugs	Fabricated metal	Other transport	Food and drink
Electrical	products	equipment	Miscellaneous
machinery	Petroleum		
Chemicals			
Instruments			

The mixed industries included some very research-intensive sectors; Machinery (non-electrical) in particular included a very wide range of products (OECD, 1970, p. 123 & 135).

For the purposes of investigation, these often have to be aggregated, electrical with electronic and instruments, chemicals with drugs and petroleum, and the non-science based sector is split into chemical-linked industries, that is textiles, food, rubber, paper and pulp, and other.

The distribution of R and D expenditure over the years for the major countries is shown in Table 9.2. The proportion going to the electrical and electronic sector is a quarter or more for all countries

TABLE 9.2 Distribution of R and D Expenditure in Manufacturing (both Industry and Government financed).

		Electrical/ Electronic %	Chemical %	Machinery %	Air and Space %	Other Transport %	Basic Metals %	Chemical Linked %	Other Manufacturing %	Total Manufacturing %
United States	1963–4	24.8	13.0	8.0	38.3	8.9	2.6	2.5	1.9	100
	1967	24.4	11.8	11.8	35.8	8.6	2.6	2.7	2.3	100
	1975	21.8	14.6	18.7	24.4	10.4	3.2	3.6	3.3	100
United Kingdom	1964–5	24.5	14.4	8.4	29.0	7.3	8.7	6.7	4.0	100
	1967	24.1	14.7	11.8	25.3	8.5	5.0	6.7	3.9	100
	1975	26.0	19.7	7.9	23.9	8.6	3.8	7.1	3.0	100
Japan	1964	30.3	27.3	5.1	(1)	11.3	9.4	8.4	8.2	100
	1967	24.5	27.0	10.8	(1)	12.5	10.6	7.7	6.9	100
	1975	26.1	22.1	9.8	(1)	18.9	9.4	6.3	7.4	100
Germany	1964	31.2	34.7	19.6	(2)	(2)	8.4	4.7	1.4	100
	1967	25.9	28.5	16.2	5.0	12.6	8.4	2.1	1.3	100
	1975	29.9	29.1	13.9	9.5	11.6	3.1	2.0	0.9	100
France	1964	28.6	19.4	7.6	24.6	5.8	5.3	4.6	4.0	100
	1967	24.6	19.0	5.6	28.8	8.6	4.4	6.1	2.9	100
	1975	31.7	19.2	5.2	20.2	11.1	4.1	6.2	2.3	100

Notes: (1) Included in Other Transport.
(2) Included in Machinery.
Sources: OECD *Technical Change and Economic Policy* (Paris, OECD, 1980), p. 31 for 1967 and 1975 figures; OECD *Gaps in Technology Analytical Report* (Paris, OECD, 1970), p. 136 for 1964 figures.

and that going to chemical ranges between 12% and 35%. The greatest difference between the countries lies in the proportion going to air and space. This is almost entirely due to the US, UK and French governments directing towards it a very high proportion, 55% or more, of their expenditure on R and D. Government finance also accounted for a very high proportion of R and D. in the air and space sector—84% and 90% in the UK and US respectively in 1964 (OECD, 1968) and 82% for the UK in 1975 (CSO *Economic Trends* July 1979, p. 119).

Now let us consider how far this information contributes to an understanding of trade. We are looking at this from the point of view of the world as a whole. The problem in this case is that because the US is so large in terms of either GNP or labour force, it contributes a greater amount of resources to R & D than other countries for almost all industries. There appear to be only a few exceptions to this, for instance in 1963–4, both the UK and Japan had a similar or greater expenditure and employed more scientists on R & D in clothing than did the US (OECD, 1970, p. 290). Thus, in terms of innovation, the US may be expected to have an advantage in almost every branch of manufacturing. How far does this show up in trade?

The most systematic study of this was carried out by Gruber, Mehta and Vernon for the US in 1962 (Gruber, Mehta & Vernon, 1967). Listing the US industries in order of R & D expenditure as a percentage of sales, they obtained a group of five industries with the highest research effort by that measure, or by the proportion of scientists and engineers employed in R & D to total employment, which was similar to the later OECD group of science-based industries. Indeed, the US R & D effort was so concentrated that these industries accounted for 89% of US R & D in manufacturing and 85% of scientists and engineers engaged in it. These industries also had a higher than average proportion of exports to sales, that is, they were more export-oriented. This might just have indicated a greater degree of specialisation in international trade. But their high ratio of net exports to sales indicated that they were also more competitive; this was 5.2% compared with − 1.1% for the other industries indicating net imports for the latter.

Further investigation also showed that in the majority of companies, R and D was directed to new products. Thus, this study tended to confirm the technological gap theory.

However, in order to establish that this could be distinguished from the factor proportions theory, Gruber, Mehta and Vernon also investigated other associations. Thus, they discovered a high correlation between the number of scientists and engineers in production, in sales and in R & D activity, but no significant correlation with capital intensity measured in terms of depreciation or net fixed assets. Thus this study would tend to confirm and explain Leontieff's paradox. The US industries with the highest exports, and net exports, are not the most capital-intensive but those employing the highest proportion of skilled labour.

Can this type of study be applied to other countries carrying out R & D? In particular, how important for the world as a whole is technological gap trade? As can be seen from Tables 8.2 and 8.3, it is clear that the industrialised countries account for most of the exports and net exports of the science-intensive products. The OECD study, *Gaps in Technology,* found that in 1963–5 exports from research-intensive industries accounted for 39% of manufacturing exports from the ten major OECD countries (Belgium, Canada, France, Germany, Italy, Japan, Netherlands, Sweden, United Kingdom and the US) if aircraft and non-electrical machinery are included, and about 19.5% when these groups are excluded. It found that the countries carrying out most of the R & D, and responsible for most of the innovation, that is the US and to a lesser extent the UK and Germany, had a high proportion of the exports of science-based products. The US in particular dominated international trade in aircraft and missiles, providing more than half the total exports of the ten major OECD countries. She also accounted for 34% of their exports of instruments, 26% of their exports of pharmaceuticals, 27% of their exports of chemicals, and 25% of electrical machinery and also 31% of non-electrical machinery (OECD, 1970, p. 208).

But the UK only accounted for 12% of the exports of aircraft and missiles, 19% of pharmaceuticals, 13% of instruments and chemicals and 16% of non-electrical machinery. Germany accounted for almost a quarter of the exports of instruments and approximately 22% of that in pharmaceuticals and chemicals.

But to what extent do these percentages reflect competitive position and to what extent just the size of the country and openness to trade? This is best seen by comparing these percentages with the country's overall share of exports of manufactures which was 22.6% for the US, 13,2% for the UK and 18.1% for Germany.

By doing this we can see that the US does, indeed, export a relatively large amount of the product of science-based industries, confirming the Gruber, Mehta and Vernon study cited earlier.

Although the UK and Germany achieved prominence in the cateogores already mentioned, they also had a higher than proportional contribution to many of the mixed and average sectors; both had a relatively high proportion of exports of motor vehicles, non-electrical machinery and fabricated metal products.

Another feature of the situation was that although these innovating countries accounted for a relatively high proportion of exports of these science-intensive products, their exports of these were not increasing as fast as those of other OECD countries, most notably Canada, Italy and Japan.

These, together with many of the other European countries, did not produce many innovations but acquired the technology of the chief innovator, the US, very rapidly. This also applied in reverse. The result is that the technological gap itself did not appear to have much effect on trade in the mid-1960s. The innovating country might have a prominent position in international trade but only for a short while; the technology was rapidly acquired by the other industrial countries.

In many cases, this technology was directly transferred by the innovator carrying out direct investment in another country. This will be considered in the next chapter. Only in the case of Japan, which discouraged all foreign investment, was the technology transferred mainly by licences.

In the last decade the whole situation appears to have changed. The US no longer appears to have such a vast technological lead. In absolute terms, the industrial R and D expenditure for the US and UK was lower in 1975 than it was in 1967 and there were fewer scientists and engineers employed to do it. (OECD, 1979B). For the US this appears to be due to a reduction in goverment finance, for the UK it is due to a reduction in private finance. Indeed, in the UK industrial intra-mural expenditure on R & D fell by 13% between 1967 and 1975 at 1975 prices; the only sector for which there was no fall was chemicals.

But expenditure on industrial R and D was very much higher in Japan in the mid-1970s than before, having risen very fast up till 1971. It was also higher in France and Germany. The same applied to the employment of scientists and engineers.

Per capita income has been rising very slowly in the US market, and since 1973 there has been a tendency towards stagnation in all industrial countries.

Most multinational enterprises are now so broadly based that it is no longer a question of responding to a particular market, producing there, and then deciding whether to set up production elsewhere, but rather a question of where production should be set up in the first place.

Above all, the incentives to innovate have changed. The high cost of labour seemed to give way in the early 1970s to the statutory measures imposed by almost all industrialised countries to reduce pollution. These raised capital costs and direct costs and in some cases appeared to shift production from areas where the restrictions were most severe or the pollutant-absorbing capacity lowest—such as chemical production in the Ruhr—to other areas. But it is rather difficult to separate out this effect on, for instance, trade in chemicals from other factors (see Walters, 1975, particularly Tables 3.1 and 3.4).

But the greatest shock was provided by the rise in the price of oil in 1973 and the continuing efforts by OPEC producers to raise it ever since. The greatest incentive now lies in the saving of fuel. This generally involves altering the process of production, and is therefore less obvious in the market for goods, except in so far as fuel-saving technology is embodied in them. Indeed, a US survey suggests that whereas in 1971 only 12% of R and D expenditure went on new processes, by 1978, this had risen to 24% (OECD, 1980).

It will also be interesting to see how far US firms do respond to this, since government intervention in the form of excise duties on oil has been kept at much lower levels in the US than in Europe—hence the incentive to innovate should be lower.

As will be described in Chapter 14, this has already affected the market in cars. A competitive advantage of both Japanese and European producers has been their earlier adoption of small fuel-efficient cars. US producers have been very reluctant to introduce these arguing that they find them unprofitable. With the threat of a continuing rise in the price of oil they have had to acquire technology from abroad either by co-operation with Japanese firms or from their own European subsidiaries.

Electronics now appears to be the major area of technological innovation. The first computers were developed in the US and Britain with some co-operation between the two (OECD, 1970).

But US firms put computers into commercial production much more rapidly and continued to develop them. The market is now regarded as comprising three segments: firstly that of large main-frame computers, secondly that of smaller personal computers, and thirdly that of micro-computers regarded in Britain as those being sold for less than £500. There are a number of large US firms, but IBM is now 'supplier of more than half of all large computers in use world wide and now also a leader in personal computers' (*Financial Times,* 30 March 1984). Its position in Europe is reinforced by '16 European plants and research and development centres which employ 100,000 people, only a handful of whom are Americans' (*Financial Times*, 28 March 1984). It appears to have achieved its dominance as much by marketing expertise as by advances in technology. Its position has been reinforced by a lack of standardisation. With such a dominant position IBM sets *de facto* standards and other firms endeavour to produce compatible equipment but their position is completely undermined if IBM changes its standards without giving advance warning. Thus there is now a move by twelve European manufacturers.to achieve some 'open' communications standards with which all manufacturers would have to comply. This would make it easier for them to compete and would also benefit the users of the products.

Although recently in Europe 75% of personal computers were imported from the US, the position is somewhat different in the field of micro-computers, in which a number of UK firms notably Sinclair and Acorn have been very successful.

The Japanese have tended to trade in components rather than complete computers. They have, for instance two thirds of the world market in 64K D-rams standard memory chips (*Financial Times* 28 March 1984). They have a reputation for high quality and are able to exploit economies of scale. Many US and European firms are dubious about the profits to be gained from standard chips, but continue to manufacture them because of the technical experience they gain by doing so. European firms endeavour to specialise in the production of specialised or custom components.

But the growth area is not only in computers but also in the application of electronic technology to telecommunications, office machinery, machine tools, consumer durables and control and display equipment of all kinds. Europe apparently has a trade surplus in telecommunications equipment even though it has to import most of the microchips and computer peripherals (*Financial Times*, 15 February 1984).

But Japan has a very strong position in consumer electronic goods, that is, colour TVs and video recorders . Recently 90% of video recorders in Europe came from Japan (Hartley, forthcoming), and Japan's JVC has established the standard system for videos.

It is difficult to identify the overall trade pattern because there is so much trade in components, and computers and most electronic equipment is subsumed under the heading office and telecommunications equipment and this accounts for only 3.5% of world trade in 1982. But it is trade which has been growing rapidly; in 1982 the US exported $17.08 billion and imported $2.10 and the EEC exported $20.22 billion and imported $22.18 billion of office and telecommunications equipment. Thus Japan and the US are net exporters and the EEC is a net importer.

This has been a cause of concern to the Europeans, who are afraid of being squeezed between US and Japanese firms. The EEC in 1983, at the behest of Philips-Grundig and the French government for Thompson-Telefunken, negotiated with the Japanese MITI an import quota of 4.55 million video recorders a year for three years. There has also been a considerable discussion about the aid to be given for research and development expenditure within the EEC and the policy to be followed.

If further restrictions are placed on European subsidiaries of US firms by the US government to prevent sales of high technology products to Eastern Europe there will undoubtedly be an even greater demand for a separate European technological base.

10 International Direct Investment and Trade

Now let us consider the general relationship between investment and trade. Foreign investment is the flow of finance that is saving from one country to another. It is a lender's response to the higher expected return in the foreign country—expected, that is, after allowing for the greater risk generally associated with lending abroad. The risk may be default, or just of a low return, perhaps because of political disturbances, or just an unanticipated change in circumstances.

A foreign investor also faces the additional hazard of a change in the relative value of exchange rates. This is regarded as very important in the provision of short-term loans (for less than a year). But it is regarded as less important in the provision of long-term loans where there is no immediate prospect of repayment or indeed where repayment may never be required. We are here chiefly concerned with long-term lending.

In the past, flows of foreign investment have been very important to both lending and borrowing countries. For instance, it has been estimated that at the beginning of this century, Britain was on average investing abroad 7% of her national income. She was the main creditor country but most of the other Western European countries were also investing abroad. However, during the 1920s the US emerged as the largest foreign investor; from 1920–9 she was investing only 1% of her income but because she was much larger than the UK, it represented about two thirds of the world total of new international investment (OECD, 1981); Thomas, 1972; Dunning, 1964; Bureau of the Census, 1960).

Such a general and continuous outflow of investment represents a persistent deficit item in the balance of payments which is generally only partly balanced by the inflow of interest and dividends earned on it. If the exchange rate is fixed, the foreign investment outflow tends to lead to deficits which in the long run have to be corrected by deflationary domestic measures, or some suppression of domestic demand. With a flexible system, it will tend to depress the exchange rate. In both cases the result will be a reduction in imports and an increase in exports. Equilibrium will be achieved only when there is a surplus on the current account equal to the net outflow of foreign investment—that is, when a real transfer, a surplus in trade of real goods and services, has been achieved which is equal to the financial transfer. Thus, from a macroeconomic point of view, foreign investment will always affect trade.

However, a country may be able to continue investing abroad without making an equivalent real transfer if other countries are willing to hold her currrency. This they may be prepared to do if they consider it useful for international transactions and that it will retain its purchasing power. They may then be willing to accumulate it as a reserve currency. In order to do so, they must be running a surplus on their current account—that is, they may be making the real transfer. Much of Britain's investment at the end of last century and the beginning of this, and the US investment in the 1950s, was financed by this method. Other countries' accumulation of sterling or dollar balances represent respectively their short-term borrowing which financed much of their long-term lending. Indeed, France's dislike of the reserve currency role of the dollar was partly due to the willingness of Frenchmen to lend short term to the US while the US firms balanced this out by the acquisition of long-term assets in France, i.e. the productive and financial assets of firms or subsidiaries.

However, the balance of payments relationships also appear to work in reverse. That is, if a country is earning a continuous surplus on its current account, it may wish to encourage long-term investment abroad in order to avoid appreciating its currency. This has applied to a succession of countries in the post-war period—firstly the US in the days of the dollar shortage which existed from approximately 1945 to 1958, then Germany and Japan from 1960 to 1973 and intermittently since then. But the surpluses of the OPEC countries have been 'recycled', that is, lent short-term rather than used for long-term foreign investment.

The political hostility evoked by foreign investment is due more to direct investment which involves foreign ownership of real assets than to portfolio investment. Most of the investment carried out during the last century and up to the First World War was portfolio investment, much of which was in railways and public utilities. Direct investment was mainly confined to the plantation and mining industries. But after the First World War US manufacturing firms began to invest directly in Europe.

Direct investment was less adversely affected by the Great Depression of the 1930s than was portfolio investment, and after the Second World War it became much more important. It continued in the extractive industries particularly in the extraction, refinement and distribution of oil, but it was in manufacturing that the greatest increase occurred.

In this book we will confine ourselves to the relationship between direct investment and trade, as it is easier to relate them by kinds of product. For this purpose we need some breakdown of investment by industry and country. The US Department of Commerce provides such information for inward and outward investment for the US, and the Business Statistics Office provides some for the UK. The UN and OECD have also made considerable efforts to obtain comparable figures for other countries and these will be used and supplemented by information derived from other official and quasi-official sources.[1]

In considering the total position, a clear distinction should be drawn between the *flow* of direct investment as mentioned above, and as it appears in the capital account of a country's balance of payments, and the accumulated *stock* or *stake* of foreign investment.

FLOWS OF FOREIGN DIRECT INVESTMENT

The flow of foreign investment may be regarded as the response of firms to economic inducements existing at the time; it does not have to be positive; firms can sell off their holdings, or they can be nationalised.

The *flow* consists of two elements. Firstly there is the financial transfer from the parent company to its foreign subsidiary or affiliate;[2] in the US such an outflow is described as 'equity and inter company account outflows'. In the UK it is the sum of three items specified in the balance of payments as:
(1) change in branch indebtedness;
(2) net acquisition of share and loan capital;
(3) change in inter-company acounts.

Comparative information provided by the OECD suggests that by the early 1960s although the US accounted for by far the largest outflow with 60% of the total of the thirteen major countries, and the UK the second largest with 9%, Germany and France accounted for only 7% and Japan 2% the contribution of the latter three increased very rapidly so that by 1974–9, they contributed 17%, 8% and 13% respectively. The US share fell to 30% and the UK share remained unchanged (OECD, 1981, pp.12 and 13).

However, these figures exclude the other important element in the flow of foreign investment, namely the reinvested profits of the foreign subsidiary.[3] For both the US and the UK, these have represented a very important source of finance for expansion, particularly as both countries have at times imposed restrictions on financing from the home country, the US from 1968 to 1974, and the UK until 1979. Thus, for the US 'Reinvested earnings of incorporated affiliates' represented between 42% and 89% of funds for foreign direct investment between 1950 and 1979 (US Dept. of Commerce, *Survey of Current Business*, February 1981) and for the UK 'Unremitted profits of subsidiaries' have represented between 33% and 82% of funds since 1958 (CSO, *United Kingdom Balance of Payments*).

Most industrial countries have inward as well as outward flows of foreign direct investment although on balance they are contributors. The position for the US from 1950 to 1979 and for the UK from 1960–80 can be seen in Table 10.1. For the US the inward flow, although still much smaller, is increasing more rapidly than the outward flow.

The developing countries are generally recipients of foreign direct investment although to differing degrees. The net flow of

TABLE 10.1   *Flow of Direct Investment from and into the US and UK 1950–80.*

	1950	1960	1965	1970	1973	1979	1980
US $ million							
Outward[1]	1096	2941	5060	7589	11,353	23,948	18,546
Valuation adjustment	−8	−902	−66	−202	82	84	8163
Addition to US investment position abroad	1088	2039	4994	7387	11,435	24,033	26,709
Inward	80	141	410	1400	2537	11,877	10,854
Valuation adjustment						114	167
Addition to investment						11,991	11,021
UK £ million							
Outward (excl. oil)		155	308	546	1621	2788	2569
Inward (excl. oil)		14	197	363	734	1818	2094
Oil outward			154	151	415	2858	1364
Inward			67	259	382	1215	1714

Note: 1. Equity and inter-company account outflows and re-invested earnings of incorporated affiliates.

Sources: US Department of Commerce, *Survey of Current Business*, particularly February 1981 and August 1981; UK Central Statistical Office, *United Kingdom Balance of Payments*, 1981 edition and 1965–75, 1964; US Department of Commerce, Office of Business Economics, *Balance of Payments, Statistical Supplement* (1963).

direct investment from the industrial OECD to the developing countries rose from $3.69 billion in 1970 to $13.49 billion in 1979. Sixty percent of the latter was accounted for by the US and most of the rest by the UK, Japan and Germany. It did not rise continuously because of the nationalisation (disinvestment) of major companies' assets by certain oil-exporting countries (OECD *Development Co-operation 1980 Review*, pp. 85 & 163). How can we assess the effect of this flow of direct investment on trade? Generally this is approached in two ways, either by considering its effect on the macroeconomic position of those countries undertaking it, or by ignoring the macroeconomic implications and just considering the effect of such investment on the location of production. The analyses of industrial economists and technological-gap theorists is an example of the latter. But let us begin by considering the former approach as exemplified by the studies carried out for the two major foreign investors, the US and UK.

US AND UK BALANCE OF PAYMENTS STUDIES

As mentioned in Chapter 3, all types of investment flows abroad appear as negative items in the balance of payments. Therefore they can be regarded as putting some pressure on it. Under a fixed exchange-rate system, the country may have to pursue more deflationary policies than it would do otherwise to maintain equilibrium. Under a flexible exchange-rate system, actual flows of investment may be expected to lower the exchange rate. To set against this is the subsequent inward flow of interest and dividends appearing in the current account which has the reverse effect.

Private foreign direct investment which involves the acquisition of real assets is only a proportion of all investment flows. Nevertheless, it was concern with the US and UK balance of payments in the 1960s that led to these two reports:

Hufbauer, G.C. and Adler, F.M., *Overseas Manufacturing Investment and the Balance of Payments,* Tax Policy research Study No. 1 (US Treasury Dept., Washington, DC, 1968) and

Reddaway, W.B. *et al.*, *Effects of UK Direct Investment Overseas: An Interim Report*, and *Final Report* (University of Cambridge, Dept. of Applied Economics, Occasional Paper No. 12 (CUP, 1967) and Occasional Paper No. 15 (CUP, 1968).

Before discussing these reports it is appropriate to emphasise the difficulty in calculating the effect of any economic phenomenon. In order to do so you must make some assumptions about what would have happened in its absence, and the results themselves will entirely depend on these assumptions. Nowhere is this more obvious than in the investigation of investment.

Firstly there is the question of the alternatives to such foreign investment. Hufbauer and Adler set the scene by distinguishing three types of possibility.

Under *Classical substitution* assumptions, direct investment completely supplements host country investment and completely replaces home investment ... therefore the act of foreign investment creates plant capacity in the host country which otherwise would *never have existed*, and at the same time *permanently deprives* the home country of that plant capacity. For example, under the classical assumptions, when IBM invests $50 milllion in France, total French investment goes up by $50 million, while total American investment goes down by $50 million.

Under *reverse classical assumptions*, direct investment fully substitutes for foreign investment but does not affect home outlays. Thus, the act of foreign investment makes *no net addition* to plant capacity abroad, *nor does it deprive* the home country of capacity would which otherwise exist. . . .

Under either the classical or reverse classical assumptions, international capital flows do not affect the *total world volume* of investment. They merely affect the location of expenditure. By contrast, *anticlassical* assumptions imply that international investment increases world capital formation. Under the anticlassical formulation no substitution takes place abroad or at home. Foreign investment thus *increases* plant capacity abroad, but *does not decrease* capacity at home. When IBM invests in France, total French investment goes up by $50 million, while American investment is unchanged. World capital formation thus goes up by $50 million.

(Hufbauer & Adler, 1968, pp. 6 & 7, authors' italics)

In most theoretical work, the classical assumption is made. It is also implicitly made in most criticisms of the foreign investment of national firms.

A firm's defence is generally based on a reverse classical assumption; it generally argues that its foreign investment was defensive; if it had not located production in the foreign country, some other firm would have done so. The reverse classical assumption must also be regarded as more consistent with the governments of both donating and recipient countries following Keynesian policies to maintain full employment. If, for instance, the firm investing abroad reduces investment at home, the government either increases the incentives for other firms to invest or carries out more investment itself. The increased investment in the recipient country, on the other hand, leads to its government introducing measures to cut aggregate demand which leads to a reduction in other forms of investment.

The efforts by the governments of developing countries to encourage foreign firms to invest certainly suggest that they regard this as an addition to their total level of investment. The question of whether it is at the cost of investment in the home country or not is a matter of debate.

As the US was such a large foreign investor, its influence on the level of activity in the rest of the world could not be ignored. So Hufbauer and Adler calculated the apparent effect of the investment under the different assumptions and thus obtained a whole array of results—this makes for difficult reading.

However, Reddaway just selected one set of assumptions which were plausible for Britain who accounted for a smaller proportion of foreign investment. He assumed that home investment would only be reduced in the social, or non-industrial spheres and thus would not appreciably affect the long-term growth of the British economy. The investment abroad did not affect the overall level of investment there because if a British firm had not invested there, some other country would have done so. British investment just meant that the foreign productive assets were owned by Britain rather than some other country. These assumptions appear to be close to the reverse classical one.

Both reports eschewed an all or nothing approach and just considered the effect of any marginal change in investment. For this purpose Hufbauer and Adler used existing data for US manufacturing firms for the period 1961–2 to 1964–5. In contrast, Reddaway carried out an actual survey of British firms for the longer period 1955–64 and in his final report considered not only manufacturing but also mining and plantations.

Both reports distinguished the *initial effects* of foreign investment from the continuing effect. The *initial effect* was due to the actual investment itself and the resulting expenditure on plant and equipment. The Hufbauer and Adler report showed that 27% of plant and equipment expenditure by manufacturing subsidiaries was spent on capital goods imports from the US (Hufbauer and Adler, 1968, Table 3.3, p. 22). Whereas the Reddaway report showed that the overseas subsidiaries of British firms purchased 14% of their capital goods from Britain (15% for manufacturing, 7% mining, 27% plantations) (Reddaway Final Report, Table X.I).

In so far as the foreign investment represents an increase in total investment abroad—that is, the classical or anticlassical assumptions apply—these figures represent the impact of foreign investment on sales of capital goods by the home country.

But if the reverse classical assumption applies, as assumed in the Reddaway report, such that British foreign investment implies ownership but no addition to investment in the recipient country, the relevant question is how much difference this ownership makes to sale of British capital goods. The Reddaway report suggested that the ownership preference was large, that is 75%, so that an increase of £100 of operating assets by a UK subsidiary resulted in an increase in imports of capital goods from the UK of £10 if it were in manufacturing, £6 if it were in mining, and £8 if it were a plantation (see Table 10.2). On adjusting to a replacement cost basis, he obtained a figure for manufacturing of 11%.

For the US, the ownership preference appears to be smaller, as an indigenous firm would have spent 23.8% of its plant and equipment expenditure on US goods (Hufbauer & Adler, 1968 Table 3.5). Therefore , if the reverse classical assumption is applied to US foreign investment, it scarcely leads to any increase in sales of US capital goods.

An additional complication is that by providing £100 of productive assets. Reddaway discovered that on average £100 worth of finance from the British parent company was associated with an additional £67 of finance from elsewhere. This immediately raises the ownership effect of investment on imports of capital goods from the UK to 18% (Reddaway Final Report 1968, p. 234).

The effect of foreign investment of exports of capital goods is important as showing part of the associated real transfer. But, of course, the real transfer need not be of capital goods; it may be achieved by any current account surplus of the lending country which, for instance, the US had for almost the whole of the period until the 1970s.

However, the US current account was not enough to cover its total net long-term capital expenditure which included government loans and private portfolio investment. For most of the period the US, like Britain, was borrowing on its short-term capital account, which took the form of other countries accumulating additional dollar and sterling liabilities. The UK has also had recourse to IMF loans, in particular in 1964–5 when it borrowed £857 million. This borrowing short and lending long is profitable so long as the return in the form of interest, dividends and capital appreciation on the foreign investment is greater than the cost of borrowing. This cost could be regarded as the interest paid on these currrency liabilities. However, Reddaway took the marginal cost of short-term borrowing for the UK as the rate of interest the IMF charged on loans, that is 3%.

The interest paid on the borrowing required to bridge the gap

TABLE 10.2 Effect of UK Overseas Direct Investment on her Exports — Comparison with US 1955-64.

	Increase in Net Operating Assets of £100[2]				Data for Sample			Inputs purchased from UK as % of output of subsidiaries	
	Initial Effect	Continuing Effect Additional £p.a.			Net Operating Assets av. 1955-63 £ million	% Increase 1955-69	UK group's stake av. 1955-63 1 million	1955	1964
		Total	Inputs	Finished goods					
UK									
Building materials	16	0	+6.9	-7.2	66.1	120.3	57.2	9.6	7.7
Food, drink, tobacco	7	0	+1.4	-1.2	514.4	48.2	447.2	0.8	0.9
Chemicals	15	-2	+2.4	-4.3	171.9	108.1	128.2	2.9	3.3
Textiles	20	-1	+3.7	-4.9	87.3	53.0	77.6	2.0	6.7
Metals and metal products	10	0	3.2	-3.4	169.8	230.4	96.5	1.2	2.4
Non-electrical engineering	11	+17	13.0	+4.2	21.2	79.3	18.0	22.3	4.4
Electrical engineering	3	+3	6.9	-3.6	60.7	90.3	48.7	3.7	2.8
Vehicles and components	21	+10	13.5	-3.2	114.1	120.0	90.1	11.8	15.4
Paper	1	0	0.1	-0.1	137.7	182.5	69.2	0.2	0.2
Total Manufacturing	10	+1	+3.7	-2.5	1343.2	93.0	1032.8	2.9	3.4
Adjusted	11[1]								
Mining	6	+1	0.8	0.0	116.5	227.2	89.3		
Plantations	18	0	0.1	0.0	95.3	25.5	92.7		
Total (excl. oil)	9	+1	3.1	-2.1	1550.0	96.1	1214.8		
Oil							918.9		
USA[1] Reverse Classical Manufacturing		3.5	0.5	+3.0					
USA Classical or Anticlassical Manufacturing	-55	-50	+5	-55					

Industries are arranged in descending order of profitability as measured by pre-tax profits (after depreciation) in relation to net operating assets.

Notes: 1. Adjusted on a replacement cost basis.
2. Estimated from information derived from 15 specified countries.

Source: W. B. Reddaway, S. J. Potter, and C. T. Taylor, *The Effects of UK Direct Investment Overseas Final Report*, University of Cambridge, Department of Applied Economics, Occasional Papers 15 (CUP, Cambridge, 1968), Table IV.1 p. 355; IV.2 and IV.3 p. 356; XI p. 370; XII.1 p. 371; XXII.6 p. 300.

between the outward financial transfer and the real transfer then became an element in the continuing effect.

THE CONTINUING EFFECT

The continuing effect of foreign direct investment shows up in the current account. Against the negative item of the interest paid for borrowing short-term must be set the profit on the investment (after tax by the host country) plus the capital appreciation of the investment.

But it is the continuing effect on trade that we are concerned with here. The reports assumed that the US and UK manufacturing firms set up foreign subsidiaries to produce the same type of goods as the parent. This accords with most of their empirical evidence, and also investigations into the technological gap theory cited in the previous chapter.

As can be seen from Table 10.2, derived from the Reddaway report, the effect on trade appeared to vary considerably between industries. Overseas investment in all except electrical engineering involved a reduction in exports of finished goods from the UK. It also always involved an increase in exports of inputs by the UK but the figure was relatively high for non-electrical engineering, and vehicles and components. The ratio of inputs from the UK in relation to the output of subsidiaries of UK manufacturing firms is also shown in the last two columns. Over the period 1955 to 1964 it rose for vehicles and components, textiles, chemicals, metals and metal products, but declined for the others.

From these figures Reddaway calculated that for manufacturing as a whole for every £100 of additional net operating assets of foreign subsidiaries of manufacturing firms, there would be a reduction in exports of finished goods from Britain of £$2\frac{1}{2}$. There would also be an increase in exports of components of £$3\frac{1}{2}$. This would represent an improvement in Britain's trade account of £1.

However, Hufbauer and Adler found that under the same assumptions, with $100 worth of additional net operating assets held abroad by the US her exports of finished goods went up by $3 and exports of components went up by $$\frac{1}{2}$. Their explanation was that:

Under reverse classical assumptions, US subsidiary firm sales replace an equal volume of native firm sales. Since native sales ordinarily displace more exports than subsidiary sales ... it follows that the net effect of overseas investment is, on this count, generally beneficial.

(Hufbauer & Adler, p. 46)

In contrast, under the classical or anticlassical assumptions, exports of finished goods from the US would fall by $5 and exports of components increase by $5 (see Table 10.2).

To conclude, these reports suggest that the effect of US and UK flows of foreign direct investment would be to provide a simultaneous increase in the demand for capital goods from the home countries but not by nearly as much as the capital flow. Also, over the long run it would generally have the effect of reducing the home country's exports of finished goods and increasing its exports of components. However, the calculations of the continuing trade effect are very sensitive to the assumptions made about the macroeconomic effect of the investment.

There have been studies of the effect of direct investment on other countries but they are rarely so comprehensive or explicit about the assumptions underlying them.

Furthermore, this type of exercise has never been repeated for the US and UK. Perhaps a reason for this is the movement from fixed to flexible exchange rates since 1971 which would make it much more difficult.

It is also no longer so easy to see the relationship between financial flows and productive capacity. Many very large multinational companies have emerged and they are being operated on a worldwide basis rather than just from the home country. Furthermore, whereas the US firms initially aimed at owning all the equity of their subsidiaries, increasingly they are now participating in various co-ownership schemes. Before 1951, 58% of the overseas manufacturing affiliates of US firms were wholly owned but by the mid-1970s this had fallen to 44%, whereas the proportion of minority-owned affiliates had risen from 11% to 28% over the same period. For European corporations with only 39% of wholly owned manufacturing affiliates before 1951, the proportion had fallen even lower to 19% by the late 1960s, with the minority owned rising from 10% to 42% over the period (OECD, 1981, Table 13, p. 50).

Thus, a change in the financial flow from the parent company may just lead to a change in branch indebtedness without any change in productive capacity. It therefore becomes extremely difficult to relate financial flows to exports of capital equipment. Nevertheless, the influence of direct investment should be remembered when investigating the trade flows of capital equipment.

Recent studies have entirely ignored the macroeconomic effects of foreign investment. Studies of foreign direct investment then just become studies of the firms undertaking it. These firms are regarded as having the nationality of the country in which they are registered for tax purposes, which is generally their country of origin and that in which they have their head office. So the foreign direct investment of, say, the US is equal to the financial transfers of US firms abroad to acquire or build up foreign subsidiaries.

Viewed in this way, a firm's decision to invest abroad is just a decision on the location of production. Partly because of the preceding arguments, but also because of the nature of the statistics available, it is easier to examine the situation in terms of stocks of investment and their changes over time than to look at flows.

STOCK OF FOREIGN INVESTMENT

The *stock* of foreign investment, or stake abroad, is the result of past *flows*. Generally, the figures are given as book values. Thus, given the stock of foreign investment held by the US at the end of 1978 of $16,784 billion you would expect the stock the next year to be equal to it plus 1979 'Equity and intercompany outflows' of $594 billion and the 'Reinvested earning of incorporated affiliates' of $184 billion. However, there is generally a valuation adjustment. This is due to the difference between the book value of an asset and the price paid for it or obtained by selling or liquidating it. Generally it is small, but if foreign assets are nationalised without complete compensation, it may be large. It may also include an element of revaluation. This is particularly important for mining companies, the value of whose assets varies with the price of the mineral produced.

Clearly, in so far as the distribution or the *flow* of foreign investment between industries is different from the distribution of the *stock* the latter will change over time. But the distribution between industries is often easier to obtain in terms of the foreign *stake* or *stock* of direct investment than in terms of the addition to that stock. Moreover, the *stock* position provides a better idea of foreign interests and control.

Let us now turn to consider some of the information available on the foreign stake of OECD industrial countries. This, as can be seen from Table 10.3, can be obtained for the major industrial countries between 1967 and 1976 and for the US and UK for earlier and later periods. These stakes are measures in current dollars and thus, because of inflation, the apparent monetary increase is much greater than the real increase. It is more meaningful to consider the relative position and relative changes. The US has by far the largest stake and even as late as 1976 accounted for about half the total

TABLE 10.3   *Stock of Direct Investment Abroad of Developed Market*
                Economies.
                Billion Dollars End of Year

	1950	1960	1967	1971	1973	1976	1980
United States	11.8	32.8	56.6	82.8	101.3	137.2	213.5
United Kingdom		12.0	17.5	23.7	26.9	32.1	
Germany		0.8	3.0	7.3	11.9	19.9	
Japan		0.3	1.5	4.4	10.3	19.4	
Switzerland			5.0	9.5	11.1	18.6	
France			6.0	7.3	8.8	11.9	
Canada			3.7	6.5	7.8	11.1	
Netherlands			2.2	4.0	5.5	9.8	
Sweden			1.7	2.4	.3.0	5.0	
Belgium, Luxembourg			2.0	2.4	2.7	3.6	
Italy			2.1	3.0	3.2	2.9	
Total of above			101.3	153.3	192.5	270.4	
All other (estimate)			4.0	5.1	6.3	16.8	
Grand Total			105.3	158.4	198.8	287.2	

Sources: OECD, *International Investment and Multinational Enterprises*, (OECD,
   Paris, 1981), Table 2, p. 39 for years 1967–76; UN, *Multinational
   Corporations in World Development*, ST/ECA/190 (UN, Department of
   Economic and Social Affairs, New York, 1973), Table 10 for 1960; US,
   Department of Commerce, *Survey of Current Business*, February and
   August 1981, for US in 1950 and 1980.

stock of foreign investment. The UK, with 11% of the total, was
the next largest holder. However, although Germany and Japan
had insignificant stakes in 1960, they added to them so fast by 1976
they each accounted for 7% of the total. In particular, whereas the
German and Japanese direct investment stakes were very small in
relation to that of the US and UK in 1960, by 1976 they represented
60% of the UK's and 14% of that of the US.

Now let us consider the distribution of these assets between
industries. In 1950, 28.8% of the overall stake of the US was held
in petroleum and 9.6% in mining (see Table 10.4a and b) By 1966,
this proportion had declined slightly to 26.8% and 7.7%. The UK
also appears to have held a high proportion of its assets in the
extractive industries. The UN figures show 22.9% in petroleum,
and 4.5% in mining and smelting in 1965. The combined US and UK
stake amounted to $25 billion in petroleum and $4.8 in mining, a
dominating stake in both these industries. Over the years, the proportion of its assets that the US has had in petroleum has declined.
This is mainly the result of nationalisation—Tanzer calculated that
'from 1956 to 1972 the multinational mining firms had 20% of their
foreign assets expropriated' (Tanzer, 1980). Since 1973 OPEC has
carried out a further series of nationalisations. Thus the pattern of

TABLE 10.4a Stock of Foreign Direct Investment held by OECD Industrial Countries in Industrial Market Economies (Ind. ME) and Developing Countries (Dev.) by Industry.
$ Billion

Holding Country	1950			1966			1971			Late 1970s		
	World	Ind. ME	Dev.	World	Ind. ME	Dev.	World	Ind. ME	Dev.	World	Ind. ME	Dev.
World (excl. CPE)												
Total	11.8			89.6	59.6	30.0						
Manufacturing	3.8			36.2	28.2	8.0						
Petroleum	3.4			25.9	14.1	11.9						
Mining & smelting	1.1 }			5.9	3.1	2.8						
Other	3.4 }			21.5	14.2	7.2						
United States[1]										1979		
Total		5.7	5.7	51.8	35.3	13.9	82.8	56.9	20.7	186.8	138.7	44.5
Manufacturing		3.0	0.8	20.7	17.2	3.5	34.4	28.3	6.0	78.6	63.5	15.1
Petroleum		1.0	2.2	13.9	7.7	5.1	21.8	12.5	7.0	38.7	30.2	6.1
Mining & smelting		1.1 }		4.0 }								
Other		1.7 }	2.7 }	13.2 }	10.4	5.3	26.6	16.1	7.7 }	69.4	44.9	23.3
United Kingdom[2]										1978		
Total (incl. oil & banks)				(16.8) [2]						50.9	41.2	10.5
Manufacturing				5.9 (5.9)	4.5	4.1	10.0	8.2	1.8	24.8	20.2	4.6
Petroleum				(3.9)			7.0	4.3	2.7			
Mining & smelting				5.9 (0.8) }	3.4	2.5 }	17.0	12.5	4.5	1.7 }	1.6	0.2
Other				(6.3) }						12.8	9.1	3.7
Total (excl. oil, banks & insurance)				11.8	7.9	3.9				39.2	30.7	8.5

Table 10.4a (continued)

Holding Country	1950			1966			1971			Late 1970s		
	World	Ind. ME	Dev.	World	Ind. ME	Dev.	World	Ind. ME	Dev.	World	Ind. ME	Dev.
Germany[3]										1976		
Total							6.8	4.9	1.9	18.7	13.0	5.6
Manufacturing							5.2	3.8	1.4	12.9	9.4	3.4
Petroleum							0.2	0.1	0.1	0.9	0.6	0.3
Mining & smelting							0.3	0.2	0.0	0.3	0.2	0.0
Other							1.3	0.8	0.5	4.8	3.0	1.8
Japan										1976		
Total							3.6	1.8	1.8	15.9	7.3	8.1
Manufacturing							1.0	0.3	0.6	5.2	3.8	1.4
Petroleum							} 1.1	0.4	0.7	4.5	1.6	2.5
Mining & smelting												
Other							1.5	1.1	0.4	6.2	4.3	1.8

TABLE 10.4b Stock of Foreign Direct Investment held by OECD Industrial Countries in Industrial Market Economies (Ind. ME) and Developing Countries (Dev.) by Industry.
% distribution for each country, and for the world in 1966

Holding Country	1950 World	1950 Ind. ME	1950 Dev.	1966 World	1966 Ind. ME	1966 Dev.	1971 World	1971 Ind. ME	1971 Dev.	Late 1970s World	Late 1970s Ind. ME	Late 1970s Dev.
World (excl. CPE)												
Total				100.0	66.5	33.5						
Manufacturing				40.5	31.5	9.0						
Petroleum				29.0	15.7	13.3						
Mining & smelting				6.6	3.5	3.1						
Other				24.0	15.9	8.1						
United States[1]												
Total	100.0	48.3	48.7	100.0	68.1	26.8	100.0	68.8	25.0	100.0	74.2	23.8
Manufacturing	32.5	25.4	7.2	40.0	33.2	6.8	41.5	34.2	7.3	42.1	34.0	8.1
Petroleum	28.8	8.5	18.4	26.8	14.8	9.8	26.3	15.2	8.5	20.7	16.2	3.3
Mining & smelting	9.6 ⎱			7.7 ⎱								
Other	29.2 ⎰	14.4	23.1	25.4 ⎰	20.1	10.2 ⎱	32.1	19.4	9.2	37.1	24.1	12.5
				2)						1978		
United Kingdom												
Total (incl. oil & banks)				(100.0)						100.0		
Manufacturing				(35.1)						48.8	39.7	9.1
Petroleum				(22.9)								
Mining & smelting				(4.5)						3.3		0.5
Other				(37.4)						25.1		7.2

Table 10.4b (continued)

Holding Country	1950 World	1950 Ind. ME	1950 Dev.	1966 World	1966 Ind. ME	1966 Dev.	1971 World	1971 Ind. ME	1971 Dev.	Late 1970s World	Late 1970s Ind. ME	Late 1970s Dev.
Germany											1976	
Total							100.0	71.9	28.0	100.0	69.7	30.2
Manufacturing							75.8	55.3	20.4	68.9	50.5	18.5
Petroleum							3.0	2.0	1.0	4.9	3.1	1.8
Mining & smelting							3.9	3.4	0.5	1.6	1.3	0.3
Other							17.4	11.2	6.2	24.5	14.9	9.6
Japan											1976	
Total							100.0	50.9	49.1	100.0	45.9	50.9
Manufacturing							26.8	9.1	17.7	32.4	8.8	23.6
Petroleum							} 31.3	10.7	20.7	28.4	10.1	15.7
Mining & smelting												
Other							41.9	31.2	10.7	39.2	27.0	11.3

Notes: 1. International and unallocated to different regions

	1950	1979	1981
Total	356	6880	5091
Petroleum	240	2502	
Other	116	4378	

2. Bracketed figures from UN 1973 ST/ECA/190.

3. Exchange rate $/£ end 1965, 2.8; end 1971, 2.5522; end 1978, 2.0410; $/DM 1976 0.3974, 1971 $/DM 0.2877.

Sources: US Department of Commerce, *Survey of Current Business*, February 1981, 'U.S. Direct Investment Abroad in 1980'; 'Trends in the US Direct Investment Position Abroad 1950–79' and August 1981, 'U.S. Direct Investment Abroad in 1980'; UK Business Statistics Office MA4 Business Monitor 1978 Supplement, *Census of Overseas Assets 1978*; Germany & Japan OECD *International Investment and Multinational Enterprises Recent International Direct Investment Trends* (OECD, Paris 1981).
World 1966, UN *Multinational Corporations in World Development* (UN, New York 1973) ST/ECA/190.

this investment in extractive industries has changed. In 1950, 64% of the US investment stake in petroleum was held in developing countries. But by 1979, this had fallen to 16%; the industrialised countries now account for most of its foreign assets in oil. The impact of these changes on developing countries can be shown in another way. Let us consider the foreign assets of the US held by industry and also in industrialised and developing countries as a percentage of the total foreign direct investment stake. In 1950, the US appears to have held roughly equal amounts of assets in industrialised and developing countries (see Table 10.4b). (The reason the percentages do not add up to 100 is because of a small unallocated percentage.) But most of the assets in industrialised countries were held in manufacturing, whereas most of the assets in developing countries were held in petroleum, mining and smelting and other. As the US reduced the proportion of its investment stake in these extractive industries in developing countries, and increased it in the industrial countries, the overall distribution of investment changed so that by 1979 three quarters of its overseas stake was in industrialised countries and only 24% in developing countries. This change occurred even though the US marginally increased the proportion of its total assets held in manufacturing in developing countries. It increased its relative investment stake in manufacturing in industrialised countries to an even greater extent but most of this increase had taken place by 1966.

The information available (see Table 10.4a and b) suggests that the UK and German pattern of foreign direct investment is similar to that of the US. But Japan holds half her overseas assets in developing countries and has a higher proportion of both manufacturing assets and extractive industry assets in developing as compared with industrial countries.

In view of the fact that a firm's degree of control is often very much greater than its actual stake, it is also worth considering the total assets of its affiliates. These are available for both the US and UK.

In 1977, the total foreign stake in the US[4] abroad was equal to $149,848 million which was held in affiliates which had total assets of $490,178 milllion, approximately three times as great. The UK 1978 foreign stake of £24,914 million consisted mainly of a stake of £15,893 million in subsidiaries, whose assets in total were equal to £39,237 million and £673 million in overseas branches, which had total assets of £2267 million.

Thus, if the total assets of foreign subsidiaries are regarded as areas of control, the US and UK companies were in a much stronger position than the foreign stake alone would suggest.

If we just limit ourselves to a consideration of the location of production, in what way would we expect this to affect trade? Here we must draw a distinction between firms in the extractive industries for minerals or fuel and manufacturing firms.

EXTRACTIVE INDUSTRIES

One of the ironies in the position of developing countries is that the primary products in which they are dominant in international trade are fuels and minerals, and it is in the extraction of these that they are so dependent on foreign direct investment.

These industries comprise some of the largest firms in the world, whether size is measured in terms of assets or sales. They grew up to supply the metropolitan power to which they belong with raw materials and fuels, but now they generally work on a multinational basis. The largest in terms of sales values in 1972 are listed in Table 10.5.

They are all oil companies, Indeed, we will here be chiefly concerned with the multinational oil companies which have accounted for the largest flow of international direct investment.

The oil industry originated in the US where oil was first drilled in 1859. Expansion was rapid but one company, Standard Oil, was built up by John D. Rockefeller to be the dominant buyer of oil and seller of refined products. Then in 1911 this company was broken up into thirty separate companies on a geographical basis by a Supreme Court ruling on anti-trust legislation. Three of these Exxon (previously Standard Oil of New Jersey), Mobil (previously Standard Oil of New York) and Chevron (previously Standard Oil of California) then expanded rapidly outside as well as inside the US so that by 1950 they were among the seven largest oil multinationals in the World. Exxon was, indeed, the largest. The others were the US firms Gulf Oil with headquarters in Pittsburgh, Texaco from Texas, Royal Dutch Shell (60% Dutch, 40% British) and British Petroleum (BP, formerly Anglo-Iranian). These are called the seven 'major' or 'seven sisters'. They have accounted for most of the international direct investment, which in turn has determined the location of production and thus trade.

However, the direction of this investment appeared initially to have depended as much on strategic and political factors as economic ones. For as the other metropolitan powers began to appreciate the uses and value of oil they encouraged their nationals to develop sources over which they could exert some political control. Initially, the Russian oil industry, centred in Baku near the

TABLE 10.5   The Largest Oil Companies.
$ million

	Nationality of	1972		1981		1982 Net profit[1]
		Sales	Assets	Sales	Assets	
Exxon	US	20,310	21,558	108,108	62,931	4990
Royal Dutch Shell	Neth./Brit	14,060	20,067	82,292	65,256	1990
Mobil	US	9166	9217	64,488	34,776	1500
Texaco	US	8693	12,032	57,628	27,489	1230
Gulf Oil	US	6243	9324	28,252	20,429	978
Socal (Chevron)	US	5829	8084	42,224	23,680	1590
British Petroleum	Britain	5712	8161	52,200	49,950	2300
Standard Oil (Indiana)	US	4503	6186	29,947	22,916	
Shell Oil (Houston)	US	4076	5172	21,629	20,118	
Conoco (Continental Oil)	US	3415	3250			
Arco (Atlantic Richfield)	US	3321	4629	27,797	19,733	
Tennaco	US	3275	4838	15,462	16,808	
Cie Française des Pétroles	France	2806	3926	22,784	13,983	
ENI	Italy	2748	7089	29,444	22,134	
Elf-Aquitaine	France	2896	3693	19,666	21,114	

Source: Fortune 1973 and 1982.
Note: 1. Financial Times, March, 1984. Gulf Oil likely to be merged with Socal.

Black Sea, provided some counter balance to US influence. But the Russian revolution resulted in Russia temporarily withdrawing from the international market.

The most fruitful area of search appeared to be the decaying Ottoman empire. The British government encouraged the six-year search for oil in Iran by William Knox D'Arcy, founder of British Petroleum, and Burmah Oil. When oil was found in 1908, the Anglo-Persion Oil Company (renamed in 1935 the Anglo-Iranian Oil Company) was formed. But by 1913 no oil had been sold because a pipeline and refinery were required. So in 1914 the British government took up £2 million of shares and just over half the voting rights.

In 1923 the French government also encouraged the formation of a company later called the Compagnie Française des Pétroles (CFP). It acquired a concession in Iraq where it discovered oil in 1927. In 1929 the French government took a 35% direct equity stake in it with 40% of the voting rights.

In the 1920s, the US companies began to show increasing interest in the Middle East because they feared their reserves were running out. This diminished as more reserves were found in Texas and

Latin America. Oil had been discovered in Mexico at the beginning of the century and in Venezuela in 1922. Shell and Esso were the companies most actively involved in Latin America. But all the major companies were constantly searching and prospecting for new and workable deposits. When a company discovered one it generally bought the concession from the owner and paid a royalty to him of $12\frac{1}{2}\%$ for every barrel of oil lifted. Frequently there was competition between the companies to gain the initial permission to prospect, and then later to gain the concession. This sometimes raised the price of the concession but there was always a high degree of uncertainty as to its value. Nevertheless, many of the concessions in the Middle East and North Africa, and even in the US, appear to have been acquired very cheaply. There also appears to have been an agreement between the British, French, and US governments not to compete for concessions (Tugendhat and Hamilton, 1975. p. 84) within the former Ottoman empire.

The situation at the outbreak of the second World War was that the US was the chief producer and consumer of oil and during the war kept Europe supplied. Oil was also being produced in Mexico but she nationalised her subsidiaries of the major companies in 1938 and they rapidly transferred their activities to Venezuela. In response to the exigencies of the war, Venezuelan production and exports were rapidly increased during the 1940s and she became and remained the largest exporter until 1970.

In the Middle east BP, then called Anglo-Iranian, was producing and exporting oil from Iran, and the CFP from Iraq, but production in the latter was disrupted by the onset of war. Deposits had also been discovered in Kuwait where Anglo-Iranian and Gulf Oil had a 50:50 concession, but they had not been brought fully into production.

After the war, as described in Chapter 12, there was a very rapid expansion in the demand for fuel as countries rebuilt their shattered industries. But the European countries and Japan had great difficulty in increasing their production of coal and these countries rapidly transferred to oil which appeared in plentiful supply.

This was because of the big seven's rapid expansion of investment in the Middle East, particularly in Iran, Iraq, Kuwait and Saudi Arabia, at first limited only by the political influence of the in metropolitan power; for instance the US reserved Saudi Arabia for a consortium of US companies, ARAMCO. The primary incentive for such investment was the lower cost of the new fields.

Adelman distinguishes three costs: finding costs of surveying and prospecting, development costs of establishing the drilling rigs and pipelines, etc., and operating costs of actually lifting the oil (Adelman, 1972). The operating costs of a field tend to increase as oil is extracted from it thus providing a continual incentive to invest in finding costs. But, a particular feature of the post-war period was that the development cost per barrel (discounted to the present period) plus the operating costs per barrel, were considerably lower in the newer territories than in the US (see Table 10.6). The cost per barrel in the US was 1.22 dollars from 1960–63. It was 38% of this in Venezuela in the late 1960s and just over a tenth of this in Libya and Nigeria. It was lowest of all in the Middle East where it barely amounted to 10 cents in the late 1960s, that is less than a tenth of the US cost. In other words, the supply schedule for oil had shifted outwards. Furthermore, most of the benefit of the lower costs were going to the oil companies as profit, because the royalties and taxes paid to the governments of the oil-producing countries were comparatively low.

The major companies were still co-operating according to their Achnacarry Agreement of 1928. This was a cartel agreement which covered the whole world outside the US and USSR.

Thus, in accordance with its provisions they were not trespassing on each other's territory and they were making their transport

TABLE 10.6   Cost per Barrel of Oil.
$ per barrel

	Development	Operating (including pipelines)	Total
United States 1960–3	1.048	0.168	1.22
Venezuela 1966–8	0.351	0.101	0.462
Africa			
Libya 1966–8	0.074	0.085	0.159
Algeria 1966–8	0.180	0.100	0.280
Nigeria 1965–6	0.094	0.070	0.164
Persian Gulf			
Iran 1963–9	0.047	0.050	0.097
Iraq 1966–8	0.025	0.045	0.070
Kuwait 1966–8	0.060	0.045	0.105
Saudi Arabia 1966–8	0.041	0.045	0.086

Source: M. A. Adelman, The World Petroleum Market (Johns Hopkins, London, 1972), p. 76.

facilities, that is tankers and pipelines, available to each other, so that the consuming areas could be supplied by the nearest or least costly producing area. The benefits of this saving in real transport costs were, however, not passed on to the consumer because of the pricing policy the companies were following. Consumers were charged prices fixed at the Gulf of *Mexico* and thus attached to the high US cost of production, plus the transport cost from that Gulf. So companies supplying South-East Asia and Europe from the Middle East were gaining a bonus equal to the fictional costs of transporting the oil across the Atlantic and back again. The first break in this occurred in 1943, when the British Ministry of War Transport objected to such exorbitant charges being made for supplying India with Middle East Oil. The next occurred when the US and Western European administrators of the Marshall Plan discovered the exorbitant sums being paid to the oil companies to supply Europe with Middle Eastern oil. Western Europe was paying approximately $4 per barrel for oil which was available in the Middle East at $1. They forced the companies to post separate prices for oil from the Middle East at the *Persian* Gulf, and also from Venezuela. The average delivered price to Western Europe then came down to $3.50 per barrel (Odell 1981, p. 121).

In spite of this price reduction the costs in the Middle East were so much lower than in the US that many other US companies were encouraged to gain a foothold there. Finding it difficult to gain concessions in the Middle East proper, they transferred their attention to North Africa.

Other industrialised countries were also anxious to sponsor national companies; in 1966 France set up the totally government owned L'Enterprise de Recherches et d'Activités Petrolières (Elf–ERAP), and Italy ENI. Japan has endeavoured to gain more control over its import oil supply generally by co-operating in oil exploration and development.

Thus, in the provision of finance the seven majors were facing increasing competition. They also faced increasing competition in the provision of technological expertise as other US oil companies entered the international arena. The USSR also began to provide technological assistance to developing countries to develop their oil resources. It has also been argued by Vernon that technology in the oil industry was approaching maturity, and thus becoming standardised and easily available on the market (Vernon, 1977).

Meanwhile, the producing countries were becoming more and more restive at the low level of payments they were receiving from the oil produced in their territories, and at their lack of control over output.

In 1948, the Acción Democrática party came to power in Venezuela, dedicated to the nationalisation of the country's oil resources, but it was quickly overthrown. When the party once more came to power in 1958 it proceeded more slowly. The oil fields were not, in fact, nationalised until 1976.

In 1949 Saudi Arabia claimed as part of its revision of its concession agreement with its four majors. Exxon, Mobil, Texas and Chevron, 50% of the net profits from selling Saudi-Arabian oil. In order to overcome the resulting impasse the US government suggested that these tax payments could be offset against tax payments to the US government. This double taxation agreement in effect meant a transfer of revenue from the US exchequer to the Saudi-Arabian one. This then became a precedent for agreement in other exporting countries.

Then in 1951 Mossadeq nationalised the Anglo-Iranian company in Iran, but the company succeeded in preventing the other organisations buying the output of the nationalised field, and exports ceased until a new agreement was reached in 1954. By this the Iranian Government retained the ownership of the oil, but contracted the working of it to the Anglo-Iranian and other companies. Production and exports then increased rapidly, but not apparently rapidly enough for the government.

However, in the 1960s, oil companies—in particular Shell and BP—were encouraged to develop the oil fields in Nigeria by the very low taxation of profits of only 38%. Production and exports were disrupted by the Biafran war, but after that continued to expand rapidly. Libya also encouraged development by relatively low taxation.

All this was taking place in a situation in which the real price of oil had been falling since 1950. Indeed, the price at which oil was actually sold was lower than the posted price and as company taxation was based on the posted price this meant a steady squeeze on company profits. See Table 12.1. This squeeze was, however, ameliorated by a reduction in transport costs due to the extension of pipelines and the building of super tankers.

The fall in the real price of oil after 1950 was partly due to the many fields being brought into operation, but it was exacerbated by the US imposition of a quota on imports in 1959, in pursuance of its aim of self-sufficiency. Thus, much of the increase in output had to be diverted to other consumers.

In order to modify their burden of taxation, the oil companies decided to reduce their posted prices of oil. They clearly did not anticipate the anger on the part of the producing countries who, largely due to the initiatives of Libya and Venezuela, combined to form in 1960 the Organization of Petroleum Exporting Countries (OPEC) to maintain the price of oil and prevent the oil companies playing one country off against another. OPEC comprises Algeria, Ecuador, Gabon, Indonesia, Iran, Iraq, Kuwait, Libya, Nigeria, Qatar, Saudi Arabia, United Arab Emirates and Venezuela. From then on the main exporting countries were persistently endeavouring to obtain a greater return per barrel of oil produced. For the first time, anxieties were expressed about the rapid rate of depletion both in Venezuela after 1958 and then in Libya when Colonel Gaddafi came to power in 1970. Then, in December 1970, OPEC declared its intention of assuming control over the supply and price of oil and demanded increased royalties and taxes on oil. The price of oil rose immediately. OPEC then began to act like a producers' cartel. Then after the Yom Kippur war of 1973, they engineered a four-fold increase in the price of oil. They also indicated that they would take over the oil companies' operations sooner than had been expected. Since then the oil fields in all the members of OPEC have been nationalised.

This brief history of the oil industry has been given in order to show that although at the beginning of the period the major oil companies, in their search for low cost oil and their avoidance of taxes, were determining the pattern of exports, by the end of the period the control of the level of output and thus of exports in the major exporting countries had been taken over by their governments. Expertise was available from other sources, and the finance for investment was never a problem, particularly when the price was raised. In any case most investment in oil had traditionally been financed out of undistributed profits.

Marketing had been more of a problem, as Mossadeq found in Iran. But as the consuming countries, notably Japan, France and Italy, began to exert more control over their channels of distribution, they became able to absorb oil from outside sources.

The multinational oil companies responded, as has been mentioned earlier, by transferring their investment to the 'safe' countries, particularly Canada, Australia, and Britain for the exploitation of the North Sea. Thus between 1966 and 1979 the stock of US direct foreign investment in petroleum in industrialised countries quadrupled, whereas in developing countries it increased by only a fifth (see Table 10.4a). As this is in current dollars there must have been a real decline in the latter. The high price of oil has also induced prospecting under government aegis in South Asia and other parts of Latin America, but the oil is generally produced by some form of joint production with either an oil company or a metropolitan power.

MANUFACTURING INDUSTRIES

In manufacturing, firms can be regarded as inherently more footloose in so far as they are not dependent on an absolutely immobile factor such as a natural resource. However, the choice of location between different countries is generally regarded as available only to large firms because they have access to the finance and financial and management expertise to be able to establish and manage subsidiaries abroad.

The general picture that emerges from empirical and theoretical studies with a strong US orientation is of large firms often in oligopolistic markets contemplating production abroad as part of a worldwide competitive strategy. They are always at a disadvantage compared with indigenous firms, who have a much greater knowledge of local markets and legal and social structures. Thus, in order to be able to compete, the foreign firm must have some ownership specific advantage, that is, some technical knowledge or expertise which cannot be purchased on the market. The firms are then in a position to exploit these advantages either by expanding production in their original domestic market and exporting to the foreign markets, or by producing in the foreign market themselves. Even if the firm could transmit this knowledge through the sale of a licence, the theory is that a firm considers that it can obtain the economic rent from its specific advantage better by direct investment (Dunning, 1974).

Innovation of the technological gap type is an example of such a specific advantage. But in this theory, elaborated by that of the product cycle, production is always initially located in the domestic market which provided the incentive for the original investment. Only in the second stage, when the product and the production process become more standardised and thus also amenable to mass production, is foreign production contemplated. Then it is likely to take place in well developed export markets. Finally, when the product and process have become standardised and are no longer susceptible to innovation, they are described as mature and production will be located where it is cheapest.

These theories provide some explanations but few economists would deny that there are other determinants of the location of production and thus of foreign investment, namely impediments to trade. These may be in the form of transport costs, or be institu-

tional in the form of tariffs or quotas on imports. The imposition
of tariffs may initially act as an inducement to an inward flow of
investment in so far as it becomes more expensive to supply the
market from outside, and it increases the price of the protected
product and thus the return from producing it. Furthermore, as
discussed in Chapter 4, most countries starting to industrialise have
imposed tariffs on imports of final consumer goods.

Trade barriers may also affect the exploitation of economies of
scale. If there were no impediments to trade, scale economies could
be exploited wherever production was situated provided, of course,
there was a sufficiently large supply of labour. But if the additional
costs of selling due to transport costs or tariff barriers are considered, they may provide a limit to the feasible size of plant which
may be sub-optimal.

But the general argument is that these large companies can
transmit finance and technical expertise to any part of the world
and that their choice of site will depend on factors described above.
The cost of production in a country will depend on the price and
supply of skilled and unskilled labour.

Does this mean that in the long run there is an inevitable tendency for manufacturing production to be transferred from
industrialised countries to the lower-waged developing ones?

In the US, firms which site manufacturing activities abroad in
low-wage countries which were previously carried out at home are
termed 'runaway' firms. They are sometimes held responsible for
US deindustrialisation, that is, the reduction in the proportion or
amount of employment in manufacturing or the reduction in
manufacturing output.

This ignores entirely the macroeconomic argument that losses of
certain types of manufacturing have been offset by gains in other
types of activity which have increased because of trade—that
changes in the pattern of trade cannot be blamed for deficient
demand in an economy.

Nevertheless, that has proved a potent political argument.

But before looking at the situation in more detail, let us consider
more carefully the type of direct investment being carried out in
relation to the original activity of the firm, as you might expect that
to determine its effect on trade.

'*Vertical*' direct investment is that which takes place in the
previous or successive activities. In the last century and the beginning of this, a considerable amount of 'upstream vertical investment' was undertaken by manufacturing firms in the production of
their raw materials—Unilever in oilseeds, Courtaulds in cotton,
etc.. But this type of investment in plantations has now become

very much less important. The nearest parallel to it is perhaps Japanese investment in the extraction of iron ore.

Now some vertical direct investment is carried out by manufacturing firms in the production of components. When, for instance, General Motors invests in a subsidiary, Delco electronics, which produces computers for its engine management systems within each of its cars, this would be described as 'upstream' vertical investment. But when Japanese car companies purchase car-distributing firms, this would be described as 'downstream' vertical investment.

A particular variation of such investment has appeared recently with multinational companies who are generally engaged in capital- or skill-intensive processes of production, farming out their labour-intensive processes to less developed countries where labour costs are lower. This has been facilitated by the tariff schedules of the US and Germany and the Netherlands which permit import duties to be placed only on the value added abroad and not on the total value of the commodity. The less developed countries have encouraged such developments by establishing special export enclaves for the purpose. Because the process is labour-intensive, the amount of investment carried out by the multinational may be small. Nevertheless, it may have an appreciable effect on trade in intermediates. Furthermore, because the multinational's investment stake is so small, it can shift this process of production from one country to another with relative ease (Helleiner 1973).

Vertical intvestment is not likely to extinguish trade. It may, however, affect the pattern of trade particularly if it consists in a manufacturing firm undertaking investment in a source of raw materials or perhaps components, and providing assistance which would otherwise not have been available to that particular country.

But in general, because countries with raw materials now have access to credit facilities and technical knowledge through the market or at least through international institutions, upstream direct investment is less likely to provide additional resources for development and therefore is less likely to affect trade. Downstream vertical investment is generally in distributing activities and as such is associated with trade and thus can scarcely be regarded as changing it.

'Horizontal' investment occurs when a firm expands its productive facilities for producing a similar type of product to that of the parent, or carrying out the same process of production; when, for instance, Ford sets up another car assembly plant outside the US.

The technological-gap theory implicitly assumes that foreign direct investment is of the horizontal variety.

With respect to trade, the foreign direct investment will reduce trade in the product concerned in the second stage of the product cycle when production is started in an importing country as a substitute for exports, although trade in components may increase. But in the third stage, in which production is located in the cheapest place, direct investment may alter the direction of trade but it is unlikely to extinguish it.

Horizontal investment may also increase trade if it leads to a greater degree of intra-industry specialisation.

The emphasis on innovation as the specific advantage of a firm suggests that the firms most likely to carry out foreign investment are those in high research intensity industries. This is consistent with the Gruber, Mehta and Vernon study of the US discussed in the last chapter. However, it does not fit the foreign direct investment pattern for the UK and Japan quite so well.

Ozawa has argued that much of Japanese foreign direct investment has been taking place in medium or low research intensity industries because they are ones in which Japan had a comparative advantage which she is now losing. The capitalists involved find it easier to transfer their expertise abroad than to adapt to the new industries emerging in Japan (Ozawa, 1979).

Finally, let us turn to the last type of direct investment, described as *'conglomerate'*. This is investment by a firm in an activity dissimilar and unrelated to the activities it already undertakes. This spreads the risks for the company of its original activities. A number of plantation companies—Lonhro, Guthrie, Waring—are conglomerates, so too are many manufacturing firms, and the oil companies are increasingly becoming so. There is no reason why this should affect trade.

Clearly, the description of any particular investment project does depend on the width of the classification used. If we take engineering and transport equipment as one manufacturing industry, General Motor's investment in Delco Electronics would be regarded as a form of 'horizontal' rather than 'vertical' investment. Also there are often some links in conglomerate investments either of a technical nature or with a weak vertical relationship. Nevertheless, this classification is still useful.

Although the type of foreign investment carried out might be expected to determine its effect on trade, this aspect has been neglected in recent studies. Multinational firms are ascribed to the industry in which lies their major interest, and they are assumed to invest abroad in similar activities, that is, they are assumed to carry out horizontal direct investment.

There is evidence to support this view in the Hufbauer and Adler, and Reddaway reports. A more recent assessment can be made for

the UK for 1978 from the statistics of the stocks of direct investment classified by the industry of the UK enterprise and also by the
industry of the overseas affiliate. In this case the situation can be
considered from the point of view of the UK parent enterprise or
the overseas affiliate. Taking the latter first, we must examine the
ownership of the affiliates. The UK stake in manufacturing
affiliates was largely held by UK enterprises within the same industry. The figures were highest at 96% for chemicals, electrical
engineering, and textiles, and lowest for rubber with 49%. On the
other hand, the UK manufacturing enterprises did not invest only
in manufacturing. Eighty per cent of their overseas stake was in
manufacturing but another 16% of their investments was in
distribution. This latter figure varied for individual sectors and was
very much higher for mechanical engineering and instrument
engineering where it amounted to 44% of the foreign stake.

Little information is published on the extractive industries. But
the UK manufacturing enterprises do not appear to hold much of
the total stock of investment in them, only 22% of that in agriculture, forestry and fishing, and 6% of that in mining, and these
assets formed less than 10% of the total assets they held abroad
(UK Business Statistics Office MA4, *Business Monitor 1978 Supplement Census of Overseas Assets 1978*, Table 17, pp. 16 & 17).

Thus, for the UK, the situation appears to be one in which the
UK manufacturing industry's investment abroad has mainly been
of a horizontal type. Vertical integration backwards accounts for
very little of the stock but there has been a certain amount of
vertical integration forward into distribution. The latter clearly
assists trade, but Reddaway also regarded it as a preliminary step
in establishing production facilities abroad.

Unfortunately, for the US there is no such simultaneous
classification of foreign assets by industry of affiliate and of parent.
But some indirect information can be gleaned by comparing the
figures of total assets of foreign affiliates[4] classified by industry of
affiliate with the statistics of them classified by the industry of the
parent. Over half the total assets of foreign affiliates were attached
to US parents in the manufacturing industries, but as these assets
were greater than the total assets held by the overseas manufacturing affiliates, the US manufacturing parents must have invested
abroad outside manufacturing. This appeared to be most likely in
trade where the stock of total foreign assets attached to US trade
companies was only 34% of the total.

The US petroleum firms accounted for an additional 28% of the
total assets of foreign affiliates. These were also greater than the
total foreign assets in petroleum which suggests some vertical or
conglomerate type of foreign investment.

Thus, although the figures provide no direct evidence, they are not inconsistent with the assumption that foreign direct investment in manufacturing is carried out by US parents in the same industry. But they do show that these US parents must also be investing in other industries.

It has already been argued that the financial transfer from the parent company represents only a small element in direct foreign investment which is becoming smaller with the borrowing from Eurocurrency markets and the proliferation of co-ownership schemes. The question then is what is the incentive for multinationals to engage in it when they have such a relatively small interest in the foreign concern, and how does this affect trade?

One obvious answer is that the multinationals find it more profitable to transfer their firm specific knowledge to produce abroad either because of lower factor prices or because of some impediments to trade. The firm always regards producing abroad as an alternative to supplying the same market from the home country.

This type of approach has been considered in terms of sales rather than assets in a recent study by Dunning and Pearce, *The World's Largest Industrial Enterprises* (Dunning and Pearce, 1981). This study is based on the Fortune selection of the largest US and non-US firms for the years 1962, 1967, 1972 and 1977. There were 831 in total at the end of the period 1978 with total sales of $2250 billion. Most of them both exported and had subsidiaries abroad.

Of the 831 firms, 54% were of US origin, 15% Japanese, and 32% European of which 9% were British. These firms were classified to the industrial group which accounted for the greatest volume of sales. These industrial groups in turn were classified according to research intensity. This was measured by the number of scientists and engineers as a percentage of total employment for the different industries in the US in 1970 (Dunning and Pearce, p. 10).

Most of the sales of the firms were within the industry to which they were allocated, indicating few vertical or conglomerate-type links. However, this did vary between industries, and the diversification percentage, that is, the percentage of sales in industries outside the industry to which a firm was classified, varied from 49% for aerospace to 14% for the motor industry. Furthermore, over the period, an increasing proportion of foreign direct investment by firms took the form of conglomerate diversification (Dunning and Pearce, p. 4).

The position of the firms in their home and foreign markets was considered entirely in terms of their sales, or production, although these clearly depended on past investment. Let us denote worldwide sales of the group as W. This was the sum of sales by the parent company P and sales by overseas affiliates and associated companies (excluding goods imported from the parent for resale) S. Overseas sales were the sum of exports by the parent (PE) and S.

The authors calculated a whole series of ratios for the 523 firms for which information was obtainable, broken down by industry and country. The overseas sales ratio shows the degree of international orientation in the different industries. The parent export ratio (see Table 10.7) shows the proportion of output by the parent that is exported. As can be seen this appears highest for Germany at 38%, then Japan at 25%, then the UK at 20%, and finally the US at 7.5%. The US and UK have the highest export ratios for high research intensity (HRI) industries, but Germany and Japan for the medium research intensity (MRI) industries.

However, it is more interesting to compare the proportion of worldwide sales that is accounted for by the parent P/W, divided between those made at home, PD/W, and those exported, PE/W, and those sales made by foreign subsidiaries, S/W (see Table 10.8).

In view of all the concern that has been expressed about runaway firms, it is interesting to see how high a proportion of sales of these very large companies is still accounted for by companies in their countries of origin. The lowest ratio of parental to worldwide sales is in petroleum at 50%. This industry is orientated towards the actual deposits of oil of which more low-cost sources have been discovered outside the parent countries.

The production of parent-company sales in the total is very much higher for the other industries. But it does vary by industry and by country. In general, the proportion of worldwide company sales accounted for by overseas subsidiaries is highest for the UK at 42%, next highest for the US at 29%, then Germany at 19% and Japan at 7%. When considered by industry groups, the ratio appears highest for the high research industries for the US at 37%, UK at 52% and Germany at 27% but low for Japan at 4% (see Table 10.8). This would appear to be consistent with stages two and three of the product cycle. But, in fact, it varies a great deal within this sector. In particular, in aerospace, the US proportion of sales by foreign subsidiaries is very low; 92% of its sales are provided by parent companies which export 26% of their output. The US is also the largest exporter of these products. This domestic orientation could perhaps be explained by its large domestic market and perhaps the greater speed of innovation than in the other HRI industries. But it is worth recollecting the dependence of this sector on the government for orders and for subsidisation of its R and D, mentioned in the previous chapter. For the UK, the information is suppressed.

Another feature of aerospace is the physical aspects of production. Large craft are being built over a considerable period of time; this involves large buildings and a considerable quantity of working capital, and also often implies considerable economies of scale. These same arguments apply to shipbuilding in which home production as a proportion of output is very high at 95% on average, of which a high proportion may be exported—51% in Japan. These physical features determining location are independent of research intensity. They do not debar foreign production but just act as an impediment to mobility for any particular firm.

The situation for the other HRI industries is different—foreign subsidiaries account for a much higher proportion of sales, between a fifth and a half (excluding petroleum) although the figures for Japan appear to be very much lower. Overseas markets are supplied by foreign production rather than exports. Indeed, to judge from the figures shown in brackets in Table 10.8, most exports of office equipment, and of the measurement, scientific and photographic group, and a high proportion of exports of the electronic and electrical appliance, and chemicals and pharmaceutical groups are of parts and components, not final products.

The figures of sales of foreign subsidiaries of other industries are lower but they are still large particularly for the UK, ranging from 14% for beverages to 61% for tobacco.

For the medium research intensity and low research intensity industries, the story appears slightly different. The US still supplies most of its market overseas by the production of subsidiaries (excluding shipbuilding). But these subsidiaries are not such a large proportion of the total group as they are of the HRI. This suggests that the firms themselves have less of a specific advantage—that the main specific advantage of US firms is in their aptitude for research and innovation associated with the HRI industries.

The UK also supplies most of its own overseas sales except for motor vehicles, by the production of foreign subsidiaries. But it is less easy to discern a trend by research intensity if petroleum is excluded. She has a high proportion of foreign subsidiary sales in the HRI industries—electronic and electrical goods, and chemicals and pharmaceuticals—for which information is available. But she also has a relatively high proportion in such resource-orientated industries as tobacco, 61%; paper and wood products, 51%, but also industrial and farm equipment, 41%, and textiles, 42%. What is specific to the firm in some of the cases is not clear but it may well be accumulated knowledge of foreign markets on the one hand, plus access to its marketing network.

In contrast, most of Japan's overseas sales are accounted for by

TABLE 10.7 The World's Largest Industrial Enterprises (1977)

	Overseas Sales Ratio[1,2]					Parent Export Ratios[1,3]					Overseas Production Ratio[4]				
	Total %	US	UK	Germany	Japan	Total	US	UK	Germany	Japan	Total	US	UK	Germany	Japan
High Research Intensity															
Aerospace	35.7	32.0	S	73.0		30.0	26.2	S	49.0		8.1	7.8	S	47.0	
Office equipment (incl. computers)	46.9	45.9	S			8.2	6.4	S			42.2	42.2	S		
Petroleum	53.2	50.8	79.4	S	4.9	5.4	3.3	30.8	S	3.3	50.5	49.1	70.2	S	1.6
Measurement, scientific & photographic equipment	46.1	46.4	27.0	S		19.3	17.3		S		33.2	35.2		S	
Electronic & electrical appliances	39.6	33.4	50.5	47.8	24.4	22.5	15.5	27.4	35.1	21.0	22.0	21.2	31.8	19.6	4.3
Chemicals & pharmaceuticals (incl. soaps and cosmetics	45.5	33.5	60.5	61.7	15.9	21.2	9.4	34.3	41.8	12.0	30.8	26.6	39.9	34.2	4.4
Total	47.5	43.2	67.0	53.8	17.4	15.8	9.5	31.6	36.6	14.3	37.7	37.3	51.7	27.1	3.7
Medium Research Intensity															
Industrial & farm equipment	44.1	37.0	55.7	48.0	32.0	28.0	18.0	25.5	44.0	30.1	22.4	23.1	40.6	7.1	2.8
Shipbuilding, railroad & transportation equipment	46.1	9.7			54.8	43.4	5.0			51.4	4.8	5.0			7.1
Rubber	32.9	33.7			31.2	5.0	3.0			26.0	29.3	31.6			7.0
Motor vehicles (incl. components)	36.6	26.7	49.9	57.4	49.4	19.8	6.7	34.7	48.3	38.1	21.0	21.4	23.2	17.6	18.2
Metal manufacturing & products	34.4	13.8	46.4	43.6	30.6	24.5	2.8	19.2	37.8	28.2	13.1	11.4	33.6	9.3	3.4
Total	37.0	25.8	49.4	49.6	39.3	22.9	7.0	24.6	42.6	33.6	18.4	20.1	32.9	12.3	8.6

Table 10.7 (continued)

	Overseas Sales Ratio[1,2]					Parent Export Ratios[1,3]					Overseas Production Ratio[4]				
	Total %	US	UK	Germany	Japan	Total	US	UK	Germany	Japan	Total	US	UK	Germany	Japan
Low Research Intensity															
Building materials	37.4	24.1	38.4	S	9.8	9.9	3.8	11.6	S	7.0	30.5	21.1	30.4	S	3.0
Tobacco	47.5	32.4	64.5	S	S	6.2	4.8	9.1	S	S	44.0	29.0	30.4	S	S
Beverages	21.3	24.6	22.9		S	3.7	1.1	10.0		S	18.3	23.8	14.3		S
Food	37.4	21.9	40.3		6.3	6.1	1.5	5.3		4.2	33.3	20.7	36.9		2.1
Paper & Wood Products	32.2	19.6	54.7	S		15.5	6.9	8.2	S		19.7	13.7	50.7	S	
Textiles, apparel, leather goods	30.2	13.9	59.7		30.0	13.6	3.5	30.9		20.1	19.2	10.8	41.7		12.4
Publishing & printing	13.2	6.7	35.2			3.7	0.5	16.0			10.4	6.3	22.9		
Total	35.1	21.4	46.9	25.2	14.8	8.8	3.2	10.5	13.8	9.5	28.9	18.8	70.9	13.2	5.9
Other manufacturing	16.4	24.7	S	17.3		10.5	9.3	S	16.5		6.6	16.9	S	1.0	
TOTAL	41.6	34.5	53.6	49.5	29.7	17.1	7.5	20.2	38.0	24.6	29.5	29.2	41.8	18.5	6.7

Notes: 1. 523 firms for which information available.
2. Overseas sales ratio = sales of overseas affiliates plus parent's exports ÷ worldwide sales of group.
3. Parent companies' exports ÷ parent companies' total sales.
4. Sales of overseas affiliates and associate companies (excluding goods imported from parent for resale) divided by total worldwide sales of group.

S = Suppressed.

Source: John H. Dunning and Robert D. Pearce, The World's Largest Industrial Enterprises (Gower, Hants., England, 1981) Tables 1.3, 6.2 and 6.4.

TABLE 10.8 The Worlds Largest Industrial Enterprises: $ Million (1977).

	Sales (1) 1978 (2)	Distribution of Worldwide Sales 1977(3)%					US Firms' Distribution of Worldwide Sales (3)%					UK Firms' Distribution of Worldwide Sales %				
		W	P/W	PD/W	PE/W (4)	S/W	W	P/W	PD/W	PE/W	S/W	W	P/W	PD/W	PE/W	S/W
High Research Intensity																
Aerospace	44,381	100	91.9	64.3	27.6(0.5)	8.1	100	92.2	68.0	24.2(0.4)	7.8	100			S	S
Office Equipment (incl. computers)	45,085	100	57.8	53.1	4.7(4.3)	42.2	100	57.8	54.1	3.7(3.4)	42.2	100			S	S
Petroleum	487,111	100	49.5	46.8	2.7(1.4)	50.5	100	50.9	49.2	1.7(1.0)	49.1	100	29.8	20.6	9.2(2.8)	70.2
Measurement scientific & photographic equipment	25,856	100	66.8	53.9	12.9(7.5)	33.2	100	64.8	53.6	11.2(6.5)	35.2	100			27.0	
Electronic & electrical appliances	219,756	100	78.0	60.4	17.6(6.4)	22.0	100	78.8	66.6	12.2(1.5)	21.2	100	68.2	49.5	18.7(2.8)	31.8
Chemicals & pharmaceuticals (incl. soap & cosmetics)	247,398	100	69.2	54.5	14.7(5.1)	30.8	100	73.4	66.5	6.9	26.6	100	60.1	39.5	20.6(9.2)	39.9
Total	1,069,587	100	62.3	52.5	9.8(3.4)	37.7	100	62.7	56.8	5.9(2.2)	37.3	100	48.3	33.1	15.3(5.1)	51.7
Medium Research Intensity																
Industrial & farm equipment	109,940	100	77.6	55.9	21.7(11.4)	22.4	100	76.9	63.0	13.9(9.0)	23.1	100	59.4	44.3	15.1(1.9)	40.6
Shipbuilding, rail & transport equipment	26,198	100	95.2	53.9	41.3(0.0)	4.8	100	95.0	90.3	4.7(0.0)	5.0	100				
Rubber	37,003	100	70.7	67.1	3.6(S)	29.3	100	68.4	66.3	2.1	31.6	100				

Table 10.8 (continued)

	Sales (1) 1978 (2)	Distribution of Worldwide Sales 1977(3)%				US Firms' Distribution of Worldwide Sales (3)%						UK Firms' Distribution of Worldwide Sales %				
		W	P/W	PD/W	PE/W (4)	S/W	W	P/W	PD/W	PE/W	S/W	W	P/W	PD/W	PE/W	S/W
Motor vehicles (incl. components)	278,412	100	79.0	63.4	15.6(9.7)	21.0	100	79.1	73.8	5.3(4.2)	21.4	100	76.8	50.1	26.7(19.5)	23.2
Metal manufacturing & products	284,139	100	86.9	65.6	21.3(2.7)	13.1	100	88.6	86.2	2.4(0.2)	11.4	100	66.7	53.9	12.8(1.6)	33.6
Total	735,692	100	81.6	63.0	18.6(6.9)	18.4	100	79.9	74.2	5.7(3.8)	20.1	100	67.1	50.6	16.5(5.8)	32.9
Low Research Intensity																
Build Materials	39,405	100	69.6	62.6	6.9(0.6)	30.5	100	78.9	75.9	3.0(0.8)	21.1	100	69.6	61.6	8.0(1.0)	30.4
Tobacco	31,300	100	56.0	52.5	3.5(0.0)	44.0	100	71.0	67.6	3.4(0.0)	29.0	100	39.0	35.5	3.5(0.3)	61.0
Beverages	30,618	100	81.7	78.7	3.0(0.6)	18.3	100	76.2	75.4	0.8	23.8	100	85.7	77.1	8.6(0.0)	14.3
Food	187,315	100	66.7	62.6	4.1(0.3)	33.3	100	79.3	78.1	1.2(0.0)	20.7	100	63.1	59.7	3.4(0.5)	36.9
Paper & wood products	66,555	100	80.3	67.8	12.5(1.2)	19.7	100	86.3	80.4	5.9(2.2)	13.7	100	49.3	45.3	4.0(0.4)	50.7
Textiles, apparel, leather goods	37,140	100	80.8	69.8	11.0(1.4)	19.2	100	89.2	86.1	3.1(0.3)	10.8	100	58.3	40.3	18.0(3.2)	41.7
Publishing & printing	14,479	100	89.6	86.3	3.3(0.2)	10.4	100	93.7	93.3	0.4(S)	6.3	100	77.1	64.8	12.3(1.2)	22.9
Total	406,812	100	70.1	64.9	6.2(0.6)	28.9	100	81.2	78.6	2.6(0.1)	18.8	100	59.3	53.1	6.2(0.8)	40.7
Other manufacturing	37,478	100	93.4	83.6	9.8(0.6)	6.6	100	83.1	75.3	7.8(2.0)	16.9				S	S
Total	2,249,569	100	70.5	58.4	12.1(4.0)	29.5	100	70.8	65.5	5.3(2.4)	29.2	100	58.2	46.4	11.8(3.5)	41.8

Notes: (1) 831 firms; (2) Table 2.2 (Dunning & Pearce 1981); (3) 523 firms; (4) 324 firms.
W = Worldwide sales of group; P = Parent companies' sales; PD = Parent companies' sales domestically; PE = Parent companies' exports—figures in brackets are the sales of parts and components to overseas subsidiaries.

Source: John H. Dunning and Robert D. Pearce, *The World's Largest Industrial Enterprises* (Gower, Hants., England, 1981).
S/W is the same as their average overseas production ratio. P/W, PD/W and PE/W can be calculated from it using their average overseas ratios and average percent export ratios.
Tables 2.2, 6.1a, 6.2, 6.3 and checked with 6.4.

exporting from the parent company. Her foreign-subsidiary sales appear largest in the medium research intensity industries plus textiles.

The difficulty in using this study as a guideline is that it does apply only to the largest firms. Although they may be the ones carrying out most of the foreign investment, it may leave out certain UK and Japanese ones that would affect the situation for certain industries. In addition, because it selects firms by size, and few European and Japanese firms can attain that size without foreign subsidiaries, it may give misleading impression of firms' preferences for supplying overseas markets from foreign subsidiaries. Smaller firms may only be able to export.

However, this is the only exercise which provides any information on comparative sales.

INTRA-FIRM TRADE

Another aspect of international investment is that a considerable proportion of international trade now takes place between related firms. The most accurate information on this appears to be that for the US. In 1970 24% of US exports of manufactures were accounted for by exports of multinational corporations (MNCs) to majority-owned foreign affiliates (MOFAs). They appeared to account for an appreciable proportion of exports in all categories of goods. But the highest proportion was achieved in chemicals, in total 36% but including plastics 88%, and what is termed 'combinations' 100%, non-electrical machinery in total 44% but with sub-categories office 75% and computing 75%, and electrical machinery with a sub-category 'other' 92%, and instruments 62% (Lall, 1978). As described in Chapters 9 and 10, to the extent that investment has taken place in high-technology industries and has led to additional exports of investment goods from the lending country you would expect additional exports of intermediates and investment goods.

A study for 1965 showed that 56% of such US exports were of finished goods for resale, another 36% were of goods for 'further processing and assembly', and capital equipment accounted for 5%. Thirty-five per cent of the total went to Canada and another 36% to Europe while developing countries accounted for less than a quarter of the total. (Bradshaw, 1969 quoted in Lall, 1978). But recently intra-firm trade has expanded rapidly within the tariff provisions 807.0 and 806.3 described in Chapter 4.

In 1977 48% of US imports came from related firms. In this

case related refers to an ownership of 5% of equity or more. The percentage of imports which were from related firms was relatively low for food except fruit and vegetables 40%, miscellaneous food 24%, beverages 24% and fish 23%. It was high for fuels with petroleum and petroleum products 57% and gas 55%, raw materials with dyeing, tanning and colouring products 70%, iron and steel 62%, chemicals were generally between 43 and 60%. For manufactured goods as a whole it was 54% with particularly high figures for transport equipment 84%, electrical machinery 63% and machinery other than electrical 60%.

It was most important in imports from other OECD countries, accounting for 61% of imports of manufactures from them and only 37% of such imports from developing countries. But it would appear that a higher proportion of such imports from developed countries are for direct resale as compared with those from developing countries (Helleiner and Lavergne, 1979). Thus for developing countries this trade appears to be contributing to production within vertically integrated firms.

TRANSFER PRICING

A problem associated with intra-firm trade is that the price of a product quoted for customs purposes may not represent its true market or 'arm's length' price but an artificial 'transfer' price set to ensure the firm collects its profits where it so desires. As already mentioned, US oil companies endeavoured to keep the price at which they imported crude oil down in order to reduce the tax and royalties they paid in the country from which they extracted it. Obversely, an exporting firm wishing to accumulate profits in the home country will set prices as high as possible. The significance of this in the valuation of international trade is difficult to ascertain. Clearly the greater the degree of competition in markets the less important it is. No account of it has been taken in this book, except in the case of oil.

NOTES

1. However, all figures should be treated with circumspection. Some idea of the difficulties involved in drawing them up is conveyed by the following remark of a British commentator on the official statistics: 'The US uses similar accounting methods and definitions of direct

investment to those in the UK, but for UK direct investment in the US at the end of 1978 our estimate is over £1 billion more than the US's estimate, and for their direct investment in the UK, our estimate is £$\frac{1}{2}$ billion more than theirs'. Business Statistics Office, *MA4 Business Monitor*, 1978, *Supplement Census of Overseas Assets*, 1978, p. 47.

2. In the US a foreign subsidiary, or affiliate, is defined very broadly as a foreign business in which a US investor holds at least 10% of the voting interest.

   In the UK 'direct investment is where the investor holds a lasting interest in an enterprise operating in an economy other than that of the investor, and where the investor has an effective voice in the management of the enterprise.' *MA4 Business Monitor, Census of Overseas Assets*, 1978.

3. Had these been included the US share would have fallen from 68% in 1961–8 to 54% in 1974–9.

4. Non-bank affiliates of non-bank US parents.

Commodity Trade

11 Agricultural Commodities

Let us now turn to trade in agricultural commodities. This is still regarded by many people as the province of underdeveloped countries with little or no manufacturing industry, who must export agricultural products in exchange for other goods, and who, therefore, are very much at the mercy of their trading partners; a situation which appears aggravated by the instability in the prices of primary products. This is the basis for the demand by third world politicians for special treatment of agricultural products in the form of stabilising or price-raising schemes, and also underlies their endeavours to increase their output and trade of manufactures.

It cannot be gainsaid that developing countries are as a whole very dependent on agriculture; FAO estimated that in 1979 60% of the economically active population of developing countries overall were engaged in it and the figure is higher for the low-income countries, in particular India and China (FAO, 1979). This may be compared with 13% for all developed countries. However, the proportion of GDP accounted for by agriculture is generally lower in underdeveloped countries because productivity in agriculture is lower than in the rest of the economy—the World Bank estimates it at only a third in India and China (World Bank, 1981).

In many cases agricultural products do account for a very high proportion of total exports particularly for the poorest countries—88% of Niger's, 84% of those of Bangladesh—but on the other hand, for the oil and mineral exporters, they may account for a very low proportion, only 6% of Nigeria's and 1% of Venezuela's in 1979. Furthermore, the dependence of some developed countries on exports of agricultural products should also be appreciated. Agricultural exports account for 75% of New Zealand's exports, 44% of Australian, 27% of Canadian, 26% of Dutch, and 23% of those of the US (FAO, *State of Food and Agriculture*, 1980, Annex Table II).

Nor can it be gainsaid that there is a considerable degree of price instability in trade in agricultural products. This has already been discussed in Chapter 2, where the standard deviation in the real price of primary products was found to be generally much greater than that for manufactures. However, the price fluctuations are generally due to the failure or success of harvests, that is, shifts in the supply schedule rather than shifts in the demand schedule. Prices thus move inversely with the harvest so as to compensate producers for a shortfall and vice versa for an abundant one. The income of producers as a whole would be entirely stabilised if they faced a stable demand schedule with an elasticity of one. If there is a shortfall in production of food or feed products which is entirely exogenous—that is, the result of climatic changes or pests—then demand is relatively stable because income elasticities are low and thus there is little fluctuation in demand with the trade cycle.

In the market for raw materials, where demand is a derived demand for the final products and tends to fluctuate with it, and where stockpiling is more important, demand-induced price fluctuations are more apparent: this was, for instance, very noticeable during the Korean War boom. But as the substitution by synthetics has increased this has tended to stabilise the price of raw materials—they have become hitched to the price of a more stable manufactured product.

Thus, although there is a considerable degree of political pressure to draw up commodity agreements with the immediate objective of stabilising prices, this does not appear to the author the most appropriate objective. Indeed, the degree to which they founder reflects the uncertainty of governments as to their effects. The whole situation is exacerbated by the efforts made by countries, or groups of countries, to stabilise the prices of products in their domestic markets, thus placing the whole burden of adjustment to fluctuations in production on the residual world market.

In this chapter we will be concerned with the long-run changes in trade and changes in its structure and the relative position of different regions and countries. In our more detailed studies of agricultural products we will confine ourselves to crops and livestock products and generally exclude forestry products and fish.

From Table 8.1 it appears that the volume of trade in agricultural products almost tripled between 1955 and 1979 and roughly doubled between 1963 and 1979. Its volume was thus increasing at half the rate of that of manufactures.

But the relative price of agricultural products in relation to manufactures was about the same in 1979 as it was in the 1960s although 11% lower than it was in 1953. However, the prices of both have increased far less than that of minerals, the overall price of which rose with that of oil. Thus the decline in the proportion of international trade accounted for by agricultural products from 35% in 1955 to 15% in 1980 is due to a slower increase in their quantity traded than of manufactures, and their slower increase in price than that of minerals.

The doubling in the volume of trade in agricultural products obscures the very divergent position of industrialised and developing countries. As mentioned in Chapter 8, exports of food and raw materials have increased far faster from industrialised than developing countries. Furthermore, Table 8.6 shows that for primary products in general and food in particular the volume of exports from industrialised countries is increasing faster than the volume of imports, whereas in developing areas, the reverse is true. Indeed, the whole pattern of specialisation appears to be changing, with the net exports of food and raw materials from developing countries declining in real terms, the net imports into industrialised countries likewise falling in real terms, and the Eastern Trading Area changing its position over the whole period from being a net exporter of food and net importer of raw materials in 1955, to a net importer of food and net exporter of raw materials in 1979.

The whole situation can be investigated more closely using FAO statistics. The FAO classification is somewhat different from that of GATT. It includes in the category of Developed Market Economies (Developed ME) all industrialised countries (by the GATT definition)[1] plus the resource-rich countries of Australia and New Zealand as Oceania, and South Africa, which with Israel[1] and Japan is regarded as in a region of other developed countries. Developing ME are equivalent to GATT's Developing Areas,[1] and the third category is similar as the Centrally Planned Economies (CPE).

The FAO definition of agricultural products is more restrictive than that of GATT in so far as it excludes synthetic rubber and textiles. We will also exclude fish and forestry products which are included in the GATT definition.

The FAO definition of food, identified by $Food_F$ is also more restrictive; it includes only commodities that are both edible and have nutritive value. It thus excludes inedible oilseeds and also coffee and tea, all of which are included in the GATT definition.

A comparison of the totals can be made from Table 11.1. It should be borne in mind that the GATT figures for agricultural trade are derived from information supplied by FAO on trade in agricultural products, fish and forestry products. So part of the differences are those of definition, in particular that the FAO figures exclude trade in synthetics. But in 1955, part of the difference was also due to the FAO figure being the trade of only

*TABLE 11.1   GATT and FAO Estimates of the Value of Agricultural
Exports, 1955; 1979–82.*
$ Billion

	$ million				
	1955	1979	1980	1981	1982
GATT					
Agricultural products[1]	33,000	262,000	299,000	292,000	272,000
FAO					
Total agriculture, fishery and forestry	29,954[2]	267,269[4]	303,226[4]	299,444	275,476
Fishery products	551[2]	13,976[6]	14,968[6]	15,382[6]	
Forestry products	2890[2]	49,181[5]	55,572[5]	51,326[5]	
Agricultural products	19,513[2]	204,051[3,4]	232,569[4]	232,576[4]	210,742[4]
as % of total	85	76	77	77	77

Notes: 1. GATT, *International Trade*, 1982/83 and earlier years.
2. FAO, *Trade Yearbook*, 1958.
3. Estimate in 1979 yearbook to be used in Table 11.2; $199,330 million.
4. FAO, *Trade Yearbook*, 1982.
5. FAO, *Yearbook of Forest Products 1970–1981*.
6. FAO, *Yearbook of Fishery Statistics*, 1981.

sixty-seven countries. The FAO estimates are constantly being revised but those available at the beginning of 1984 show a rise in trade in agricultural products, fish and forestry products from $30 billion in 1955 to $303 billion in 1980 at current prices. Since then, trade has been declining. In this chapter we exclude fish and forestry products, to concentrate on agricultural products proper, which account for 77% of the total.

As can be seen from Table 11.1, the value of agricultural trade rose from $19.5 billion in 1955 to $204 billion in 1979. This represents a ten-fold increase. But the value of trade in the different agricultural products did not grow proportionally, as can be seen from Table 11.2. This is based on the 1958 and 1979 Yearbooks in which in the latter the total for 1979 was given as $199 billion.

Within the total, the most dramatic change was the fall in the proportion of agricultural raw materials from 26% of the total in 1955 to 9% in 1979. The three different types of raw material—natural rubber, textile fibres and hides and skins—all contributed to this fall. Even allowing for a significant unallocated element in 1979, FAO now regards 90% of agricultural trade as being in food and feeding-stuffs and only 10% in raw materials.

Another noticeable feature is the continuing importance of cereals which have risen slightly from 14.4% of the total in 1955 to 15.6% in 1979. The proportion of trade accounted for by fats,

TABLE 11.2 *Value of World Exports of Agricultural Products—Breakdown for 1955 and 1979.*

	1955		1979	
	$ million	Per cent	$ million	Per cent
Food & Feeding Stuffs				
Animals live			4637	2.3
Meat	1279	6.6	19,018	9.5
Dairy products	1179	6.0	11,436	5.7
Milk			3921	2.0
Butter			2860	1.4
Cheese			3760	1.9
Eggs			895	0.4
Cereals	2815	14.4	31,004	15.6
Wheat & flour			13,385	6.7
Rice			4032	2.0
Barley			2039	1.0
Maize			9912	5.0
Fruit & vegetables	1717	8.8	10,113	5.1
Sugar	673	3.4	8168	4.1
Coffee, tea, cocoa, spices	2748	14.1	19,235	9.7
Coffee			12,238	6.1
Cocoa			4822	2.4
Tea			1693	0.8
Beverages	558	2.8	5505	2.8
Wine			4531	2.3
Beer			974	0.5
Tobacco	718	3.7	3882	1.9
Fats, oils, oilseeds	1398[1]	7.2[1]	23,303	11.7
Edible oils & lard			8050	4.0
Raw Materials				
Natural rubber	1479	7.6	4027	2.0
Natural fibres	3126	16.0	10,969	5.5
Cotton			6728	3.4
Wool			3330	1.7
Hides & skins	500	2.6	3369	1.7
Total—Agricultural Products	19,513	100.0	199,330	100.0

Notes: When 1955 not given they are not separately available.
  1. Excludes linseed & oil, castor seed & oil, & tung oil and oilseed but includes feeding stuffs amounting to $331 million
Sources: FAO *Trade Yearbook* 1958; FAO *Trade Yearbook* 1979; FAO *Commodity Review & Outlook 1980–81*.

TABLE 11.3 *Volume of Trade in Agricultural Products (A) and Food (F)[2] 1961–5 to 1978–80.* 1969–71 = 100.

		Export Volume						Increase 1961–5 to 1978–80	Import Volume						Increase 1961–5 to 1978–80
		1961–5[1]	1969–71	1973	1974–6	1978–80	1982		1961–5[1]	1969–71	1973	1974–6	1978–80	1982	
Developed ME	A	78	100	134	134	179	197	129	81	100	115	113	124	128	53
	F	75	100	137	138	186	207	148	75	100	117	116	129	131	72
N. America	A	89	100	154	145	206	220	131	87	100	113	108	115	108	32
	F	98	100	160	153	219	239	123	76	100	113	107	110	101	45
W. Europe	A	65	100	128	138	177	206	172	83	100	113	113	126	130	52
	F	63	100	126	136	176	205	179	79	100	114	116	130	135	65
Oceania	A	82	100	113	102	130	129	59	89	100	104	121	112	140	26
	F	78	100	120	114	154	149	97	87	100	109	137	130	188	49
Other Developed	A	77	100	104	99	115	120	49	61	100	131	121	136	142	123
	F	62	100	108	105	125	128	102	51	100	134	131	155	159	204
Developing ME	A	87	100	108	105	117	129	34	79	100	117	134	200	236	153
	F	87	100	108	109	127	145	46	80	100	120	138	209	252	161
Africa	A	95	100	110	98	84	87	–13	81	100	116	131	209	265	158
	F	102	100	105	93	79	80	–23	79	100	119	131	222	284	181
Latin America	A	85	100	107	106	129	134	52	78	100	123	137	220	225	182
	F	78	100	109	110	135	141	73	78	100	126	142	235	239	201

Table 11.3 (continued)

		Export Volume						Increase 1961–5 to 1978–80	Import Volume						Increase 1961–5 to 1978–80
		1961–5¹	1969–71	1973	1974–6	1978–80	1982		1961–5¹	1969–71	1973	1974–6	1978–80	1982	
Near East	A	79	100	114	91	96	108	22	70	100	111	173	280	372	300
	F	84	100	122	100	134	170	60	69	100	113	180	302	400	338
Far East	A	89	100	109	117	138	167	55	84	100	119	119	151	167	80
	F	95	100	110	131	167	224	76	88	100	122	120	149	167	69
Centrally Planned	A	76	100	106	106	105	106	38	83	100	149	140	186	221	124
	F	74	100	101	98	94	90	27	86	100	168	152	215	271	150
Asia	A	79	100	127	112	115	97	46	77	100	161	127	217	262	182
	F	76	100	124	108	103	89	36	72	100	148	119	202	258	181
USSR & E.Europe	A	75	100	100	104	103	106	37	82	100	143	142	175	209	113
	F	73	100	93	95	91	92	25	91	100	174	163	219	274	141
World	A	82	100	121	119	147	161	79	82	100	120	119	145	159	77
	F	78	100	124	124	158	175	103	78	100	123	125	156	175	100

Notes: 1. Extrapolated with index based on 1961–5.
2. Food excludes fish. As defined by FAO, Food comprises commodities that are considered edible and contain nutrients. Thus it excludes inedible oils and also tea and coffee, which have no nutritive value.

Source: FAO Trade Yearbooks, 1976, 1979 & 1982.

oils and oilseeds has also risen from 7.2% in 1955 to 11.7% in 1979. The proportion of trade accounted for by meat has risen from 6.6% to 9.5%, although that accounted for by dairy products appears to have fallen slightly. There is a marked decline in the proportion accounted for by coffee, tea and cocoa from 14.1% in 1955 to 9.7% in 1979, and also tobacco from 3.7% to 1.9% and apparently a slight decline in the proportion accounted for by fruit and vegetables.

In surveying these figures it should be appreciated that some of the decline, particularly in exports of textile fibres, may be due to the product being exported in a more processed form as, say, yarn, cloth or clothing.

It should also be appreciated that the changes are the net result of changes in quantity and price. We have already considered changes in overall volume, and changes in the volume of trade of industrialised countries and developing countries taken as two groups. FAO also provides volume figures for the trade of different regions since 1961–5 for agricultural products in total and for Food$_F$ narrowly defined.

These are shown in Table 11.3. These FAO quantitative indices confirm the general picture that emerged from the GATT figures. But they show that there was scarcely any change in the volume of trade between 1981 and 1982; the change in value was almost entirely due to a drop in price.

The exports of developed MEs are increasing faster than their imports and this is true of the individual regions and true not only for all agricultural products but also for Food$_F$. The only exception to this is other industrialised countries, which includes Japan, Israel, and South Africa and this is mainly due to the level and increase in Japanese imports.

Comparing 1978–80 with 1961–5, West European exports of agricultural products appear to have increased faster than for any other region of the world—they increased by more than 50% from the early 1960s to 1969–71 and then by another 77% to 1978–80. North American exports did not increase as fast in the earlier period but they have increased faster since, more than doubling between 1969–71 and 1978–80. In comparison, Oceania's exports have increased relatively slowly, standing only 59% above their level in 1961–5.

The volume of imports of developed MEs as a whole was 53% greater in 1978–80 than in 1961–5. But they increased much more slowly into Oceania. They increased much faster into other developed MEs, increasing by 64% between the early 1960s and 1969–71, and then increasing by 123% to 1978–80. Their increase in imports of food was even faster—it doubled between 1961–5 and 1969–71 and then increased by 55% to 1978–80. Most of this increase is due to Japan.

The obverse of this situation is shown by the developing MEs whose imports of agricultural products by volume are increasing faster than their exports. This is true for the separate regions and generally for $Food_F$ as well as agricultural products as a whole. The only exception is for $Food_F$ in the Far East where exports are increasing faster than imports.

African exports of both agricultural products as a whole and $Food_F$ are now lower than they were in either 1961–5 or 1969–71. The exports of agricultural products by the Near East fluctuated but exports of $Food_F$ have been increasing recently reaching 70% above the 1969–71 level in 1982. The volume of exports by the other developing ME regions rose by between 50% and 80% between 1961–5 and 1978–80.

But the imports of most of the developing MEs have more than doubled over the period. Indeed, imports by the Near East have approximately quadrupled. Only in the Far East have imports of $Food_F$ increased at a slightly slower rate than exports but at 69% over the period from 1961–5 to 1978–80, this is faster than that of most of the developing MEs.

The shift in the position of the Centrally Planned Economies can also be seen from Table 11.3. From the early 1960s to 1969–71, exports of agricultural products and $Food_F$ by the USSR and Eastern Europe had been increasing faster than imports but then the situation rapidly reversed itself; exports of agricultural products fluctuated around that level and imports rapidly increased by 75% between 1969–71 and 1978–80. The turn round was even more exaggerated for $Food_F$ exports which fell after 1969–71 and the imports of which more than doubled. Imports of $Food_F$ in 1982 were 274% of their 1969–71 level. For the Asian CPE dominated by China, imports had all along been increasing faster than exports but after 1973 exports fell while imports continued to increase rapidly reaching, in 1982, 258% of their 1969–71 level.

VALUE OF TRADE

We have already considered the exports and overall balances of trade for the major groups of countries using GATT figures in Tables 8.3, 8.4 and 8.5 let us now consider the major contributors to these balances. Comprehensive coverage is only provided by FAO from 1969 onwards, but figures for some countries, in

TABLE 11.4 Value of Agricultural Trade 1955–82
($ million).

	1955		1969–71		1973		1978–80		1982	
	Exports	Net Exports	Exports	Net Exports	Exports	Net Exports	Exports	Net Exports	Exports	Net Exports
Developed ME			30,817	−3937	59,674	−12,484	128,575	−14,612	139,622	−17,455
N. America	4329	−924	9027	+1675	21,427	+10,119	42,300	+20,887	46,256	+24,980
of which USA	3295	−1256	7138	+1060	18,145	+9079	36,554	+19,298	38,230	+21,354
Canada								1587	8026	3626
W. Europe	5787	(−9388)	17,411	−10,565	30,423	−20,297	72,658	−30,578	77,676	−23,178
of which UK	909	−4844	1486	−4327	2450	−6500	7056	−8300	7376	−6610
Germany	222	−2415	1291	−5046	3205	−8204	8864	−13,957	10,643	−12,481
France	980	−1185	3227	−50	7082	+969	15,347	+1637	15,755	+2842
Netherlands	991	+201	3123	+1041	5939	+1866	14,285	+4029	15,098	+4816
Italy	479	−440	2944	−546	1987	−5272	5193	−8265	5645	−7637
Oceania	2169	+1863	3245	+2907	6087	+5625	10,082	+8931	12,155	+10,762
of which Australia	1468	+1248	2266	+2018	4253	+3930	7262	+6403	8657	+7629
Japan	217	−1292	338	−3689	372	−8482	733	−15,278	821	−15,414
Developing ME	983	(+762)	17,262	+7912	27,723	+11,183	61,198	+13,105	58,048	−384
Africa			3673	+2148	5443	+2728	10,277	+1832	8601	−1757
Latin America	3300	(+2612)	7321	+5020	12,505	+8335	28,949	+17,968	26,443	+14,836
of which Brazil	1274	+994	1898	+1588	4181	+3411	7744	+5618	8034	+6243
Argentine	860	+729	1443	+1313	2457	+2206	5183	+4694	4999	+4634

Table 11.4 (continued)

	1955		1969–71		1973		1978–80		1982	
	Exports	Net Exports	Exports	Net Exports	Exports	Net Exports	Exports	Net Exports	Exports	Net Exports
Near East	671	(+435)	1865	+203	3200	+65	4667	−9770	5235	−14,756
Far East	3141	(+1636)	4255	+580	6408	+204	16,667	+3048	17,327	+1511
of which India	557(a)	+149(a)	644	−33	1012	+178	2103	+920	2349	+828
Indonesia	642	+563	470	+235	750	+165	2310	+935	1516	+183
Malaysia	967(b)	+397(b)	770	+443	1192	+656	3502	+2329	2972	+1592
Centrally Planned			4638	−1670	7884	−4951	13,227	−17,473	13,072	−22,527
Asia CPE			1422	−75	2205	−715	3905	−2888	3658	−4218
of which China			1007	+229	2011	−223	3438	−2652	3265	−4176
E. Europe and USSR			3496	−1595	5679	−4236	9322	−14,584	9414	−18,309
of which USSR			1580	−720	1844	−3223	2629	−11,534	2779	−16,600
World			52,717	−3131	95,281	−6252	202,999	−18,981	210,742	−24,657

Regions as given in 1978 FAO Trade Yearbook. Bracketed figures indicate information is not complete.

Notes: (a) 1957.
(b) Includes Singapore.

Sources: FAO Trade Yearbook, 1958, 1974, 1978, 1980, 1982.

particular the developed ones, are available for earlier periods. In
Table 11.4, the FAO figures of agricultural exports f.o.b. are given.
Net exports are calculated by subtracting from them the imports
c.i.f. which are greater than the value of imports f.o.b.by the cost
of insurance and freight. Thus, net exports do not sum to zero but
to some negative figure representing transport costs. Nevertheless,
making a mental allowance for such c.i.f. costs, which FAO
estimates add approximately 12% to the f.o.b. value of imports, it
is still possible to make rough comparisons cross-sectionally and
over time.

As a measuring rod, let us use the unit value index for
agricultural products with 1975 = 100 which stood at 50 in 1955
and 49 in 1969–71, rose to 143 in 1978–80, and then fell to 129 in
1982. [Constructed from the unit value indexes for Food and
Agricultural Non Food with 1975 weights, see Table A2.]

As is consistent with the volume figures, the value of exports by
the developed market economies is increasing far faster than the
price index, quadrupling between 1969–71 and 1978–80. Those of
the developing market economies are increasing somewhat faster,
and those of the centrally planned economies have fluctuated. The
countries most responsible for these increases can be seen in the
table. Most noticeable is the US, which in 1982 accounted for 27%
of world exports of agricultural products, and France and the
Netherlands with 11%. These are now the largest exporters of
agricultural products in the world—much larger than any developing country—even those with abundant land and labour such as
Brazil, and also larger than resource-rich countries such as Canada
and Australia.

Exports of the other developed countries did not rise as fast—
those of Oceania increased in value only just faster than the price
index. Those of Japan only doubled in value between 1969–71 and
1978–80 and thus showed a decline in real terms.

The difference in the performance of the developed countries
raises the question of causation—but we will return to that later.

The exports of developing market economies also increased in
real terms but the performance of the individual regions differed
markedly. The more rapid increase in the volume of exports by
Latin America and the Far East shows up in the value figures, and
the decline in the volume of agricultural exports by Africa and the
Near East shows up in the slowly growing value figures.

However, if we are concerned with changes in specialisation in
the world as a whole, it is net exports that we should consider.

As can be seen from Table 11.4 the strong position of the US
emerges yet again—she was by 1978–80 by far the largest single net

exporter. Furthermore, this represents a very great change from 1955 when she was a small net importer.

France and the Netherlands appear far less of agricultural specialists because of their high proportion of imports. Nevertheless, their real exports have been increasing over the whole period far faster than their imports, so that France changed from being a net importer in 1955 to a net exporter in 1978–80 and the Netherlands changed from being a very small net exporter to a large one. However, they are far less important as *net* exporters than the traditional agricultural countries Australia, Brazil and Argentina.

But what is most interesting is the appearance of Japan as the largest net importer by 1978–80. Her net imports of agricultural products in 1978–80 were over twelve times their monetary value in 1955 and therefore had increased far faster than the price index.

However, recently it is the centrally planned economies that have shown the greatest changes. Their net imports increased ten times in value between 1969–71 and 1979–80. This was partly due to China's shift from a small net exporter to a sizeable net importer. But it was mainly due to Russia's very rapid increase in net imports. In 1982, the USSR was the largest net importer of agricultural products.

German net imports of agricultural products had doubled between 1955 and 1969–71 in monetary and real terms but since then they have remained constant in real terms. But in 1982 Germany was the third largest net importer of agricultural products after Japan. She was followed by Italy and Britain in that order. Italian net imports have increased as fast as the Japanese. Britain's net imports declined from 1955 to 1969–71 in monetary and real terms, and in real terms this decline appears to have continued from 1969–71 to 1978–80 as their value did not increase as fast as the price index. She thus appears to be moving steadily away from the traditional position that she still held in 1955 as the largest agricultural importer in the world.

In terms of regions the Near East has now emerged as a major net importer of agricultural products and by 1982 Africa had become a minor one.

In considering the way this pattern of specialisation has changed over time, an immediate question suggests itself, i.e. are the changes the result of shifts in comparative advantage or are they the direct result of the commercial policies pursued by governments?

This is a very difficult question to answer. It requires a distinction to be drawn between the changes that are due to economic expansion, which in Chapter 7 is considered as the outward movement of the production possibility curve due to the increased supply of factors of production and technological change, and the increase in consumption associated with it; and on the other hand, deliberate government intervention which alters the relative price of agricultural commodities and thus the incentives to produce and consume.

The terms of trade between agricultural products and manufactures were approximately the same in 1978–80 as in 1961–5. Therefore, in the absence of any changes in government intervention within countries, the whole of the changes in trade would be due to exogenous changes in production and consumption within countries.

Let us for the moment work on that hypothesis and consider the

TABLE 11.5   Resources Devoted to Agriculture 1961-5 to 1979

| | Population engaged in Agriculture | | | | Arable and Permanent Crop Land Area | | | |
| | millions | | | Increase 1965 to 1979 % | million hectares | | | Increase 1961–5 to 1979 % |
	1965	1970	1979		1961–5	1969–71	1979	
Developed Areas								
W. Europe	28	23	17	− 39	105	99	95	− 10
N. America	4.8	3.9	2.8	− 42	222	232	233	+ 5
of which US	4.1	3.2	2.2	− 46	180	190	188	+ 4
Other developed[1]	15	13	10	− 33	19	20	20	+ 5
of which Japan	13	10	7	− 46	6	5.5	4.9	− 27
Oceania	0.6	0.6	0.5	− 17	34	42	44	+ 29
Total of above	49	40	31	− 37	381	393	392	+ 3
Developing ME								
Africa	80	87	99	+ 24	167	139	150	− 10
Latin America	35	36	39	+ 11	116	146	161	+ 38
Near East	33	33	36	+ 9	75	85	87	+ 16
Far East	239	257	284	+ 19	248	256	268	+ 8
Total	388	415	460	+ 19	607	628	667	
Eastern Trading Area								
USSR & E. Europe	59	49	40	− 32	277	280	278	0
of which USSR	39	30	23	− 41	229	233	232	1
Asian CPE	260	286	290	12	129	114	112	− 14
Total	319	335	330	+ 3	406	393	389	− 4
World Total	756	790	822	+ 9	1394	1415	1449	+ 4

Note: 1. Israel, Japan (incl. Bonir & Ryukyu Is). South Africa.
Sources: FAO *Production Yearbook* 1980, 1976; *FAO Fertilizer Yearbook* 1980, 1978.

factors that have contributed to the changes in production and consumption. Let us begin by considering the resources devoted to production.

In Table 11.5 we identify the first factor, labour, as the economically active population engaged in agriculture, This has declined in all the regions of the developed world by 37% on average from 1965 to 1979. The only region in which it has declined less than this is Oceania and the other developed areas, in the latter entirely due to South Africa and Israel. It has declined most, that is by 46%, in the US and Japan. In the developing ME countries it has increased by 19% overall over the period. This increase in total, and for the separate regions, is less than half as great as their population increase. In the centrally planned economies there is a

Table 11.5 (continued)

Permanent Pasture Land				Consumption of Fertilizers $N_1 + P_2O_5 + K_2O$			
million hectares			Increase 1961–5	1000 MT p.a.			Increase 1961/2–65/6
1961–5	1969–71	1979	to 1979 %	1961/2–65/6	1969/71	1979/80	to 1979–80 %
74	74	71	−4	12,264	17,263	21,825	78
282	266	266	−6	9928	16,034	22,639	128
261	244	242	−7	9406	15,231	20,821	121
88	84	82	−7	2130	2724	3370	58
0.1	0.3	0.6	+357	1798	2105	2344	30
459	465	462	−1	1195	1478	1838	54
902	890	882	−2	25,517	37,499	49,672	95
688	636	634	−8	288	657	1184	311
493	523	539	+9	1298	2872	6751	420
188	282	281	+49	496	1140	2969	499
36	36	35	−3	1407	3726	9548	579
1406	1477	1490	+6	3494	8403	20,475	486
387	390	389	1	7682	17,751	27,846	262
372	375	374	1	4133	10,180	17,358	320
349	365	349	0	1733	4934	13,741	693
736	755	738	0	9415	22,685	41,587	342
3044	3123	3110	+2	38,426	68,587	111,734	191

decline in the agricultural labour force in the USSR and Eastern
Europe but apparently an increase in the Asian regions; the figure
for the latter is entirely dependent on the FAO estimates for China.

Let us take the next factor of production as land. This comprises
areas of very different fertility, weather, water supplies and ease of
cultivation. However, we are concerned with changes at the margin
in the amount employed, rather than the absolute level of productivity. For this purpose, two measures have been selected, arable
and permanent crop land area, and permanent pasture land—the
latter less intensively cultivated than the former. The latter is much
larger than the former except in the densely populated regions of
Europe, Japan and the Far East. The arable and permanent crop
land areas have increased since 1961–5 in most of the developed
ME regions with the exception of Europe, and it has increased in
most of the developing MEs with the exception of Africa. It
appears to have fallen in the Asian CPE but this is entirely due to
China, the estimate for which must necessarily appear somewhat
tentative. But the area of permanent pasture land has declined or
remained stagnant in all areas except Latin America and the Near
East.

It would be desirable to have some comparable figures on investment in agriculture. Clearly there has been a great deal of investment in machinery and also in land improvement in irrigation
schemes, etc. But unfortunately, comparable figures on investment
are just not available.

So far we have considered the increase in primary factors of production available to agriculture. However, there is also the element
of technological change which would contribute to a shift in productive potential. It leads to an increase in output for any given
combination of primary inputs. In agriculture, much of it is
associated with the introduction of higher-yielding crops which,
when there is an adequate water supply, are more responsive to
fertilisers and the benefits of which can be measured in terms of
yield per acre. However, this depends on the increased application
of fertilisers. The consumption of fertilisers thus represents not
only the use of an input but also the degree to which modern
technology has been adopted.

In Table 11.5 we can see the change in the consumption of
fertilisers in the different regions of the world since
1961/62–1965/66. It has increased very rapidly, that is four-fold
or more in developing ME regions and also apparently the Asian
CPE and the USSR. According to FAO estimates it now stands
about eight times its previous level in the Asian CPE and seven
times its previous level in the Far East.

In the developed MEs as a whole it has only increased by 95%, increasing only slowly in the regions of Oceania, Other Developed countries and Western Europe. But in the US and North America as a whole it has more than doubled. These differences between the industrialised regions reflect the different positions that had already been attained by 1961–5. Applications of fertilisers in Western Europe and other developed countries were already very high at respectively 117.2 and 112.7 kilograms of fertiliser, that is nitrogen, phosphate and potash ($N + P_2O_5 + K_2O$) per hectare of arable land and permanent crops. The latter figure encompassed the high figure for Japan of 305.2. these figures for Western Europe also varied with applications of 442.5 in Belgium—Luxembourg, 311.8 in West Germany, 534.9 in the Netherlands, but 132.0 in France, 164.8 in Denmark, and 198.9 in the UK. Applications in countries with traditionally more extensive agricultural systems were much lower: for the US it was 52.2, Canada 12.4 and Australia 24.5. Thus, the scope for raising yields by raising fertiliser inputs assuming some logarithmic yield functions, tended to be lower in Western Europe and Japan than elsewhere (FAO, *Fertilizer Yearbook*, 1978).

The overall use of these resources, labour, land and fertilisers, the latter both providing an indication of technological change and representing an input from the manufacturing sector, should give some idea of the shift in productive capacity. They suggest that in the developing ME there is a general increase in productive capacity in agriculture due to an increase in the use of all three. For the developed ME it depends on how far the increased consumption of fertilisers compensates for the reduction in labour and also, in the case of Europe for land. Investment may be expected to increase the shift.

Turning to Table 11.6, the actual change in production can be seen. Production is, indeed, increasing fastest in the developing ME with an increase of 60% overall in Food$_F$ production between 1961–5 and 1978–80. Among the developing ME regions, Latin America showed the fastest increase in Food$_F$ production of 73% and Africa the slowest with 37%. The increase in production of the centrally planned economies was just slightly lower than in the developing ME at 54% between 1961–5 and 1978–80. The developed ME showed the slowest increase in production of only 37% for agriculture and 41% for Food$_F$. Among them, Oceania showed the fastest increase in the production of both, and other developed countries showed the slowest increase in production. The increase in the production of Food$_F$ by the US was 46% from 1961–5 to 1978–80, but that of Western Europe was only 39%.

TABLE 11.6 The Increase in Agricultural Production and Population in the 1960s and 1970s
1969–71 = 100².

		Production of Agricultural Products (A) and Food (F)						Population		
		1952–6	1961–5	1969–71	1973	1978–80	Increase 1961–5 to 1978–80 %	1963	1979	Increase 1963–79 %
								million		
WORLD	A		84	100	108	124	48	3,160	4,336	37
	F		83	100	108	125	51			
Developed ME										
W. Europe	A	68	86	100	106	120	39	336	371	10
	F	68	86	100	106	120	39			
N. America	A	77	89	100	105	122	37	208	244	17
	F	73	85	100	105	123	45			
of which USA	A		89	100	106	122	37	189	220	16
	F		85	100	105	123	46			
Other developed	A	60	82	100	100	108	31	116	148	27
	F	61	81	100	101	108	34			
Oceania	A		82	100	109	123	50	13.5	17.4	29
	F		82	100	116	134	63			
Total	A	60	87	100	105	119	37	674	780	16
	F		85	100	106	120	41			

Table 11.6 (continued)

		Production of Agricultural Products (A) and Food (F)						Population		
		1952–6	1961–5	1969–71	1973	1978–80	Increase 1961–5 to 1978–80 %	1963	1979	Increase 1963–79 %
								million		
Developing ME										
Africa	A	66	84	100	101	114	36	230	366	59
	F	68	84	100	100	115	37			
Latin America	A	62	82	100	106	134	63	232	359	55
	F	61	79	100	107	137	73			
Near East	A	60	81	100	104	130	61	141	212	50
	F	60	81	100	104	134	65			
Far East	A	62	81	100	108	130	60	842	1215	44
	F	61	81	100	108	131	62			
Total	A		82	100	106	128	57	1448	2157	49
	F		81	100	106	130	60			
Centrally Planned										
Asia CPE	A		82	100	111	134	63	713	1024	44
	F		83	100	110	134	62			
USSR & E. Europe	A		81	100	115	121	49	326	375	15
	F		87	100	116	120	49			
of which USSR	A		80	100	116	119	48	225	264	17
	F		80	100	117	118	48			
Total	A		82	100	113	126	54	1038	1399	35
	F		82	100	113	126	54			

Table 11.6 (continued)

		Production per head					Estimated		
		1961–5	1969–71	1973	1978–80	Increase 1961–5 to 1978–80 %	Increase in GNP per head 1963–79 %	Income elasticity of demand for food	Increase in demand per head 1963–79 %
WORLD	A	96	100	102	105	9	65	0.2–0.4	13–26
	F	95	100	102	106	12			
Developed ME									
W. Europe	A	91	100	104	114	26			
	F	90	100	104	114	27			
N. America	A	97	100	103	113	16			
	F	93	100	102	114	23			
of which USA	A	96	100	103	113	18			
	F	92	100	103	114	24			
Other developed	A	91	100	95	94	4			
	F	90	100	96	95	6			
Oceania	A	94	100	104	108	15			
	F	92	100	111	117	28			
Total	A	93	100	102	111	19			
	F	91	100	103	112	23			
Developing ME									
Africa	A	100	100	93	88	– 12	13[3]	0.4–0.8	5–10
	F	100	100	92	89	–11			
Latin America	A	100	100	98	106	+6	63	0.4–0.8	25–50
	F	96	100	99	107	12			

Table 11.6 (continued)

		Production per head				Increase 1961–5 to 1978–80 %	Estimated		
		1961–5	1969–71	1973	1978–80		Increase in GNP per head 1963–79 %	Income elasticity of demand for food	Increase in demand per head 1963–79 %
Near East	A	98	100	96	102	+4	50	0.4–0.8	20–40
	F	98	100	96	105	+7			
Far East	A	97	100	101	104	+8	25[4]	0.4–0.8	10–20
	F	96	100	101	105	+10			
Total	A	98	100	98	102	4			
	F	97	100	98	103	7			
Centrally Planned									
Asia CPE	A	93	100	105	117	25			
	F	93	100	105	117	26			
USSR & E. Europe	A	87	100	112	112	28	(44)[6]		
	F	87	100	113	112	28			
of which USSR	A	87	100	113	109	26	(41)[5]		
	F	86	100	114	109	27			
Total	A	91	100	108	112	23			
	F	91	100	108	112	23			

Notes: 1. FAO definition excludes tea and coffee and non-edible oils.
2. Indexes extrapolated to 1961–5 with index based on 1961–5 and linked at 1969–71, and then with index based on 1952–6 and linked at 1961–5.
3. 1960–70, 1.7% p.a. 1970, 0.0% p.a.
4. Asia — GNP grew 1.8% p.a. from 1960–70 and 1.1% p.a. from 1970–80.
5. 1970–9.
6. China 1970–9.

Sources: FAO *Production Yearbook* 1980, 1976, 1978 & 1958; IBRD *World Development Report* 1981 Table 1.1.

However, changes in trade depend not only on changes in output but also in consumption. This depends partly on changes in population. As can be seen from Table 11.6, this has increased very much faster in the developing countries, by 49% from 1963 to 1979, than in the developed countries where it increased on average by only 16% over the same period. The increase for the centrally planned areas was 35% but this depends heavily on the FAO estimates for China, which accounts for most of the population of the Asian CPE. The increase for the USSR and Eastern Europe at 15% was comparable to that for the developed ME.

This scale effect of changes in population can be taken account of by calculating the change in agricultural and food production per head. This has increased for all regions in the world except for Africa and other developed countries—see Table 11.6. The increases are greatest for the USSR and Eastern Europe and food for Oceania at an additional 28% between 1961–5 to 1978–80. But they are also high in the rest of the centrally planned economies and in Western Europe and for food in North America.

The other exogenous factor apart fom population accounting for an increase in consumption is the increase in income per head. The World Bank's estimates of these are shown in the fourth from last column in Table 11.6. The effect of increases in income per head depends on the income elasticity of demand for food. The income elasticity for food declines with income. Most estimates are of expenditure elasticities, but as expenditure increases roughly in proportion with income per head for any given country, we can take them as estimates. If we take the range of income elasticities to be between 0.2–0.4 for the developed economies, and 0.4 to 0.8 for the developing ME, we can see from the last column the estimated range of consumption that would occur at constant prices.[2]

From these calculations it can be seen that the lower increases in output of food by the developed ME has been offset by a lower increase in demand due to increases in population and income per head, whereas in the developing ME the increase in production is not sufficient to supply both the increase in population and the estimated increase in demand per head engendered by the increase in *per capita* income even if the lower range of income elasticities is employed. It would appear that the difference in the growth of demand especially for food between the developed ME and developing ME in conjunction with the increase in production would itself be sufficient to account for the changes in trade between 1961–5 and 1979.

What about the situation in the CPE? Food production is shown to have increased quite fast, whereas the population of the Eastern European sector has not, thus the increases in food supplies per head of population have increased by 26% for the Asian CPE and 28% for USSR and Eastern Europe since 1961–5, and 17% and 12% since 1969–71, that is more than twice the world average.

How is this consistent with the general shift of the centrally planned economies from being net exporters to net importers of food as can be seen from the GATT figures Table 8.5, with, as can be seen from Table 11.3, exports of food and agricultural products stagnant or declining since 1969–71 while imports have increased rapidly?

Furthermore, how can the increase in production in the USSR and Eastern Europe plus the shift in trade be consistent with the recent desperate food shortage in Poland?

If we take the World Bank figure of an increase in *per capita* income of the USSR and Eastern Europe of 41% between 1970 and 1979, demand would increase in proportion with output if the income elasticity of demand for food was 0.34. In that case, net imports of food might be expected to increase at the same rate as the total output of food i.e. 20%. In fact, they have increased far faster.

If we take the GATT definition of food, net imports of the USSR and Eastern Europe were $0.43 billion in 1970 rising to $8.60 billion in 1979, that is a twenty-fold increase. The GATT unit value index for agricultural products stood in 1979 at 280% of its level in 1970. This suggests that in real terms net imports of food in 1979 were seven times their level in 1970. Thus, consumption of food must have risen far faster than that implied by a situation of constant prices and income elasticity of 0.34.

An income elasticity for food of 0.34 is relativeley high for an industrialised country; you would expect one higher still if the *per capita* income and consumption of food was low in the first place. The only comparative information available on this is the figures on *per capita* food supply per day supplied by FAO. The available figures on calorie intake for Eastern European and Western European countries are shown in Table 11.7. These show the calorie intake in Eastern European countries (Hungary, Romania, and Poland) as being comparable with those of the Western European countries although there are clearly considerable divergences between them. Calorie consumption increased by 5% from 1969–71 to 1977–9 in Hungary and Poland but by 13% in Romania bringing it nearer the level of the other two and higher than that of many Western European countries. More significantly, as with Western European countries, the consumption of calories

TABLE 11.7 Food Supply — calories per caput per day.

	Total				Animal Products			
	1969–71	1977–9	Absolute Increase	% Increase	1969–71	1977–9	Absolute Increase	% Increase
Developed								
W. Europe								
Belgium, Lux.	3668	3800	132	3.60	1286	1426	140	10.89
Denmark	3359	3345	−14	−.42	1375	1414	39	2.84
Finland	3108	3122	14	0.45	1270	1322	52	4.09
France	3337	3412	75	2.25	1124	1235	111	9.88
Greece	3087	3365	278	9.01	566	757	191	33.75
Italy	3472	3517	45	1.30	653	832	179	27.41
Norway	3033	3218	185	6.10	1083	1172	89	8.22
Sweden	2955	3065	110	3.72	1133	1249	116	10.24
Switzerland	3456	3472	16	0.46	1174	1304	130	11.07
UK	3323	3275	−48	−1.44	1275	1200	−75	−5.88
Yugoslavia	3330	3510	180	5.41	613	802	189	30.83
E. Europe								
Hungary	3369	3553	184	5.46	1134	1268	1134	11.82
Poland	3356	3515	159	4.74	1044	1196	152	14.56
Romania	3020	3411	391	12.95	520	810	290	55.77

Source: FAO, *Production Yearbook 1980*, Table 97, p. 247.

from livestock products has increased far faster than the total at 12%, 15% and 56% respectively. In Poland as in many Western European countries, the increased consumption of livestock products accounts for almost the whole of the increased calorie intake; in certain Western European countries—Belgium, Luxembourg, Denmark, Finland, Italy and Sweden—the increase in calories derived from livestock products appears to have led to a decline in calorie intake from elsewhere. The UK is the exception to the above and her position will be discussed later.

Thus there is no evidence to suggest that food consumption was unusually low in quantitative terms or in terms of the proportion accounted for by livestock products in Eastern European countries and thus no reason to expect a particularly high income elasticity of demand for food. It is, of course, possible that in such highly planned economies with the availability of other consumer goods determined by the state, that the income effects may be different from the rest of the world. However, although the intake of calories from livestock products increased fast in both absolute and proportional terms, the increase for Hungary and Poland was lower than that for Greece and Italy. Only in Romania was it exceptionally high and her intake was very low in the first place.

If we multiply the calorie figures by the population, it appears that the total consumption of calories has increased by 14% for Poland, 9% for Hungary and 24% for Romania between 1969–71 and 1977–9. But the consumption of calories derived from livestock products has increased by 24%, 16% and 71% respectively. It is probably difficulties in producing the latter that cause the problem, as will be discussed later, particularly as these figures are greater then the percentage increase in total output of Poland and Romania.

So far we have considered all changes in production as though they were exogenous changes and we have identified as exogenous changes in consumption those arising from increases in income and population. To what extent can government policies help explain these changes? We are here concerned with government policies that work through the market by altering prices. In this case, as we wish to explain *changes* in trade, we are concerned with *changes* in protective policies.

A straight tariff or increase in tariff, as was explained in Chapter 6, raises prices to both consumers and producers inducing both a reduction in the amount consumed and an increase in the amount produced and for both reason reduces the amount of the commodity imported. But the world situation since 1968 appears confusing; the prices of all commodities entering world trade started to increase more rapidly after 1968, and there was also a sharp rise in relative agricultural prices in the early 1970s. From 1971 onwards there was a general movement away from the fixed exchange-rate system that had existed before and a realigning of rates. This has meant that protective policies such as those of the EEC which have aimed at stabilising domestic prices have often involved fluctuating degrees of protection.

The main blocks of countries which provide positive protection to their agriculture are the US, Japan and the EEC.[3] The form and changes in the level of protection have been discussed in Chapter 5.

However, it is difficult to distinguish the effect of protection from the instability in the world market as a whole. Only in Britain could the movement to a higher food price level be clearly distinguished with identifiable effects on consumption. Between 1970 and 1979, British *real* expenditure per head on food, beverages, and tobacco increased by 10%, but on food alone increased by only 2% although total private consumers' expenditure per head increased by 21%. It was this that showed up as a reduction in total calories, and also calories per head from 1970 to 1979 in Table 11.7.

However, Table 5.5 does show one interesting contrast between the US and the EEC. Since 1968, producer prices of livestock products have increased faster than those of cereals in the US, whereas in every country of the EEC the prices of cereals have increased faster.

In Japan the actual price of food to consumers fell during the early 1960s and then rose slightly more rapidly than the price of other products. There is not much systematic information available on prices to producers.

There is not enough information to assess the effect of changes in relative food prices. But in any case, the whole Japanese situation has been dominated by the rise in population of 1% a year and the very rapid rise in *per capita* income. Expenditure on agricultural products has risen but this has largely represented a substitution of livestock products for cereals. Direct calorie consumption per head has remained stable but consumption of rice has fallen and that of livestock products has risen.

Thus, no general conclusion can be drawn about the effects of government intervention on the market for agricultural products in industrialised countries. When considering total changes in trade, the changes in protection cannot easily be brought in as a single additional explanatory variable.

For developing countries it is even more difficult to distinguish the effect of government intervention in the market from long-run changes. This is even more true when the government has direct control of resources for investment or of direct inputs such as fertilisers as it has in many developing countries and in the centrally planned economies. Over the period since the early 1960s, and even more since 1970, there has been a clear shift in the position of many governments in favour of more resources being devoted to agriculture. The 27% of investment devoted to agriculture in the USSR national plan is just one example of this.

However, in this chapter we are concerned to explain not only the change in the balance of agricultural trade by different regions and countries, but also the structure of international trade.

An important feature for most countries has been an increase in the *per capita* consumption of livestock products as income rises. The only countries in which this has not occurred have been those in which there has scarcely been any increase in *per capita* income (Ghana, Uruguay) or those in which the price of food has risen markedly in relation to that of other products (UK).

This shift in consumption towards livestock products has important implications for agriculture because 100 calories derived from livestock products represents some multiple of that for feed—generally the estimates are approximately three times that for pigs and poultry, meat and eggs and milk and may be seven times that for beef. In any free market you would expect the marginal conversion rates to be reflected in the relative prices of the products. Thus you would expect the relative price for 100 calories consumed in the form of meat to be three or more times greater than that consumed in the form of bread, and you would expect that beef with a higher conversion ratio to be higher than that of pork.

What effect has the increase in demand for livestock products had on trade? You might expect that it would lead to an increase in imports of livestock products by the more densely populated countries from the land-abundant countries of Australia, New Zealand and Canada. On the other hand, the livestock products could be supplied by the domestic industry, whose elasticity of supply would not only depend on the elasticity of supply of the primary factors such as land and labour to it but also the elasticity of supply of feedingstuffs.

In fact, as can be seen from Table 11.2, the value of trade in meat has increased from 6.6% of the total in 1955 to 9.5% in 1979 but the proportion of trade accounted for by dairy products has declined.

This may be due to the protective policies followed by countries in which the increase in consumption of livestock products is taking place. But our study of the EEC and Japan suggests that it is not that the protection afforded livestock products is increasing, but that under the existing protective system, production of livestock products has increased very rapidly and thus the derived demand for feedingstuffs. Furthermore, there is some evidence that as the production of livestock in a country increases, the consumption of feedingstuffs increases more than proportionally. With a fairly low stocking ratio of animals to land, the livestock may be fed on grass, forage, and waste from other processes. But production can only be increased by the greater feeding of concentrates. The concentrates are largely of cereals and oilseed cake. Trade in both of these has increased as a proportion of the total as can be seen from Table 11.2.

TRADE IN CEREALS

Let us begin by considering cereals. Unfortunately, the amount used directly for human consumption throughout the world is not

TABLE 11.8   Trade in All Cereals, Exports (E), Imports (M) and Net Exports (NE) Prewar to 1982 million metric tons per annum

	Average 1934/5–1938/9			Average 1951/2–1955/6			Average 1961/2–1965/6		
	E	M	NE	E	M	NE	E	M	NE
World	42.35			46.56			90.38		
Developed	14.27	31.26	− 16.99	32.84	31.46	+ 1.38	71.19	46.28	+ 24.91
N. America	8.03	2.30	+ 5.73	25.96	2.02	+ 23.94	52.86	1.05	+ 51.81
US	2.71	1.84	+ 0.87	14.52	1.86	+ 12.66	39.63	0.39	+ 39.24
W. Europe	2.46	26.34	− 23.88	3.20	24.53	− 21.33	9.73	14.29	− 4.56
Oceania	3.02	0.07	+ 2.95	3.23	0.21	+ 3.02	7.02	0.17	+ 6.85
Japan	0.42	2.36	− 1.94	0.05	4.00	− 3.95	0.09	7.85	− 7.76
Developing	20.57	8.79	+ 11.78	11.20	12.72	− 1.52	15.49	27.36	− 11.87
Africa	1.14	0.71	+ 0.43	1.32	1.04	+ 0.28	0.78	2.86	− 2.08
Latin America	11.05	2.15	+ 8.90	5.01	4.00	+ 1.01	9.21	6.31	+ 2.90
Near East	0.88	0.27	+ 0.61	1.62	1.36	+ 0.26	1.14	4.99	− 3.85
Far East	7.50	5.61	+ 1.89	3.22	6.24	− 3.02	4.36	13.03	− 8.67
India	0.35	2.27	− 1.92	–	2.20	− 2.20	–	5.79	− 5.79
Centrally planned	7.94	2.16	+ 5.78	2.86	1.22	+ 1.46	3.66	14.11	− 10.45
Asia	2.43	1.39	+ 1.04	0.89	0.03	+ 0.86	1.43	5.94	− 4.51
China(a)	1.11	1.39	− 0.28	0.72	0.02	+ 0.70	0.99	5.78	− 4.29
USSR & E Europe (b)	5.51	0.76	+ 4.75	1.79	1.19	+ 0.60	2.23	8.17	− 5.94
USSR	1.30	0.11	+ 1.19	1.30	0.30	+ 1.00	1.36	4.11	− 2.75

Sources: See Table 11.9.

known, although it is known for most of the industrialised countries. The most important cereal in direct consumption is wheat, used chiefly to make bread but also to make pasta. In English-speaking countries, hard wheat is generally required for bread and durum wheat for pasta—both types of wheat have a high protein content and are sold at a premium. But soft wheat is also used in bread and confectionery. Soft wheat may be used as a feedingstuff, particularly for poultry if its price is low enough. Rye is another bread grain but is now of scarcely any importance in international trade. Rice is the second most important grain for human consumption; it is the staple grain in South-East Asia but it is not important in international trade, accounting for only 6% of the total by weight but 13% by value in 1979.

The other grains—barley, maize, sorghum, millet, oats—are predominantly used as feedingstuffs although they may be used either in industry or for some particular food or drink, e.g. maize for breakfast foods, starch, and now as a basis for sweeteners, and

Table 11.8 (continued)

Average 1969–71			*1973*			*Average 1978–80*			*1982*		
E	M	NE	E	M	NE	E	M	NE	E	M	NE
110.53			164.49			204.52			220.83		
79.77	57.88	+21.89	134.36	66.63	+67.73	172.69	74.57	+98.12	184.40	73.62	+110.78
50.09	0.89	+49.20	98.83	1.17	+97.66	122.79	1.15	+121.64	127.21	1.30	+125.91
36.33	0.37	+35.96	82.41	0.26	+82.15	103.31	0.20	+103.11	100.60	0.40	+100.20
18.87	40.74	−21.87	25.65	45.48	−19.83	31.96	47.41	−15.45	37.87	46.02	−8.15
8.87	0.06	+8.81	7.55	0.01	+7.54	14.29	0.04	+14.25	14.67	0.03	+14.64
0.68	14.72	−14.04	0.58	18.61	−18.03	0.56	24.08	−23.52	0.57	24.37	−23.80
18.14	32.54	−14.40	16.77	44.80	−28.03	23.31	67.07	−43.76	29.00	75.81	−46.81
0.82	4.26	−3.44	0.08	6.55	−5.75	0.50	12.06	−11.56	0.43	15.35	−14.92
11.63	8.15	+3.48	10.34	12.44	−2.10	13.28	20.71	−7.43	15.97	18.37	−2.40
0.94	6.69	−5.75	1.07	6.84	−5.77	1.71	17.49	−15.78	2.12	23.93	−21.81
4.75	13.23	−8.48	4.56	18.73	−14.17	7.83	16.49	−8.66	10.48	17.80	−7.32
0.03	3.65	−3.62	0.43	3.69	−3.26	0.91	0.41	+0.50	0.60	2.40	−1.80
12.62	18.74	−6.12	13.36	46.22	−32.86	8.44	60.45	−52.01	7.43	71.85	−64.42
2.29	7.89	−5.60	3.78	12.89	−9.11	2.17	17.18	−15.01	1.00	21.45	−20.45
2.04	5.23	−3.19	3.61	9.06	−5.45	1.59	4.99	−13.40	0.67	20.37	−19.70
10.33	10.84	−0.51	9.58	33.33	−23.75	6.27	43.27	−37.00	6.43	50.40	−43.97
8.18	2.68	+5.50	5.81	24.38	−18.57	2.88	27.19	−24.31	2.22	40.0	−37.88

barley for beer. Bearing this in mind, let us turn to consider trade in cereals. We will consider it in quantitative terms (see Table 11.8). As can be seen from Table 11.8, the pattern of trade established in the mid-1950s was very similar to the pre-war situation except for the decline in the position of the Far East and Latin America in the export markets and the growing importance of North America, particularly the US. Over the next twenty-five years, the whole situation changed dramatically. US net exports tripled between the early 1950s and 1960s, then stabilised, and then tripled again between 1969–71 and 1978–80. The US now exports three times the total quantity of cereals entering world trade in the mid-1930s and two and three quarter times that in the mid-1950s. Whereas the developing countries' deficit in the cereal market is equal to the total quantity of cereals entering the world market in the 1950s. This deficit is contributed to by each of the developing ME regions, even Latin America, which in the 1930s was a major exporter, accounting for a quarter of world exports.

But this shift in the position of the developing ME was matched by the shift in the position of the CPE. The CPE were, apart from China, net exporters of cereals before the war, were approximately self-sufficient by the early 1950s, but had moved into deficit by the early 1960s. This deficit fell somewhat to 6 million tons in 1969–71 but since then has grown to 64 million tons in 1982, 29% or world exports. The greatest change is perhaps that of net imports into the USSR and Eastern Europe which grew from 0.51 million tons in 1969–71 to 37.46 million tons in 1978–80; this represents an increase from $1\frac{1}{2}$ Kg to 100 Kg per head of the population of that region. In 1982, the region's net imports had risen to 44 million tons.

Among industrialised countries, Japan has also expanded her net imports rapidly from 3.95 million tons in the early 1950s to 23.52 million tons in 1978–80. On the other hand, the net imports of Western Europe are lower than they were pre-war or in the 1950s.

TRADE IN WHEAT

Within this total trade in grain, the special position of wheat should be considered. As the traditional bread grain, it has been accorded special status in most of the Western industrialised countries. In the US, many special provisions have been directed at it and as we have seen in the EEC, its initial price differential was high, far higher than on the world market. Because these measures provided an incentive for increased production it also featured largely in the surplus disposal programmes of the US and later of the EEC. This encouraged consumers in Japan and in developing countries, who in any case were influenced by Western tastes, to increase their bread consumption. The slow increase in rice production also contributed to this. The result of this combination of factors can be seen in Tables 11.8 and 11.9.

The developed MEs, which were net importers of wheat before the war and net exporters to the extent of 5 million tons in the early 1950s, have now become very large net exporters to the extent of 59 million tons in 1978–80 and 75 million tons in 1982. This is due to the very rapid increase in US exports of wheat so that in the 1970s it stood at more than four times its level in the early 1950s, whereas Western Europe changed from being a net importer of 12 million tons in the early 1950s to a net exporter of 8.6 million tons by 1982. Japanese net imports increased to $5\frac{1}{2}$ million tons which was not enough to change the overall position of developed countries.

In contrast, the developing ME countries, which were small net exporters of wheat in the pre-war period, emerged in the post-war period as net importers to the extent of 5 million tons in the early 1950s and their net imports increased seven-fold to 34 million tons in 1978–80. This represented 15.7 Kg per head of population within these regions. They then increased to 40 million tons in 1982. Net imports have increased for each region but within the Far East, India's position has fluctuated from being a net importer to a marginal net exporter.

The position of the centrally planned economies has also changed quite dramatically. The USSR and Eastern Europe were net exporters of wheat in the pre-war period and were still net exporters in the early 1950s but were in 1978–80 net importers of 12.34 million tons. This represented net imports of 33 Kg of wheat per head of population. The position of the Asian CPE is largely determined by that of China whose net imports increased to 10 million tons of wheat in 1978–80. By 1982, their net imports had risen to 22 million tons into the USSR and Eastern Europe and 15 million into China.

The other cereal which is used for direct human consumption is rice. But only 11 million tons of it were exported in 1978–80, so it only represented 6% of international trade by weight. Furthermore, most of the trade took part between the developing countries of the Far East. The developing ME countries of the Far East accounted for 39% of world exports and 33% of world imports, and China accounted for an additional 13% of world exports. The only other major exporter was the US, which accounted for 22% of world exports.

Apart from wheat and a small amount of rice, most of the trade

TABLE 11.9   Trade in Wheat, Exports (E), Imports (M) and Net Exports (NE) Prewar to 1982 million metric tons per annum.

	Average 1934/5–1938/9			Average 1951/2–1955/6			Average 1961/2–1965/6		
	E	M	NE	E	M	NE	E	M	NE
World	18.28			26.50			49.76		
Developed	11.02	13.85	− 2.83	21.98	16.67	+ 5.31	44.32	16.51	+ 27.81
N. America	6.35	0.78	+ 5.57	17.47	0.49	+ 16.98	32.75	0.09	+ 32.66
US	1.54	0.73	+ 0.81	8.93	0.48	+ 8.45	20.59	0.09	+ 20.50
W. Europe	1.38	12.58	− 11.20	1.92	13.53	− 11.61	5.27	12.57	− 7.30
Oceania	2.93	0.05	+ 2.88	2.54	0.21	+ 2.33	6.21	0.17	+ 6.04
Japan	0.36	0.35	+ 0.01	0.04	1.90	− 1.86	0.09	3.29	− 3.20
Developing	4.51	3.60	+ 0.91	3.60	8.53	− 4.93	4.53	19.76	− 15.23
Africa	0.48	0.27	+ 0.21	0.32	0.62	− 0.30	0.15	1.75	− 1.60
Latin America	3.40	1.72	+ 1.68	2.59	3.48	− 0.89	4.13	5.10	− 0.97
Near East	0.23	0.17	+ 0.06	0.65	1.16	− 0.51	0.18	4.06	− 3.88
Far East	0.40	1.43	− 1.03	0.04	3.22	− 3.18	0.07	8.74	− 8.67
India	0.28	0.06	+ 0.22	—	1.40	− 1.40	—	4.88	− 4.88
Centrally planned	2.75	0.90	+ 1.85	0.93	0.61	+ 0.32	0.91	11.85	− 10.94
Asia	—	0.76	− 0.76	—	—	—	—	5.22	− 5.22
China(a)	—	0.76	− 0.76	—	—	—	—	5.22	− 5.22
USSR & E. Europe(b)	2.75	0.13	+ 2.62	0.93	0.61	+ 0.32	0.91	6.63	− 5.72
USSR	0.63	0.07	+ 0.56	0.73	0.06	+ 0.67	0.87	3.83	− 2.96

Notes: (a) In 1934/5–1938/9 includes Taiwan.
(b) Except for 1934/5–1938/9 excludes trade between centrally planned economies.
Regional definitions those of FAO *Trade Yearbook*, 1980.
Wheat includes wheat equivalent of flour.

in cereals is for feedingstuffs. So by deducting the figures for wheat from that of cereals from Tables 11.8 and 11.9 the pattern of trade in feedingstuffs can be obtained. (It includes trade in rice but as stated this is small and a third takes place within the region of the Far East.) This shows quite clearly the growing dominant position of the US. Her exports of cereals for feed in the pre-war period were only 1.17 (2.71 − 1.54) million tons, that is 5% of world exports, by the 1950s this had risen to 5.59 (14.52 − 8.93) million tons which was 28% of world exports, and by 1978–80 it had risen to 67.62 (103.31 − 35.69) million tons which was 59% of world exports (2.54 million tons of this were rice).

The other major exporters of cereals as feedingstuffs in 1978–80 were Western Europe with exports of 15.40 million tons, Latin America with 9.62 million tons and the Far East with 7 million

Table 11.6 (continued)

	Average 1969–71			1973			Average 1978–80			1982	
E	M	NE	E	M	NE	E	M	NE	E	M	NE
54.75			81.57			86.21			104.70		
44.22	18.61	+25.61	70.13	19.26	+50.87	78.65	19.78	+58.87	95.04	20.41	+74.63
27.62	0.03	+27.59	51.36	—	+51.36	50.84	—	+50.84	61.25	0.06	+61.19
16.79	0.03	+16.76	38.44	—	+38.44	35.69	—	+35.69	41.62	0.06	+41.56
9.14	13.50	−4.36	12.71	13.59	−0.88	16.56	13.49	+3.07	22.53	13.95	+8.58
7.41	0.03	+7.38	5.66	—	+5.66	11.01	0.03	+10.98	11.00	—	+11.00
0.05	4.63	−4.58	0.04	5.39	−5.35	0.10	5.72	−5.62	0.25	5.71	−5.46
2.50	22.65	−20.15	4.39	29.72	−25.33	5.55	39.32	−33.77	4.77	44.34	−39.57
0.10	2.82	−2.72	0.08	4.57	−4.49	0.02	7.93	−7.91	0.01	9.35	−9.34
2.14	6.22	−4.08	3.14	8.72	−5.58	3.62	11.09	−7.47	4.00	11.51	−7.51
0.05	5.40	−5.35	0.60	5.33	−4.73	1.14	11.52	−10.38	0.64	13.49	−12.85
0.21	8.08	−7.87	0.56	10.95	−10.39	0.77	8.61	−7.84	0.12	9.81	−9.69
0.01	2.87	−2.86	0.41	2.24	−1.83	0.50	0.34	+0.16	N.A.	2.40	?
8.04	12.38	−4.34	7.05	27.73	−20.68	4.49	28.33	−23.84	4.89	42.83	−37.94
0.01	5.54	−5.53	0.01	7.67	−7.66	0.01	11.50	−11.49	—	15.75	−15.75
0.01	4.47	−4.46	0.01	5.95	−5.94	—	9.65	−9.65	—	14.75	−14.75
8.03	6.85	+1.18	7.04	20.06	−13.02	4.49	16.83	−12.34	4.88	27.08	−22.20
7.08	1.77	+5.31	5.05	15.63	−10.58	2.66	11.91	−9.25	1.97	22.16	−20.19

Rice: 1934/5–1938/9 cereal data include rice average of calendar year 1934–8.

1951/2–1955/6 cereal data include rice average of calendar year 1952–6.

1961/2–1965/6 cereal data include rice average of calendar year 1962–6.

Sources: FAO *Trade Yearbooks*, 1974, 1975, 1980, 1982; FAO *World Grain Trade Statistics*, 1965/6, 1973/4; FAO *Rice Reports* 1966, 1967, 1970.

tons. But these regions were also large importers, so North America was the only large net exporting region of feedingstuffs and of its total of 70.8 net exports of cereals for feed, 67.45 were supplied by the US.

Clearly, a counterpart to the growing net exports of the US must have been the growing net imports of other parts of the world. The first of the most significant deficit regions to emerge appears to be the USSR and Eastern Europe. Up to 1969–71, its cereal imports were mainly of wheat but since then its imports of other grains have grown very fast from 3.99 million tons in 1969–71 to 26.50 million tons in 1978–80; the latter represents a net deficit of 25 million tons of cereals other than wheat. Since then it has declined slightly.

The second major deficit region is Japan, whose imports of cereals other than wheat grew from 2.10 in the 1950s to 18.36 million tons in 1978–80. Her net imports increased from 2.09 million tons in the 1950s to 17.90 million tons in 1978–80 and 18.34 in 1982.

Western Europe's imports of other cereals have also grown from 11.00 million tons in the 1950s to 33.92 in 1978–80. There is a considerable amount of intra-European trade but her net imports of cereals other than wheat grew from 9.72 in the 1950s to 18.52 million tons in 1978–80 and then fell to 11.73 in 1982.

It might be noted that in all these areas protective policies are followed, particularly with respect to livestock. In both the USSR and Eastern Europe and Japan, there is no systematic relation between domestic prices and international prices. In the EEC the protection afforded to milk products and beef tends to be higher than that afforded to feed grains.

OILSEEDS, OILS AND FATS

Oilseeds, oils and fats are the next most important category of agricultural exports; it has increased rapidly from $1,398 million in 1955 to $23,303 in 1979. Oilseeds, generally seeds or nuts, but sometimes fruits, are used mainly for the extraction of culinary or industrial oils. The world production and trade of the main groups and the most important oils are given in Table 11.10. The edible vegetable oils and palm oils are highly substitutable for each other in consumption. In a true Arrow sense, they each comprise a bundle of characteristics such that the largest UK producer of margarine could alter its intake of oils according to a linear programme of their characteristics and the New York price to produce margarine of the same specifications but the lowest cost. In human consumption, they compete directly as oil with butter and lard and also indirectly in their use in margarine and shortening. Marine oils are also used in margarine and shortening. Generally, the cheaper vegetable and animal oils are used in the production of soap with 10–20% of lauric acid oils, that is, palm kernel and coconut oils, to produce the lather.

The non-edible oils, the chief of which are linseed and castor, are excluded from the FAO definition of food and feedingstuffs but included in the GATT definition of food. During the Second World War, linseed oil was modified for human consumption, and castor

TABLE 11.10: *Fats, Oils and Oil Seed (Oil Equivalent) World Production and Exports 1950–4 to 1979*
1000 tonnes

	World Production				World Exports		
	1950–4	1969–71	1979–80	1980–1[p]	1950–4	1969–71	1979[p]
Edible Vegetable Oils	8514	19,804	29,381	32,600	1375	5397	10,067
Cotton seed	1569	2425	3011	3230	171	306	372
Peanut	1610	3233	3382	3166	568	803	741
Soyabean	1864	6078	11,681	14,391	367	2657	6105
Sunflower	875	3714	4661	5520	98	868	1236
Rape seed	939	1947	3663	3449	65	519	1252
Olive	980	1363	1554	1390	53[a]	98[a]	129[a]
Palm Oils	3480	4436	7700	8366	2039	2299	4030
Coconut	1891	2183	2822	3017	1134	1156	1234
Palm kernel	381	480	646	662	370	325	380
Palm	1161	1727	4085	4537	527	808	2411
Industrial Oils	1332	1735	1387	1461	581	739	662
Linseed	1007	1110	744	815	406	449	381
Castor	200	348	386	388	119	236	238
Animal Fats	9485	12,446	14,519	14,463	1170	2515	3936
Butter (fat content)	3311	3916	4957	4957	358	508	881
Lard	3837	4105	4012	3956	295	459	520
Tallow grease	2336	4424	5550	5550	517	1549	2535
Marine Oils	989	1250	1336	1203	630	713	620
TOTAL	23,708	39,671	54,327	58,093	5795	11,663	19,315

Notes: [p]Preliminary; [a]Net exports.
Sources: USDA, *Agricultural Statistics*, 1959, 1973, 1979, 1981.

oil can be used for medicinal purposes. But their main uses are as raw materials in which they face considerable competition from synthetics.

In the last century it was the European need for additional supplies of fats and oils that led to the development of trade. By 1938, the demand for oilseeds still emanated chiefly from Europe, but the US and Japan had emerged as substantial importers. In terms of oil equivalent, trade was greatest in copra (dried coconut), groundnut, linseed, palm oil, soyabean, and palm kernels in declining order of importance. The export flow was from the developing countries of West Africa and Asia to the industrialised countries. Apart from palm oil and olive oil obtained from the fruit, which has to be extracted *in situ*, the exports were in the form of seed, which was crushed in the industrialised countries. The residual oilseed cake and meal, which was very rich in protein, was used as an animal feed. The subsequent trade in oil and cake by the industrialised countries is excluded from the exports which we are here considering.

The joint production of oils and oilseed cake is a very important feature of the market in oilseeds. Furthermore, the proportions differ between them. The proportion of oil is highest for copra with 64%, medium for palm kernels and groundnuts with 47% and 45% of oil respectively, lower for sunflower and rape seed with 35% and lowest for soyabeans and cottonseed with 17% and 16% respectively.

During the war, US farmers were encouraged to expand their production of oilseed, in particular of groundnuts and soyabeans. They emerged with almost double their previous level of output in a situation in which the output of the rest of the world was much lower; the production in most of the countries of the Commonwealth had declined slightly and that of Indonesia and the Philippines was only about a tenth of its previous level. Indeed, the world output of oils and fats only reached its pre-war level by 1949 and even then, trade was still 20% lower. There was considerable anxiety about the world shortage of fats and oils and thus the British colonial authorities endeavoured to expand the production of oilseeds in their dependencies in Africa. In these circumstances, the US contributed supplies to the rest of the world under various forms of aid agreement including the European Recovery Programme. By 1949, the US had become the largest exporter.

Since then, world production has increased rapidly (see Table 11.10). In 1969–71 in terms of oil equivalent, it was two thirds greater than it was in 1950–4 and it has increased by about a half since then. Trade increased even faster even though, as can be seen from Table 2.3, there was a negative trend in the *real* price of oilseeds, oils and fats and oilcake from 1968 to 1980. Exports in terms of oil equivalent doubled between 1950–4 and 1969–71 and then increased by another two thirds to 1979. But the composition of the trade has changed. Several factors have contributed to this.

First let us consider demand. Studies on the income or expenditure or income elasticity of demand for oils and fats for food, show that it tends to be lower the higher the level of income. Thus, you would expect demand per head to be increasing faster in the developing than in the developed countries. Unfortunately, the only comparative information on such consumption is for the latter. As can be seen from Table 11.11, between 1955/6 and 1978 the *per capita* consumption of oils and fats for food increased in all the countries shown, very fast in Japan where it quintupled over the period, but more slowly in the others; in the UK it increased by only 4% over the period. For a number of EEC countries, notably Belgium, the Netherlands and Germany, it has recently started to decline. These changes in consumption are, of course, the combined effects of changes in income and price, although you would expect price changes to be a more important determinant of composition than the overall level of consumption. An additional determinant of composition is the trend against animal fats induced apparently by fear of their high cholesterol level.

For instance, although the consumption of oils and fats per head in the US increased by 16% between 1955/6 and 1978, the consumption of butter more than halved and the consumption of lard fell by four fifths, while the consumption of margarine increased by 39%, that of shortening by 63%, and the consumption of edible oils used as such more than doubled. Changes of this magnitude are difficult to attribute to price changes when the real price of butter fell over the period, albeit less than that of margarine and vegetable oils. Similarly, it is unlikely that the recent decline in consumption of butter in some of the European countries can be attributed to price changes except in Britain, where her accession to the CAP led to an increase in the *real* price of butter of 47% from the beginning of 1974 to the end of 1978.

Another usage of edible and lauric-acid oils is in soap, including washing powders. There are few statistics on consumption but taking as a proxy production figures, this appears to be on the increase in all developing countries. However, in most industrialised countries, it is declining because of substitution by synthetic detergents. Indeed, in the US, *per capita* consumption has fallen from 8.6 Kg p.a. in 1950 to 1.8 in 1979 (USDA, *Agricultural Statistics*, 1981).

TABLE 11.11 Per capita Consumption of Fats and Oils for Food in OECD Countries 1955/6 to 1978
Kg per head per year of oil equivalent

	1955/6		1964				1978			
	Total	Butter	Total	Butter	Vegetable Oils and Fats	Margarine and Prop. Fats	Total	Butter	Vegetable Oils and Fats	Margarine and Prop. Fats
North America										
Canada	19.1	7.5	20.1	6.9	2.2	3.2	23.1	3.8	4.2	4.8
United States	21.2	3.6	21.5	2.5	6.4	9.8	24.5	1.6	9.6	12.3
Japan	2.7		6.8	0.2	5.0	—	13.3	0.5	10.5	—
West Europe										
EEC (6)	19.8	4.5	24.1	5.3	3.2	12.6	27.5	7.2	3.7	10.0
Belgium, Lux.	24.6	9.3	28.3	8.1	8.9	3.3	26.5	8.0	10.8	3.6
France	18.7	6.0	22.8	7.1	3.6	9.1	25.4	5.7	5.2	3.6
Germany	25.6	5.7	26.2	7.3						
Italy	11.2	1.2	17.2	1.3	13.2	1.0	23.9[P]	1.7	20.0	1.5[P]
Netherlands	30.4	2.5	31.7	4.0	2.3	20.9	32.9[P]	2.7	3.8	17.7[P]
EFTA	20.9	5.1	22.0	6.1						
United Kingdom	21.9	5.4	21.9	7.0	14.9		22.8[P]	5.9	6.4[P]	7.4
Oceania										
Australia		7.7	14.3[a]	7.7	1.1	4.2[a]	14.2	4.3	5.1	7.9
New Zealand		15.7		15.7				11.1		
OECD Total	17.9	4.0	20.7	4.2						

Notes: [P]Provisional; [a]For 1965.
Sources: OECD, *Food Consumption Statistics 1964–1978* (OECD, Paris, 1981) for countries for 1964 and 1978; OECD, *Agricultural Statistics 1955–1968* (OECD, Paris, 1969) for countries for 1955/6 and totals for 1955/6 and 1964/5.

Thus, to summarise, the decline in the consumption of soap, together with the low increase in population and the low income elasticity of demand for fats and oils for food on the part of high-income countries would lead you to expect a relatively low increase in their consumption of vegetable oils. But demand for them has been boosted by their substitution for animal fats. To what extent this is due to an exogenous trend and to what extent to the protective policies pursued by the industrialised countries, in particular the very high price of butter in the EEC, the author leaves others to determine. However, the buoyancy of the market in industrialised countries in the earlier part of the period is indicated by the increase in consumption in various countries; a ten-fold increase in Japan between 1952 and 1970, an increase of 73% in the US, 85% in Germany, 121% in France, 59% in the Netherlands, but a decline of 16% in the UK (CEC, *Vegetable Oils and Oilseeds*, No. 21 and No. 9, *Estimates of New Supplies*).

However, most developing countries appeared unable to take advantage of this situation. They increased their output of oilseed except for groundnuts, but this increase was diverted to home consumption and there was a comparatively small increase in exports. These increased from 3,243 thousand tons of oil equivalent in 1950 to 3,715 in 1970, an increase of 15% over twenty years (CEC, *Vegetable Oils and Oilseeds*, 1956 and No. 21). This situation is particularly noticeable for palm crops, which are entirely supplied by developing countries. As can be seen from Table 11.10, between 1950–4 and 1979–80, production of coconut and palm kernels increased by 49% and 70% respectively, but exports remained stagnant or declined. Exports of palm oil did increase but this was almost entirely due to one country, Malaysia, who between 1952 and 1980 increased her exports of palm oil by 2 million tons.

In addition, the developing countries were anxious to obtain some of the value added in processing by crushing their oilseed crops domestically. So, whereas in 1938 almost all palm kernels and groundnuts were exported as such, by 1955 these proportions had been reduced to 91% for palm kernels and 59% for groundnuts.

The major crushing firms in the industrialised countries realised that this could make some of their equipment redundant and were, therefore, pleased to be able to acquire soyabeans from the US.

Meanwhile, the US was rapidly expanding her production and exports of soyabeans. By 1950, she had net exports of 757 thousand tons; by 1954 these had doubled and by 1959 they had doubled yet again. A factor contributing to this rapid increase was a shift in the relative demand for the products of oilseeds from oil to cake. The use of oilseed cake as fodder had been rapidly increasing in the US, by 81% between 1950 and 1970 and almost all of it was soyabean meal. The demand for oilseed cake also increased in other countries. The result was that after falling with fluctuations between 1951 and 1959, the price of soyabean meal then increased. But the price of soyabean oil continued to fall until the late 1960s. In 1980, the actual price of soyabean oil was 90% higher and that of soyabean meal 176% higher than in 1950. In real terms, the price of both were lower than they were in the mid-1960s (World Bank, 1981).

The increase in the demand for oilseed cake reinforced the demand for soyabeans which produce a high proportion of cake of a high protein content.

In the EEC, the demand for oilseed cake was strengthened by the adoption of the CAP which, as described in Chapter 5, established high rates of protection and therefore prices for livestock products and cereals but did not impose tariffs on the imports of oilseeds or oilseed cake. As can be seen in Table 11.12, soyabean imports have increased rapidly, induced in part by the fall in the price of soyabean meal in most EEC countries in contrast to the rise in the price of feed grains. This is particularly marked for the UK where although the price of soyabean meal rose by 0.8% a year between 1973 and 1979, the price of barley and oats rose by 15% p.a. and maize by 12.6% p.a.

The Commission has argued that 'Soya is not a cereal substitute: it is a major and independent source of protein for animal production in the Community ... it has undoubtedly contributed substantially to the holding of production costs and to technical efficiency.' (Commission of the European Communities, 1980, pp. 97–105.)

However, it is misleading to regard it only as a new form of technology because as the Commission elsewhere states, a high-grade protein such as oilseed cake in combination with a low-priced feedingstuff such as manioc can replace in a compounder's formula an equivalent quantity of maize, barley or feed wheat.

The rapid increase in the marketable supplies of oilseeds for fodder in the EEC, by 45% between 1972/3 and 1978/9 (see table 11.12), in contrast with the relatively stable level of cereals must be regarded at least partially as a response to the relative price structure which has been distorted by the CAP.

But in so far as it has led to an increase in the level of protein used in livestock feed, it may, as the Commission states, have added to technical efficiency but in the form of increasing output and thus adding to the EEC surpluses of milk and milk products and beef.

As the US is the chief supplier of soyabeans, this increase in con-

TABLE 11.12 Feedingstuffs in the EEC (9) 1972 to 1980
million tonnes

	1972	1973	1974	1975	1976	1977	1978	1979	1980
Imports[1]									
Soyabean			9.1	8.2	9.2	9.0	10.8	11.7	12.2
Soya cake & meal			3.4	3.4	4.2	4.1	5.8	6.2	6.4
Manioc				2.2	3.0	3.8	6.0	5.4	5.7
Cereal brans				1.5	2.3	2.2	1.9	2.0	2.0
Maize gluten feeds				0.9	1.1	1.5	1.7	2.0	2.5

Animal Feedingstuffs Marketable[2]								
Years	1972/73	1973/74	1974/75	1975/76	1976/77	1977/78	1978/79	1979/80
Cereal	71,982	73,265	71,144	68,705	68,558	68,882	72,257	71,646
Oilseeds	14,496	13,954	14,471	16,629	17,473	18,024	20,988	23,011

Sources: 1. Commission of the European Communities, *The Agricultural Situation in the Community, 1980 Report*, p. 97.
2. Eurostat, *Yearbook of Agricultural Statistics 1977–1980*, p. 216, published in 1982 and previous years, (Animal Feedingstuffs Marketable).

*TABLE 11.13   Net Exports of Fats and Oils (Oil Equivalent) and Oilcake
and Meal (Protein Basis) in 1980 by Region.*
1000 tonnes

	Fats & Oils[1]	Oilcake and Meal[2]
Developed Countries	690	− 4950
N. America	8430	11,620
US	5887[1]	
W. Europe	− 5470	− 11,360
EEC	− 4830	− 9370
E. Europe & USSR	− 910	− 3020
USSR	− 720	− 540
Oceania	390	10
Others	− 1750	− 2200
Japan	− 1840[3]	− 2080[3]
Developing Countries	− 610	4560
Latin America	1100	5120
Africa	− 790	150
Near East	− 1870	− 200
Far East	740	− 580
Asian CPE	− 590	− 550
World	20,990[4]	19,920[4]

Notes: 1. Including oil equivalent of oilseeds.
2. Including cake equivalent of oilseeds.
3. Imports.
4. Exports.
Sources: FAO, *Commodity Review and Outlook, 1981−82.*
1. 1978, USDA, *Agricultural Statistics 1981,* p. 142. Total fats and oils.

sumption has compensated her for the adverse effect of the variable
levy system on her exports of feedgrains. The real value of US
exports of feedgrains to the EEC fell between 1973 and 1980. But
her total exports of fodder to the EEC, that is feedgrains, oilseeds,
and oilseed cake, increased in real terms, that is, they increased
from $2174 million to $5232 million, an increase of 158% over the
period, which was greater than the increase in the general price index of 81%. In 1973, 69% of the total was oilseed cake, and soyabean and cake alone accounted for 64%. By 1980, 77% was oilseed
and cake, and soyabean and cake alone accounted for 69%. The
response of the EEC to this situation was to try and increase its production of oilseeds, and its output of sunflower seed doubled
between 1974 and 1979, but it was not successful with other
oilseeds. Recently it has succeeded in increasing the use of cereals
for fodder.

Finally let us look at the overall situation in the two markets
for oilseeds, that is, for oils and fats, and for oilcake and meal.

TABLE 11.14 *Exports by Value of Oilseeds and Products and Butter in 1980.*
$ million

	Oilseeds	Fats and Oils[1]	Of which Butter	Oilcakes and Meals	Total
Developed Countries	7680	10,410	3395	3420	21,520
N. America	7080	2250	1	1830	11,160
US[2]	6794	2030[3]	1	1718	10,596
W. Europe	460	6950	2903	1530	8940
EEC (9)	420	6080	2864	1250	7750
E. Europe & USSR	60	460	88	10	530
USSR	10	180	26	10	190
Oceania	40	570†	398		610
Developing Countries	1910	4680	19	2950	9541
Latin America	1250	1330	5.6	2360	4940
Africa	140	380	0.7	110	640
Near East	90	30	1.2	40	150
Far East	340	2870	11.2	430	3640
Asian CPE	130	40	–	10	170
World	9590	15,100	3413	6380	31,060

N.B. Developed Countries include Eastern Europe and the USSR.
Notes: 1. Including animal fats and marine oils.
2. Fiscal year 1 October–30 September.
3. 1244 vegetable oils & waxes, 785 animal fats.
Sources: FAO, *Commodity Review and Outlook, 1981–82;* USDA, *Agricultural Statistics, 1981;* FAO, *Trade Yearbook, 1980.*

Exports of oilseeds are attributed to the two according to their oil and protein content. As can be seen from Table 11.13, the developed countries (including Eastern Europe and the USSR) have an overall balance of net exports of oils and fats but this is entirely due to the net exports of North America, in particular the US. Western Europe is a large net importer and so is Japan, and Eastern Europe as a whole is in deficit. Among the developing regions, the Near East is a large net importer, and the only regions with net exports are Latin America and the Far East, the former due to a rapid expansion of oilseed production and exports, particularly of soyabeans by Argentina and Brazil, and the latter, as mentioned, due to palm oil exports by Malaysia.

The developed countries are net importers of oilcakes and meal even though North America is a major net exporter. Most of the net imports go to the EEC, but Eastern Europe and Japan are also major importers. Most of the net exports from developing countries are provided by Latin America.

However, a better idea of the value of trade is given in Table 11.14. As can be seen, the US accounts for a third of the value of world exports. Most of her exports are of oilseeds and she accounts for 71% of world exports of oilseeds. Latin America is the other major source of oilseeds.

The developed countries account for most of the exports of fats and oils. The EEC exports $6 billion of these but almost half is butter. About half of this butter goes to other members of the EEC: the other half is exported to non-members and must, therefore, be subsidised. The EEC accounts for 84% of world exports of butter.

In the oilseed cake market, as we have already seen, Europe is the largest deficit market—indeed, the EEC accounts for half all imports by quantity. The major suppliers of oilseed cake are Latin America and North America—most EEC exports go to other members.

NOTES

1. But GATT includes Israel among Developing Countries.
2. Clearly this analysis involves simplification in so far as the income of the agricultural population is partly dependent on their production. To take expenditure elasticities as a proxy for income elasticities assumes a constant relationship between households' expenditure and *per capita* income of a country.
3. The level of support provided in East Europe and the USSR is difficult to determine.

12 Fuels

Now let us turn to consider trade in fuels. Public attention in the last decade has been focused on oil and the dependence of the world on a few Middle Eastern suppliers for most imports, a dependence of which most people only became fully aware when the OPEC producers quadrupled the price of oil in 1973–4, which not only raised the price of fuel but also pushed the world economy into a turmoil from which it has never fully recovered (see Table 12.1).

We have already discussed in Chapter 10 the shift in the balance of power from the large oil multinationals to OPEC. Here we are concerned with the growth in consumption and trade in oil that led to this dependence on Middle Eastern producers. But as the major use of oil is as a fuel, this is just part of a larger phenomenon, namely the growth and change in the market for fuels. Fuels are sources of heat and energy and as such, oil competes with other hydrocarbons such as coal and natural gas, and also hydroelectricity and electricity generated by nuclear power plant.

In studying the market in fuels, the first problem is that of a numeraire. What measure can be applied to different fuels in order to aggregate them? Normally, some measure of calorific value is taken and the totals are expressed directly in terms of energy as calories or joules, or in thermal equivalents of metric tons of coal (m.t.c.e.) or in metric tons of oil (m.t.o.e.). One of the problems in doing so is that some fuel is consumed directly such as petrol in cars, coal, natural gas, or fuel oil for heating, but that a considerable amount is used indirectly to generate electricity which is then used by the consumer. The generation of electricity from primary fuels is very inefficient; with just over a third of the energy of the primary fuels obtained, the rest is wasted (although sometimes the waste heat is used for subsidiary purposes). Nevertheless, for the purpose of measuring fuel consumption, it is the use of the primary fuel that must be counted.

But then a problem arises in the measurement of hydroelectricity and nuclear power; should this direct production of electricity be counted as its actual production of calories, or should it be counted

TABLE 12.1 The Price of Petroleum and Coal Entering
International Trade 1950 to 1983

	Crude Oil: Saudi-Arabian		Coal US	At Constant 1980$[1] Crude Oil	Coal
	posted price $/barrel	realised price $/barrel	$/tonne	realised $/barrel	$/tonne
1950	1.71	1.71	9.84	8.30	43.40
1951	1.71	1.71	9.63	6.95	39.15
1952	1.71	1.71	9.72	6.79	38.57
1953	1.84	1.84	9.25	7.69	38.54
1954	1.93	1.93	8.97	8.18	38.01
1955	1.93	1.93	9.38	8.04	39.08
1956	1.93	1.93	10.59	7.85	43.05
1957	2.01	1.86	11.03	7.24	42.92
1958	2.08	1.83	10.74	6.75	39.63
1959	1.92	1.56	10.34	6.05	40.08
1960	1.86	1.50	10.00	5.68	37.88
1961	1.80	1.45	10.06	5.47	37.96
1962	1.80	1.42	10.08	5.42	38.47
1963	1.80	1.40	10.06	5.30	38.11
1964	1.80	1.33	10.14	4.96	37.84
1965	1.80	1.33	10.22	4.84	37.16
1966	1.80	1.33	10.24	4.73	36.44
1967	1.80	1.33	10.57	4.67	37.09
1968	1.80	1.30	10.80	4.87	40.45
1969	1.80	1.28	11.48	4.78	42.84
1970	1.80	1.30	14.77	4.38	49.73
1971	2.21	1.65	17.35	5.14	54.05
1972	2.47	1.90	19.16	5.38	54.28
1973	3.30	2.90	20.90	6.41	49.64
1974	11.59	9.78	44.52	18.74	85.29
1975	11.53	10.72	54.27	17.93	90.75
1976	12.38	11.51	53.56	18.93	88.09
1977	13.33	12.40	54.26	18.79	82.21
1978	13.66	12.70	55.74	16.26	71.37
1979	17.28	17.00	56.50	18.99	63.13
1980	31.03	28.50	55.70	28.50	55.70
Jan/June 1981	34.41	32.00	59.39	28.50	55.70
1982		33.34[3]	62.95[3]		
1983	29.00[2]				

Notes: 1. Prices deflated by the c.i.f. unit value index of manufactures (SITC 5–8).
Coal is bituminous.
2. *Financial Times*, 19 April, 1983.
3. Calculated using indexes with base 1975 = 100 published in the UN,
Monthly Bulletin of Statistics.
Source: World Bank, *Commodity Trade and Price Trends* (Johns Hopkins,
London, 1981).

as equivalent to the amount of fossil fuels required to produce that amount of electricity assuming some average efficiency in thermal power stations? The first method is employed by the UN and attributes a lower importance to the production of such electricity than does the second method, which is employed by the OECD and the EEC for both hydroelectricity and nuclear power. This should be borne in mind in considering the succeeding figures.

The world market in fuels has certain distinctive features. It is based on the extraction of fossil fuels in places where the reserves are found. As the reserves become depleted, the cost of extracting additional units of fuel rises. Thus the firms concerned are forever surveying and prospecting for additional reserves. This has become extended across national boundaries by the large multinational oil firms, as discussed in Chapter 10.

Furthermore, fuels are often costly or difficult to transport. Coal for instance is bulky—that is, it has a low monetary value in relation to its weight or volume. In 1979, the US Department of Energy estimated that transport costs accounted for between a quarter and two thirds of the import price of coal into Western Europe. Thus, most trade in the first half of this century was intra-regional, mainly between European countries. Now it is almost entirely limited to trade among developed countries including those of Eastern Europe and the USSR. In 1953 it accounted for 31% of trade in fossil fuel but by 1970 this had fallen to 16% (UN, 1979).

Gas is perhaps even more difficult to transport. Methane, butane and propane can be liquified and transported by tanker, but the first Atlantic crossing with liquified natural gas only occurred in 1958. It is easier and cheaper to transport gas by pipeline but that requires both a considerable amount of investment and political agreement and stability.

Oil is the easiest and cheapest to transport either by tanker or pipeline and the US Department of Energy estimated that in 1979 transport costs represented only 10% of the import price of crude oil at Rotterdam (quoted in GATT, *International Trade, 1980/81*). Thus, oil has had highest ratio of trade to production at 53% in 1978, compared with 8% for solid fuels and 13% for natural gas. It increased as a proportion of value of trade in fossil fuels from 69% in 1953 to 84% in 1970 and 90% in 1975 (UN, 1979).

The result of this uneven distribution of reserves in relation to consumption coupled with the difficulties of transportation has been that the absolute and relative prices of fuels have differed quite considerably between different countries. The differences have, if anything, been exaggerated by the differing taxation and pricing policies followed by different governments.

The most comparable data available is for industrialised countries, for which the differing prices of fuel and also of feedstocks into the chemical industry act as a frequent bone of contention in international negotiations with respect to trade in metals, chemicals and chemical products such as synthetic rubber and fibres for which they are most important. Some idea of the price spread can be gained from Tables 12.2 and 12.3. In general, the US and Canada have had the lowest price for fuel and West Germany the highest.

Clearly, to the degree that these cross-sectional price differences represent differences in transport costs, they merely reflect the comparative advantage of different countries. But much of the difference represents the deliberate price and tax policies of governments.

The US government has endeavoured to provide encouragement to its domestic oil and gas industries by the tax concessions mentioned in Chapter 10. In 1959 it also imposed quotas on imports of oil. The result of the latter was that up to 1973, the price of domestically produced oil tended to be slightly higher than that of imported crude oil. But in its concern to keep the price down to consumers, it introduced oil price controls in 1972. The result was that between 1973 and 1979 the import price of oil rose far faster than that of domestically produced oil (see Table 12.2). But recently, these controls have been removed.

In the case of natural gas, the price control element is the most important and even the Natural Gas Policy Act of 1978 has scarcely modified this. Thus, the average price of imported gas has been approximately double that of domestically produced, which is in brackets in Table 12.2 and has increased considerably faster since 1973.

Consumer taxes also tend to be very low. As can be seen from Table 12.3, the total of state and federal taxes were only 3.7 cents a litre of gasoline in 1980 having fallen in real terms since 1973.

In most European countries, as can be seen from Tables 12.2 and 12.3, the government raises prices to consumers of gasoline by the imposition of much heavier taxes. In 1973, the taxes imposed by the chief EEC governments represented more than half its retail price.

In terms of the argument in Chapter 6, these taxes could be regarded as a distortion and thus as one of the impediments to international trade. But trade in fossil fuels includes an aspect not considered so far, namely the finite nature of the total supply. Marginal cost prices only reflect the values placed by consumers and producers already in the market on a good. They do not reflect the interests of future generations for whom one more additional unit used now will represent one less available in the future. In so far as a high level of taxation discourages consumption and encourages fuel-saving forms of production, it may just be regarded as a conservation measure imposed to avoid the squandering of a commodity in finite supply. But in order to be effective, this policy should be extended to the US and Canada, which, as can be seen from Table 12.4, have the highest *per capita* levels of consumption. A more consistent policy should also be followed with respect to the different fuels.

However, considerable changes in the price of fuel have also occurred over time. In Table 12.1 the posted and realised price of crude oil from Saudi Arabia and the price of coal exported from the US are shown since 1950.

In terms of current dollars, the price of coal rose slowly until 1957, then fell and then started rising after 1963. In real terms, that is deflated by the international price index of manufactures and thus in 1980 $, it fluctuated around $39 per tonne until about 1968 when its price started to rise to a peak of $90.75 in 1975. Since then, it has fallen but it is still higher in real terms than it was before 1973.

The posted price of oil rose to 1958 then fell slightly to $1.80 in 1961 where it stayed until 1970. However, after 1956, oil was actually sold at a considerable discount on the posted price—this was mentioned in Chapter 10. This realised price reached a low of $1.28 in 1969.

The oil exporting countries' increasing dissatisfaction with the return they were getting, and their formation of OPEC, has been considered in Chapter 10. The oil exporters began complaining about the rising price of manufactures that they purchased with their oil revenues. By 1970, the oil companies also wished to raise the oil price and thus shortly afterwards there was an increase in the posted price from $1.80 a barrel in 1970 to $2.21 in 1971 and $2.47 in 1972. Then, after the Yom Kippur war of 1973, in a series of decisions, OPEC raised the price of crude oil to $11.59 a barrel by 1974. This quadrupling in the price of oil ensured a dramatic reversal in the trend in the price of fuel. The price of other fuels rose as demand shifted to them. OPEC raised the price of crude oil again in the late 1970s. The posted price was more than doubled between 1978 and 1980. However, between 1982 and 1983 the price of oil fell by about 15%; in January 1984, the weighted average price was $28.57 per barrel (*Financial Times*, 6 February 1984).

Furthermore, OPEC extended its demands to natural gas and in June 1980 issued the following communique:

The Conference reiterates OPEC member countries' determination to set gas prices in line with those of crude oil in order to achieve a coherent

TABLE 12.2 Prices of Traded Fuels in some Industrialised Countries and their Increase between 1973 and 1979
$ per tonne

	(1) 1960	(2) 1973	(3) 1979	(4) Price $\frac{1979}{1973}$ %	(5) Ex. $\frac{1979}{1973}$ rate[5] %	(6) Increase in domestic prices (4) ÷ (5) %
US[1] [2]						
Crude oil	18.53(21.70)	25.07(28.62)	126.32(92.93)	504(325)		504(325)
Anthracite	(8.56)	(15.29)	(41.81)	(273)		(273)
Bituminous coal	10.01(4.56)	20.89(8.84)	56.61(25.89)	271(293)		271(293)
Natural gas[3]	0.20(0.126)	0.32(0.198)	2.13(1.079)	666(545)		666(545)
W. Germany[4]						
Crude oil		30.94	152.02	491	145	339
Anthracite		25.55	67.48	264		182
Other hard coal		20.12	49.69	247		170
France[4]						
Crude oil		26.05	134.20	515	104	495
Anthracite		32.42	75.54	234		225
Other hard coal		26.35	48.78	185		178
Italy[4]						
Crude oil		31.30	134.39	429	70	613
Anthracite		31.95	69.35	217		310
Other hard coal		28.65	61.84	216		309

Table 12.2 (continued)

	(1) 1960	(2) 1973	(3) 1979	(4) Price $\frac{1979}{1973}$ %	(5) Ex. rate[5] $\frac{1979}{1973}$ %	(6) Increase in domestic prices (4) ÷ (5) %
Netherlands[4]						
Crude oil		25.93	136.45	526	139	378
Anthracite		40.75	92.98	228		164
Other hard coal		26.63	55.07	207		149
Belgium[4]						
Crude oil		26.46	144.82	547	132	414
Anthracite		42.46	88.35	208		158
Other hard coal		30.66	56.28	184		139
UK[4]						
Crude oil			133.65		95	
Anthracite			101.29			
Other hard coal			64.45			

Notes: 1. Bracketed figure is the domestic producers' price as near the point of production as possible.
2. Non-bracketed figures represent price of imported Venezuelan crude oil, exports of bituminous coal and average price of imported natural gas.
3. Per million BTU.
4. Average frontier values.
5. Exchange rate = dollars per unit of domestic currency.

Sources: see Table 12.3.

TABLE 12.3   Retail Prices of Oil Products in the Chief Industrialised Countries 1973 and 1st January 1980. US cents per litre

	1973 Retail Price	1973 Tax	1980 Retail Price	1980 Tax	Retail Price 1980/1973 %	Tax 1980/1973 %	CPI 1980/1973 %	Change in real value of tax per litre from 1973–9 %
US								
Gasoline	10.57–11.89	2.91	31.44ᶠ–33.82ᴾ	3.70	284	127	185	–31
Diesel fuel			23.06					
Heating fuel	6.02		25.84					
United Kingdom								
Gasoline	18.08–18.97	12.15–12.15	59.37–59.93	26.57–26.71	316	220	239	–8
Diesel fuel	18.35	12.15	63.98	29.73	349	245		+3
W. Germany								
Gasoline	22.89–25.90	16.92–17.22	57.92–60.67	31.22–31.55	234	183	131	+40
Diesel fuel	23.83	16.01	60.12	30.06	252	188		+44
France								
Gasoline	44.10–45.49	30.21–31.82	72.59–77.58	43.31–46.14	171	145	184	–21
Diesel fuel	29.13	18.02	52.67	26.00	181	144		–22
Italy								
Gasoline	26.13–27.85	20.12–20.66	74.35–76.69	47.52–48.77	275	236	248	–5
Diesel fuel	13.75	8.91	33.95	7.10	247	80		–68

Table 12.3 (continued)

	1973 Retail Price	1973 Tax	1980 Retail Price	1980 Tax	Retail Price 1980/1973 %	Tax 1980/1973 %	CPI 1980/1973 %	Change in real value of tax per litre from 1973–9 %
Netherlands								
Gasoline	** *** 25.79–26.8	** *** 18.93–19.08	** *** 66.28–68.00	** *** 36.96–37.22	254	195	152	+28
Diesel fuel	13.29	6.65	44.64	16.21	336	244		+61
Belgium								
Gasoline	** *** 26.21–27.57	** *** 20.56–20.81	** *** 72.02–73.39	** *** 38.95–39.14	266	188	162	+16
Diesel fuel	14.99	8.99	47.05	30.96	314	344		+112
Japan								
Gasoline			62.79	25.02		177		
Diesel fuel			42.80	11.31				
Heating fuel			30.93					

** = Two Star, *** = Four Star, r = regular, p = premium.

EEC prices and tax for 1 January of stated year but converted using average exchange rate for the year in question, quote in Eurostat *Agricultural Price Statistics 1969–80*. Change in exchange rates in terms of US cents per unit of other currency as obtained from *Statistical Abstract of the US*.

Sources: EEC countries—Eurostat *Energy Statistics Yearbook 1979*; US and Japan Chase Manhattan Bank, *The Petroleum Situation*, April 1981; US Dept. of Commerce *Statistical Abstract of the United States, 1982–83*; UN *Yearbook of Labour Statistics 1981*, for General Consumer Price Index (CPI).

marketing policy for their hydrocarbons. Therefore, the major gas importing countries should consider the oil-gas equivalency as a necessary
incentive to develop gas resources economically, and thus allow gas to
contribute substantially to the satisfaction of world energy needs.

It was not stated where the gas-oil parity should occur or with what
grade of oil. But Algeria initially demanded that France and the US
should pay parity with Algerian crude high quality oil which would
have been $6.11 per million BTUs and temporarily stopped
deliveries to France and the US in support of this claim.

Some idea of the effect of these decisions on the prices in the
main Western industrialised countries can be gained by comparing
Tables 12.1, 12.2 and 12.3. The price of crude oil is always quoted
in dollars, and from Table 12.1 it can be seen that the realised price
of Saudi-Arabian crude increased from $2.70 to $17.00 between
1973 and 1979, that is, it increased more than six-fold. The increase
in the price of crude oil at the frontiers of the chief European
countries was generally lower, around five-fold, as can be seen
from Table 12.2. The increase was appreciably lower only for Italy.
The difference in these price rises reflects the element of transport
costs in entry to Europe. These did not rise with the price of oil;
on the contrary, they tended to fall as consumption was reduced.

The price of coal has also risen (see Table 12.2), but it is now
only $2-2\frac{1}{2}$ times greater than it was before. Bearing in mind that
the calorific value per ton of coal is between $\frac{1}{2}$ and $\frac{3}{4}$ of that of oil,
it can be seen that whereas in 1973 oil was generally cheaper in
terms of calorific value, by 1979 it was coal that was cheaper.

In considering the effect of these international trade prices on
domestic prices, it should be remembered that there have been
considerable changes in the dollar values of the main European
currencies. These are shown in the penultimate column of Table
12.2. Over the period, the Deutschmark, Dutch guilder and Belgian
franc had appreciated by a third or more, whereas the Italian lira
had depreciated by 30%. The resulting increase in price of crude oil
and coal in terms of domestic currency is shown in the last column
of Table 12.2. Of course, for the US the price rises remain exactly
the same. But for the countries with the appreciating currencies the
apparent rise in the price of crude oil is lower.

Now let us compare the change in the price of crude oil with the
change in domestic prices of refined products. Increases in price of
the latter tend to be lower still. This is partly because most
countries impose taxes on oil products, in particular gasoline and
diesel fuel and the UK also imposes one on heating oil. In Table
12.3, the retail prices and taxes on gasoline (four-star signified by

** and two-star **) and diesel fuel are shown. In all the EEC countries, tax represented more than half the retail price in 1973 but by 1980 this proportion had dropped considerably. Thus the EEC governments have cushioned consumers against the rise in price of fuels by reducing their percentage rate of tax. Indeed, in the US, France and Italy and for gasoline in the UK, the real value of the tax imposed per litre fell. Thus part of the OPEC price rise has been paid by the governments of the consuming countries and to that extent it represents a transfer of revenue from them to the governments of the exporting countries. Unfortunately, comparable figures are not available for Japan, but for 1980 the rates of tax in Japan appear comparable to those of the EEC countries.

The rate of tax in the US is very much lower than that of the EEC countries. But partly as a result, the rise in retail price of gasoline and heating fuel has been generally greater than in European countries.

However, since 1980, the UK has raised taxes on gasoline until in 1982 they were 153.7% in real terms of their 1978 level and recently Belgium, France and Italy have raised their excise duties to offset the fall in crude-oil prices, and gasoline taxes have been raised in the US (OECD, *Economic Outlook*, December 1983B).

In conclusion, there still appears to be a wide variation in price of refined products in industrialised countries, and this appears to be largely due to tax policies of their respective governments. The taxes imposed by the federal and state governments in the US are very low compared with those of major European countries and Japan. But until 1983 the real price of energy was increasing in all countries. Between 1973 and 1982 real final energy prices tripled for industry, doubled in the residential/commercial sector and rose by 50% in the transportation sector in the seven major countries (US, Japan, Germany, France, UK, Italy, Canada) (OECD, 1983B).

These variations in domestic prices between countries and over time should be remembered as we now turn to consider the statistics of consumption.

CONSUMPTION OF FUEL

The UN figures for the total consumption of commercial energy are shown in Table 12.4 in terms of million metric tons of oil equivalent (m.t.o.e.) for regions and the chief countries within regions for 1950, 1973 and 1978 and for individual countries for 1981. Consumption is defined thus: Consumption = Production + Imports − Exports − Bunkers ± Stock changes. Fuel for bunker-

TABLE 12.4 *Consumption of Commercial Energy in Oil Equivalents—Total and* per capita *in 1950, 1973, 1978 and 1981 and Distribution between Solid Fuels (S), Liquid Fuel (L), Natural Gas (NG) and Hydro and Nuclear and Geothermal Electricity (H&N).*

	1950						1973					
	Total m.t.	Per capita Kgs.	Percentage Distribution				Total m.t.	Per capita Kgs.	Percentage Distribution			
			S	L	NG	H&N			S	L	NG	H&N
Developed ME	1268	2193	57	29	12	2	3280	4375	22	52	22	2.8
N. America	808	4865	41	39	19	2	1833	7883	20	45	32	2.6
US	758	4977	40	39	20	1	1687	8020	20	45	33	1.9
W. Europe	391	1293	85	12		2.4	1040	2878	25	59	12	3.5
UK	150	2965	91	9			206	3689	39	47	13	1.3
Germany	85	1694	96	3		1	246	3965	34	53	12	1.3
France	54	1300	80	17		2.5	158	3033	19	69	9	3.2
Italy	13	284	49	33	3	15	115	2088	7	76	13	3.3
Netherlands	13	1325	83	17			54	4051	5	38	56	−
Belgium	20	2282	89	11			42	4346	27	55	18	−
Japan	31	377	85	4		10	290	2668	19	77	2	2.4
Oceania	20	1971	73	25		1.8	62	3026	40	50	6	3.2
Developing ME	95	86	39	55	4	1.8	462	251	16	67	13	3.6
Caribbean	22	320	6	79	13	1.5	116	870	5	70	23	2.5
Mexico	10	386	7	78	14	1.7	45	802	7	63	26	3.1
Venezuela	3	613		69	31		22	1940	1	46	51	2.4
Other American	22	231	21	73	2	4	94	558	5	79	9	6.7
Argentina	9	535	11	88		0.2	31	1272	3	75	21	0.8
Brazil	7	135	30	61		9	43	423	7	81	0.5	11.5
Middle East	6	95	40	60			62	559	8	65	26	0.8
Iran	1	51					23	747	3	59	36	1.0
Far East	35	53	71	25	2	1.1	147	137	36	56	5	2.9
India	24	67	86	13		0.9	61	106	64	31	1	4.3
Indonesia	3	37	19	60	20	1	12	92	1	92	6	1
Korea	0.7	35	75	23		1	22	650	46	54		0.5
Africa	10	50	33	66		1	40*	115	11	75	8	6.4
CPE	333	411	86	11	3		1520	1198	57	27	16	1.1
CP Europe	304	1131	84	13	3	0.4	1139	3191	48	31	21	1.1
USSR	195	1084	79	17	3	1	799	3201	49	35	24	1.3
GP Asia	30	54	99	1		0.2	361	418	83	15	1	1.6
China	29	55	100			0.2	347	407	84	14	1	1.0
World	1696	683	61	27	10	1.7	5261	1363	32	46	20	2.4

Note: To convert from coal equivalents to fuel oil equivalents, multiply by 0.680272. N. America = US + Canada.

Sources: UN Department of International Economic and Social Affairs Statistical Papers, *World Energy Supplies 1973–78* and *World Energy Supplies 1950–1974*, Table 5 for figures for 1950, 1973 and 1978. UN 1981 *Yearbook of World Energy Statistics*, Table 3 for 1981 figures.

Table 12.4 (continued)

	1978						1981				
Total m.t.	Per capita Kgs.	S	L	NG	H&N	Total m.t.	Per capita Kgs.	S	L	NG	H&N
3369	4326	23	52	22	3.6						
1861	7642	20	47	30	3.2	1781	7009	22	43	31	4
1702	7737	21	47	30	2.3	1613	7018	23	42	31	3
1066	2888	24	56	16	4.6						
198	3546	37	40	21	1.8	178	3192	38	36	24	2.1
251	4092	32	49	17	2.0	238	3861	34	44	19	2.8
158	2971	20	63	12	5.3	152	2807	21	53	16	10
125	2197	6	71	19	3.8	129	2251	9	67	19	4
51	3624	6	38	55	0.9	55	3887	7	49	44	1
41	4134	24	51	23	2.4	36	3665	29	43	25	3.3
299	2602	17	74	5	3.0	289	2459	21	66	8	5
75	3368	41	44	11	4.0	71	3078	37	44	14	5
637	305	15	67	14	4.1						
144	924	6	71	20	2.9						
63	941	8	68	20	2.9	86	1161	5	70	23	2.5
27	2033	1	49	46	3.9	31	2168	0	52	43	4
119	624	7	75	9	9.1						
34	1274	3	69	25	1.9	33	1182	3	64	30	4.5
62	540	9	75	2	13.8	63	521	9	72	1.7	17
105	822	6	65	28	1.3						
43	1230	2	54	44	0.8	24	601	2.1	75	22	1
211	175	32	58	7	3.0						
77	121	66	28	2	4.6	94	137	65	29	1.7	5
28	189	1	84	14	0.7	25	166	1	30	18	1
34	925	38	61	–	1.1	38	974	38	61	0	1.3
56	139	8	75	11	6.2	78	174	6	71	19	0.5
1950	1437	54	27	18	1.4						
1392	3726	43	31	24	1.4						
983	3742	35	35	29	1.6	1056	3946	33	34	31	1.9
558	567	81	17	1	1.3						
521	569	80	18	1	1.1	393	397	76	20	3	1.4
5956	1411	32	45	20	2.9	5841	1302	31	43	22	3.8

ing refers to fuels supplied to ships and aircraft engaged in international transport irrespective of the flag of the carrier.

In 1950, out of a total of 1696 m.t.o.e. consumed (excluding bunkering), three quarters was accounted for by the developed market economies. The centrally planned economies (CPE) accounted for another 20% and the developing market economies the remainder. World consumption increased rapidly, at an average rate of 5% p.a. between 1950 and 1973; the increase for developing countries was somewhat faster at 7.1% p.a. and for CPEs at 6.8% whereas it was 4.1% p.a. for developed countries. These rates of increase then fell after 1973 to 2.5% per annum for the world as a whole, with near stagnation in the developed areas; their consumption was, for instance, only 2.7% higher in 1978 than in 1973. Thus, out of a total consumption in 1978 of 5956 m.t.o.e., $3\frac{1}{2}$ times the level in 1950, 57% was consumed by developed market economies, 11% by the developing market economies and 33% by the CPEs.

A comparison of the level of consumption in different regions and countries can be made by taking the *per capita* consumption. From the figures in Table 12.4, North America, in particular the US, has by far the highest level of consumption. In 1978, consumption in the US was almost three times the level of that in Japan and Western Europe as a whole although only about twice the level of the UK, Germany, the Netherlands and Belgium. Consumption in these Western European countries was at about the same level as that in the USSR and Eastern Europe. It was, however, very much higher than in any of the developing countries. Consumption in most developing countries was very low; it was even low in countries like Mexico and Venezuela which are major producers and exporters of oil.

The problem with assessing the *per capita* consumption figures and, for instance, relating them to income, is that they depend greatly on usage in transport and industry.

The consumption of fuel in industry also depends on a country's degree of industrialisation and type of industry. The reduction of metal ores is very fuel-intensive; for instance, the production of a ton of iron or steel requires about 0.6 of a ton of coal (Aylen, 1982).

But over and above the problem of outlets is the degree to which the primary source of fuel is consumed directly, or indirectly, in the form of electricity. This is because even with present technology, the generation of electricity from a fossil or nuclear fuel provides only 35–41% of the energy of the primary fuel as will be seen in Table 12.6).

Now let us turn again to Table 12.4 to consider the distribution of consumption between solid fuels (S) mainly coal, liquid fuels (L) petroleum products in various forms, natural gas (NG) and hydroelectric and nuclear-power generated electricity (H and N). From this it can be seen that in 1950 Western Europe and Japan depended on coal for 85% of their energy requirements. Their industrialisation had been based on coal of which they have indigenous reserves, or which, as in the case of France, the Netherlands and Austria, they could obtain from nearby European countries. Among the large European countries, the ratio of coal was significantly lower only for Italy.

The situation in the centrally planned economies was similar; they relied on coal for 86% of their requirements and apparently China was totally dependent on it. But the USSR, which has indigenous supplies of oil, obtained only 79% of her energy from coal.

The US, with domestic reserves of oil and natural gas as well as coal, showed a much greater dependence on liquid fuels and gas which in 1950 accounted for 39% and 20% respectively of consumption.

The majority of the developing countries, particularly in Latin America and, as might be expected, the Middle East, were also much more dependent on oil. This again reflects dependence on an indigenous or nearby source of fuel. Of the major countries, only India and Korea with their own coal reserves, had a pattern of consumption similar to that of Europe, and were dependent on coal for at least three quarters of their requirements.

Since 1950, the pattern of consumption has changed markedly. The consumption of coal in *developed countries* as a whole remained static between 1950 and 1973 and most of their increase in energy requirements came from oil, and to a lesser extent natural gas. Hydroelectricty and nuclear power still represented a small, albeit growing, proportion of the total—but refer above to problems of measurement. In spite of the increase in price of oil since 1973, the distribution of consumption between the different fuels was very much the same in 1978 as in 1973.

The *developing countries* have also become increasingly dependent on oil; it now accounts for two thirds of their total consumption overall although very much less in a few countries. In India, for instance, it accounted for only 28% of consumption in 1978. Her consumption of coal has increased but not proportionately, but her consumption of natural gas has been increasing very rapidly although it accounted for only 14% in 1978.

In the *centrally planned economies* the consumption of coal has

increased over the whole period even in CP Europe but the consumption of oil has increased faster, and the consumption of
natural gas even faster, so that in 1978 the consumption of the
latter was 38 times greater than in 1950.

In studying the changes in the distribution of consumption
between the different fuels, the question arises whether these are
due to the growth of particular end uses and therefore the degree
to which these are demand-induced. For instance, Western Europe,
Japan, CP Europe and India all obtained around 85% of their
energy requirement from coal in 1950 yet by 1978 this had fallen
to 24%, 17%, 43% and 66% respectively and oil accounted for
56% 74% 31% and 28% of these respectively. Does this reflect the
rapid growth in motor transport in the first two and the restriction
on it in the last two?

Unfortunately there is not enough comparative information on
the use of fuel to give a complete answer to this.

ENERGY BALANCES

But OECD has calculated some energy balances for the industrialised countries. Let us consider them for the three most
industrialised regions—North America, Western Europe and
Japan. We will only be concerned with consumption by the final
consumer and thus will exclude all energy used up by the energy
industries themselves—these figures will, therefore, be lower than
those of the UN except in so far as OECD places higher values in
terms of oil equivalent on hydroelectricity and nuclear power. Let
us distinguish between the final direct consumption of fuels in
which their different attributes may be important, and indirect consumption in electricity generation.

In Table 12.5 we show the direct consumption of solid fuels (S),
liquid fuels (L) and gas. Some of the gas in 1960 was produced
from coal or as a by-product in the smelting of iron ore, but most
of it was natural gas.

DIRECT CONSUMPTION OF SOLID FUELS IN
INDUSTRIALISED REGIONS (TABLE 12.5)

Let us begin by considering the direct consumption of solid fuels.
In each of the areas most of this was in industry and in 1960
approximately half of this was in iron and steel.

Let us for a moment consider the production of iron and steel in more detail. In the reduction of the iron ore, coal is used not only as a fuel but also as a chemical agent—its hydrocarbons react with the oxide in the ore to leave the pure metal. Gas and oil can be used in the same way. On the other hand, electricity may be used when no reduction is required—as, for instance, in melting down scrap metal. The direct use of fuels in the iron and steel industry of a country will, therefore, depend on its size, its efficiency, and the degree to which it is based on ore or scrap metal. In view of the decline in the output of the iron and steel industry in Europe, it is not surprising that the direct use of fuels in it declined between 1973 and 1979. But, as can be seen, the consumption of electricity which is mainly used to process scrap metal actually increased slightly.

In spite of difficulties, the iron and steel industry in the US has not shown such a decline, and its consumption of direct fuels increased by 22% between 1960 and 1979. The consumption of electricity increased between 1960 and 1973 and then remained static.

In Japan, the iron and steel industry has been expanding and it has become by far the largest direct consumer of coal. The Japanese industry is also a more efficient user of fuel than those of other countries due to its general use of continuous casting and larger blast furnaces and converters.

In Europe, the other major direct use of solid fuel is for residential use but this is not true of North America and Japan.

DIRECT CONSUMPTION OF OIL IN INDUSTRIALISED REGIONS (TABLE 12.5)

Now let us turn to consider oil. The major single direct use of oil is in transport, and in the US its usage for this purpose more than doubled from 248 m.t.o.e. in 1960 to 502 in 1979. It increased even faster in Japan and at 53 m.t.o.e. in 1979 was $7\frac{1}{2}$ times its level in 1960. But this was still only a tenth of the US level. In Western Europe the use of oil for transport appears to have tripled between 1960 and 1973 and then increased by another 23% to 1979. In each of the regions, most of the oil for transport was for road transport but in North America and Western Europe, just over a tenth was for air transport. However, between 1979 and 1982, the consumption of gasoline declined by 3.3% per annum in N. America, 5.8% per annum in Japan and 4.0% per annum in Western Europe (GATT, *International Trade, 1982/83*, p. 71).

A certain amount of oil is used not as a fuel but as a raw material in the production of white spirit and products such as naptha which

TABLE 12.5 Energy Consumption — Direct and Indirect Use of Fuels in Industrialised Regions, 1960–79. m.t.o.e.[1]

	1960					1973					1979				
	Direct use		Gas	Electricity		Direct use		Gas	Electricity		Direct use		Gas	Electricity	
	S	L		Actual	PEEE[2]	S	L		Actual	PEEE[2]	S	L		Actual	PEEE[2]
North America															
Industry	80	62	110	41	120	78	104	211	77	219	84	123	156	81	232
Iron & steel[3]	42		8	5	13	35	6	16	8	23	43	5	13	8	24
Chemical												75	4	11	49
Transportation	2	248			1		437			1		502			1
Road		208					364					424			
Air		26					56					60			
Residential	28	123 (+41)	104	33	96	8	180 (+84)	203	97	274	5	134	134	65	185
Commercial												6	70	46	132
Other[4]												2 (+80)	–	10	27
Total final consumption	109	474	215	75	217	86	805	414	174	493	89	847	360	203	577
OECD Europe															
Industry	116	45	7	24	82	79	149	52	53	142	66	174	69	62	165
Iron & steel[3]	56	7	–5	5	15	54	18	7	8	22	44	11	11	10	27
Chemical											4	72	25	15	40
Transportation	20	57		2	6	2	163		3	7	1	196		3	9
Road		44					132					164			
Air		5					19					20			

Table 12.5 (continued)

	1960					1973					1979				
	Direct use			Electricity		Direct use			Electricity		Direct use			Electricity	
	S	L	Gas	Actual	PEEE[2]	S	L	Gas	Actual	PEEE[2]	S	L	Gas	Actual	PEEE[2]
North America															
Residential	96	37 (+14)	9	13	46	41	178 (+83)	45	45	123	37	130	59	38	102
Commercial												27	19	18	48
Other[4]											1	24 (+32)	2	6	15
Total final consumption	232	154	16	39	134	122	570	97	101	272	105	582	149	126	338
Japan															
Industry	20	9	1	6	22	35	65	2	25	57	30	85	3	28	69
Iron & steel	7	2		1	4	33	11	1	6	14	27	7	1	7	16
Chemical[3]												35	1	5	11
Transportation	4	7		1	1		38		1	3		53		1	3
Road		5					30					37			
Air							2					4			
Residential	5[5]	4[5] (+2)[5]	1[5]	1[5]	5[5]	2[5]	47[5] (+38)[5]	1[5]	9[5]	21[5]	3	33	5	10	25
Commercial											-	-	1	4	11
Other												4 (+13)	-		1
Total final consumption	29	20	2	8	28	37	188	7	35	81	33	188	10	44	109

Notes: 1. m.t.o.e. = million metric tons of oil equivalent where one ton oil equivalent equals 10^7 K cal.

2. PEEE = primary energy equivalent of electricity.

3. In 1979 includes both uses for energy and non-energy purposes by the chemical and petrochemical industries. For 1960 and 1973, all naptha is included in non-energy uses.

4. Bracketed figure = non-energy use not included elsewhere.

5. Residential + Commercial + Other.

Source: OECD, *Energy Balances of OECD Countries, 1960/74, 1975/79.*

are used as the base for synthetic fibres and rubber. In the 1973 and 1979 figures, all consumption by the chemical industry is counted as fuel and only other non-fuel use is separately identified. In contrast, in 1960 an estimate has been made of the total non-fuel use.

DIRECT CONSUMPTION OF GAS IN INDUSTRIALISED REGIONS (TABLE 12.5)

Finally, let us consider gas. As can be seen from Table 12.4, in 1950 only North America among developed regions consumed any significant amount of natural gas and the same was true in 1960. Some of the gas consumed in Western Europe in 1960 was town gas and some of it was a by-product of blast furnaces. But then, as natural gas became tapped in Holland and later from the North Sea, the consumption of natural gas in Western Europe increased very rapidly. However, the consumption of gas in Japan remained very low. As can be seen from Tables 12.5 and 12.6, most of the gas in North America and OECD Europe was consumed directly, divided fairly evenly between industrial use on the one hand and residential and commercial use on the other.

Thus we can say that in the direct consumption of fuels, gas is spread between the different outlets, whereas the single most important use of coal is in the production of iron and steel, and of oil is for road transport. Substitution between fuels is possible for iron and steel, but not to any appreciable extent for motor vehicles—although Brazil has introduced 10% of alcohol into her petroleum.

GENERATION OF ELECTRICITY IN INDUSTRIAL REGIONS (TABLES 12.5 & 12.6)

Let us now turn to consider the indirect use of fuels, that is, in the generation of electricity. This is a usage for which, at least in the long run, there is a very high degree of substitution between the different fuels.

As can be seen from Tables 12.5 and 12.6, all the fossil fuels and natural gas have been used to produce electricity. But the proportion of electricity generated in nuclear plants and from hydro-electricity and geothermal units has been increasing rapidly. If we measure the latter in terms of their fossil-fuel equivalents (unlike Table 12.4), in 1979 it accounted for between 30 and 35% of electricity generation.

TABLE 12.6   Generation of electricity.
$(m.t.o.e.)$[1]

	North America			OECD Europe			Japan		
	1960	1973	1979	1960	1973	1979	1960	1973	1979
Electricity generated[2]	87	203	239	49	120	148	10	52	51
Solid fuels	118	240	307	88	120	150	14	9	14
Oil	15	88	87	12	86	81	5	61	60
Gas	48	101	85	2	25	30		2	13
Nuclear[3]	0.13	25	74	1	18	42	–	2	17
Hydro & geotherm[3]	70	117	127	64	75	96	14	18	21
PEEE[4]	251	573	680	166	324	397	34	92	125

1. m.t.o.e. ≡ million metric tons oil equivalent—one ton oil equivalent is defined as 10^7 K cal.
2. Difference between figures for electricity generation in this table and consumption in Table 12.2 is due to electricity consumption by the sector itself and losses.
3. Fossil fuel equivalent needed to produce the given output.
4. PEEE ≡ Primary energy equivalent of electricity consumed.
Source: OECD, Energy Balances of OECD Countries, 1960/1974, 1975/1979.

The solid-fuel input into electricity generation has been increasing in North America and Western Europe but not proportionally and in 1979 it accounted for only 45% and 35% of their inputs respectively. In Japan, the input of solid fuels tended to decline to 1973 and then increased slightly but it accounted for only 11% of the fuels used in electricity generation in 1979.

In all three areas there was a very marked increase in the use of oil and gas for electricity generation between 1960 and 1973 so that by 1973 they together accounted for a third of the fuel used for this purpose in North America and Western Europe and 68% in Japan. Oil itself accounted for 15% of this use in the US, 27% in Western Europe and 66% in Japan. The amount of oil used for this purpose then declined slightly between 1973 and 1979 and as the output of electricity continued to increase, oil fell as a proportion of fuel used for this purpose to 13%, 20% and 48% in the areas respectively.

Econometric studies have also been made of the demand for different fuels, and calculations have been made of their price elasticities. Pindyck, in The Structure of World Energy Demand carried out an econometric study of the demand for fuels in the period up to 1974, particularly of industrialised countries. He took it as comprising three sectors—residential, industrial and transport. In analysing residential consumption he assumed that consumers would increase their expenditure on fuel in proportion to their income if prices remained the same, i.e. the long run income elasticity of demand for fuel was 1. His calculations suggested a price elasticity of demand for coal of around 1, or oil somewhat higher and for gas higher still between 1.20 and 2.09. The price elasticity of demand for electricity was the lowest at 0.7 or less.

For industrial demand he obtained a very low price elasticity for electricity but price elasticities of near 1 for oil and 2 for coal in the US and Canada but lower in Europe and Japan. In particular, the industrial price elasticity of demand for oil was very low in Japan reflecting the great importance attached to it as a non-polluting fuel. The price elasticity of demand for gas was high—between 1.3 and 2.34 for Europe but much lower in the US and Canada. In industry there was also a fairly high cross-elasticity of demand with capital and labour.

His investigation into transport yielded low price elasticities of demand for the relevant liquid fuels except for motor gasoline for which it was 1.61. But the elasticity of demand with respect to GDP was very high for aviation gasoline and jet fuel, but less than 1 for diesel fuel and motor gasoline.

This examination of the use of fuels does suggest some explanation for the changes in consumption. If oil had only been used as a fuel for road and air transport their rapid growth would have provided the main explanation for the growth in its consumption. But, in fact, oil has been used for many other purposes for which it is highly competitive with other fuels. This is shown by the high price elasticities, and the considerable variation in the composition of fuel inputs for residential and industrial use both between countries and over time.

This suggests that part of the explanation lies in the more rapid expansion in supply, that is shift in the supply curve, in oil than in coal between 1950 and 1973. The fall in the real price of oil induced an increase in consumption in all outlets.

Why was there so little change in the relative consumption of fuels between 1973 and 1978 with the rise in the price of oil? The answer appears to be that in 1973 oil accounted for 46% of the world consumption of energy, and the elasticity of supply of none of the other fuels was sufficiently large to make any difference to the world market, at least in the short run. Indeed, the US, the largest consumer, found it impossible even to maintain her output of natural gas. However, in the industrialised countries, as can be seen from the above, there was some shift. In electricity generation there was a reduction in the percentage input of oil and a very rapid increase in the use of nuclear power. But the distribution of fuels in overall consumption is also affected by the decline in the iron and steel industry in Europe, which was one of the main direct users of coal in that area.

In the oil-importing developing areas for which there is less information, economic growth has entailed a rapid growth of transportation which, as it has been road rather than rail (but not of private cars), has involved a continuing expansion in the consumption of liqud fuels. In 1979 their consumption of motor gasoline accounted for 16%, gas-diesel oils 28% and residual fuel oils 42% of their total consumption of petroleum products, and usage had increased by 3%, 7% and 4% per annum respectively between 1973 and 1979 (GATT, *International Trade, 1980/81*, p. 69).

We have so far considered the changes in the consumption of fuel and suggested that changes in its distribution between fuels appear to be due more to changes in the supply of different fuels than to changes in the composition of demand. This has been very important to international trade.

SUPPLY OF FUELS (TABLE 12.7)

Let us consider the supply situation. In the period immediately after the Second World War, one of the greatest difficulties faced by the Western European countries and Japan was in increasing their output of coal on which, as has already been mentioned, they were very dependent. One manifestation of this was a series of fuel crises; in Britain in 1947 for instance, a shortage of coal led to electricity being cut for daytime household use for weeks on end.

The US was as dependent on oil as on coal and was the largest producer of oil in the world but she had not been able to increase her production of oil as fast as her consumption and by 1948 had become a net importer of oil.

The largest exporter of oil in the immediate post-war period was Venezuela. Her production had been increased very rapidly by the oil companies in response to the exigencies of war. By 1950, as can be seen from table 12.8, she was exporting 64 m.t.o.e. and was the largest exporter in the world.

Fortunately for the industrialised countries, some of the immense oil reserves in the Middle East had already been discovered. In 1950, as can be seen from Table 12.8, Iran, Kuwait and Saudi Arabia were already producing oil and exporting respectively 12, 16 and 20 m.t.o.e. Between 1950 and 1970 there was a very rapid development of Middle-Eastern oil. Most of this was carried out by the seven major oil companies discussed in Chapter 10. The US companies which had grown up on the exploitation of US oil found the Middle East a very profitable area because the cost of extraction was so much lower than in the US and even

TABLE 12.7 Production of Primary Fuels in 1950, 1973–9 and 1981 — Solid (S) Liquid (L), Natural Gas (NG) and Hydro, Nuclear and Geothermal Electricity (H&N).

m.t.o.e.

	1950				1973				1979				1981			
	S	L	NG	H&N	S	L	NG	H&N	S	L	NG	H&N	S	L	NG	H&N
World	1075	541	168	29	1506	2873	1063	128	1776	3245	1276	198	1816	2910	1308	220
Developed	745	295	156	26	680	662	747	94	767	701	752	138				
North America	355	291	155	13	347	615	615	48	424	561	570	69	445	551	555	71
US	344	287	153	8.5	352	515	549	31	405	476	499	46	423	477	491	46
Western Europe	331	4	1	9	220	20	126	37	210	115	174	53				
Japan	26			3	15	1	3	7	12	0.5	3	13	12	0.4	2	15
Oceania	15			0.4	45	20	4	2	50	22	8	3	53	22	10	3
Developing	34	202	3	1.4	65	1711	79	17	84	1810	118	30				
Africa	2	3	0		4	289	8	3	3.4	334	22	5	4	238	27	4
Other American developing	4	102	2	1.2	7	272	35	9	10	281	47	17				
Middle East	2	86			5	1059	24	0.5	6	1080	26	1.4				
Far East	25	11	1	0.4	49	91	11	4	64	120	30	7				
Centrally Planned	296	44	9	1.4	842	501	238	17	1032	717	397	30				
CP Europe	266	44	9	1	562	449	232	13	624	610	384	22				
USSR	150	38	5	1	334	430	193	11.5	359	584	332	19	365	610	379	22
CP Asia	29				280	51	6	4	408	106	13	8				

For 1950 to convert from coal equivalent to oil equivalent, multiply coal equivalent by 0.680272. To convert from Kilowatt hours to tons oil equivalent multiply by .0845776 Developed North America = US + Canada. Developing Africa = Africa – South Africa. Liquid fuel ≡ oil.

Sources: UN, *1979 Yearbook of World Energy Statistics* (UN, New York, 1981), Tables 4 & 9; UN *World Energy Supplies 1950–71* (UN, New York, 1976), Table. 2; UN *1981 Yearbook of World Energy Statistics*, (UN, New York, 1983) Table 3.

Venezuela. They did, however, continue to expand output in the latter although at a somewhat lower rate.

The result of this was that world ouput doubled between 1950 and 1960. By 1960, the largest exporter was still Venezuela, who accounted for 28% of world trade of 381 m.t.o.e., but the contribution of Iran, Iraq, Kuwait and Saudi Arabia had risen to 32, 45, 75 and 53 m.t.o.e. respectively.

The search for oil continued and reserves were discovered in Libya and Nigeria from which exports began to emerge in significant quantities in the 1960s (see Table 12.8). By 1970, world production was more than double its level in 1960 but because most of the increase had come from countries with low levels of consumption, exports were three times as great. The largest net exporter was Iran with 165 m.t.o.e., then came Saudi Arabia and Libya with 160, Kuwait with 129 and Venezuela with 128 m.t.o.e.

Faced with the apparently ever-increasing supplies of cheap oil, the European countries began to close down the production of their high-cost coal mines. This was carried out as a deliberate policy by the European Coal and Steel Community (ECSC) the treaty for which was signed by its six members—France, Germany, Italy, Belgium, Netherlands and Luxembourg in 1951, and in Britain as a policy of the National Coal Board. Japan appears to have followed suit.

Thus, between 1950 and 1973, coal production of Western Europe fell by a third, and of Japan by 42%, and it continued falling in these two areas until 1978 (see Table 12.7). Furthermore, although the production of the three other types of fuel oil, natural gas and H & N electricity had increased rapidly, total output of primary energy in Japan was 16% lower in 1973 than 1950. Total output in Western Europe was 16% higher largely due to the very rapid expansion of natural gas. But this increase in production was nowhere near as great as the increase in consumption.

This was true even of North America where output of primary energy had doubled between 1950 and 1973. Indeed, by 1973, the US inability to follow a policy of self-sufficiency had become so evident that her quota on oil imports had been dropped. Natural gas production which had increased very rapidly to 1970 had begun to fall. This was partly due to the price restrictions the government had imposed on it.

TRADE IN CRUDE OIL

Thus, as can be seen from Table 12.9, net imports of primary energy into Western Europe increased from 120 m.t.o.e. in 1955 to

TABLE 12.8   Major Producers' Production (P), and Net Exports (NE) of
Crude Petroleum.
million metric tons

	1950		1953		1955		1960		1963		1968	
	P	NE	P	NE	P	NE	P	NE	P	NE	P	NE
Developed												
US	284	−20	342	−30	362	−38	380	−51	409	−57	501	−65
Canada	4	−11	11	−11	18	−11	26	−12	37	−8	57	−3
Developing Oil Exporters												
M. East												
Iran	32	12	1		16	10	53	32	74	54	142	118
Iraq	7	6	28	27	33	32	47	45	57	54	74	70
Kuwait	17	16	43	42	55	53	85	75	105	92	133	117
S. Arabia	27	20	41	31	48	37	65	53	89	74	153	132
U.Ar.Emir.									2	2	24	24
Africa												
Libya									22	22	126	125
Nigeria							0.8	0.9	4	4	7	7
Far East												
Indonesia	7	−1.3	10	−	12	1	20	9	22	12	30	20
Caribbean America, Developing												
Mexico	10	2	10	0.5	13	1	15	−	17	1	22	−
Venezuela	78	64	92	70	113	85	150	105	170	116	190	129
Centrally Planned Economies												
USSR	38		53	1	71	1	148	17	206	30	309	59
China	0.2	−	0.6	−	1	0.4	5.5	0.6	7.5	0.1	15	
UK	0.2	−9	0.2	−26	0.2	−28	0.1	−45	0.1	−53	0.1	−83
World	520	141^E	657	197^E	803	257^E	1092	381^E	1354	529^E	1993	920^E
OPEC					284		440		580		943	

E = Exports.

Sources: UN Dept. of International Economic and Social Affairs Statistical Office, *World Energy Supplies 1973–1978* (UN, New York, 1979), Table 10. UN Dept. of Economic and Social Affairs Statistical Office, *World Energy Supplies 1950–74* (UN, New York, 1976), Table 6, 1979, *Yearbook of World Energy Statistics,* (UN, New York 1981) and 1981 *Yearbook of World Energy Statistics* (UN, New York, 1983) Table 16.

758 in 1973, whereas in Japan they increased from 7 to 308 m.t.o.e. over the same period. US net imports increased from 18 m.t.o.e. in 1955 to 295 in 1973.

The result of this was that while in 1955 net imports of fuel accounted for 26% of Western European consumption, 27% of Japanese and 2% of North American, by 1973 this had risen to 71%, 108% and 14% respectively (the figure in excess of 100 for Japan reflects stock accumulation and the provision of bunkers).

Table 12.8 (continued)

1970		1973		1978		1979		1980		1981	
P	NE	P	NE	P	NE	P	NE	P	NE	P	NE
475	− 66	454	− 161	428	− 305	422	− 310	422	− 247	422	− 207
62	3	88	7	64	− 18	73	17	70	− 18	63	− 18
191	165	293	264	263	224	160	121	74	40	65	36
76	73	100	95	126	117	170	161	130	121	45	37
151	129	152	133	112	89	126	105	84	64	56	43
188	160	378	348	415	385	476	440	496	461	491	450
38	38	74	74	90	89	90	87	83	82	73	71
160	160	105	105	96	90	101	95	88	82	55	48
54	51	102	99	95	91	115	109	104	97	71	64
43	30	67	49	80	67	78	57	78	46	79	47
22	−	23	− 3	62	19	75	27	97	41	115	55
194	128	176	111	114	65	124	74	115	68	112	66
353	63	429	72	572	108	580	115	603	115	609	113
24	0.4	51	1	104	10.6	106	13.4	106	12.5	101	14
0.1	− 101	0.1	− 112	53	− 43	77	− 20	79	− 4	88	− 18
2273	1165[E]	2780	1573[E]	3010	1589[E]	3126	1675[E]	2974	1480[E]	2789	1293[E]
1166	1000	1541	1367	1488	1302	1539	1342	1342	1129	1125	927

Thus Japan was almost entirely dependent on imports. Most of these imports were of oil which accounted for 85% of the net imports of the developed countries from the rest of the world in 1973 (see Table 12.9).

In contrast, the production of all fuels increased rapidly in the developing regions after 1950 (see Tables 12.7 and 12.9). Most of this increase was of oil. Some countries, as already described, emerged as major exporters. The others generally did not succeed in increasing their production as much in absolute terms as their consumption and thus their fuel deficit increased.

As already mentioned, oil was the primary source of fuel for most of them and it accounted for most of the increased consumption and most of any deficit. The Far East, in particular, showed an increasing fuel deficit and an even greater oil deficit.

TABLE 12.9 Production (P) and Consumption (C) of Commercial Energy and Net Exports in Total and of Oil, 1950, 1973, 1979 and 1981

m.t.o.e.

	1955		Net Exports		1973		Net Exports		1979		Net Exports		1981		Net Exports	
	P	C	Total	Oil	P	C	Total	Oil	P	C	Total	Oil	P	C	Total	Oil
Developed	1383	1479	−193	−162	2183	3195	−1335	−1149	2358	3407	−1363	−1183				
N. America	940	924	−48	−49	1625	1823	−258	−154	1625	1895	−382	−327	1632	1781	−219	−225
US	906	891	−18	−38	1430	1676	−297	−161	1426	1721	−400	−310	1436	1613	−233	−207
W. Europe	375	468	−120	−99	403	1016	−758	−717	551	1084	−670	−586				
Japan	34	45	−12	−7	26	282	−306	−251	28	302	−314	−240	29	289	−285	−194
Oceania	17	24	−10	−5	64	53	−2.3	−12	82	66	9	−6	88	68		−7
Developing	364	127	206	159	1872	455	1298	1128	2042	642	1259	1117			1316	
Africa	4	9	−7	−1	304	40	256	255	364	68	279	256	272	78	175	163
Other America developing	154	58	76	−8	323	205	72	−44	355	275	41	−36				

Table 12.9 (continued)

	1955		Net Exports		1973		Net Exports		1979		Net Exports		1981		Net Exports	
	P	C	Total	Oil	P	C	Total	Oil	P	C	Total	Oil	P	C	Total	Oil
Middle East	163	17	140	124	1089	63	983	934	1113	92	978	929				
Far East	43	42	−3	−	156	146	−8	−16	221	216	−26	−36				
Centrally Planned	520	495	13	−0.4	1598	1466	51	13	2176	1939	117	40				
CP Europe	459	433	14	0	1256	1125	57	12	1641	1427	108	32				
USSR	307	300	0.5	1	967	799	107	72	1297	1000	187	115	1376	1056	222	113
CP Asia	61	62	−0.4	−0.4	342	340	−5	1	535	512	9	8				
World Total	2267	2102	492^E	252^E	5570	5115	2157^E	1573^E	6496	5951	2385^E	1675^E	6255	5841	2019^E	1293^E
Bunkers			47				166				150					
OPEC	291	23	255		1600	85	1469	1367	1613	127	1437	1342				+927

Consumption = Production + imports − exports − bunkers + stockchanges.
Bunker data refers to fuels supplied to ships and aircraft in international
transportation, irrespective of the flag of the carrier.
Oceania = Australia + New Zealand.
Liquid fuels consumption excludes non-energy petroleum products.
E = Exports North America = US + Canada.
Developing Africa = Africa − South African customs union.

Sources: *UN 1979 Yearbook of World Energy Statistics* (UN,
New York, 1981), Tables 4, 9 and 21.
UN World Energy Suppliers 1950–1974 (UN, New
York, 1976) Table 2.
UN Yearbook of World Energy Statistics (UN, New
York, 1983), Tables 3 and 16.

In order to enforce the price rise of 1973, OPEC had to reduce its supplies of oil.

Indeed, some Western economists dismissed the idea of OPEC being a succesful cartel on the grounds that it required co-operation between members to restrict production, and every individual member has an incentive to support it in principle while breaking it in practice.

Subsequent events proved these economists wrong. There is always, of course, a certain amount of disagreement among producers about what price to aim for and how the production cuts required to enforce the price rise are to be apportioned. Certain countries, notably Venezuela, Libya and Kuwait, have also been concerned to reduce what they regard as too high a rate of depletion. Generally, the least populous countries find it easiest to reduce output because they cannot spend all their revenue anyway. On the other hand, Saudi Arabia, accounting for 22% of world exports in 1973 and 26% in 1979, has always shown some concern for the effect of oil price rises on the world economy.

The result has been that the exports of all OPEC members are lower than they would be otherwise. The countries which appear from Table 12.8 to have sustained the greatest cuts in exports between 1973 and 1979 are Iran, Kuwait and Venezuela with reductions in net exports of 54%, 21% and 33% respectively. Production and exports then continued to fall in Iraq, Kuwait, Venezuela and Libya and Nigeria. They also fell in Iran until 1982 when production was suddenly increased by 50%.

The price rise did provide a considerable inducement to production elsewhere, particularly of reserves the extraction of which would have been too costly to contemplate otherwise. Thus a rapid expansion of production in the North Sea became economically feasible. Surveying efforts were also intensified in areas which up till then had remained comparatively neglected; often they were areas in which the oil companies felt they would be allowed little freedom of action. As a result, production in India and Egypt has been increased rapidly. Such populous countries are not likely to be net exporters; all supplies will be required for internal consumption and their newly-found reserves will merely assist them in reducing their fuel deficit.

But clearly, to the degree that other countries succeed in replacing OPEC production, OPEC has to cut its own ouput even more severely. Thus, in 1973, OPEC accounted for 55% of world output but by 1979 this had fallen to 49%, and by 1981 to 40%.

Meanwhile, the output in the centrally planned economies had also expanded rapidly. At the beginning of the period, the Western powers feared that the USSR might have acquisitive designs on the Middle-Eastern supplies of oil. But the USSR had been one of the earliest producers of oil, with production concentrated near Baku near the Black Sea, and she discovered additional reserves in Siberia. Output was expanded very rapidly from 38 m.t.o.e. in 1950, to 429 in 1973 and 609 in 1981. Most of her exports went to other centrally planned European countries. Romania also produced oil, and by 1973 the CP Europe as a whole had net exports of 12 m.t.o.e. to the rest of the world. The price rise of 1973 induced CP Europe to expand its exports to other areas so that in 1979 these stood at 32 m.t.o.e.

OVERALL ADJUSTMENT OF DEFICIT AREAS SINCE 1973

Now let us turn to consider adjustments in the main deficit areas since 1973 beginning with that of the industrialised countries (see Table 12.7).

After 1973 output remained static in Japan apart from a rapid increase in H & N electricity. Production of liquid fuels, natural gas and H & N electricity expanded rapidly in Western Europe, but, as mentioned, coal continued to decline. The US was unable to maintain her output of natural gas but increased her output of coal. Oceania increased its ouput of all four types of fuel. Thus, between 1973 and 1979, as can be seen from Table 12.9, the US increased her net imports of fuel from 257 to 400 m.t.o.e. and Japan increased hers slightly from 306 to 314 m.t.o.e.; these two countries were by far the largest net importers of fuel. But net imports into Western Europe had fallen and Oceania had become a larger net exporter. Net imports for developed countries as a whole had increased from 1355 m.t.o.e. in 1973 to 1363 in 1979. Almost all the net imports were of oil which for industrialised countries as a whole accounted for 86% of the total in 1979.

The further doubling of the price of oil between 1978 and 1980 intensified efforts to save energy and to substitute away from oil. The consumption of fuels overall declined for most developed countries and the consumption of oil declined even faster; between 1979 and 1982, the annual *reduction* in total consumption was 6.8% in North America, 7.9% in Japan and 6.4% in Western Europe (GATT, *International Trade* 1982/83, p. 71). The reduction in the relative consumption of oil was balanced by an increase in the relative consumption of coal and hydro and nuclear electricity and for some countries, as will be discussed, an increase in the relative consumption of natural gas.

The developing countries also increased their output (see Table 12.9). If we exclude that of OPEC, it rose from 272 m.t.o.e. in 1973 to 429 m.t.o.e. in 1979, an increase of 58%. Consumption increased from 370 to 515 m.t.o.e., an increase of 39%. So, in terms of fuel equivalents, they were reducing their deficit, but not in financial terms because of the very much higher price of fuel.

There is little information on recent trends in the production and consumption of deficit areas, but they also appear to be substituting away from oil (GATT, *International Trade* 1982/83, p. 70). It remains to be seen whether the recent reduction in the price of oil of 15% since 1982 has any impact on these trends (OECD, *Economic Outlook*, December 1983).

TRADE IN NATURAL GAS

A side effect of the OPEC reductions in the output of oils has been the rapidly increasing importance of natural gas on the world market. In 1979 the US was still the largest producer but other countries had been responsible for the increase in production of 40% since 1970 (see Table 12.10). The largest of these was the USSR where output increased from 6670 to 14,160 terajoules over the period, so that in 1979 she accounted for more than a quarter of world output. She is estimated to have a third of the world's reserves. Output has also increased very rapidly in the Middle East and exports increased ten-fold over the period.

The natural gas of Algeria and Libya can be liquified and exported in tankers and there are plans to tap the large Nigerian reserves in this way (*Financial Times*, 20 December 1983). But not all natural gas can be liquified and the process is expensive. It is estimated that it costs $5.25 per million BTU to ship liquified natural gas (LNG) from OPEC to Europe compared with a weighted average gas price of $4 per million BTU in Europe (EIU quoted in *Financial Times*, 2 March 1984). Thus, it is not worth collecting the gas produced as a by-product of oil in the Middle East unless it can go by pipeline.

The production figures shown in Table 12.10 do not include gas that is flared at the pithead, and the near doubling of production in the Middle East between 1970 and 1979 was due to the provision of more pipelines. OECD estimated that even in 1980, 12% of the world's gross output of natural gas was flared or lost (IEA, 1982).

Four-fifths of trade in natural gas now goes through pipelines (GATT, *International Trade*, 1980/81). Investment in them enabled trade in natural gas to quadruple between 1970 and 1979

TABLE 12.10 *Natural Gas — the Major Traders, their Production (P), Net Exports (NE) and Trading Partners. Quantities In Thousand Terajoules*

	1970		1973		1978		1979		1980		1981		Percentage of 1980 Exports going as Imports of			
	P	NE	P	NE	P	NE	P	NE	P	NE	P	NE	US	W. Europe	Japan	CPE
Developed																
N. America																
US	22,860	−817	23,410	−1030	20,654	−981	21,275	−1289	21,102	−1013	20,910	−898	100			
Canada	2113	811	2794	1068	2856	929	3041	1055	2781	840	2746	803	100			
W. Europe																
Netherlands	1116	398	2498	120	3048	1605	3100	1767	3012	1790	2664	1629		100		
Norway					658	599	890	860	1065	1024	1058	1023		100		
Developing																
Middle East																
Iran	451	34	707	317	668	285	700	211	279	9	235	10				100
UAE	9	0	33	0	92	69	84	66	115	102	146	104			100	
Far East																
Indonesia	47	0	64	0	353	199	482	326	607	449	653	460			100	
Brunei	8	2	77	59	351	299	377	309	399	318	390	304			92	
Africa																
Algeria	64	61	163	99	737	252	608	442	660	241	662	380	40	60		
Libya	0	0	120	120	184	153	183	153	196	166	185	166		100		
Nigeria	4	0	12	0	101	0	51	0	31	0	200	0				
CPE																
USSR	6670	−9	8217	−160	12,967	964	16,160	1355	15,149	1940	16,165	2063		48		50
World	38,440	1653[E]	45,284	2298[E]	51,742	6062[E]	54,376	7159[E]	54,921	7527[E]	55,759	7538[E]	14	56	12	14
OPEC	1108	95	1838	536	2520	939	2541	974								

Production excludes flared gas. E = Exports.

Source: UN, 1981, *Yearbook of World Energy Statistics*, Tables 35 and 36 except for OPEC figures from UN, 1979, *Yearbook of World Energy Statistics*, Tables 35 and 36.

(see table 12.10). However, exports of oil and gas by pipeline are subject to disruption by wars and political unrest, particularly in the Middle East. Syria has closed the Iraq oil export pipeline to the Mediterranean (*Financial Times*, 14 December 1983). The Iraq-Iranian war has also disrupted Iranian exports of natural gas which fell from 211 terajoules in 1979 to about 10 in 1980 and 1981 (see Table 12.10). Indeed, in 1982, world exports of natural gas declined slightly as did world consumption and production. The Netherlands' export prices rose by 8% but there was no rise in import prices to the US and Japan (GATT, *International Trade, 1982/83*).

Another feature of this dependence of trade on pipelines is that it leads to a very great geographical concentration of trade, as can be seen from Table 12.10. Thus, in 1980, all Canadian exports went to the US, all Dutch and Norwegian exports went to Western Europe, and all Indonesian and most Brunei exports went to Japan. USSR exports were split between other Eastern European countries and Western Europe. But the CP European economies also took all Iranian exports. Forty per cent of Algerian exports went by tanker to the US. It is interesting to see how a trans-Mediterranean pipeline affected this trade.

The concentration of this trade leads to difficulty in negotiating the price. Italy, for instance, agreed in 1977 to buy Algerian gas and constructed and financed a 1500 mile trans-Mediterranean pipeline at a cost of $3 billion. But Algeria then pressed for a higher price than that in the original agreement, and France was willing to pay it. Eventually in September 1982, Italy agreed to pay $5.40 per million BTU and agreed that the price be linked to a basket of crude oils. In 1983, Italy received the first deliveries through the pipeline (*Financial Times*, 14 December 1983). On the other hand, Algeria lost its trade to the US because of its demand for an oil equivalent price (*Financial Times*, 2 March 1984).

The other major project is the 2700 mile pipeline from Siberia to Western Europe. This was opposed by the US government, which was reluctant to see Western Europe dependent on the USSR for a major source of fuel. It tried to prevent the transfer of technology for this purpose by placing embargoes on US-made or US-designed turbines for compressors in the pumping stations (*Financial Times*, 26 September 1983). The Western European governments strongly objected to this intervention and were anxious both to obtain the gas and the contracts for construction amounting to $4 billion. So much so that it has been estimated that due to subsidies, half the French and Italian exports and credit facilities were paid for by their own taxpayers (*Financial Times*, 27 September 1983). Gas is only expected to come through it in any quantity in 1985 (*Financial Times*, 12 January 1984).

There is also the question of whether Britain should be connected by pipeline to the continental gas grid which could mean that she eventually receives gas from the USSR or Algeria, or possibly exports it if the UK government removes the ban on this. The Norwegians apparently think this would reduce their bargaining position for their exports of gas to Britain from their fields in the North Sea. (*Financial Times*, 2 March 1984).

In terms of economic efficiency, there is an argument for expanding facilities for trade and obtaining a more uniform price structure throughout the world.

13 Textiles and Clothing

Now let us consider trade in textiles and clothing, trade which, as mentioned in Chapter 4, has provoked industrial countries to the erection of a vast and elaborate system of import regulation.

TOTAL TRADE

Let us first consider what has actually happened. GATT has calculated that in 1975 the volume of trade in textiles and clothing (measured at 1970 prices) was approximately three times its level in 1963. Industrialised countries' exports of textiles were 246% and 309% of their 1963 level. Developing countries' exports of textiles plus clothing were, in 1975, more than five times their level in 1963 in real terms (GATT, 1978, Table F1). World exports of textiles and clothing then increased by a third between 1975 and 1979 (OECD, 1983, Table 17).

In terms of value, trade in textiles and clothing now forms a lower proportion of manufacturing trade than it did in 1955. The proportion of trade in textiles has been consistently declining from 11% in 1955 to 5% in 1981, whereas the proportion of trade in clothing was initially increasing from only 2% in 1955 to 4% in 1973 where it has remained.

DISTRIBUTION OF EXPORTS

The distribution of exports from industrial countries on the one hand, and developing countries on the other has also changed. In Table 13.1, the figures for selected years from 1955 to 1981 are shown. In 1955 almost all exports came from industrial countries. Textiles were far the most important at $3.78 billion compared with $560 million of clothing. Forty-seven per cent of the textiles went to other industrial countries, and 40% went to developing countries. But two thirds of their exports of clothing went to other industrial countries and only 29% to developing countries.

TABLE 13.1 Exports (E) of Textiles and Clothing by Industrial (I) and Developing (D) Countries 1955–81. billion dollars at current prices

	1955 E	I	D	1963 E	I	D	1973 E	I	O	NO	1975 E	I	O	NO	1980 E	I	O	NO	1981 E	I	O	NO
		% sent to			% sent to			% sent to				% sent to				% sent to				% sent to		
Industrial																						
Textiles	3.78	47	40	5.31	65	25	17.12	72	5	14	19.73	69	7	13	38.40	69	8	14	36.30	64	10	15
Clothing	0.56	66	29	1.50	79	18	6.92	88	1	6	9.00	86	3	6	20.15	86	4	7	18.70	80	6	7
Developing[1]																						
Textiles	0.66	32	58	1.10	48	39	4.05	52	9	26	4.45	44	11	31	11.50	43	10	34				
Clothing	0.08	50	50	0.30	70	27	3.82	85	3	8	5.36	84	6	6	14.55	82	7	8				

O = OPEC countries.
NO = Non-OPEC countries.
Note: 1.Developing 1955–63 represents all developing countries but 1973 onwards only non-OPEC countries.
Sources: GATT, International Trade, 1979/80 and 1981/82; GATT, Network of World Trade by Areas and Commodity Classes, 1955–76, (Geneva, 1978).

The developing countries, with a much smaller proportion of trade, sent most of their textiles to other developing countries but distributed their exports of clothing evenly between industrial countries and the developing ones.

Since then, exports from developing countries have been increasing much faster than from industrial countries, and most of this increase has gone to industrial countries. Their exports of clothing also increased faster than exports of textiles so that by 1975 they were exporting more clothing than textiles. The figures after 1973 must be qualified to the extent that previous years include OPEC, whereas 1973 onwards excludes it. This does not affect exports of clothing, but in 1973 OPEC exported $0.28 billion of textiles to North America and Western Europe and in 1975 $0.25 billion.

After 1973, industrial and developing countries increased the proportion of exports they sent to OPEC. The developing countries also appear to have shifted their exports of textiles towards other developing countries so that by 1980 they accounted for a third, a smaller proportion than in 1955 and 1963 but a very much larger volume.

The situation for the main industrial countries or groups of countries since 1963 is shown in somewhat more detail in Tables 13.2 and 13.3. As can be seen, all were increasing their exports and imports in terms of value.

Let us first consider the situation in textiles—see Table 13.2. The country with the largest positive and growing balance was Japan, and she also had a positive balance in relation to each of the main groups of countries, apart from a temporary negative balance with developing countries in 1973.

Over the same period, the US changed from being a net importer of textiles in 1963 and 1973 to a net exporter by the end of the 1970s. This was due to an increase in exports to both industrial and developing areas, coupled with a very much smaller increase in imports. Imports from industrial areas other than Canada but including Southern Europe increased by only 10% by value between 1973 and 1979 and thus the US moved into a positive balance with them, but this was removed by a fall in her exports after 1980. After 1973, imports from developing countries increased less rapidly than exports such that the US moved into a small positive balance with them in 1979; this balance has since declined.

The EEC had a positive balance over the whole period. This was due to a positive balance with EFTA and the ETA and generally with developing areas. The positive balance with the Southern European and other industrial areas became negative in the mid-1970s.

Canada and EFTA had a negative balance overall and with each of the groups of countries except for the emergence of a small positive balance between EFTA and the developing countries in 1981.

The most important markets for international trade in clothing are the US, EEC and EFTA. The US had a negative balance with all areas; her overall net imports have been increasing fast and in 1982 were five times their level in 1973 by value—see Table 13.3. This was due to an almost five-fold increase in imports from developing countries.

Most of the trade of EEC countries is with each other. But in relation to the rest of the world, the EEC has a positive balance with EFTA and other industrial countries but a negative balance with all the others. The EEC's net imports have also been rising fast due to a five-fold increase in net imports from developing countries between 1973 and 1980 but since then they have declined.

The trade situation just described is largely the result of the increasing protectionism of the industrial countries with respect to products from developing countries. As can be seen, in many cases net imports of textiles from developing countries have been reduced or net exports increased since 1973, particularly from the US. The EEC moved from a positive to a negative balance in textiles in 1980 and then back to a positive one in 1981.

However, in clothing, the net imports from developing countries have increased consistently fom 1973 to 1980 but then net imports into the EEC fell and those into the EFTA remained static.

However, these value figures give a misleading impression to the extent that inflation means that increases appear greater than they are in physical terms. Furthermore, all the restraints on trade are in physical terms. The relationship between the sectors should also be considered—that is, cotton yarn may be exported as such, or incorporated into fabric, and the fabric may be exported as such, or made up into clothing or household goods. To this extent, an increase in exports of clothing may offset a reduction in exports of textiles.

But let us first consider why trade in textiles and clothing has been the area of so much conflict between industrial and developing countries, before considering in more detail the effect of intervention.

SCOPE OF TEXTILE AND CLOTHING INDUSTRIES

Before investigating the significance of trade to different countries, let us first consider the activities the industries themselves comprise.

TABLE 13.2   Trade in Textiles 1963 to 1982
billion dollars

Country and trading partners	Imports					Exports					Balance of Trade				
	1963	1973	1980	1981	1982	1963	1973	1980	1981	1982	1963	1973	1980	1981	1982
US total	0.68	1.58	2.54	3.07	2.85	0.49	1.22	3.62	3.61	2.77	−0.19	−0.36	1.08	0.54	−0.08
Canada	0.01	0.04	0.07	0.08	0.10	0.11	0.30	0.62	0.66	0.50	0.10	0.26	0.55	0.58	0.40
Other industrial	0.40	0.92	1.13	1.34	1.30	0.13	0.46	1.33	0.94	0.75	−0.27	−0.46	0.20	−0.40	−0.55
Developing	0.27	0.59	1.14	1.34	1.16	0.19	0.33	1.28	1.40	1.17	−0.08	−0.26	0.94	0.06	0.01
ETA	0.00	0.02	0.19	0.30	0.28	0.00	0.03	0.16	0.31	0.14	0.00	0.01	−0.03	0.01	−0.14
Canada total	0.27	0.78	1.28	1.41	1.13	0.03	0.15	0.31	0.33	0.29	−0.24	−0.63	−0.97	−1.08	−0.84
US	0.12	0.36	0.75	0.80	0.61	0.01	0.06	0.09	0.11	0.12	−0.11	−0.30	−0.66	−0.69	−0.49
Other industrial	0.11	0.28	0.30	0.35	0.29	0.01	0.05	0.10	0.09	0.07	−0.01	−0.23	−0.20	−0.24	−0.22
Developing	0.03	0.09	0.17	0.20	0.16	0.01	0.02	0.06	0.08	0.06	−0.02	−0.07	−0.11	−0.12	−0.10
ETA	0.01	0.04	0.06	0.08	0.06	0.00	0.00	0.01	0.01	0.00	−0.01	−0.04	−0.05	−0.07	−0.06
EEC (10) total	2.36	9.14	22.94	19.09	18.27	3.35	11.16	24.02	21.02	19.89	1.01	2.02	1.08	1.94	1.62
Intra-trade	*	*	*	*	*	1.68	6.60	14.89	12.50	12.03	*	*	*	*	*

Table 13.2 (continued)

Country and trading partners	Imports					Exports					Balance of Trade				
	1963	1973	1980	1981	1982	1963	1973	1980	1981	1982	1963	1973	1980	1981	1982
EFTA	0.20	0.59	1.66	1.49	1.50	0.48	1.19	2.70	2.26	2.14	0.28	0.60	1.04	0.77	0.64
S. Europe	0.06	0.35	1.06	0.98	1.09	0.10	0.46	0.91	0.81	0.80	0.04	0.11	−0.15	−0.17	−0.29
Other industrial	0.14	0.46	1.70	1.29	1.07	0.30	0.94	1.18	1.25	1.20	0.16	0.48	−0.52	−0.04	+0.13
Developing	0.25	0.98	3.08	2.32	2.16	0.54	1.09	2.65	2.67	2.36	0.29	0.11	−0.43	0.35	0.20
ETA	0.05	0.27	0.80	0.70	0.67	0.06	0.55	1.25	1.07	0.96	0.01	0.28	0.45	0.37	0.29
EFTA[a] total	0.68	2.00	4.39	3.64	3.40	0.38	1.41	3.31	3.11	2.99	−0.30	−0.59	−1.08	−0.53	−0.41
Intra-trade	*	*	*	*	*	0.09	0.48	0.80	0.68	0.62	*	*	*	*	*
EEC	0.46	1.14	2.70	2.23	2.11	0.19	0.57	1.70	1.54	1.54	−0.27	−0.57	−1.00	−0.69	−0.57
S. Europe	0.02	0.11	0.17	0.13	0.14	0.02	0.08	0.12	0.11	0.10	0.00	−0.03	−0.05	−0.02	−0.04
Other industrial	0.05	0.08	0.17	0.15	0.13	0.02	0.12	0.10	0.13	0.13	−0.03	0.04	−0.07	−0.02	0.00
Developing	0.03	0.13	0.40	0.32	0.30	0.03	0.08	0.38	0.45	0.43	0.00	−0.05	−0.02	0.13	0.13
ETA	0.02	0.08	0.20	0.16	0.14	0.01	0.05	0.18	0.17	0.15	−0.01	−0.03	−0.02	0.01	0.01
Japan total	0.04	1.13	1.65	1.63	1.60	0.90	2.45	5.10	5.85	5.09	0.86	1.32	3.45	4.22	3.49
Industrial	0.04	0.41	0.60	0.56	0.55	0.26	0.46	0.83	1.00	0.98	0.22	0.05	0.23	0.44	0.43
Developing	0.00	0.56	0.74	0.76	0.74	0.51	1.55	3.40	3.76	3.23	0.51	0.99	2.66	3.00	2.49
ETA	0.00	0.16	0.31	0.31	0.31	0.02	0.15	0.55	0.70	0.52	0.02	−0.01	0.24	0.39	0.21

Note: (a) Excluding Portugal.
Source: GATT, *International Trade 1981/82, 1982/83.*

TABLE 13.3 Trade in Clothing 1963 to 1982
billion dollars

Country and Trading Partners	Imports						Exports					Balance of Trade					
	1963	1967	1973	1980	1981	1982	1963	1972	1980	1981	1982	1963	1967	1972	1980	1981	1982
US Total	0.39	0.65	2.17	6.94	8.12	8.79	0.09	0.29	1.22	1.26	0.99	−0.30	−0.47	−1.88	−5.72	−6.86	−7.80
Industrial areas[2]	0.28		0.66	0.75	0.83	0.85	0.04	0.09	0.55	0.51	0.35	−0.24		−0.57	−0.20	−0.32	−0.50
Developing areas	0.11		1.49	5.82	6.71	7.13	0.05	0.18	0.63	0.70	0.58	−0.06		−1.31	−5.19	−6.01	−6.55
ETA	0.00		0.02	0.36	0.56	0.79	0.00	0.00	0.00	0.00	0.00	0.00		−0.02	−0.36	−0.56	−0.79
EEC (10) Total	0.78	1.31	5.81	20.32	17.98	17.04	1.01	4.96	14.58	12.96	12.66	0.23	0.25	0.85	−5.74	−5.02	−4.38
Intra trade		0.87					0.50	3.39	9.88	8.34	8.17						
EFTA[1]	0.07		0.26	0.90	0.79	0.74	0.17	0.68	2.36	2.06	2.16	0.10		0.42	1.46	1.27	1.42
S. Europe	0.02		0.48	1.42	1.29	1.45	0.01	0.11	0.23	0.21	0.21	−0.01		−0.37	−1.19	−1.08	−1.24
Other industrial areas	0.04		0.10	0.60	0.49	0.32	0.17	0.41	0.74	0.72	0.80	0.13		0.31	0.14	0.23	0.48
Developing areas	0.14		1.18	5.83	5.69	5.24	0.13	0.23	1.15	1.42	1.13	−0.01		−0.95	−4.68	−4.27	−4.11
ETA	0.01		0.36	1.28	1.13	1.04	0.01	0.11	0.17	0.15	0.13	0.00		−0.25	−1.11	−0.98	−0.91
EFTA[1] Total	0.25	0.45	1.37	4.74	4.21	4.16	0.13	0.66	2.08	1.98	1.79	−0.12	−0.23	−0.71	−2.66	−2.23	−2.37
Intra-trade	0.13						0.13	0.32	0.86	0.70	0.64						
EEC	0.17		0.69	2.48	2.18	2.25	0.07	0.24	0.95	0.83	0.78	−0.10		−0.45	−1.53	−1.35	−1.47
S. Europe	0.01		0.11	0.30	0.26	0.28	0.00	0.01	0.01	0.01	0.02	−0.01		−0.10	−0.29	−0.25	−0.26
Other industrial areas	0.02		0.03	0.18	0.15	0.10	0.02	0.03	0.06	0.06	0.06	0.00		−0.	−0.	−0.	−0.
Developing areas	0.02		0.18	0.79	0.80	0.80	0.00	0.01	0.03	0.03	0.03	−0.02		−0.17	−0.76	−0.77	−0.77
ETA	0.01		0.04	0.16	0.13	0.11	0.00	0.04	0.18	0.35	0.26	−0.01		0.00	0.02	0.22	0.15

Notes: 1. Excluding Portugal.
2. Including S. Europe.

Sources: GATT, International Trade, 1981/82, 1982/83; OECD, Textile Industry in OECD Countries (Paris, OECD, 1976) for 1967 statistics.

The textile industry is here defined to *exclude* the production of man-made fibres, but to *include* all the cleaning, combing, and spinning of fibres to produce yarn, and then the weaving or knitting of yarn to produce cloth. Bleaching, dyeing, texturising and finishing of yarn and cloth are also included.

Products for the household require little further processing. In Western Europe these account for about 22% by weight of fibres consumed, with sheets and pillowcases as 6%, towels and towelling as 3%, blankets 2%, drapery (curtains) and upholstery 10%. Another 17% is accounted for by carpets (Cable, 1979, p. 19).

Products for industry such as tyre cord and conveyor belting also go directly to the industry concerned. These now account for approximately 11% of total fibre consumption. Figures for the UK suggest that in the 1950s the proportion going to industry was higher (Briscoe, 1971).

This is a classification by weight of fibre. A classification by square yardage would give somewhat different results. It would, for instance, reduce the proportion going to carpets because the weight per square yard is so high.

The remaining output of the textile industry goes to the clothing industry, which accounts for about one half of fibre consumption. Here the fabric is cut up, sewn up, and pressed. But knitted products such as stockings often require little further processing, so firms in the knitting industry can be regarded as extending their activities into the production of clothing.

RAW MATERIALS

The raw materials of the textile industry are expensive and thus the products of the textiles and clothing industries have a high value in relation to their weight or bulk and therefore in relation to transport costs. Thus it has often been profitable to trade the raw materials, and for trade to take place at each stage of manufacture, depending on the relative costs of manufacturing in different locations. This is because there are generally economies of scale associated with each process, but the next process often requires a mixture of inputs.

Here we must distinguish the subdivisions of the textile industry. These are based on the traditional raw materials, mainly because of the physical form and strength of the fibres; for instance, silk is a continuous filament, cotton has a staple length of $\frac{3}{8}-1\frac{1}{2}$ inches (sea island cotton up to $2\frac{1}{2}$ inches), wool up to $2\frac{1}{2}$ inches for woollen goods, over $2\frac{1}{2}$ inches for worsted goods and carpets, linen (flax)

12–20 inches, jute up to 7 feet, and this is one of the main determinants of the spinning process.

The initial attempts to produce a man-made fibre were as a
substitute for the most expensive natural one, namely silk. The first
satisfactory ones were based on naturally occurring cellulose and
are sometimes described as regenerated artificial fibres or
cellulosics. The most common of these is now viscose rayon. In this
book they will all be called rayon. In the pre-war period, the largest
ouput was that of the US, with Japan, Germany, the UK and Italy
following in declining order. The output of the Axis powers had
been built up because they anticipated being cut off from supplies
of natural fibres during the coming war. After the war it was some
time before their production reached pre-war levels.

The first synthetic fibres formed by the polymerisation of non-
fibrous materials were discovered by Carothers for du Pont in the
US in 1928–9. Research was concentrated on polyamides, and in
1935 polyamide 66, that is nylon 66, was chosen for commercial
development. Production was increased very rapidly to meet the
needs of the Second World War, particularly for parachutes.

The polyesters (Dracon, Terylene) were not developed commercially until after the Second World War and the acrylics (Orlon,
Acrilan and Courtelle) were developed during the 1950s.

These synthetics are essentially plastics which can be produced in
the form of a filament. Their properties are somewhat different
from those of natural fibres. They are generally stronger. From the
point of view of the consumer, they are less moisture-absorbent
and soft to the touch and are, therefore, less comfortable to wear;
on the other hand, they are generally crease-resistant and resistant
to deterioration by sunlight (important for curtains).

All man-made fibres can be extruded either as a continuous filament as a substitute intitially for silk, or they can be produced to
any staple length so that they can be spun with, or instead of,
cotton, flax or wool. Initially, they were absorbed by the traditional
textile industry.

Indeed, the large chemical firms producing the synthetic fibres
tend to regard the indigenous textile industry as the natural outlet
for them. They have acquired an interest in its viability; in Britain
this has been consolidated either by direct takeovers as by Courtaulds (producer of acrylic and polyamide fibres) or, as in the case
of ICI (producer of polyamide and polyester fibres), by financing
another firm, Viyella International to do so. They have also held
minority shareholdings in other firms (Briscoe, 1971). Most of the
other large industrialised countries have producers of synthetic
fibres and they also export synthetic yarns and fabrics. They also

tend to regard imports as leading to a reduction in the size of their outlet, whether these imports are of cotton or synthetic goods.

The situation in the US is somewhat different from that in Europe. On the one hand, the US unlike the other industrialised countries, is a major producer of cotton, At one point, the US was subsidising the export of raw cotton but not home consumption. The US cotton textile producers complained that they were being discriminated against and in 1964, the subsidy was also extended to them.

On the other hand, there was a dramatic decline in the US production of wool yarn and wool fabric; in 1973 it was about a quarter of its level in 1950. This appears to have resulted from the mergers of firms in the US wool industry with those using or producing man-made fibres in the early 1950s (Rainnie, 1965, pp. 42–3).

ATTRACTIONS FOR COUNTRIES BEGINNING THEIR INDUSTRIALISATION

Several features make the textile industry attractive to countries beginning their industrialisation. Firstly, in all countries there is an already existing domestic market for textiles and so in its initial stages, production, particularly of cotton goods, is a matter of import substitution. Secondly, the machinery is easily obtained and the skills to operate it are easily acquired.

This is not so true of clothing. Although there is a domestic market for Western-type clothing in Latin American countries and some Asian countries with indigenous Chinese populations, this is not true of all developing countries. Furthermore, the importance of design and fashion makes it a more difficult market in which to operate. Fashion, changes over time and differs between countries, so do colour ranges, and even sizing. Therefore, more entrepreneurial skill is required in production. In addition, for fashion garments, the operations of cutting and machining may require a considerable degree of skill. Thus it is not surprising that a clothing industry is established much later than textile manufacturing, and that the first developing countries to establish themselves as international clothing producers were those with Chinese populations, namely Hong Kong and Taiwan—the Chinese style of women's clothing being not unlike the Western one, and the populations in these countries having a high degree of literacy. Nor is it surprising that one of the greatest areas of competition is in T-shirts, which are simple to make, and jeans, men's shirts and pullovers which have a very standardised construction.

Furthermore, both the textile and clothing industries are labour-intensive, that is, they require a relatively large amount of labour in relation to capital for production. There are many studies showing this. The labour intensity of the industries, which will be discussed later, means that wage rates are of paramount importance.

However, the initial establishment of a mechanised textile industry is an aspect of industrialisation. In Britain, the cotton industry was in the vanguard of the industrial revolution and at its zenith in the 1880s, exported four fifths of its output. At the time it was also pursuing a policy of free trade. But almost all other countries have industrialised behind tariff or other trade barriers. In this way, the US, Japan and other European countries fostered their textile industry.

By 1913, the desire of other developing countries to establish their own textile industries was clear, as was the emergence of Japan and India as Britain's main competitors. But the world trading position became much more adverse, as described in Chapter 2, due to the disruption caused by the two world wars with the Great Depression in between. Shipping difficulties during the wars provided a particular inducement to countries with their own supplies of raw material.

The effect of these developments was that although textile production increased by almost 50% between 1913 and 1955, world trade in yarn and fabrics actually declined. The increases in production had come mainly from underdeveloped countries and Japan. Most of the underdeveloped countries had been import-substituting, but as their production grew they increasingly tended to enter the export market. The development of wool manufacturing particularly combing, took place much later than cotton manufacturing. Indeed, many countries did not begin to process their raw wool till the second World War, and production was based from the beginning on the export market, as most wool-producing countries did not have a large enough domestic market to support it (Briscoe, 1971).

TRADE IN COTTON PRODUCTS

Cotton products continued to be the most important category entering international trade, accounting for 48% of textiles and 47% of clothing exports in 1957 (GATT, 1966, Tables 2 and 6). But as described in Chapter 3, cotton textiles were regarded by industrial countries as 'sensitive' products and thus were excluded from the rounds of tariff reductions. Most European countries also had import restrictions on them, although these were gradually removed for intra-European trade firstly by negotiations under the OEEC and then in the six nations of the EEC by the Treaty of Rome. These restrictions were chiefly directed at Japan. Faced with such closed markets, she directed most of her textile exports to the US who, eventually, in 1956 also imposed some 'voluntary' restrictions on them.

But what the European countries did not quite appear to have envisaged was the reversal of trading positions with developing countries. This was particularly true of Britain, who, with the Commonwealth preference scheme, had low or zero tariffs on many textile products on a reciprocal basis of preference with her former dependencies. Her exports of cotton textiles had already started declining in 1949. Then, after 1953, imports of cotton cloth began increasing rapidly. Most came from India and Hong Kong, as Commonwealth products entered free of duty. In 1958, imports of cotton cloth became greater than exports. By then the cotton industry had begun its campaign for greater protection. The government was at first unwilling to impose any trade barriers on Commonwealth goods, but eventually said that it was willing to police a 'voluntary' agreement. Such an agreement was arrived at in 1959 for imports of cotton cloth; India, Hong Kong and Pakistan were given quotas of 175, 164 and 38 million square yards respectively.

This did not, however, stem the flow of imports. Other countries rushed in to seize their opportunity: imports of piece goods from Spain increased six-fold between 1959 and 1960, to become greater than those of Pakistan and half those of Hong Kong. Imports of cotton yarn had also begun to increase rapidly. It was not surprising that Hong Kong was unwilling to renew the agreement in 1962. The British government then stepped in and raised Hong Kong's quota for 1961 by 10 million square yards, and established a quota for 1962 of 100 million square yards of piece goods, 65 million square yards of made-up goods, and 20 million which could be used for either. These quotas, together with prevailing quotas for India and Pakistan, were then continued, but were later extended to cover the cloth content of made-up articles; so that by 1965 the basic quotas were 195 million square yards from India, and 42.4 from Pakistan, for all cloth and made-up articles. The imports of yarn were also limited to their level in 1961.

Meanwhile, as one country after another invaded the British market, the government attempted to reach a quota agreement or 'understanding' with them, such as, for instance, had existed for many years under the Anglo-Japanese commercial treaty of 1954. The government also agreed to the categorisation of imports—particularly for Hong Kong—which the British industry hoped would reduce the total. Even so, by 1963 retained imports equalled 30% of the United Kingdom production of cotton cloth.

In 1966 this was replaced by a quota system for all underdeveloped and semi-industrialised countries, excluding the Sino-Soviet bloc. India and Hong Kong opted for individual quotas, which were retained at their previous level of 195 and 185 million square yards of cloth and made-up articles respectively, together with 11.5 and 6.3 million pounds of yarn respectively.

The others were covered by global quotas of 4.25 million lbs. of yarn and 59.9 million square yards of cloth (categorised into 46.5 of grey cloth, 5.0 of finished cloth, 3.4 of household textiles and 5.0 of apparel) for the first six months. These arrangements were later modified by allocating part of the global quota to the participating countries on an individual basis. This system of control, with quotas for individual categories of goods and some allocation by countries, was to be continued until 1970, but from 1967 the level of import quotas was raised by one per cent each year. There were special quota arrangements by value of imports from China and for other countries of the Sino-Soviet bloc. Imports of goods from Japan were still regulated by the Anglo-Japanese commercial treaty. Imports from all the other OECD countries and Australia and New Zealand were admitted without restriction. The non-Commonwealth countries faced a tariff, except those in EFTA.

Thus, within ten years, there was a complete *volte-face* in regard to cotton textile imports. Free entry for Commonwealth products was replaced, for those taking advantage of it, by a quota system, the most rigid form of protection. As each attempt to block a particular source encouraged another, the quota system was gradually extended to cover almost all underdeveloped and semi-industrialised countries. But even a global quota for cotton textiles then appeared to be encouraging the imports of man-made fibre cloths, which remained outside it (Briscoe, 1971).

The experience of Britain illustrates the position of other European countries with respect to cotton goods, although they were generally less export-orientated in the first place and retained more restrictions on their imports. In 1953 the major European countries all exported more cotton fabric than they imported and were generally net exporters of cotton yarn, as can be seen from Tables 13.4 and 13.5. From 1953 to 1960, imports increased more rapidly than exports so that the net exports of the EEC(6) fell from 107 to

86 million Kg of cotton fabric, and 30 to 18 million Kg of yarn. However, the trade flows were still largely between member countries, with 59% of the value of cotton fabric and 68% of yarn of EEC members' imports coming from other members of the EEC, and another 25% of cotton fabric and 19% of cotton yarn coming from EFTA. Only 16% of fabric and 12% of yarn came from outside the OEEC. This can be compared with Britain, who obtained 64% of her cotton fabric imports and 67% by value of yarn imports from outside the OEEC, mainly from developing countries (OEEC, 1961, Tables 35 and 37).

Under the LTA, the EEC quota on imports from developing countries was raised by 88%—see Chapter 4—and between 1960 and 1979, its imports of both cotton yarn and cotton fabric more than doubled in quantity and the EEC's exports of cotton fabric fell by a quarter.

The other traditional sector of the textile industry was the wool industry. This, in turn, was divided into the worsted and woollen sectors. In the worsted sector, longer stapled wool, that is over $2\frac{1}{2}$ inches, is required and in an intermediate process all the shorter stapled wool is combed off leaving what is termed a wool top. The tops are then spun to form a yarn in the usual way. In the woollen sector, wool of a shorter staple is used and the yarn is softer. A considerable amount of trade used to take place at each stage of the production process, that is in tops, wool yarn, and wool fabric, as can be seen from Table 13.4. This may be because differentiating features such as mixtures of colour are introduced into the yarn, that is, at a much earlier stage than in the cotton industry.

The trade of the original six members of the EEC appeared to be generally increasing until 1973 in wool tops, yarn and wool fabric—see Table 13.6. But British exports of wool tops and wool fabrics were declining. This trade was largely between European countries themselves; for instance, in 1960, of $316 million exports of yarn by OEEC countries, 80% were imported by other OEEC countries. The major exporters of yarn were France with $107 million, Belgium and Luxembourg with $68 million and the UK with $57 million. Only the UK exported any appreciable amount, that is 39%, outside the OEEC (OEEC, 1961).

Total OEEC exports of woollen and worsted fabrics amounted to $477 million in 1960 of which 60% was to other OEEC countries and 24% to the US and Canada. The major exporter was the UK with $184 million and Italy with $124 million. The UK exported two thirds to countries outside Europe, mostly to Canada and the US.

Unfortunately, figures for Japan cannot be obtained for the

TABLE 13.4 Trade in Cotton Yarn 1953–1982
million Kg

	Exports					Imports				
	1953	1960	1970	1973	1982[1]	1953	1960	1970	1973	1982[1]
Industrial Countries										
US	9.6	5.9	7.1	8.3	16.3	4.4	6.9	9.6	10.3	10.9
Canada	0.01	0.1	–	–	–	3.5	4.0	6.3	7.2	–
Germany	1.5	3.1	6.8	10.0	24.7	4.5	19.4	49.4	80.1	114.5
Belgium/Lux.	21.5	20.8	11.5	16.3	21.5	1.4	8.5	21.6	38.2	50.1
Netherlands	5.0	9.2	12.6	13.1	8.4	12.6	16.7	17.8	20.9	21.1
France	8.2	11.6	18.2	23.0	15.7	1.4	0.3	7.3	17.4	43.7
Italy	14.5	19.8	22.4	27.9	34.1	0.7	2.2	16.1	33.8	65.7
EEC (6)	50.6	64.6	71.5	90.3	104.4	20.7	47.1	112.2	190.4	295.1
UK	23.8	13.5	8.2	13.8	5.0	1.6	17.5	16.8	17.3	36.2
EFTA										
Japan	9.6[1]	39.1[1]	7.1	8.0	5.5	–	–	12.9	50.0	110.5

Table 13.4 (continued)

	Exports					Imports				
	1953	1960	1970	1973	1982[1]	1953	1960	1970	1973	1982[1]
Other OECD										
Greece	0.2	1.5	12.0	26.0	58.0	0.8	0.1	0.2	0.4	–
Spain	0.2	5.8	15.4	12.7	26.6	–	0.01	0.03	9.1	–
Turkey	–	0.1	16.8	32.8	58.5	2.2	0.03	–	–	–
Portugal	0.5	9.0	19.8	28.3	11.8	0.04	0.04	0.1	0.2	–
Developing[1]										
Hong Kong	14.2	15.2	13.1	7.4	3.5	–	–	36.4	79.3	134.7
Taiwan	–	–	–	1.2	33.0	–	–	–	6.0	–
South Korea	–	–	–	–	20.3	–	–	–	–	–
India	7.3	6.9	30.6	11.9	9.9	0.9	–	–	–	–
Pakistan	–	41.0	87.2	163.3	112.5	9.3	–	–	–	–
Egypt	5.5	20.0	43.4	45.2	47.6	–	–	–	–	–
Brazil	–	–	–	29.4	64.8	–	–	–	–	–

Notes: 1. The Textile Statistics Bureau, *Quarterly Statistical Review*, Autumn 1983.
2. Supplemented by GATT, *A Study on Cotton Textiles*, (GATT, Geneva, 1966).
Sources: Data is derived from OEEC and OECD publications except those with a superscript 1 which are derived from the reviews of the Textile Statistics Bureau previously The Textile Council and previous to that The Cotton Board.
OECD, *Textile Industry in OECD Countries, 1974–75*; OECD, *Industrial Statistics 1900–1962*, (Paris, OECD, 1964).

TABLE 13.5 Trade in Cotton Fabric 1953 to 1982
million Kg

	Exports					Imports				
	1953	1960	1970	1973	1982[1]	1953	1960	1970	1973	1982
Industrial Countries										
US	(502.4)	72.2	34.0	56.0	(143.3)	–	33.6	78.0	110.0	(695.0)
Canada	–	17.36	6.2	11.1	–	21.6	29.5	26.2	40.7	–
Germany	23.2	28.5	26.8	47.7	97.3	6.7	28.7	38.0	54.8	76.8
Belgium/Lux.	19.0	27.4	20.8	27.5	43.9	2.3	9.6	14.4	24.7	39.1
Netherlands	23.0	34.0	24.5	30.0	30.9	9.4	24.0	22.3	30.1	37.4
France	49.3	53.3	33.0	43.6	65.5	3.1	3.8	30.0	61.3	94.9
Italy	14.4	11.7	8.6	14.6	33.6	1.0	3.0	45.5	58.6	92.1
EEC (6)	129.0	154.9	113.7	163.4	271.2	22.5	69.0	150.2	229.5	340.3
UK	83.4	42.4	20.4	23.7	21.2	14.7	102.7	67.6	95.6	95.8
EFTA										
Japan	(764.2)	151.7	60.2	36.2	(362.2)	–	–	15.5	108.1	–

Table 13.5 (continued)

	Exports					Imports				
	1953	1960	1970	1973	1982[1]	1953	1960	1970	1973	1982
Other OECD										
Greece	0.5	0.1	1.1	2.1	9.5	2.3	2.8	2.3	3.1	4.6
Spain	3.3	16.3	6.2	2.0	5.8	0.1	0.0	0.8	1.7	3.7
Turkey	–	1.9	3.6	5.5	10.6	11.1	0.0	–	–	–
Portugal	10.2	10.5	17.5	20.9	12.6	0.2	0.3	3.2	3.8	3.5
Developing[1]										
Taiwan	–	–	47.3	48.4	64.9	–	–	–	1.9	5.9
South Korea	–	3.9	22.3	33.6	32.9	–	–	1.3	4.5	4.8
Brazil	–	–	–	25.6	26.4	–	–	–	–	–
Egypt	–	12.6	–	–	18.4	–	–	–	–	–
India	(598.5)	(661.7)	(443.9)	(631.9)	(253.4)	–	–	(366.4)	(418.3)	–
Hong Kong	(122.2)	34.7	(491.3)	(460.7)	(399.5)	–	–	–	–	757.0
Pakistan		61.0	396.5	(501.6)	(571.3)	–	–	–	–	–

Note: 1. Supplemented by the Textile Statistics Bureau, previously the Textile Council, prior to that the Cotton Board's *Quarterly Statistical Review*, information on woven cotton piece goods. Bracketed figures in million square metres.

Sources: OECD, *Textile Industry in OECD Countries, 1974–75;* OEEC, *The Textile Industry in Europe, 1960–61;* OECD, *Industrial Statistics 1900–1962,* (Paris, OECD, 1964); GATT, *A Study on Cotton Textiles,* (GATT, Geneva, July 1966).

TABLE 13.6 Trade in Wool Products 1953 to 1973
million Kg

	Exports				Imports			
	1953	1960	1970	1973	1953	1960	1970	1973
Wool Tops								
Germany	1.9	1.3	4.2	8.2	2.0	5.2	13.9	17.1
Belgium/Lux.	6.2	8.1	9.6	10.1	9.0	13.4	23.9	17.3
Netherlands	0.1	0.6	1.8	1.6	5.1	7.5	6.7	3.6
France	16.5	26.1	32.0	38.9	2.0	2.2	1.8	2.8
Italy	0.1	0.1	0.4	0.2	5.9	4.9	9.8	18.0
EEC(6)	24.9	36.3			24.1	33.2		
UK	31.8	38.2	21.1	21.4	2.2	0.6	3.4	3.1
EFTA	32.8	38.6			14.5	15.7		
Japan			5.2	2.5			3.4	27.4
Wool Yarn								
Germany	2.2	3.9	4.7	6.2	11.4	32.5	28.9	19.5
Belgium/Lux.	11.1	18.4	28.1	19.4	2.6	4.0	7.7	7.8
Netherlands	1.9	5.2	7.2	6.2	8.3	11.2	12.3	10.1
France	15.9	28.9	22.3	16.5	0.2	0.7	2.8	3.8
Italy	1.2	6.4	11.0	8.7	0.2	0.7	3.2	2.4
EEC(6)	32.4	62.8			22.9	49.1		
UK	13.1	14.9	15.8	18.3	1.4	2.4	3.1	5.4
EFTA	15.6	20.4			11.0	15.4		
US	0.1	0.1	0.2	0.2	1.0	2.3	3.7	2.3
Canada	–	0.1	0.2	0.2	1.4	1.5	1.7	1.3
Japan			17.0	5.1			1.8	6.0
Wool Fabric								
Germany	1.3	3.8	6.4	9.7	8.1	24.0	21.9	26.5
Belgium/Lux.	4.3	11.2	3.6	3.5	2.2	4.7	4.6	5.1
Netherlands	4.2	5.9	6.0	5.3	3.0	5.8	7.8	7.6
France	4.1	6.0	7.5	7.9	0.8	3.0	5.0	8.2
Italy	15.7	42.7	47.4	44.7	0.9	1.9	2.0	2.7
EEC(6)	29.6	69.6			15.0	39.4		
UK	27.1	25.8	20.1	19.6	2.4	6.4	5.3	12.5
EFTA	28.9	28.8			11.7	19.4		
US			0.2	0.5			11.3	5.8
Canada			0.2	0.1	6.0	5.8	4.4	6.5
Japan			10.1	2.0			2.7	4.0
Total OECD			108.0	99.2			80.5	80.6

Sources: OECD, *Industrial Statistics, 1900–1962* (Paris, OECD, 1983), IV Textiles.
For 1953 and 1960 data, except Wool Tops.
OEEC, *The Textile Industry in Europe 1960–1961*, (Paris, 1961).
OECD, *The Textile Industry,* 1974–75, 1962, and 1976.

earlier years, but it is interesting to see from Table 13.6 that her imports of wool products seemed to be increasing rapidly in the early 1970s.

In the 1950s and early 1960s there was still a jute industry in the larger European countries. This produced jute yarn and fabric for the carpet industry, and also sacking. The six EEC countries' imports of both yarn and cloth tended to increase more rapidly than exports and their output declined after the mid-1950s. This was partly in response to the decline in consumption of sacking.

Britain had the largest jute industry in Europe, which she protected through the Jute Control Board, acting as a monopoly importer. But from 1963 onwards protection was reduced. Indeed, the European countries gradually ceded their jute trade to Asian producers as the US had done long before in recognition of their lack of competitiveness and the increasing substitution of paper bags for sacks.

Finally let us consider carpets and rugs. There is very little information on trade in these. In terms of employment, the US and UK appear to have the largest industries with 62 and 31 thousand workers in 1979 respectively. In the late 1960s the UK was exporting between 10 and 20% of her output. She benefited from her membership of EFTA in so far as she increased her share of all the other member countries' markets between 1958 and 1966. On the other hand, as she was outside the EEC, her share of that market fell (The Federation of British Carpet Manufacturers, 1967).

Before considering the increasing intervention by industrial countries in their trade in textiles and clothing, let us first consider what appears to underlie the competitive advantage of the developing countries, and whether it shows any sign of changing.

THE LABOUR INTENSITY OF THE TEXTILE AND CLOTHING INDUSTIES

First let us consider the question of factor intensity. Labour and capital are regarded as the only two factors required for production and therefore labour intensity can be shown by a relatively large amount of labour or small amount of capital required per unit of output.

An early exercise by the UN using horsepower as a proxy for capital, showed that within each country horsepower per person engaged in textiles was lower than the average for all manufacturing between 1938 and 1958 and that it was even lower in clothing (UN, 1960).

An alternative approach is by an examination of the output, that is value added by the industry which is the difference between its total final sales and its purchase of raw materials and intermediate products from other industries. This is equal to the return to the factors of production. If a high proportion goes on wages and salaries which can be regarded as the return to labour, then a low proportion goes as a return to capital. If the return to capital is proportional to the amount employed, then a low proportion of value added going as a return to capital and a high proportion going in the form of wages and salaries indicates a labour-intensive industry. By this measure, the UN study showed that within each country textiles was more labour-intensive than average and the clothing industry was more labour-intensive still.

These figures cannot, of course, be used to compare the capital intensities of the same industry in different countries, because although you would expect more capital to be substituted for labour in a high-wage economy such as the US, compared with a low-wage economy such as Hong Kong, this might be balanced out in the proportion of wages and salaries to total output by the higher US wage level.

A later study of factor intensities in the 1960s included a calculation of:

(a) the amount of capital employed per worker;
(b) value of the capital stock divided by the wage bill;
(c) profits per worker;
(d) profits divided by the wage bill.

By all four measures, the textile industry appeared less capital-intensive, that is, more labour intensive than the average for manufacturing, and clothing appeared more labour-intensive still, for the European countries considered. (Sometimes the UK capital intensity in textiles appears relatively high, but this is because the production of man-made fibres, a capital-intensive chemical process, has been included with textiles.)

Furthermore, ranking industries in order of capital stock per employee for Germany in 1968 and the US in 1964, clothing appears at the bottom of the scale as the most labour-intensive manufacturing industry, and textiles near the middle (UN ECE, 1977).

However, it has been persistently argued that the capital intensity of the textile industry is rising (see, for instance, the OECD studies *Modern Cotton Industry: A Capital Intensive Industry* and *Textile and Clothing Industries*). It has even been said that it is now more capital-intensive than the average manufacturing industry.

But all these figures of capital intensity should be treated with circumspection. By a capital-intensive industry, the reader may visualise an industry in which a large amount of expensive equipment is required by the worker to carry out an operation. In passing, it should be noted that technologically advanced spindles and looms are available throughout the world and that many of the recently industrialised countries have a higher proportion of modern equipment than have the older European industries—and that this would be reflected in the value of the capital stock.

However, the overall magnitudes given above are the result not only of the amount of equipment used by a worker but also for how long the equipment is worked. A remarkable feature of the international textile industry is the vast divergence in number of hours worked by machinery.

COSTS IN THE COTTON TEXTILE INDUSTRY

Information on costs in the cotton textile industry was collated by GATT (GATT, 1966). In Tables 13.7 and 13.8, average productivity of the machinery per hour is shown, together with the number of hours the machinery works per year for the larger industrial and developing countries.

Firstly, let us consider spinning. productivity is shown in kilograms of yarn produced per spindle hour. In 1964, it did not generally appear lower in developing countries than in the EEC, UK and Japan. Indeed, the highest output per spindle hour was achieved in Hong Kong, and the next highest in the US.

As mentioned, the hours worked per spindle varied considerably between countries. These have been increasing in all countries, but in 1964 were higher in the developing countries than in Japan or Western Europe. The greatest utilisation was achieved in Hong Kong with spindles on average working 8200 hours per year, next were South Korea, Turkey and Pakistan. Thus the output per spindle, the net result of productivity per spindle hour, and hours worked was generally greater in developing countries than in Western Europe or Japan. In 1964 it was highest in Hong Kong with 166.43 Kg per spindle per year, and next highest in the US with 126.54. Assuming the costs of the machines to be the same, and depreciation to depend on the age of the machine rather than its output, the greater the output per spindle, the lower the capital costs per kilogram of yarn produced. Thus, even the capital costs of the developing countries appear relatively low compared with those of Western Europe and Japan. This has to be qualified in so far as a lower ouput per spindle hour may be due to a finer count

TABLE 13.7   *Productivity and Machine Utilization in Cotton Spinning, 1953 and 1964.*

	Yarn production per spindle hour Kgs/hour	Hours worked per spindle per year		Yarn production per spindle in place Kgs per year	Average count English
	1964	1953	1964	1964	1964
US	0.0197	5513	6416	126.54	
EEC (6)	0.0163	2891	3852	62.85	23.00
Belgium	0.0163	3218	4400	71.54	20.40
France	0.0154	2540	4100	63.03	22.00
Germany	0.0178	3223	3656	65.03	23.80
Italy	0.0154	2829	3488	53.77	24.32
Netherlands	0.0171	3256	4660	79.59	22.50
UK	0.0152	1645	2862	43.53	21.10
Japan	0.0171	4084	3840	65.55	31.40
Hong Kong	0.0201		8280	166.43	24.00
Pakistan	0.0138	4435	6482	89.53	30.00
Taiwan	0.0185		6401	118.48	20.00
South Korea	0.0168		6590	110.40	22.80
Egypt	0.0139	4388	7119	98.70	23.30
Turkey	0.0178		4529	116.56	20.60
Spain	0.0117		4167	48.86	22.00
Portugal	0.0176	3422	4932	86.42	22.11

Spindles in ring equivalent.
2 shifts = 4160 hours. English count — the finer the yarn the higher the count.
Sources: GATT, *A Study on Cotton Textiles* (Geneva, GATT, 1966), Part II.

of yarn being produced—but as can be seen, this is not enough to dispose of this conclusion.

In weaving, the production of cloth per loom hour varied considerably between countries in 1964—see Table 13.6. This was partly due to the variation in the proportion of automatic looms which was 100% in the US and 86% and 85% respectively in Italy and Hong Kong. These figures do not appear quite consistent with the output per loom hour which appeared higher in Belgium and Germany than Italy but this may be due to the former two countries working their automatic looms much longer than the rest. The hours worked per loom are again much lower in Western Europe and Japan than in most of the developing countries with the longest

TABLE 13.8 *Productivity and Machine Utilization in Cotton Weaving, 1953 and 1964.*

	Cloth production per loom hour kgs/hour	Hours worked per loom per year		Cloth production per loom in place Kgs per year		Proportion of automatic looms[1]		
	1969	1953	1964	1953	1964	1953	1964	1977
US	0.754	5529	6411	3876	4834	100	100	100[2]
EEC (6)	0.784	2280	3349	1386	2753		74	
Belgium	0.851		376	1957	4136	28	52	87[2]
France	0.754	2139	3403	1196	2568	42	69	93[2]
Germany	0.870	2467	3506	1729	3057		77	99[3]
Italy	0.737	2107	2927	1091	2158	64	86	96[2]
Netherlands	0.749	2682	4061	1486	3043	22	67	100[3,4]
UK	0.751	1817	2800	1049	2102	11	37	76[3]
Japan	0.497	3885	4350	1314	1794		24	39[3]
Hong Kong	0.527		8160		4300		86	
India	0.578	4409	4992	2553	2884		12	
Pakistan	0.733	4092	5657		2651		64	
Taiwan	0.430		3830	1401	1646		54	
South Korea	0.663		3713		2394		28	
Egypt	0.581	5032	6472	3121	3763	45	66	
Brazil	0.400		5695					
Turkey	0.720		5760		4148	55	100	
Spain	0.600		3252	620	1951	15	36	
Portugal	0.480		3578	965	1716	12	28	57[3,4]

Notes: 1. Or semi-automatic looms.
2. OECD, *Textile and Clothing Industries* (Paris, OECD, 1983) p. 24 (1977 data).
3. OECD, *Textile Industry in OECD Countries 1977* (Paris, OECD, 1972), Table S4.
4. 1976.
Source: GATT, *A Study on Cotton Textiles* (Geneva, GATT, 1966), Part II.

hours shown by Hong Kong with 8160 and the next highest for the US. The output per loom was generally higher in the developing countries than Western Europe or Japan but the highest figure of all was for the US, followed by Hong Kong. Again, output per loom may be expected to be inversely related to capital costs except in so far as the slower looms are also cheaper.

Of course, far more machines than just the basic spindles and looms are generally used. But the same argument applies. The longer the machinery is used, the lower the depreciation per unit of output. This is because depreciation is due to obsolescence rather than wear and tear.

So it would appear that due to the greater utilisation of machinery, capital costs in both spinning and weaving were lower in the major developing countries than in the EEC, UK or Japan.

In relation to the approach made so far, labour productivity should be considered in terms of the manning of machines; the higher the number of persons employed per spindle hour, the lower labour productivity in spinning.

However, the figures generally provided are of overall labour productivity, which is dependent on the output per machine hour as well as on the number of people manning the machine. The GATT figures of overall labour productivity taking the US as 100 are shown in Table 13.9. However, although labour productivity in Hong Kong and India appears relatively so low, particularly in spinning, this is balanced out by even lower wage costs.

Another study consistent with the previous ones shows this in terms of labour cost per pound of cotton yarn spun and per yard of cloth woven—see Table 13.10.

The total cost of producing 20s yarn and cotton polyester shirting in different countries is shown in Table 13.8. Total costs in Hong Kong, India and Pakistan were lower both because labour costs were lower and because of a greater utilisation of machinery which reduced depreciation per unit of output. The price of the input cotton for yarn, and yarn for cloth, also contributed to the variation in price of the final product. This is, of course, where trade protection for an intermediate is transmitted as higher costs for subsequent processing. For both cases, the costs of production of Portugal, Hong Kong, India and Pakistan were substantially below those of the US, UK, France and West Germany.

TABLE 13.9   Production per Worker per annum.
US = 100

	Yarn	Cloth
USA	100	100
UK	29	68
France	39	70
Italy	25	44
Hong Kong	33	48
India	17	35

Source: GATT, A Study on Cotton Textiles (Geneva, GATT, 1966), p. 67.

TABLE 13.10   The Textile Councils Estimate of Production Costs

	Production Costs: 20s Yarn				Production Costs: Polyester/Cotton Shirting		
		Spinning				Weaving	
		Clean			Yarn		
	Total	cotton	Labour	Depreciation	Total	cost	Labour	Depreciation
		cents per kilo yarn				cents per square metre cloth		
USA	107.6	73.6	13.4	5.3	31.3	21.4	5.1	0.3
UK	107.1	69.9	18.3	2.4	32.6	22.1	4.8	1.2
France	95.9	68.8	10.1	7.5	30.4	18.0	5.8	1.2
West Germany	100.3	70.3	12.6	7.5	33.2	19.0	6.4	1.3
Portugal	88.2	64.2	8.8	4.4	26.3	17.3	3.2	0.8
Hong Kong	85.5	66.4	7.1	2.9	26.7	19.3	2.9	0.5
India	86.4	61.9	9.3	4.4	26.3	17.9	3.1	0.7
Pakistan	83.1	61.5	5.7	6.0	24.3	17.7	2.0	0.8

Source: The Textile Council, Cotton and Allied Textiles (Manchester, The Textile Council, 1969), pp. 37 & 40.

DEVELOPMENTS IN TRADE UP TO 1973

In face of the clear cost advantage of developing countries, how much effect do the LTA and other agreements directed at reducing and controlling imports of cotton textiles into European and North American countries appear to have had on trade, production, and employment?

The LTA does appear to have allowed a considerable increase in imports into the signatory countries such that they generally moved from being net exporters to net importers.

As can be seen from Table 13.4, the US net imports of cotton yarn increased between 1960 and 1970 to 2.5 million Kg per annum, but were very small compared with those of other industrial countries. The EEC (6) changed from being a net exporter of 17.5 million Kg in 1960 to a net importer of 46.7 million in 1970 and net imports increased still further to 100 million Kg in 1973.

The US trade in cotton fabric was more significant—see Table 13.5—changing from net exports of 38.6 million Kg in 1960 to net imports of 44 million in 1940 and 54 million Kg in 1973. The EEC moved from having net exports of 85.8 million Kg in 1960 to net imports of 36.5 in 1970 and 66.1 in 1973.

The UK, covered by other agreements, increased her net imports of cotton yarn from 4 to 8.6 million Kg between 1960 and 1970 and then they were reduced to below the 1960 level. Her net imports of cotton cloth fell from 1960 to 1970 from 60.3 to 47.2 million Kg, but then increased again to 73.7 in 1973. She imported far more than any of the other industrial countries in relation to both population and consumpion.

Let us now consider the situation in the internal market of the chief importing countries.

EFFECT OF PROTECTION ON INTERNAL MARKETS

In the US, the production of cotton yarn and fabric continued to increase with fluctuations until the mid-1960s and then declined. But in the European countries, protection did not lead to any increase in output of cotton textiles. The output of both cotton yarn and cotton cloth has persistently declined in Britain. In the EEC (6) as a whole, the output of cotton yarn and cloth reached a maximum in 1960 and has been on a downward trend with fluctuations since then.

The quota on cotton goods provided a barrier which made it easier for the man-made fibre producers to gain acceptance for their products, particularly the new synthetics. They also acquired an interest in the viability of the industry; in Britain they were largely responsible for its rationalisation. It might be argued that there would have been a shift in consumption towards synthetics anyway. But the association of the man-made fibre producers with the industry assisted their adoption. The man-made fibre producers provided technical and financial assistance, co-operated in the development of machinery which could take advantage of synthetic fibres, and promoted their products by advertising in conjunction with textile or clothing producers, wholesalers or retailers. The importance of this absorption, particularly for synthetics, is made clear from the figures of output. Between 1953 and 1960, the production of cellulosics in Europe increased by 40% but the output of synthetics increased nearly eight fold.

In the US and Canada, synthetics had already begun to replace cellulosics and thus there was a decline in the production of continuous filament rayon, and the consumption of the staple fibre scarcely increased.

Most of this increased output was fed into the traditional textile industry. But man-made fibres are clean and can be produced more uniformly than cotton, and also a considerable amount is produced as a continuous filament which needs no spinning but just twisting together to produce a yarn. For all these reasons, less labour was required. Furthermore, because the synthetics are stronger, much faster machinery could be developed for them in both spinning and weaving and this also reduced the labour required.

Thus the labour force of the cotton textile industry has been declining faster than output. Between 1962 and 1969 the labour force in the cotton industries of the EEC (6) countries and of Britain fell by about a third, but that of the US by only 5%.

But man-made fibres are not used only in the traditional spinning and weaving sectors but also in knitting. The knitting industry comprises three sectors: flat weft knitting similar to ordinary hand knitting; warp knitting similar to crocheting; and circular knitting similar to circular hand knitting but much faster as several rows can be knitted at a time, but with no facility for changing the number of stitches. Knitting saves preparation time because no warp has got to be set up. Circular knitting can also produce cloth at a much faster rate than can weaving. These features account for the rapid growth of knitting, particularly for synthetic yarns. Indeed, the only sector of the European textile industry to have shown an increase in employment between 1964 and 1971 has been knitting (OECD, 1971–2).

So the imposition of barriers on the imports of cotton goods has not accounted for any increase in domestic production but rather a shift to synthetics and knitting rather than weaving. It has not led to an increase in employment in the traditional sectors; if any has occurred, it has been in the knitting sector.

Has this forced a shift in consumption which would not have occurred anyway? This is not clear. In the 1950s there was a fashion for nylon shirts and nylon sheets which were generally warp-knitted. Was this just due to their easy care properties or was it partly due to the much greater advertising of them than of the equivalent cotton products? Later these came to be replaced by cotton and polyester products said to be superior because of their warmer feel and greater absorbency, which were derived from the cotton in the mixture. How far did their acceptance depend on the advertising and design efforts of the man-made fibre producers?

There were similar fashions in knitted garments for women: acrylic and bulked polyester (Crimplene) dresses, for instance.

These fashions, however, did persuade producers in developing countries to try and circumvent the LTA by providing man-made and mixture fabrics which were not included in it. The most common of these was a mixture of polyester and cotton. The polyester appears to have come largely from Japan.

There was also an endeavour, particularly by the more advanced developing countries to trade up by selling clothing rather than fabric. They may have been assisted by the shift in fashion in

Europe in the early 1970s to more casual wear, which included jeans and T-shirts. The effect of this was a very rapid increase in imports from developing countries into industrial countries as can be seen from Table 13.3.

In 1973 the total value of imports of clothing into the US was more than three times as large as it was in 1967, in Japan it was 36 times as great over the same period, and in the EEC (9) it was four times as great. Furthermore, imports into the EEC from non-member countries had been increasing even faster, and were about six times their level in 1967. Exports of these three areas were also increasing but not nearly as fast (OECD, *Textile Industry*, 1974–5). The result of this was that, whereas in 1967 the EEC and Japan were both net exporters of clothing, by 1973 they were net importers.

TRADE SINCE 1973

This was the background to the MFA described in Chapter 4. The MFA included most fabrics in its scope and thus put an end to circumvention of the LTA. It also permitted bilateral negotiations.

As stated in Chapter 4, the US had already in 1971 negotiated quota agreements on imports of textile products not covered by the LTA from Japan, and clothing from Taiwan, South Korea and Hong Kong. The MFA just gave these legal recognition, and the US the opportunity to extend them (Keesing and Wolf, 1980, p. 39). The effect on trade was that the quantity of imports measured in million square yards_of apparel and other textiles declined from 1972 onwards. It rose slightly in 1976 but the imports of textiles other than apparel were in 1979 only half their 1972 level although those of apparel were slightly higher. The result was that imports in square yardage equivalent were, at 4648 million square yards overall in 1979, 25% lower than they were in 1972. There was a significant fall in imports from Japan such that they were in 1979 only 29% of their 1971 level. Imports from Europe and other industrial countries fluctuated but were lower after 1972 than before. Imports from Hong Kong, Taiwan and South Korea fluctuated but in 1979 were 7% above their 1972 level. Imports from other developing countries increased faster, particularly those from China which rose from 0.2 million square yards in 1971 to 231 million square yards in 1979.

Thus, within the overall reduction in imports of textiles and clothing into the US, there appears to have been a diversion away from Japan and other industrial countries to developing countries.

Imports from Hong Kong, South Korea and Taiwan, while only slightly abover their 1972 level, had risen as a percentage from 29% to 42% of the total (Keesing and Wolf, 1980, Table 3.6, p. 85). Thus the US, in subsequent efforts at restriction, has endeavoured to reduce the quotas of these three countries.

As described in Chapter 4, in 1975 the EEC had also begun to extend its system of import control by a negotiation of bilateral agreements with the leading developing countries. This involved a reduction in quotas on products from Hong Kong, Taiwan and South Korea. But it could not impose the same degree of restraint on countries with which it had signed preferential agreements, nor on other industrial countries for fear of retaliation.

In imposing its restrictions on imports, the EEC also distinguished products by their degree of 'sensitivity'—it divided textile and clothing products into groups. Group I contained the most 'sensitive' products, namely cotton yarn, cotton fabric, fabrics of synthetic fibres, T-shirts, pullovers, trousers, blouses and shirts. The least increase was to be permitted for these products.

The effect of these restrictions on the volume of imports can be seen in Table 13.11. Between 1976 and 1980, imports of MFA products from outside the EEC (9) increased by 20% but those of Group I only increased by 4.4%. But imports from low-cost countries increased at lower rates than these, implying that there must have been some diversion of trade from low-cost countries to other industrial countries. The chief of these was the US, who became the largest single supplier of textiles and clothing to the EEC. US exports of synthetics were assisted by the low price of feedstock to US producers of synthetic fibres and US trade in general was assisted by the low value of the dollar; when this began to rise in 1980, US exports to the EEC began to fall.

Imports of all MFA products into the EEC (9) from low-cost countries increased by 11% between 1976 and 1980. But imports from Mediterranean countries in this group increased very much faster—Greece by 27.4%, Spain by 27.6% and Portugal by 34%, and they also increased faster from ACP countries, both these groups being covered by preferential agreements. Imports from countries tied by bilateral agreements increased much more slowly, by only 9.3%, and these countries, together with Portugal, appear to have borne the brunt of the restrictions on imports of sensitive goods to an increase of only 1.2% from low-cost countries.

This general picture of trade diversion from developing to developed countries is also borne out by the distribution by value of trade in textile and clothing products, particularly the sensitive items. The proportion of world exports by value of cotton fabric,

TABLE 13.11   EEC Imports of MFA Products.
1000 tonnes

		1976	1980	Increase 1976–80 %
Extra EEC	All	1448.9	1739.8	20.1
	Group I	779.6	813.7	4.4
Low-cost countries	All	1092.8	1214.8	11.2
	Group I	645.5	653.2	1.2
of which developing	All	595.7	678.4	13.9
	Group I	368.5	390.2	5.9
of which ACP	All	15.5	18.3	18.1
	Group I	14.2	15.5	9.2
State-trading	All	174.2	185.3	6.4
	Group I	60.5	66.5	9.9
Mediterranean	All	361.4	420.3	16.3
	Group I	240.3	245.7	2.2
of which Greece	All	82.9	105.6	27.4
	Group I	58.4	69.8	19.5
Spain	All	47.1	60.1	27.6
	Group I	22.7	24.9	9.7
Portugal	All	54.8	73.5	34.1
	Group I	30.3	29.0	− 0.04
Bilateral-agreement countries	All	651.3	711.8	9.3
	Group I	380.8	385.6	1.3

Source: Michael Noelke and Robert Taylor, *EEC Protectionism Present Practice and Future Trends,* pp. 267 and 270. (Brussels, European Research Association, 1981).

both grey and bleached, supplied by developing countries declined between 1973 and 1980, and that of cotton yarn remained stationary. But the developed countries continued to be the most important import market except in continuous synthetic woven fabric.

In clothing, developed countries still account for around nine tenths or more of all imports. But the proportion of some sensitive items exported by developing countries declined dramatically. For instance, between 1976 and 1980, the proportion by value of world exports of trousers by developing countries fell from 53% to 35%, of cotton blouses from 38% to 28%, of men's shirts from 96% to 71% and of jerseys and pullovers from 70% to 33% (UN, *1980 Yearbook of International Trade Statistics*, Vol. II, New York, 1981).

Thus, the overall figures for trade in textiles and clothing shown in Chapter 8, and their apparent decline in significance in relation to other manufactures, is the result of a deliberate suppression of imports from developing countries by the more advanced industrial ones. Quotas on imports have been imposed in the face of consistent evidence that the production costs of developing countries remain lower even after the various reorganisation and rationalisation schemes carried out by governments. Furthermore, these barriers have been most stringently applied to imports from the most efficient and highly developed of the developing countries, namely Hong Kong, Taiwan and South Korea.

This has led to trade diversion to higher-cost but competitive countries, in particular those with which the EEC has preferential agreements, and also the US. The US was competitive because of her very high productivity, particularly in weaving and also because, as already mentioned, of her more continuous utilisation of machinery, generally 24 hours a day, which brings down capital costs. Her competitive edge was reduced after 1980 by the appreciation of the dollar.

Protection in the EEC may also have been successful in leading to an increase in output or at least a maintenance of output of some of the countries imposing the barriers. But most of this has not been in the traditional sector on whose products the import barriers have largely been placed, but in the competing knitting sector which is more capital-intensive and uses a higher proportion of synthetic fibres. Employment in the traditional sectors has declined and any increase in the knitting sector has not been sufficient to compensate for this except perhaps in Italy.

The cost of this has been borne by the consumer in the form of higher prices. How much higher is a matter of controversy. The Consumer's Association in Britain estimated that the MFA raised prices of basic imported clothing by 15–40%. It also led to the exporting country trading up into higher-valued items and therefore had a disproportionate effect on supplies and therefore prices of low-valued products such as children's wear, T-shirts, etc.

There is also the interesting question of who gains the economic rent or benefit from the quota that arises from the difference between the price at which the goods can be acquired on the world market and the price at which they can be sold on the domestic market of the importers.

14 Road Motor Vehicles

Road motor vehicles might be regarded as a prime example of an innovation as described in Chapter 9 However, they really represented the culmination of a series of innovations in a number of different European countries notably Germany, France and Switzerland with the Karl Benz automobile of 1885 being regarded as the first commercially feasible petrol-driven automobile. But there then followed a whole series of inventions which emerged from workshops throughout Western Europe and the US which led to great improvements and modifications in design of the engine and the body of the car.

European production was undertaken by craftsmen in workshops to individual designs; the cars were large and relatively powerful but expensive. At the turn of the century, the largest industry was in France.

In contrast, the US producers had to concentrate on much lighter vehicles which could traverse their dirt track roads. The US industry also moved early towards a standardisation of parts. Henry Ford was a great advocate of bringing down the price by mass production so that cars could be available to the general public. He founded the Ford Motor Company in 1903, and in 1908 introduced the Model T Ford which incorporated parts that were standardised and machined to close tolerances, and which were, by 1913, put together on a moving assembly line. In that year he produced 100,000 vehicles and by 1919 about a million. Such an output meant that all economies of scale in the production of parts and components could be exploited.

In 1908, Mr Durant had also founded the General Motor Corporation (GM) which was a merger of eleven automobile companies plus fourteen other producing electrical lights, parts, and accessories. It also began to expand very rapidly (Sloan, 1965). By 1929 the US industry as a whole reached its pre-war peak of 4.6 million vehicles. Although complete world statistics are not available, output of the US industry in the period between 1910 and 1939 appears to have been greater than that of the rest of the world put together.

The US firms were interested in exporting to Europe, the other centre of car consumption and production. But from the outset it was clear that European demand for cheaper cars was different partly because the level of the vehicle taxation in Europe was dependent on engine size. The price of petrol was also much higher in Europe and taxes were later shifted from engine size to fuel.

So, in order to benefit from their innovations in production technology, US firms began to set up assembly and then production units in Europe and often developed specially small cars for the market.

The consumption lag and imitation lags were very small. For instance the Model T Ford was being exported to Britain by 1909 and assembly was started there in 1911, which was gradually extended to include more and more production. Then Ford started production with its first UK designs in a large green-field site in Dagenham in 1932. However GM established itself in Europe entirely by acquisition of Vauxhall in Britain in 1925 and Opel in Germany in 1929 (Sloan, p. 197).

The McKenna import duties of $33\frac{1}{3}$% on cars (see Chapter 4) acted as an additional incentive to supplying the British market by domestic production rather than exports. As the rising tide of nationalism throughout Europe led to increasing tariff levels—for instance the German duty on motor vehicles was 13% in 1925, 20% in 1929 and 40% in 1937 (Jones, 1981, Table 17)—this also became true of other European Countries.

Indeed with the double incentive of tariffs and the advantage of local production, Ford and GM had established themselves in a number of Latin American countries. Australia, South Africa, Japan and India. Chrysler, the third largest US company, also acquired assembly facilities in Belgium, Britain and Canada.

These assembly and production facilities fared much better during the Great Depression than US exports, which fell from 546,200 in 1929 to 70,000 in 1932. Furthermore, apart from the subsidiaries in Japan, which were gradually driven out by the Japanese government during the 1930s, they provided the basis for the post war network of overseas subsidiary production by the US companies.

In Britain, Ford was the largest producer in 1914 but in the 1920s Morris and Austin introduced mass-production techniques which lowered the costs and prices of their cars, and they expanded rapidly. The British Industry was less affected by the Great Depression than that of the US and other European countries, partly because of a lower decline in real income, so that at its worst ouput only fell by 15% (Maxcy and Silberston, 1959, p. 14). Morris and

Austin became the largest producers of cars, and Morris and Ford the largest producers of (mainly light) commercial vehicles.

By 1938 the largest industry in the world was still that of the US, producing 2 million cars and half a million commercial vehicles. The UK was the second largest, producing 431 thousand cars and 104 thousand commercial vehicles, followed by the German industry and then the French. The Japanese industry was very small and produced mainly commercial vehicles.

The US emerged from the Second World War with production almost entirely geared to commercial vehicles, output of which was twice its pre-war level. But US ouput of cars soon exceeded its previous peak in 1929. The UK production of commercial vehicles was also greater than pre-war but she did not attain her 1938 ouput of cars until 1949. Germany also took some time to recover.

Then began a period of very rapid expansion in which all industrial countries shared. This was the result of the very rapid increase in *per capita* incomes in the post-war period up to 1970 the reduction in the relative cost of motoring because of the fall in the real price of oil described in Chapter 12, and an apparent change in tastes away from public to private transport. The last was cumulative in so far as when a public service starts making losses, the frequency and geographical extent of the services are generally cut in order to stem these losses. This erosion of service quality makes private transport appear more desirable.

However, there is generally assumed to be some saturation level of ownership which varies between countries according to family structure, road mileage and congestion in cities. It is assumed to be approached asymptotically.

As can be seen from Table 14.1, the European ownership level in 1953 was far below that of the US at 291 and Canada at 166 per 1000 of population. The average for the EEC (6) was only 31. The European saturation level may be below the US level because of less extensive road networks in relation to population but it was clear that it certainly had not been reached. Ownership in all European countries increased rapidly so that by 1982 the figures in France and Germany were greater than those of the US in 1962. An additional inducement to ownership of a car was provided by the major investment in motorways undertaken throughout Europe.

The increase in the total ownership of passenger cars and commercial vehicles can also be seen in Tables. 14.1 and 14.2. The very high figures for the EEC shold be noted, with Germany achieving an increase of 414% in ownership of passenger cars between 1953 and 1962. The average increase for the EEC was 227%. The lower increase of 135% in the UK reflected her slower increase in

TABLE 14.1 *Expansion of the Market for Passenger Cars, 1953–82.*

	Passenger cars per 1000 inhabitants				Passenger cars in use 1000 units				Passenger cars—new registrations 1000 units	
	1953	*1962*	*1973*	*1982*	*1953*	*1962*	*1973*	*1982*	*1973*	*1982*
US	291	351	481	556	46,422	65,929	101,985	124,821	11,351	7754
Canada	166	242	354	435	2514	4550	7866	10556	945	727
EEC (6)	31	106			4848	18,284	50,550[2]	71,598[2]	5997[2]	6881[2]
France	56	147	280	370	2386	7007	14,620	20,300	1746	2056
Germany	26	119	275	385	1277	6558	17,036	24,036	2031	2156
Italy	13	60	244	345	613	3007	13,424	19,400	1449	1900
EFTA	45	114			3908	10,383	8,144[1]	11,500[1]	937[1]	1,039[1]
UK	56	126	247	286	2862	6730	13,815	16,075	1661	1555
Japan			133	217			14,474	25,539	2934	3038
Australasia							5567	7675	563	566

Notes: 1. Remaining EFTA members, Switzerland, Sweden, Portugal, Norway, Finland & Austria.
    2. Of France, Germany, Italy, Netherlands, Belgium only.
Sources: Society of Motor and Manufacturers and Traders, *The Motor Industry of Great Britain, 1983*. Tables 36 & 16 for 1973 and 1982. (Taxes are excluded from the UK figures). Also Table 47; OECD *Industrial Statistics 1900–1962*. (Paris, OECD, 1964).

income. The increase was also very much slower in the US and Canada. This partly reflects their slower increase in income but also their approach to a saturation level.

The sales or registration of new vehicles represent partly the additions to total stock and partly the replacement of depreciated stock. The total of such registrations reached a maximum in Western Europe in 1973.

But as a country approaches its saturation level, the sales of new cars tend to fall to replacement levels. The frequency of replacement or the average age of car may in turn depend on income levels and the costs of using a car.

Thus, much of the rapid expansion in Western European industries shown in Tables 14.3 and 14.4 was to supply home markets. But the output of the major countries increasingly became associated with their trading position.

This is intertwined with the position of producing firms. They are acting in a market which could be described as one of oligopoly with distinctly differentiated products which are nevertheless substitutable by products from other firms. Each producer has the

TABLE 14.2   Expansion of the market for Commercial Vehicles 1953–82
thousand units.

	Commercial vehicles in use				New registrations	
	1953	1962	1973	1982	1973	1982
US	9832	13,094	23,668	35,622	3029	2430
Canada	877	1200	2004	3294	235	205
EEC (6)	2250	3622	5178^2	6881^2	562^2	705^2
France	1038	1823	2100	2890	270	363
Germany	634	846	1347	1648	138	124
Italy	313	552	1084	1615	83	152
EFTA	1561	2450	948^1	1310^1	$[100]^1$	$[150]^1$
UK	1142	1657	1875	1850	307	231
Japan			10,526	15,797	1982	2223
Australasia					130	177

Notes: 1. Remaining EFTA members Switzerland, Sweden, Portugal, Norway,
Finland and Austria.
2. Of France, Germany, Italy, Netherlands and Belgium only.
Sources: Society of Motor Manufacturers & Traders, The Motor Industry of Great
Britain, 1983, for figures for 1973 and 1982, Tables 36 and 16. Taxis are
included with commercial vehicles for UK for 1973 and 1982; OECD,
Industrial Statistics 1900–1962 (Paris, OECD, 1964) for 1953 and 1967
figures.

choice of the size and type of vehicles he produces, their quality and
the method of production.

As already mentioned, the large US car firms introduced mass
production and they grew by takeovers and direct expansion
together with their market to be able to exploit all economies of
scale. By 1954, 91% of car production in the US was accounted for
by the largest three producers and by 1969 this dominance had
increased to 97%, with General Motors producing 4.9 million,
Ford 2.6 million and Chrysler 1.5 million. The next largest was
American Motors with 0.2 million (Rhys, 1972, p. 124). The firms
are vertically integrated, producing most of their components,
engines, gearboxes, and bodies (but not tyres), as well as carrying
out final assembly, but the geographical distribution of the plants
became fairly widespread as production was moved away from
Detroit to green-field sites with more plentiful supplies of labour.

The Canadian car industry is really an extension of the US
industry. Furthermore, since the 1964 trade agreement there have
been no duties on trade in cars and components between the US
and Canada.

The European industry is quite different from that of the US. At the beginning of the post-war period there was a large number of producers in the UK and France and Germany. They are generally classed as volume car producers, or specialist producers of luxury or sports cars or ultra-utilitarian ones. None of these had an output anywhere near that of GMC or Ford in the US and therefore could not exploit such economies of scale. This appears to have been the factor inducing a whole series of mergers in the European industry. The mergers included the specialised as well as the volume car producers.

The chief volume car producers in the UK in 1947 were Morris, Austin, Ford, Standard, Vauxhall (GM) and Rootes and the main specialist producers were Rover, Singer and Jaguar. Morris merged with Austin in 1952 to form the British Motor Corporation (BMC) which acquired Pressed Steel in 1962 and Jaguar in 1966. Rootes took over Singer in 1955 and then was saved from bankruptcy by Chrysler in 1964 which acquired complete control in 1967. The Leyland Motor Corporation, specialising in buses and trucks, acquired Standard in 1961 and Rover in 1967. Then, under the auspices of the government's Industrial Re-organisation Corporation (IRC), it merged with BMC in 1968 to form British Leyland which then accounted for 47% of the British output of cars and 43% of commercial vehicles. The IRC was aiming for some rationalisation of production so that more economies of scale could be obtained. But although the group was initially profitable, it was saddled with more problems than it could cope with in the form of geographically dispersed assembly lines, too many models and too few new ones, low labour productivity or overmanning which because of poor industrial relations was very difficult to improve, and out-of-date equipment. It almost sank beneath these problems and had to be rescued and nationalised by the government in 1975. Then in 1976 the UK government also provided Chrysler UK with a loan of £162.5 million in order to prevent its liquidation. The government did not wish to nationalise it but it also wished to maintain employment particularly at its works in Scotland and also the export of knock-down kits to Iran.

Thus the UK industry emerged with one indigenous firm depending on government support and the subsidiaries of the main US firms, that is Ford UK, Vauxhall (GMC) and Rootes (Chrysler) with the last in a precarious state.

The chief French producers were Renault, Citroen, Peugeot and Simca. Renault had been nationalised in 1946. Ford had a 15% share in Simca, which Chrysler bought in 1958 and gradually increased to obtain full control in 1972. The French government consistently resisted the efforts of Ford and GM to expand in France by setting up additional assembly facilities and thus they sited the plants in Germany and Belgium respectively. Fiat also tried to gain complete control of Citroen and was refused, eventually selling out to Peugeot. Peugeot-Citroen in 1978 took over Chrysler Europe, which included Simca and the British operations, renaming them Talbot. Most of the latter was closed down in 1980 but Talbot is still producing in the UK. Peugeot-Citroen has run into the same sort of problems as BL, with difficulties in assimilating and rationalising its acquisitions. Talbot's output rapidly declined and its losses continued to mount resulting in losses for the whole Peugeot group since 1979 (*Financial Times*, 9 January 1984).

The chief German producers were Volkswagen, established by the state in 1937 and emerging as the dominant producer in the post-war period with 46% of output, Opel (GM), Mercedes, and Ford (Rhys, 1972, p. 146). Volkswagen concentrated until the 1970s on the production of one model, which enabled it to reap the same kind of economies of scale as the US producers; in 1956 it produced 1.5 million cars.

Italy is dominated by Fiat, a privately owned company specialising in small cars but which also absorbed the specialist producers, Ferrari in 1965 and Lancia in 1970. Alfa Romeo, a specialist producer, is owned by the state.

The luxury-car producers Mercedes Benz, Alfa Romeo and Lancia already mentioned and BMW (Germany), Volvo (Sweden) and Saab (Sweden) together account for a relatively small proportion of new registrations: 12% in the EEC in 1982 (SMMT). Their fortunes have varied considerably and to increase competitiveness many of them have introduced small cars, Alfa-Romeo with the assistance of Nissan (Maxcy, 1981, p. 198).

Most large European producers of cars also produced commercial vehicles. These were often extensions of their car models. But there remained a number of specialist firms devoted to the production of large trucks, vans and buses. However, the largest European producer is now Daimler-Benz (part of the Mercedes group) which produced 250,000 commercial vehicles in 1982.

Thus the European market gradually became dominated by the large indigenous producers of the major countries generally owned or supported by their governments—Fiat, still privately owned, was the major exception. These have been described as the European champions, that is carriers of the national flag, and the international competition was regarded as taking place between them and the US multinationals.

This competition largely took the form of choice of models and the European firms were often able to gain markets at the expense of the US multinationals by their earlier and more effective development of really small and fuel-efficient cars.

INTERNATIONAL TRADE UNTIL 1973

But to revert to the immediate post-war period, it was the US industry that was the largest and strongest and the main source of both passenger cars and commercial vehicles for the rest of the world. However, these exports soon declined and resumed their traditional flow to Canada and Latin America. The dollar shortage also meant that European countries were unwilling to spend them on US cars. Even when this faded away at the end of the 1950s, US-built cars did not appeal to European tastes. They were cheaper in terms of price per unit weight but they were relatively large and had a low mileage per gallon. They did not appeal to middle-income Europeans faced with less road space and a higher price of petrol, and wealthy Europeans preferred the luxury cars of their specialist producers to the mass-produced American ones.

It was the UK that early established herself as the major exporter of passenger cars exporting 226,300 cars in 1948, that is two thirds of her output (see Table 14.3). This was partly because of the early post-war recovery of the industry and the greater allocation of steel to the industry for exporting, by the British government desperately anxious to improve the British trading position. Just as in the inter-war period, she continued her exports to the Commonwealth but also exported to Europe and the USA. The Commonwealth markets that Britain had supplied in the past became more and more constricted if not closed by tariff barriers and quotas of countries anxious to establish their own industries such as Australia and India, or merely wishing to restrict entry of what were regarded as luxury goods. The US was also affected by this.

After 1950, Germany and France and then Italy began to expand their output and exports rapidly, as can be seen from Tables 14.3 and 14.4. UK exports increased to 1963 but not nearly as fast as those of other European countries. By 1963, Germany was the largest exporter of passenger cars and was exporting 1.2 million. The exports of France, Germany and Italy then continued to increase rapidly to 1973, whereas those of the UK declined slightly and continued to decline after 1973. Those of France and Italy also declined after 1973, whereas those of Germany continued to increase. Most of these exports were to other European countries.

TABLE 14.3 Production and Exports and Imports of Passenger Cars by Industrial Countries, 1948–82 thousand units.

	Production: passenger cars					Exports: passenger cars					Imports: passenger cars				
	1948	1955	1963	1973	1982	1948	1955	1963	1973	1982	1948	1955	1963	1973	1982
US	3909	7920	7644	9667	5075	207	218	144	509	356	28	58	409	2437	3319
Canada	167	375	532	1227	787	27	12	16	892	680	17	49	60	630	595
EEC (6)	174	1490				79	580				—	218			
France	100	553	1521	2867	2777	54	113	530	1446	1464	1	10	147	463	990
Germany	30	705	2414	3650	3762	6	357	1217	2173	2194	—	17	133	768	840
Italy	44	231	1105	1823	1297	14	61	292	656	437	0.1	3	191	418	905
Belgium		[2]	285	969	950	4	25	146	786	903		120	56	250	463
UK	335	898	1608	1747	888	226	391	616	599	314	1.1	20	48	505	944
Sweden	4	33	147	342	295	1	3	68	183	233	8.5	90	153	145	162
Spain	0.2	14	79	706	930				158	460	2.5	16	15	18	65
Japan			408	4471	6887			31	1451	3770	—		9	37	36
Industrial countries	4590[1]	10,730[1]	15,899	27,931	24,105	540[1]	1217[1]	3084	8960	11,010		671[1]	1841	7064	9860

Notes: 1. OECD — excludes Japan.

2. Belgium is regarded as assembling rather than producing cars in 1955.

Sources: OECD, *Industrial Statistics 1900–1962* (Paris, OECD, 1964) for 1948 and 1955 figures; GATT, *International Trade 1980/81 & 1982/83* (Geneva, GATT, 1982) for 1963, 1973 and 1981 figures.

TABLE 14.4 Industrial Countries' Production, Exports and Imports of Trucks and Buses 1948–82 thousand units.

	Production					Exports					Imports				
	1948	1955	1963	1973	1982	1948	1955	1963	1973	1982	1948	1955	1963	1973	1982
US	1376	1249	1464	3014	1913	211	180	123	152	129	1	1	18	190	707
Canada	97	79	99	347	448	21	6.5	7	230	395	4	9	6	144	102
EEC (6)															
France	98	172	214	351	372	19	30	74	107	140	1	1	13	119	130
Germany	30	204	254	299	301	–	68	115	175	203	–	2	4	26	37
Italy	15	39	75	135	156	5.7	7.5	13	49	91	–	1	14	26	70
Belgium	–	–	19	82	48	3	5	6	78	46	–	30	14	25	34
UK	173	340	404	417	269	79	141	159	163	91	2	2	3	37	73
Sweden	7.8	17.5	21	37	54	2	8	13	26	50	5	4	9	11	21
Spain	0.4	1.7	53	116	140	–	–	–	14	45	4	4	2	4	5
Japan	–	–	876	2612	3850	–	–	67	617	1821	–	–	3	1	1
Industrial countries Total	1799[1]	2109[1]	3524	7515	7683		451[1]	582	1626	3083		120[1]	192	732	1454

Note: 1. OECD excluding Japan.
Sources: See Table 14.3

But in the 1950s the European producers began to export small cars to the US. Their rapid expansion provoked the US firms to retaliate by introducing 'compact' cars of their own, first from their European subsidiaries and then from production in the US (Maxcy, 1981, p. 100). This reduced the sales of British and French cars, but Volkswagen managed to retain and improve its position. Then GM and Ford gradually increased the size of their compacts.

Then another wave of imports into the US started in 1969. The three US firms responded in the same way, imports from the subsidiaries were resumed and then, in 1968, the US producers announced plans to manufacture European type 'sub compacts'. But imports continued to rise, reaching 2.4 million in 1973 and 3 million in 1981, but fell to 2.2 million in 1983.

In the case of commercial vehicles, the US retained its position as the major exporter for most of the 1950s (see Table 14.4) although these were mainly to Canada. In the immediate post-war period the UK was the second largest exporter of commercial vehicles. Neither consumption nor trade, in terms of units, increased as fast as in cars. This is partly because if a greater load has to be carried, it is often more efficient to use a larger truck or goods vehicle rather than acquire another one and this does not show up in these statistics. UK exports continued to increase until in 1963 she became the largest exporter of commercial vehicles. But German exports were increasing very rapidly and soon overtook those of Britain; they continued to increase after 1973 whereas UK exports declined. These exports were generally sent to other European countries but some were also sent to developing countries where they were regarded as investment rather than consumption goods and therefore had to face lower tariff barriers. Indeed, most of the increase in real net exports of road motor vehicles by industrial countries as a whole to the rest of the world, noted in Chapter 6, must be in the form of commercial vehicles.

COSTS OF PRODUCITON

The description above suggests that most of the competition was in the form of the type of vehicles produced. But after the acute shortage of the early post-war period, the costs of production became increasingly important.

The distinctive feature of car production is that it represents the assembly of so many different components. Rhys estimates over 4000 separate items (Rhys, 1972, p. 260). In Europe about 60% of these are purchased by the vehicle manufacturer from outside sources. The economies of scale then depend on the economies associated with each of the different processes carried out by the manufacturer himself. The Central Policy Review Staff (CPRS) calculations of the minimum efficient size (m.e.s.) of car production, that is the one below which a car manufacturer was at a competitive disadvantage, for the main operations are shown in Table 14.5.

In the past, every time a model was changed some processes had to be retooled. But apparently with the recent introduction of more computer-controlled machinery and robots, it is now possible to introduce different models on to the same assembly line.

Assuming a m.e.s. is achieved, then variable costs represent a high proportion, 84% of the total in 1968, according to Rhys. But this was because of the high proportion of bought-in components. In terms of the UK industry in 1975, with four volume car producers, the CPRS calculated than an output of 1.8 million p.a. was required for them to break even, and variable costs would then represent 63% of the total (CPRS, 1975, p. 24). The EEC found that for the motor vehicle industry as a whole the capital stock per employee was slightly higher than the average for manufacturing in Germany in 1968 and the US in 1964 (UN ECE, 1977, p. 45).

However, capital is very mobile between the different locations, not only financial capital which determines new investment, but also the machines themselves can be moved around. This means that a very important determinant of competitiveness is labour costs. An important determinant of these in turn is labour productivity. As can be seen from Table 14.6, in 1955 by far the highest labour productivity in terms of vehicles produced per employee per year was that of the US. The figures are weighted to allow for different size distribution of cars, and two estimates are given. The UK had the second highest productivity, closely followed by Germany and France and then Italy. The productivity of all coun-

TABLE 14.5   Economies of Scale in Car Production

Manufacturing operation	Minimum efficient size (m.e.s.)
	(Identical units per plant p.a.)
Casting of engine block	100,000
Engine and transmission machining, and assembly	500,000
Final assembly	250,000

Source: Central Policy Review Staff, *The Future of the British Car Industry*, p. 16 (London, HMSO, 1975).

TABLE 14.6   *Productivity: Vehicles Produced Per Employee Year.*

	CPRS estimates[1]			D.T. Jones' estimates[2]			
	1955	1965	1973	1955	1965	1973	1978
US	11.1	13.9	14.9	19.3	23.2	31.6	20.9
UK	4.2	5.8	5.1	4.1	5.8	5.8	4.7
Germany	3.9	7.1	7.3	3.9	6.4	7.7	8.6
France	3.6	6.1	6.8	3.6	6.2	6.9	6.6
Italy	3.0	7.4	6.8	3.0	6.3	7.1	6.2
Japan	1.2	4.4	12.2	2.2	5.9	13.1	16.3

Sources: 1. Central Policy Review Staff, *The Future of the British Car Industry* (London, HMSO, 1975), p. 80.
       2. Daniel T. Jones, *Industrial Adjustment and Policy; Maturity and Crisis in the European Car Industry: Structural Change and Public Policy*, Sussex European Papers No. 8 (University of Sussex, Sussex European Research Centre, 1981).

tries increased up to 1965 but faster for Japan, Italy, Germany, and France than for the UK. The productivity of the US, Germany and France then continued to increase whereas according to the CPRS that of the UK and Italy fell. The productivity of Japan had meanwhile been increasing so fast that in 1973 it was well above that of the European countries and catching up with that of the US.

Allowing for differences in wage rates and capital costs, the net effect was that the cost and prices of mass-produced European cars in the 1950s were very much the same; because they were so similar, competition alone would have ensured some equivalence in prices (Maxcy and Silberston, 1959, Appendix C). It was more difficult to compare British with American prices because the cars were so different; in terms of price per pound of car they were very similar but in terms of price per unit of horse power the American cars were considerably cheaper.

By 1975, the number of labour hours required to produce both identical and comparable cars was between 67% and 166% higher in Britain than on the continent. The lower British wage rates were not sufficient to compensate for this in the cost of production (CPRS, 1975, pp. 80 and 81).

This situation persisted, with Ford stating in 1981 that forty manhours were required to produce a car in Halewood, UK, which was almost double the twenty-one hours required in Saarlouis, West Germany, and that the UK wage costs were not relatively low enough to compensate for this, with the result that identical Escort models cost $1000 more to produce in Halewood (quoted by Sinclair, 1983, p. 66).

It must be emphasised that these comparisons have been made of the costs of production between *countries*; the same factors apply to US subsidiaries and indigenous firms. The higher costs of production in Britain applied to all firms operating there. With prices kept down within each market by competition, the British car industry was relatively unprofitable. Indeed in 1970–3, Chrysler UK and Vauxhall were making losses even though car sales were booming. British Leyland and Ford (UK) were obtaining 5.6% and 5.9% as a return on shareholders funds, barely above that obtained on government stock. This discouraged investment in Britain (CPRS, 1975, p. 63).

Before considering the changes in trade, some reference should be made to the trade barriers discussed in Chapter 4. These were being reduced between European countries by the formation first of all the EEC and EFTA and then in 1973 by the free trade area in manufactures gradually established between them. The external tariffs of the EEC for cars and commercial vehicles were higher than those of the US (see Table 4.2). But the common external tariff on motor vehicles was reduced by the Tokyo round to 11% in 1972.

Thus, most European producers faced a tariff-free market much larger than their domestic one and until 1973 these markets were expanding very rapidly. Not only the indigenous producers but also the subsidiaries of US firms took advantage of this. Indeed multinationals are always in favour of customs unions and free-trade areas because they enable producers to supply customers within them from the cheapest member country. Both Ford and GM began to take an integrated view of their operations in Europe. They developed the concept of a world car whose components are completely standardised and can be produced and assembled anywhere.

GROWTH OF THE JAPANESE INDUSTRY

The first factor that radically changed the outlook for both the US and European producers was the emergence of the Japanese industry. Initially it was very small and devoted mainly to the production of commercial vehicles—in 1947 total output was only 11,320 units (Rhys, 1972, p. 188). It was also protected by very high tariff barriers. But by the 1960s production, particularly of cars, was increasing rapidly. By 1963, as can be seen from Tables 14.3 and 14.4, 408 thousand cars and 876 thousand commercial vehicles were produced—by 1975 car output had increased tenfold and commercial vehicle output threefold. By 1979, Japan was producing more commercial-vehicles than the US and by 1980 more passenger cars.

Before 1939, almost all the cars were produced by Toyota and Nissan, with two smaller producers, Daihatsu and Toyo Kogyo. These firms also dominated the production of commercial vehicles. With the rapid expansion of demand in the 1950s and 1960s the commercial-vehicle producers, Isuzu, Hino and Fuji and Mitsubishi, began car production as did the motor-cycle makers Suzuki and Honda. Many of the firms used foreign expertise, for instance, Isuzu built a Rootes and Hino a Renault model under licence and Nissan received help from Austin.

However, there were a series of mergers in the later 1960s with Toyota taking over Hino in 1966 and Daihatsu in 1967, and Nissan taking over Fuji in 1969. Toyota is now the third largest producer in the world and Nissan the fourth with Toyo Kogyo and Honda the ninth and tenth respectively (*Financial Times*, 20 October 1983).

After 1963 Japanese exports increased even more rapidly than production. Most of these exports were directed initially at the US market. They were of relatively small fuel-efficient cars. These aroused a considerable amount of resentment on the part of the US producers because the Japanese had such heavy protective barriers around their own market. These Japan was gradually persuaded to reduce, but it still appears difficult to obtain the necessary certificates of roadworthiness.

The next major shock to the system of trade was provided by the quadrupling of the oil price in 1973–4, and then the doubling from 1978 to 1980. This not only led to macroeconomic instability and deflation as described in Chapter 3, but it also raised the cost of running cars and commercial vehicles and increased the importance of fuel efficiency.

The Japanese, as small-car producers, gained from this and you might have expected the European producers also to do so, but as mentioned previously British Leyland was encountering great difficulties with its organisation and the slump finally tilted it towards bankruptcy.

Ford and GM continued to drag their feet with respect to the introduction of small cars in the US, arguing that they were not profitable. Only in 1978, when the US government laid down fuel-efficiency requirements, did these two companies take this situation seriously. But even by 1980, 90% of US output was of cars of 3000 cc or over whereas most Japanese and European output was of 2000 cc or less (Noelke and Taylor, 1981, p. 124). The result was that imports of small cars from Japan and Europe increased rapidly. In response to the rising costs of production in Germany as compared with the US, Volkswagen also began producing their Rabbit model in Pennyslvania in 1978 (now called Golf, as in Europe).

These US firms produced smaller cars in Europe but even so never produced minis, that is those under 1000 cc, again on the basis that it was too difficult to make a profit. They did, however, improve their operating efficiency by pursuing standardisation and Europeanisation. This led to a considerable amount of trade between European countries both in components and final products on which it is rather difficult to obtain satisfactory statistics.

A similar type of policy was pursued by the European multinationals, although British Leyland was forced to contract, whereas the French firms Renault and Peugeot-Citroen set out on an expansionary path, but soon lost their momentum and the Peugeot group began making heavy losses.

In 1983 Renault had the largest share of the Western European market with 12.6% of new registrations closely followed by Ford; Fiat had 12%, Volkswagen-Audi 11.9% and Peugeot-Citroen-Talbot 11.7%. The Japanese had 10.1% of the market (*Financial Times*, 5 March 1984).

Japanese production and exports continued to increase both to the US and Europe, and also to other countries. It was widely acknowledged that Japanese producers had a higher labour productivity and lower cost of production than of those of the US or Europe. By 1981, it was estimated that Japanese man hours per car on the assembly line had fallen to 14, whereas in the US it was 29, and with lower labour costs in Japan, $12.50 compared with $19 per hour in the US, this resulted in a cost differential of $1,600–$1,700. Even allowing for other costs and transportation across the Pacific this still left a cost advantage to the Japanese of $1,500–$2,000 per car (Abernathy quoted in Sinclair, 1983, p. 68).

Japan's higher labour productivity was partly due to a greater degree of automation, particularly investment in robots. This assisted in the very tight control of quality. Lower costs were also the result of a lower proportion of working capital. Japanese firms were estimated to carry $159 worth of stocks and work in progress for each car they produce in comparison with $755 for US firms (Sinclair, 1983, p. 69). This was achieved because of the stability and continuous running of the component, bodywork and assembly plants, such that the latter needed to hold very few stocks. This could not be achieved in the US or Europe where plants were more geographically dispersed, run less continuously and there was sometimes the threat of strike action.

Thus, although the US and European firms improved their operating efficiency by the greater standardisation of parts and the sourcing of production in the lowest-cost location, they were still not able to produce at as low a cost as the Japanese—they faced both higher wages and higher working-capital costs.

From this they argued for greater protection from the Japanese, and as can be seen from Chapter 4 most of the industrial countries with indigenous producers introduced quotas on Japanese imports.

In the past when large firms have been faced with actual or threatened barriers to their exports in a major market they have generally responded by directly investing in production in the market. This is, of course, the chief reason for the establishment of the subsidiaries of US firms in Europe.

But Japanese firms have generally been reluctant to invest in other industrial countries because they have not been able to transfer their cost advantages to them. As a result, the higher the local content rules, that is the lower the proportion that can be supplied from Japan, the less willing they are to carry out the investment.

In the EEC a car is regarded as a product of the EEC if it is assembled there, and can then be freely traded. The product of an EFTA member country can also be freely traded if it contains a 60% EEC content.

But trouble has already arisen over the British Leyland production of the Triumph Acclaim which has an approximately 30% Japanese content. The Italians claimed that the British content was only 60% and threatened to treat it as a Japanese car and as such to include it in their import quota of 2400 Japanese cars.

The arguments about content rules and quotas on Japanese goods continue. In the US the United Auto Workers are anxious to have very high domestic-content rules whereas the position of the US firms depends on their links with Japanese firms. GM, which in 1983 owned 34% of Isuzu and 5% of Suzuki, was more anxious to collaborate with them in the production of a new small car than to impose restrictions on Japanese imports. Under pressure from the US government, Nissan has recently established a plant for producing pick-up trucks in Tennessee, and Honda is producing cars in Ohio. Nissan has holdings in Europe but had to be forced by the Spanish government to take control of Motor Iberica in 1978.

Both Toyota and Nissan have assembly or production units in Australia which compete with the already established GM and Ford subsidiaries there.

But generally Japanese firms prefer to collaborate with other firms in industrial countries rather than to invest there. Indeed because of the expense and necessity of bringing out more fuel-efficient models there is an increasing amount of collaboration between major vehicle producers.

However, Japanese firms are as willing as European and US firms to invest in developing countries—this is partly to supply the highly protected home markets but also increasingly to supply components to the group. For the assembly or production of cars, Latin America is the most popular location followed by the more developed Asian countries. But in 1980, the seven Japanese car firms owned thirty-eight assembly plants in Asia (Sinclair, 1983, p. 70).

In 1977, more than a fifth of the output of the world's large motor-vehicle companies originated from overseas, 21.4% of the output of US firms and 23.3% of the output of UK firms (see Table 10.8). This figure excludes the value of goods imported from the parent company either for resale or in the form of parts and components for incorporation in the subsidiaries' products. The figure for the Japanese firms was lower at only 18.2% (Dunning and Pearce, 1981, Table 6.1a).

But the effect of the establishment of plants has been—as described in Chapter 10—to lead to a fall in exports of final goods and an increase in exports of parts and components. By 1982 exports of parts accounted for a third of the value of all industrial countries' exports of automotive products. It was highest for the US at 68%, then came the UK with 57%, Italy with 47% and France 40%. For Japan it was comparatively low at 16% (GATT, *International Trade 1982/3*, p. 88).

PRESENT POSITION

Thus, international trade in motor vehicles is the result of competition between a number of very large companies which can themselves determine the location of production. Their competitive success appears to depend largely on their choice of vehicles, thus the advantage European, and then Japanese, companies had over the US firms was in their earlier development and production of small cars.

It also depends on their costs of production. The US firms were in a position to fully exploit economies of scale in passenger-car production from the beginning of the period. The main European firms grew large enough to do so but apart from Volkswagen they tended to produce too many models tc take full advantage of such economies. Otherwise, the chief determinant of costs of production appears to be the country in which production is located, which determines labour productivity and wage levels.

The Japanese appear to have absolutely lower costs of production for all these reasons. But they are being faced by increasing barriers to their trade.

How does this leave world trade? As might be expected from the previous discussion, trade in parts has been increasing faster than trade in finished vehicles. However, trade in passenger cars is still the most important. In 1982 out of total exports by industrial countries of $126 billion, $59 billion were of passenger cars, $24.5 billion were commercial vehicles, and $43 billion were parts, that is 47%, 19%, and 34% respectively. Of total world exports of road motor vehicles, 93% by value were accounted for by industrial countries, who, in turn, accounted for 70% of world imports (GATT, *International Trade* 1982/83). Thus trade, particularly in passenger cars, is largely between industrial countries, which is why most of this chapter has been devoted to this. However, as was seen from Chapter 8, the industrial countries as a whole have been increasing their net exports of road motor vehicles to the rest of the world.

Let us now consider the present network of trade in terms of units. The figures in Tables 14.7 and 14.8 of passenger cars, and commercial vehicles, are those provided by the SMMT and differ slightly from the GATT ones[1] but the general picture is the same. Japan is by far the largest exporter of passenger cars and commercial vehicles. Half her passenger cars go to North America, a quarter to the EEC and EFTA. The rest go mainly to developing countries, of which OPEC is the most important, accounting for 9%. Her exports of commercial vehicles are distributed somewhat differently, with only a quarter going to the US, 12% to the EEC and EFTA and 49% going to developing countries. She is by far the largest exporter to Asia mainly because of her exports of 129 thousand commercial vehicles to Indonesia and 219 thousand to Saudi Arabia. Indeed, 29% of her total exports are to OPEC countries.

Turning to other industrial countries, it can be seen that almost all US and Canadian exports of passenger cars are to each other. Most of the exports of European countries are to each other but West Germany exports 271 thousand and Sweden 104 thousand cars to North America. The distribution of commercial vehicles is again wider. Almost all Canadian exports go to the US but only 54% of US exports go to Canada, the remainder going mainly to developing countries particularly OPEC ones, which account for

TABLE 14.7 Cars[2]: Chief Trade Flows of Major Exporters in 1982.
(1000 units)

Origin	North America	EEC	EFTA	Latin America	Destination Developing: Asia	Developing: Africa	OPEC[1]	South Africa	Oceania	Japan	Total
US	334	5	2	14	20	0.6	23	0.1	—	3	379
Canada	684	—	1	0.5	18	—	17	—	—	1	704
UK	14	124	13	5	72	12	53	55	13	1	313
France	74	742	105	45	46	130	97	10	8	1	1194
Italy	6	321	56	8	16	12	7	7	3	1	437
W. Germany	271	1688	373	8	55	15	25	8	9	25	2517
Sweden	104	46	17	—	9.0	2	4	—	6	1	186
Japan	1845	642	247	139	565	76	353	3	223	—	3770
GRAND TOTAL											9499

Notes: 1. Already included in the figures for developing countries.
2. Complete and chassis.
Source: Society of Motor Manufacturers and Traders, *The Motor Industry of Great Britain, 1983*, Table 73.

TABLE 14.8 *Commercial Vehicles: Trade Flows of Major Exporters in 1982.*
(1000 units)

					Destination						
Origin	North America	EEC	EFTA	Latin America	Developing: Asia	Developing: Africa	OPEC[1]	South Africa	Oceania	Japan	Total
US	68.8	3.8	1.0	12.6	33.9	4.1	37.6	0.4	1.3	0.1	127.1
Canada	387.6	0.8	3.1	0.6	8.2	0.3	—	—	0.1	—	400.9
UK	—	15.6	15.3	1.2	25.9	10.0	25.0	10.7	2.6	—	90.9
France	3.1	62.5	9.8	3.8	6.5	66.3	38.5	—	1.0	—	156.1
Italy	2.7	61.6	4.8	0.2	3.4	5.0	5.1	0.2	—	—	90.7
W. Germany	4.8	82.3	27.8	1.4	51.3	15.1	49.3	12.2	1.8	—	207.5
Sweden	0.5	13.5	8.6	0.3	9.8	2.2	8.8	0.3	1.0	—	38.5
Japan	452.3	135.7	76.2	103.7	666.2	120.1	530.4	81.9	172.9	—	1820.4
									GRAND TOTAL		2932.1

Note: 1. Already included in the figures for developing countries.
Source: Society of Motor Manufacturers and Traders, *The Motor Industry of Great Britain, 1983.*

30%. Although a high proportion of European exports go to other European countries, a higher proportion is sent to developing countries, over half of which goes to OPEC countries.

Thus a considerable proportion of trade represents the swapping of products by industrial countries particularly trade within North America and within Europe. Intra-North America trade accounted for 17% of the total value of trade in road motor vehicles in 1982, and intra Western European trade accounted for $34\frac{1}{2}$%, with intra-EEC trade alone 22%. This intra-area trade has been reinforced by the trade barriers placed on imports from countries outside, particularly Japan. It has undoubtedly led to trade diversion within the EEC, for instance, the UK would have undoubtedly imported more Japanese cars and fewer European if Japan had not been restricted to 11% of the market.

This intra-European trade is partly a response to consumers' demand for differentiated products. But intra-area trade also represents the global strategy of multinationals who endeavour to achieve economies of scale by confining the location of particular processes and particular models to as few sites as possible, trading the products according to demand in the different markets. Inevitably much of the 'sourcing' is dependent on the costs of production, and countries whose relative costs have risen, such as the UK, have lost production and exports in the process. In the two years 1980 and 1981 Italy and Belgium were net importers of road motor vehicles and parts, the UK had a small deficit in 1979 which moved into a surplus in 1980 and 1981 and then reverted to a deficit in 1982, whereas Germany had a growing and France a declining surplus.

The world's major exporter of both passenger cars and commercial vehicles is Japan and her costs of production are so far below those of other industrial countries that she could easily retain her position and expand were it not for the increase in the trade barriers imposed on her products by other industrial countries. These led to a decline in her exports in terms of units although not in terms of value in the early 1980s. The response of the Japanese to these restrictions in the US has been to trade up into somewhat larger cars crammed with electronics thus becoming even more competitive with the US producers.

Although it provides some incentive for Japanese firms to set up production in the US they lose most of their cost advantages by doing so. Furthermore if they cease to export cars to the US market this frees production facilities in Japan, which are likely to be used to provide cars and commercial vehicles for third markets or to produce other goods for export.

NOTES

1. The SMMT include chassis with the finished product.

15 Conclusion

This book has related the main changes in international trade that have occurred over the post-war period. The beginning of the period saw the establishment of a superstructure of international institutions devoted to stablising and liberalising the international monetary system, reducing trade barriers and encouraging multi-lateralism in trade and economic growth. In this they were largely successful in the 1950s and 1960s. Trade did increase very fast, faster even than incomes which themselves were increasing at unprecedented rates.

Now at the end of the period the whole system appears to have gone into reverse. Exchange rates have become flexible although countries have agreed to refrain from competitive changes in them. Industrial countries are increasingly imposing import quotas, or voluntary export restraints (VERS) as they are euphemistically called, on individual products of individual countries and sometimes these are reduced over time. Large countries and regional organisations are increasingly relying on their size to extract concessions from other countries or prevent discrimination against them. Indeed in the US Houses of Congress there is even a demand for reciprocity in trade, which would undermine completely the remaining multilateralism in world trade.

What caused this turnround? One of the underlying problems even in the period of expansion was that the developing countries felt they were deriving too little of the benefits from trade. As a group they are net exporters of primary products and net importers of manufactures even though their exports of manufactures increased rapidly over the period. They objected to the industrial countries' continued protection of agriculture, and increasing restrictions on imports of textiles and clothing and other simple manufactures from developing countries.

However, developing countries were not only concerned with access to the markets of industrial countries. Following the work of Prebisch (1959), they increasingly focused on the terms of trade, in particular the terms of trade between primary products and manufactures.

The author has argued that for many primary products this is not an appropriate target because developing countries account for too small a proportion of trade. In 1955 industrial countries accounted for the same value and proportion of export trade in food, raw materials and ores and minerals as developing countries. But exports from industrial countries then increased more rapidly so that by 1982 developing countries accounted for less than a third of world trade in these categories.

Taking agricultural products alone, the US is now the largest individual exporter with exports of $38 billion in 1982, 18% of world trade. This must be compared with the total exports of developing market economies of $58 billion, 28% of the total. The largest single exporter among them is Brazil with $8 billion (see Table 11.4). Furthermore, the overall postition of the developing market economies fluctuates; generally they are net exporters but in 1982 they were net importers due to the deficit position of the Near East and to a lesser extent Africa. Over a third of US exports of food go to developing countries.

Only in fuels was the pattern of specialisation clear. Almost all trade was in oil; the industrial countries were all net importers of it, and a few developing countries were net exporters of it. Most of the reserves had been discovered and developed by individuals and companies from industrial countries.

Production in the Middle East and then Africa was increased rapidly and after the mid-1950s the real price fell. Western Europe and Japan, which had in 1950 relied on coal for 85% of their fuel requirements, transferred to oil closing down high-cost coal mines in the process. The US also increased her net imports. Thus the conflict of interests between developing exporting countries and importing industrial countries appeared very clear. The former benefited from a higher price of crude oil in relation to manufactures and also a higher proportion of the price retained in the form of royalties and tax. This was the basis for the OPEC price increases of the 1970s and the spate of nationalisations.

As related, this caused great macroeconomic problems of adjustment for the rest of the world caused both by the acceleration of inflation due to the higher price of fuels, and the reduction in world aggregate demand because not all of the increased revenues were spent.

Industrial countries and developing countries responded differently to this situation.

The US and UK governments initially tried to maintain their level of domestic aggregate demand but then felt it necessary, as did the governments of other industrial countries, to reduce it in order to correct their balance-of-payments deficit and to control inflation. Unemployment in the industrial countries began rising and the rapid growth of the post-war era came to an end. The combination of high unemployment and high and variable rates of inflation in most countries, which governments appeared unable to control, led them to abandon Keynesian stabilisation policies and increasingly to favour monetary policies. These were directed at controlling inflation. It was argued that if the government reduced its expenditure and thus the growth of the money supply the private sector would have a greater incentive to expand. This in turn was assumed to lead to greater employment.

Yet the high levels of unemployment persisted. Governments became more responsive to the demands of their import-competing industries for protection in order to maintain employment. Thus quotas were placed on imports of textiles, clothing, footwear and other simpler manufactures from developing countries, and on cars and some consumer and office products from Japan.

It has been argued in this book that such protective measures raise the price of the product to consumers and producers in the country concerned and thus attract inflows of capital and labour into its production. Employment in the industry is likely to be higher than it would be otherwise, unless the capital investment is so labour-saving that it offsets this. But with a given level of aggregate demand the flow of capital and labour into this industry is obtained by a deflection from other sectors of the economy where they would have earned a higher return in terms of world prices. In other words, protection lowers the efficiency of the economy as a whole and thus potential real income.

Furthermore if the country retains the same overall balance of payments position the protection will not increase overall employment. Any reduction in imports will just lead to an appreciation in the exchange rate which will reduce exports. A slight qualification has to be made if the import substitutes are more labour-intensive than the exports.

In the UK consumers have fared particularly badly. In 1973 she joined the EEC which entailed abondoning her cheap food policy for the expensive CAP one. From 1973–9 the price index for food and beverages rose by 16% p.a., faster than the consumer price index which of course included the rise in price of fuels. The EEC became increasingly protectionist both with respect to textiles and clothing and a whole range of products from Japan. Indeed it has been argued in Chapter 4 that the institutional structure of the EEC gives far more weight to producer than consumer interests.

In joining the EEC Britain also adopted the VAT which proved the pretext for governments to gradually shift the tax burden from direct income tax to indirect tax and taxes on employment. The net result was that between 1973 and 1979 the consumer price index rose by 15.6% p.a. which was faster than that of any major industrial country except Italy.

Employment scarcely increased over the period and real GDP only increased by 1.4% p.a. in spite of the development of North Sea oil. Because of this, Britain moved from a balance-of-payments deficit in oil of £941 million in 1973 to a deficit of £731 million in 1979 and then a surplus which rose to £4605 million in 1982. Indeed this movement from a deficit to surplus in oil is being blamed for the declining surplus in manufactures. But it is not enough to explain the rise in unemployment and the difficulty of reducing it.

The Conservative government elected in 1979 applied a monetarist policy to the inflation limiting the growth of the money supply and stated that employment depended on keeping wage costs down. It nonetheless increased the national insurance taxes on employment. Nor did it ever consider the contribution of protectionist policies to rises in the cost of living and increased wage demands. Employment has barely increased and unemployment is now (January 1984) at 12.5% which is very high by historical standards and in relation to other industrial countries.

The non-oil developing countries pursued different policies. They were also very dependent on imports of oil. But with widespread poverty they did not regard a reduction in aggregate demand as an acceptable policy. Instead they continued their policies of expansion in spite of trade deficits by borrowing on the international market. Funds were freely available as great efforts had been made to recycle the OPEC surpluses through the private capital market. Most of the non-oil developing countries moved into large deficits on their current account. The exceptions were apparently China and some of the 'newly industrialising countries' such as Taiwan and Hong Kong, whose exports continued to increase in spite of the increasing obstacles being placed in the way of their trade by the industrial countries. After 1980 the deficits of the developing countries became more serious. Their export earnings declined with the decline in world trade and the real burden of their debt denominated in dollars rose as the dollar appreciated; so did the cost of financing it as the industrial countries raised their interest rates. Many of the countries ran into severe difficulties and had to negotiate some rescheduling of their debt. This was generally accomplished by cutbacks in their investment plans and reductions in imports.

This in turn affected the industrial countries, particularly their investment goods industries which export to developing countries. The problems of commercial-vehicle producers have already been mentioned in Chapter 14. Overall industrial countries' exports of engineering products and chemicals to non-oil developing countries declined so that in 1982 they were lower than in 1980. They have also declined to oil-exporting developing countries whose revenues from oil have been declining since 1980.

Thus, much as the industrial countries would like to forget about their dependence on developing countries it nevertheless exists, and it is not just confined to trade in fuels. Industrial countries may conduct their macroeconomic and commercial policies as if the only problems were those of adjustment between themselves, but in the long run they must also adjust to developing countries. In 1982 15% of their exports went to non-oil developing countries and 10% to oil exporters, and each group accounted for 14% of their imports. These proportions may appear small but in view of their very different factor endowments and relative costs, potential or actual benefits from trade are very great. Furthermore, since 1973 the incomes of developing countries have often increased faster than those of industrial countries.

In relation to world trade the US still appears in a dominant and assymetric position. Her monetary, fiscal and commercial policies not only affect her own position but the relative position of all other countries in world trade. Recently she has been running a fiscal deficit, which she has financed by borrowing fom the rest of the world. This has required high interest rates which she has imposed on the international monetary system even though it has aggravated the serious balance-of-payments position of developing countries. The inflow of funds has also led to an appreciation of the dollar and thus reduced the profits of her exporters and those producing import substitutes. This in turn has led to a demand for greater protection.

In addition, the government has been trying to prevent the transfer of technology to the Eastern Trading Area by restricting exports of products which incorporate it not only from the US but also from firms abroad which use US technology.

Interference of either kind could have considerable effects on the world economy. The US is at the moment a major exporter of high-technology and agricultural products and a major net importer of fuels and medium-technology mass-produced products such as motor vehicles and household appliances, and also clothing, textiles, and other consumer goods.

US limits on movements of high-technology products must be expected to reduce her exports in future. For instance any further restrictions on exports to the USSR by firms in the EEC—beyond those already imposed by the EEC countries themselves—will provide the EEC with an even greater incentive to develop its own technology, at considerable real cost.

The arguments against the increase in protection of import-competing industries remain as before. It may increase the returns and even employment in these industries but only at the cost of reducing them in the export industries if the balance of trade remains the same. If it is used as a means of increasing the surplus (or reducing the deficit) on trade or current account the increase in aggregate demand and employment this represents is at the cost of increasing unemployment in the countries which supplied the exports. In short, discrimination in trade is not an appropriate method of achieving macroeconomic objectives.

TABLE A1   The Growth in Output, Population, and Output per head of Population. percentage per annum

	Growth in real output						Growth in population			Growth in output per head of population	
	1955–68	1968–73	1973–9	1980	1981	1982	1955–68	1968–73	1973–9	1968–73	1973–9
	(1)	(2)	(2)	(6)	(6)		(1)	(2)	(2)	(2)	(2)
Total OECD	4.7	4.7	2.7	1.2	2.0	−0.5	1.0	1.1	0.8	3.7	1.9
OECD Europe	4.8	5.0	2.5	1.3	−0.1	0.6	0.8	0.9	0.6	4.1	1.9
EEC	5.3	4.9	2.5	1.0	−0.3	0.5	0.8	0.7	0.3	4.2	2.2
US	4.0	3.3	2.6	−0.2	3.0	−2.4	1.3	1.1	1.0	2.2	1.6
Japan	10.2	8.8	3.6	4.9	4.0	3.2	1.0	1.3	1.1	7.3	2.5
Germany	5.1	4.9	2.4	1.8	−0.1	−1.0	0.6	0.8	−0.2	4.1	2.6
France	5.7	5.9	3.1	1.1	0.3	1.6	0.7	0.9	0.4	5.0	2.7
UK	2.8	3.2	1.4	−2.6	−1.3	2.3	0.6	0.3	—	2.9	1.4
Italy	5.5	4.6	2.6	3.9	0.1	−0.3	0.9	0.7	0.6	3.9	2.0
Canada	4.5	5.6	3.3	1.0	4.0	−4.2	2.1	1.3	1.3	4.3	2.1
	1950–2 to 1964–6	1963–73	1973–6				1950–2 to 1964–6	1970–8			
	(3)	(4)					(3)	(5)			
Argentina	3.3		2.3[5]				1.3	1.3			
Brazil	5.2	8.2[4]	8.2[4]				3.1	2.8			
Mexico	6.1	7.1	4.0[4]				3.3	3.3			
Pakistan	3.8		6.4[5]				2.4	3.1			
Philippines	5.6		6.3[5]				3.2	2.7			
Taiwan	8.3	10.4	5.0[4]				3.5	2.0			
Korea		10.3	10.8[4]					1.9			
Hong Kong		9.0	7.1[4]					1.9			

Sources: 1. OECD, The Growth of Output 1960–1980 (Paris, OECD, 1980), Tables 3 and 4.
2. OECD, Historical Statistics 1960–1981 (Paris, OECD, 1983).
3. I. Little, J. Scitovsky and M. Scott, Industry and Trade in Some Developing Countries, (Development Centre of the OECD, Paris, 1970), Table 2.11 and Table A2.10.
4. OECD, The Impact of the Newly Industrialising Countries (Paris, OECD, 1979), Table 23.
5. World Bank, World Development Report, 1980 (New York, IBRD, 1980), Tables 2 and 17.
6. OECD, Economic Outlook, December 1983.

TABLE A2 *World Export Price Indexes of Primary Commodities 1975 = 100.*

	Primary commodities	Primary commodities and petroleum	Agricultural non-food			Minerals and fuels	Minerals and fuels excluding crude petroleum	Fuels			Non-ferrous metals		
			Food	Total	Oilseeds, oils, and fats		Total	Coal	Crude petroleum	Natural gas	Total	Copper	Aluminium
1950	32		43	65	56	15	15	19	15		41	41	37
51	40		47	90	70	16	15	20	15		55	50	41
52	34		47	65	57	17	15	22	15		56	59	48
53	32		47	59	55	17	16	23	16		50	58	49
54	33		50	59	56	17	16	22	16		49	56	50
55	31		45	60	51	17	16	22	16		59	74	54
56	-31-		-45-	-59-	-55-	-18-	-17-	-26-	-16-		-61-	-74-	-61-
57	32		45	59	53	18	17	26	17		49	50	65
58	30		44	52	50	18	17	22	17		44	45	62
59	29		41	55	50	17	16	21	16		49	53	62
1960	29		40	56	47	17	16	21	16		51	55	64
61	-28-		-39-	-54-	-49-	-17-	-15-	-21-	-15-		-49-	-52-	-63-
62	28		40	51	45	16	15	21	15		48	53	59
63	29		43	53	48	17	16	23	15		48	53	56
64	30		45	54	49	17	16	23	15		57	63	59
65	30		44	55	54	17	16	24	15		64	77	61
66	30		45	55	53	17	16	24	15		74	101	60
67	-29-		-44-	-51-	-49-	-17-	-16-	-24-	-15-		-68-	-88-	-62-
68	29		43	51	47	17	16	23	15		71	95	63
69	30		45	53	48	17	16	24	15		83	116	67

Table A2 (continued)

Year	Primary commodities	Primary commodities and petroleum	Food	Agricultural non-food		Minerals and fuels	Minerals and fuels excluding crude petroleum	Fuels				Non-ferrous metals		
				Total	Oilseeds, oils, and fats			Total	Coal	Crude petroleum	Natural gas	Total	Copper	Aluminium
1970	31	47	47	54	56	19		17	32	15	34	86	114	71
71	34	49	49	56	57	22		21	36	19	37	74	88	72
72	38	55	57	62	55	24		23	38	22	34	74	87	67
73	57	84	87	101	97	33		31	48	30	51	106	145	68
74	103	107	111	120	145	96		99	85	100	57	131	167	87
75	100	100	100	100	100	100	100	100	100	100	100	100	100	100
76	106	106	105	112	98	105	99	106	95	106	118	109	114	104
77	117	118	120	124	120	114	101	116	100	117	128	117	106	131
78	119	121	121	132	127	115	100	117	106	117	125	126	111	149
79	154	138	136	159	145	161	108	165	112	170	131	167	161	173
1980	226	157	159	167	130	271	134	281	127	295	183	186	177	205
81	235	146	141	154	125	299	149	310	125	325	251	163	141	189
82	222	132	125	136	103	287	151	298	116	311	272	142	120	169
83*	200	132	122	149	133	248	136	257	104	268	251	147	134	170

Sources: UN Monthly Bulletin of Statistics, December 1983; UN Statistical Papers (1979), Methods Used in Compiling the United Nations Price Indexes for Basic Commodities in International Trade Series M No. 29 Rev. 2. (New York). Copyright, United Nations (1985). Reproduced by permission.
*Provisional.

Select Bibliography

Adelman, M. A. (1972), *The World Petroleum Market* (London; Johns Hopkins).

Alexander, Sidney S. (1952) *The Effects of a Devaluation on a Trade Balance* (IMF Staff Papers Vol. II).

Aylen, J. (1982) 'Plant size and efficiency in the steel industry: an international comparison', *NIER*, No. 100.

Baer, W. (1961–2), 'The economics of Prebisch and the ECLA', *Economic Development and Cultural Change*, Vol. 10.

Balassa, B. (1974), 'Trade Creation and Trade Diversion in the European Common Market', *Manchester School*, Vol. 42, June.

Balassa, B. and Associates (1971), *The Structure of Protection in Developing Countries* (Baltimore and London; Johns Hopkins for the IBRD and Inter-American Development Bank).

Baldwin, R. E. (1970), *Non-tariff Distortions of International Trade* (Washington D.C., The Brookings Institution; London, Allen and Unwin).

Barker, T. S. and Han, S. S. (1971), 'Effective Rates of Protection for United Kingdom Production', *Economic Journal*, Vol. 81.

Basevi, G. (1966), 'The United States Tariff Structures Estimates of Effective Rates of Protection of United States Industries and Industrial Labour', *Review of Economics and Statistics*, Vol. 48.

Briscoe, Lynden (1971), *The Textile and Clothing Industries of the United Kingdom* (Manchester; Manchester University Press).

Bureau of Agricultural Economics, (BAE) (1981), *Japanese Agricultural Policies*, Policy Monograph No. 1. Australia.

Cable, Vincent (1979), *World Textile Trade and Production* (London; Economist Intelligence Unit, Special Report No. 63).

Caves, R. E. (1960), *Trade and Economic Structure* (Cambridge, Massachusetts; Harvard University Press).

Caves, R. E. (1965), ' "Vent for surplus" models of trade and growth' in Baldwin, R. E. *et al.* (eds,), *Trade, Growth and The Balance of Payments, Essays in Honor of Gottfried Haberler* (Chicago and Amsterdam; Rand McNally and North Holland).

Central Policy Review Staff (CPRS) (1975), *The Future of The British Car Industry* (London, HMSO).

Commission of the European Communities (1980), *The Agricultural Situation in the Community 1980 Report* (Brussels).

Commission of the European Communities (1982), *The Agricultural Situation in the Community 1982 Report* (Brussels).

Commission of the European Communities, *9th Financial Report on the European Agricultural Guidance and Guarantee Fund* (Brussels).

Conan, A. R. (1966), *The Problem of Sterling* (London; Macmillan).

Consumers' Association (1979), *The Price of Protection* (London; Consumers' Association, August).

Cooper, C. A. & Massell, B. F. (1965), 'A New Look at Customs Union Theory', *Economic Journal*, Vol. 75.

Corden, W. M. (1971), *The Theory of Protection* (Oxford; OUP).

Deane, Phyllis and Cole, W. A. (1967), *British Economic Growth 1688–1959* (Cambridge; CUP).

Dow, J. C. R. (1961), *The Management of the British Economy 1945–60* (London; NIESR, CUP).

Duncan, W. C. (1973), *US–Japan Automobile Diplomacy: a study in economic confrontation* (Cambridge, Mass: Ballinger).

Dunning, John, H. (1964), 'Capital Movements in the Twentieth Century' in John H. Dunning (ed.) *International Investment* (Penguin, 1972).

Dunning, John H. (ed.) (1972), *International Investment* (Harmondsworth, England, Baltimore, USA; Penguin).

Dunning, John H. (ed.) (1974), *Economic Analysis and the Multinational Enterprise* (London; Allen and Unwin).

Dunning, John H. and Pearce, Robert D. (1981), *The World's Largest Industrial Enterprises* (Farnborough, Hants., England; Gowen).

EEC (1962), *Treaty Establishing The European Economic Community, Rome 25th March, 1957* (London; HMSO).

EEC Statistical Office (1971), *Yearbook of Agricultural Statistics*.

EFTA Secretariat (1969), *The Effects of EFTA* (Geneva; EFTA).

Ellsworth, P. T. (1961), 'The terms of trade between primary-producing and industrial countries', Inter-American economic Affairs, Vol 10, No. 1, 1961 reprinted in Livingstone, I. (ed.), *Economic Policy for Development* (Penguin, 1971).

European Parliament, *Normanton Report*, European Parliament Working Documents 438/77. Committee on Economics and Monetary Affairs, Rapporteur, Normanton M. T., *Report on the crisis in the textile industry* adopted 16 December 1977.

Federation of British Carpet Manufacturers (1967), *Annual Report for the Year to 31st December 1966* (London).

Findlay, R. and Grubert, H. (1959), 'Factor intensities, technological progress and the terms of trade', *Oxford Economic Papers*, Vol. 2.

Ford: Dennis Hackett (1978), *The Big Idea: The Story of Ford in Europe* (Nottingham, England; Ford Motor Co.).

Freeman, Christopher (1974), *The Economics of Industrial Innovation* (Penguin).

GATT (1958), *Trends in International Trade* (Geneva; GATT).

GATT (1963), *Long-Term Arrangement Regarding International Trade in Cotton Textiles*, Entered into force 1 October 1962 (Geneva; GATT).

GATT (1966), *A Study in Cotton Textiles* (Geneva; GATT).

GATT (1974), *Arrangement Regarding International Trade in Textiles*, Entered into force 1 January 1976 (Geneva; GATT).

GATT (1978), *Networks of World Trade by Areas and Commodity Classes 1955–76* (Geneva; GATT).

GATT (1979), *The Tokyo Round of Multilateral Trade Negotiations* (Geneva; GATT).

Gruber, William H., Mehta, D., and Vernon, R. (1967), 'The R and D Factor in International Trade and International Investment of United States Industries', *Journal of Political Economy*, Vol. 75, No. 1.

Helleiner, G. K. (1973), 'Manufactured Exports from Less Developed Countries and Multinational Firms', *Economic Journal*, Vol. 83, pp. 21–47.

Helleiner, G. K. and Lavergne, R. (1979), 'Intra-Firm Trade and Industrial Exports to the United States', *Oxford Bulletin of Economics and Statistics*, Vol. 41 (November).

Hilgerdt, Folke, League of Nations (1945), *Industrialization and Foreign Trade* (League of Nations).

Hirsch, Seev (1965) 'United States Electronic Industry in International Trade', *National Institute Economic Review*, No. 34, November.

Hirsch, Seev (1967), *Location of Industry and International Competitiveness* (Oxford, Clarendon Press).

Hufbauer, G. C. (1966), *Synthetic Materials and the Theory of International Trade* (London, Duckworth).

Hufbauer, G. C. and Adler, F. M. (1968),*Overseas Manufacturing Investment and the Balance of Payments*, Tax Policy Research Study No. I. (Washington D.C., US Treasury Department).

IEA (1982) *Natural Gas* (Paris, OECD).

Johnson, D. G. (1973), *World Agriculture in Disarray* (London, Fontana for the Trade Policy Research Centre).

Johnson, H. (1957), 'Factor Endowments, International Trade and

Factor Prices', *Manchester School of Economic and Social Studies XXV*, 270–83.

Johnson, H. G. (1959), 'Economic Development and International Trade', *Nationaløkonomisk Tidsskrift* 97 Bund 5-6 Heft.

Johnson, H. G. (1961), *International Trade and Economic Growth Studies in Pure Theory* (Cambridge, Mass.: Harvard University Press).

Johnson, H. G. (1965), 'Optimal Trade Intervention in the Presence of Domestic Distortions', in R. E. Caves, P. B. Kenen and H. G. Johnson (eds.), *Trade, Growth and the Balance of Payments* (Amsterdam, North Holland).

Jones, Daniel T. (1981), *Maturity and Crisis in the European Car Industry: Structural Change and Public Policy* (University of Sussex, Sussex European Research Centre).

Keesing, Donald B. and Wolf, M. (1980), *Textile Quotas against Developing Countries* (London, Trade Policy Research Centre).

Kindleberger, C. P. (1956), *The Terms of Trade: A European Case Study* (New York and London, MIT and John Wiley; and London, Chapman and Hall).

Kindleberger, C. P. and Lindert, P. H. (1978), *International Economics* (Illinois, Irwin-Dorsey).

Kravis, I. B. (1956), 'Availability and other influences on the commodity composition of trade', *Journal of Political Economy*, Vol. 64.

Krueger, A. I. (1978), 'Impact of LDC Exports on Employment in American Industry', International Economics Seminar Group Annual Conference, University of Sussex.

Lall, S. (1978) 'The Pattern of Intra-Firm Exports by US Multinationals', *Oxford Bulletin of Economics and Statistics*, Vol. 40.

Leontief, W. W. (1954), 'Domestic Production and Foreign Trade: the American Capital Position Re-examined', *Economic Internazionale VII*, 3–32.

Leontief, W. W. (1956), 'Factor Proportions and the Structure of American Trade: Further Theoretical and Empirical Analysis', *Review of Economics and Statistics* 37, 386–407.

Lewis, W. A. (1952), 'World Production, Prices and Trade 1870–1960', *Manchester School of Economics and Social Studies*, Vol. 21, pp. 139–91.

Linder, S. B. (1961), *An Essay on Trade and Transformation* (New York, Wiley).

Lipsey, R. G. (1957), 'The Theory of Customs Unions: Trade Diversion and Welfare', *Economica*, Vol. 24.

Maddison, A. (1965), *Economic Growth in the West* (New York, 20th Century Fund).

Major, R. L. and Hays, S. (1970), 'Another Look at the Common Market', *NIER*, No. 54, November.

Maxcy, G. (1981), *The Multinational Motor Industry* (London, Croom Helm).

Maxcy, G. and Silberston, A. (1959), *The Motor Industry* (London, Allen and Unwin).

Meadows, D. H. and Dennis, L., Randers, J., Behrens, W. W. III (1974), *The Limits to Growth* (London and Sydney, Pan).

Meyer, F. V. (1978), *International Trade Policy* (London, Croom Helm).

Minhas, B. S. (1962), 'The homohypallagic production function, factor-intensity reversal and the Heckscher-Ohlin Theorem', *Journal of Political Economy*, 70, 138–56.

Minhas, B. S. (1963), *An International Comparison of Factor Costs and Factor Use* (Amsterdam, North Holland).

Myint, H, (1958), 'The "Classical Theory" of International Trade and the Underdeveloped Countries', *Economic Journal* 68, 317–37.

McCrone, G.' (1962), *The Economics of Subsidising Agriculture: a study of British policy*, University of Glasgow Social and Economic Studies, New Series 1 (London, Allen and Unwin).

MacDougall, G. D. A. (1951), 'British and American Exports: A Study Suggested by the Theory of Comparative Costs', *Economic Journal*, 61, No. 244.

MacDougall, G. D. A. (1958), 'The benefits and costs of private investment from abroad: a theoretical approach', *Economic Record* 36, 13–35.

Noelke, M. and Taylor, R. (1981), *EEC Protectionism: present practice and future trends* (Brussels, European Research Associates).

Odell, P. R. (1981), *Oil and World Power*, 6th edition (Penguin).

OECD (1956), *Agricultural Policies in Europe and North America* (Paris, OECD).

OECD (1965), *Modern Cotton Industry: A Capital Intensive Industry* (Paris, OECD).

OECD (1967A), *Agricultural Policies in 1966* (Paris, OECD)

OECD (1967B), *The Overall Level and Structure of R & D Efforts in OECD Member Countries* (Paris, OECD).

OECD (1968), *Statistical Tables and Notes: A Study of Resources Devoted to R & D in OECD Member Countries in 1963/64* (Paris, OECD).

OECD (1970), *Gaps in Technology Analytical Report* particularly pp. 123, 185 and 206 (Paris, OECD).

OECD (1971), *The Conditions for Success in Technological Innovation* (Paris, OECD).

OECD (1972), *Policy Perspectives for International Trade and Economic Relations* (Paris, OECD).

OECD (1974A), *Agricultural Policy in the US* (Paris, OECD).

OECD (1974B), *Agricultural Policy in Japan* (Paris, OECD).

OECD (1979A), *The Impact of the Newly Industrialising Countries* (Paris, OECD).

OECD (1979B), *Trends in Industrial R & D in Selected OECD Member Countries* (Paris, OECD).

OECD (1980), *Technical Change and Economic Policy* (Paris, OECD).

OECD (1981), *International Investment and Multinational Enterprises* (Paris, OECD).

OEEC (1961), *The Textile Industry in Europe* 1960–61 (Paris, OEEC).

Ozawa, T. (1979), 'International Investment and Industrial Structure: New Theoretical Implications from the Japanese Experience' *Oxford Economic Papers*, Vol. 31.

Paige, D. and Bombach, G. (1959), *A comparison of national output and productivity of the United Kingdom and the United States* (Paris, OEEC).

Patterson, G. (1966), *Discrimination in International Trade, The Policy Issues 1945–1965* (Princeton, Princeton University Press).

Pindyck, R. S. (1979), *The Structure of World Energy Demand* (Cambridge Mass., MIT Press).

Pollard, S. (1969), *The Development of the British Economy 1914–1967*, 2nd edition (London, Arnold).

Posner, M. Y. (1961), 'International Trade and Technical Change', *Oxford Economic Papers*, Vol. 13, pp. 323–41.

Prebisch, R. (1959), 'Commercial Policy in the Underdeveloped Countries', *American Economic Review*, papers and proceedings.

President's Science Advisory Committee (1967), *Report of the Panel on the World Food Supply*, Vol. 3, Ch. 7 (Washington D.C., U.S. Government Printing Office).

Rainnie, G. F. (1965), *The Woollen and Worsted Industry* (Oxford, Clarendon Press).

Reddaway, W. B. with Perkins, J. O. N., Potter, S. J., and Taylor, C. T., (1967), *Effects of UK Direct Investment Overseas: An Interim Report*, University of Cambridge, Dept. of Applied Economics, Occasional Papers No. 12 (Cambridge University Press).

Reddaway, W. B. with Potter, S. J., and Taylor, C. T., (1968),

Effects of UK Direct Investment Overseas Final Report, University of Cambridge, Dept. of Applied Economics Occasional Papers, No. 15 (Cambridge University Press).

Rhys, D. G. (1972), *The Motor Industry: An Economic Survey* (London, Butterworth).

Rojko, A. *et. al.* (1978), *Alternative Futures for World Food in 1985* (Washington D.C., USDA).

Rossides, E. T. (1977), *US Customs Tariffs and Trade* (Washington D.C., The Bureau of National Affairs).

Rowe, J. O. F. (1965), *Primary Commodities in International Trade* (Cambridge, CUP).

Rybczynski, T. M. (1955), 'Factor Endowment and Relative Commodity Prices', *Economica* Vol. 23, 352–9.

Samuelson, P. A. (1949), 'International Factor-Price Equalisation Once Again', *Economic Journal*, 59, June.

Saul, S. B. (1960). *Studies in British Overseas Trade 1870–1914* (Liverpool, Liverpool University Press).

Schulz, T. W. (ed.) (1978), *Distortions of Agricultural Incentives* (Bloomington, USA, Indiana University Press): Schulz, T. W., 'On Economics and Politics of Agriculture'; Johnson, D. G. 'International Prices and Trade in Reducing the Distortions of Incentives'; Brown, Gilbert T., 'Agricultural Pricing Policies in Developing Countries'.

Sinclair, Stuart (1983), *The World Car: The Future of the Automobile Industry* (London, Euromonitor Publications Ltd).

Sinha, R. (1982), *Japan's Options for the 1980s* (London and Canberra, Croom Helm).

Sloan, A. P. (1965), *My Years with General Motors* (New York, MacFadden).

Spraos, J. (1980), 'The Statistical Debate on the Net Barter Terms of Trade Between Primary Products and Manufactures', *Economic Journal*, Vol. 90, pp. 107–28.

Stolper, W. F. and Samuelson, P. A. (1941), 'Protection and Real Wages', *Review of Economic Studies* 9, 58–73.

Tanzer, M. (1980), *The Race for Resources* (London, Heinemann).

Thomas, B. (1972), 'The Historical Record of International Capital Movements to 1913' reprinted in John H. Dunning (ed.), (1972), *International Investment* Penguin).

Tracy, M. (1964), *Agriculture in Western Europe* (London, Cape).

Tugendhat, C. and Hamilton, A. (1975), *Oil the Biggest Business*, revised edition (London, Eyre Methuen).

Turner, L., *et. al.* (1982), *The Newly Industrialised Countries: Trade and Adjustment* (London, Allen and Unwin for the Royal Institute of International Affairs).

Tyszynski, J. (1975), 'World Trade in Manufactured Commodities 1899–1950', *The Manchester School of Economic and Social Studies*, Vol. 19.

UK Business Statistics Office, *MA4 Business Monitor 1978 Supplement Census of Overseas Assets 1978*.

UN (1960), *Pattern of Industrial Growth 1938–58* (New York, UN Dept. of Economic and Social Affairs).

UN (1981), *1979 Yearbook of World Energy Statistics* (New York).

UN (1983), *1981 Yearbook of World Energy Statistics* (New York).

UNCTAD (1975), *Operation and Effects of the Generalized System of Preferences*, TD/B/C.5/42 (New York).

UNCTAD (1978), *The Generalized System of Preference and the Multilateral Trade Negotiations*, TD/B/C 5.52, p. 17, Rev. 1 (New York, UN).

UNCTAD (1981), *Dimensions of Corporate Marketing Structure*, TD/B/C.1/219 (New York).

UNCTAD (1983), *Review of Trends, Developments and Restrictions in Trade in Manufactures and Semi-Manufactures, including Areas of Special Interest to Developing Countries, and of Developments Arising from the Implementation of the Results of the Multilateral Trade Negotiations*, International Trade in textiles, with special reference to the problems faced by developing countries, TD/B/C.2/215 (Geneva).

UN Dept. of Economic and Social Affairs Statistical Office (1976), *World Energy Supplies 1950–74* (New York).

UN Dept. of Economic and Social Affairs Statistical Office (1979), *World Energy Supplies 1973–78* (New York).

UN ECE (1977), *Structure and Change in European Industry* (New York).

UN ECLA (1950), *The Economic Development of Latin America and its Principal Problems* (New York), written by Prebisch.

UN Statistical Papers Series M (1979), No. 29, Rev. 2, *Methods Used in Compiling the United Nations Price Indexes for Basic Commodities in International Trade* (New York).

US Bureau of the Census (1960), *Historical Statistics of the United States, Colonial Times to 1957* (Washington D.C., Bureau of the Census).

Vanek, J. (1963), *The Natural Resource Content of the United States Foreign Trade 1870–1955* (Cambridge, Mass., Institute of Technology Press).

Vernon, R. (1966), 'International Investment and International Trade in the Product Cycle', *Quarterly Journal of Economics* 80, 190–207.

Vernon, R. (ed.) (1970), *The Technology Factor in International*

Trade, National Bureau of Economic Research (New York, Columbia University Press).

Vernon, R. (1977), *Sovereignty at Bay* (New York, Basic Books; London, Longman).

Viner, J. (1950), *The Customs Union Issue* (Carnegie Endowment for International Peace).

Walters, I. (1975), *International Economics of Pollution* (London, Macmillan).

Wells, L. T. Jr. (ed.) (1972), *The Product Life Cycle and International Trade*, Division of Research Graduate School of Business Administration, (Boston, Harvard University).

World Bank or International Bank for Reconstruction and Development (IBRD) (1978), *World Development Reports* (New York and Oxford, OUP).

World Bank (1981), *Commodity Trade and Price Trends* (London, Johns Hopkins)

Yates, P. L. (1943), *Commodity Control* (London, Cape).

Yates, P. L. (1959), *Forty Years of Foreign Trade* (London, Allen and Unwin).

Young, S. Z. (1973), *Terms of Entry: Britains Negotiations with the European Community 1970–1972* (London, Heinemann).

Statistical Series

(Produced annually except where stated otherwise)

CEC, *Vegetable Oils and Oilseeds* (London, CEC)
CSO, *Economic Trends*, monthly (London, HMSO)
CSO, *United Kingdom Balance of Payments* (London, HMSO)
Eurostat, *Yearbook of Agricultural Statistics* (Brussels)
FAO, *Commodity Review and Outlook* (Rome)
FAO, *Fertilizer Yearbook* (Rome)
FAO, *Production Yearbook* (Rome)
FAO, *Rice Report* (Rome)
FAO, *The State of Food and Agriculture* (Rome)
FAO, *Trade Yearbook* (Rome)
FAO, *Yearbook of Fishery Statistics* (Rome)
FAO, *Yearbook of Forest Products* (Rome)
GATT, *International Trade* (Geneva)
OECD, *Development Co-operation Review* (Paris)
OECD, *Economic Outlook*, twice yearly (Paris)
OECD, *Foreign Trade by Commodities*, Series C (Paris)
OECD, *The Iron and Steel Industry* (Paris)
OECD, *The Textile Industry* (Paris)
UN, *Monthly Bulletin of Statistics* (New York), monthly
UN, *Statistical Yearbook* (New York)
UN, *Yearbook of International Trade Statistics* (New York)
UN, *Yearbook of World Energy Statistics* (New York)
USDA, *Agricultural Statistics* (Washington D.C.)
US Department of Commerce, *Statistical Abstract of the US* (Washington D.C.)
US Department of Commerce, *Survey of Current Business*, monthly (Washington D.C.)

Index